George Washington
and Political Fatherhood

George Washington and Political Fatherhood

The Endurance of a National Myth

HEINZ TSCHACHLER

McFarland & Company, Inc., Publishers
Jefferson, North Carolina

ALSO BY HEINZ TSCHACHLER

The Monetary Imagination of Edgar Allan Poe:
Banking, Currency and Politics in the Writings
(McFarland, 2013)

The Greenback:
Paper Money and American Culture
(McFarland, 2010)

Frontispiece: George Washington, "*Des Landes Vater.*" Archives & Special Collections, Franklin & Marshall College, Lancaster, Pennsylvania.

ISBN (print) 978-1-4766-8109-2
ISBN (ebook) 978-1-4766-3917-8

LIBRARY OF CONGRESS AND BRITISH LIBRARY
CATALOGUING DATA ARE AVAILABLE

Library of Congress Control Number 2020000404

© 2020 Heinz Tschachler. All rights reserved

No part of this book may be reproduced or transmitted in any form
or by any means, electronic or mechanical, including photocopying
or recording, or by any information storage and retrieval system,
without permission in writing from the publisher.

Front cover image: *Washington*, 1976 (Library of Congress)

Printed in the United States of America

McFarland & Company, Inc., Publishers
Box 611, Jefferson, North Carolina 28640
www.mcfarlandpub.com

To the memory
of my father,
Karl Tschachler

Table of Contents

Acknowledgments ix
Prologue: Enter George Washington 1

I. Daddy Issues: Presidents as Fathers 13
1. On Fathers, Past and Present 15
2. George Washington Becomes the Father of His Country 29

II. Political Sovereignty and Metaphorical Fathers 47
3. Strict Father Washington? 49
4. Inventing George Washington 61
5. Representing the Republic 71

III. One Whom Memory Oft Recalls 81
6. Symbolic Alliances 83
7. Expressions of Consent 94
8. The Father of the Fatherless 106

IV. From the Civil War through the Bicentennial of 1932 121
9. North and South 123
10. National Myths 133
11. Towards the Bicentennial of 1932 147

V. The Preservation of Our Folklore 159
12. George of Many Perceptions 160
13. Washington's Unique Greatness 178

Epilogue: If George Washington Had Not Been the Father of His Country 192
Notes 203
Bibliography 243
Index 247

Acknowledgments

I began work on this book in earnest in 2014. My plan was to complete it within three years. Yet no end was in sight in 2017. By then I had learned that on average book projects had a 40 percent chance of failure. I should have quit then and there. Although I must have sensed that persevering was not reasonable, I gathered myself together and carried on. Now that the book is completed, I know that I have learned valuable lessons from the experience. The first is that realistic planning is important. The second is that because of my predictably irrational perseverance I completed the endeavor, had followed through, as it were. The model of setting a goal and following through was not new for me. I had come across it in Barack Obama's book *Dreams from My Father*, when the Illinois state senator-to-be adopts the role of father to his younger half-brother Bernard. It is impossible to determine whether Barack Obama consciously imitated George Washington, but one of the most fitting descriptions of the Father of his Country is, in Richard Brookhisers words, that of "a man who follows through. This is why it was particularly appropriate that [he] came to be known as the father of his country, for he was the founder, above all others, who followed through." At the end of the day, I even had a logical explanation for why I intuitively decided not to quit: The process of writing provided me with a cue to persevering; this cue gained me access to information stored in my memory; the information, the result of studying biological and political fathers, finally provided the answer.

The pioneering scholars and visionaries, whose excellent work I was able to build on and whose ideas provoked further thought, do not need an acknowledgment; their works are cited throughout and listed in the bibliography. One who is neither cited nor listed in the bibliography is the late Philip Roth. As he told the *New York Times* in January 2018, writing a book entails silence, as in a room at the bottom of a pool. I am deeply grateful, therefore, to the many people who shared their thoughts and opinions with me as I developed my plans for this book. I apologize for not listing them all. A few individuals played a major role in making the book happen. Particular thank-yous go to Stefan "Steve" Rabitsch (Graz, Austria) and Daniel Shanahan (Charles University, Prague) for reading portions of the manuscript, offering valuable comments, providing a plethora of leads and useful hints and, beyond that, for remaining steadfast friends, inspiring colleagues, and intellectual companions. I am also indebted to Mark Thistlethwaite (Texas Christian University, Fort Worth), Nadja Gernalzick (University of Vienna), and Raymond W. Gibbs, Jr. (University of California, Santa Cruz). For their help in tracing the pictures I thought I needed and securing the rights to use them in a publication I thank Susan Ishler Newton (Winterthur Museum, Winterthur, Delaware), Jennifer Johns and Alex Till (Pennsylvania Academy of the Fine Arts, Philadelphia), Robert Kelley and Douglas Mudd (American Numismatic Association Money Museum, Colorado Springs, Colorado), Julie Zeftel (Metropolitan Museum of Arts, New York), Hillery L. York and Kay Peterson (Division of Work and Industry, National Museum of American History, Smithsonian Institution), Christopher M. Raab (Archives & Special Collections, Franklin & Marshall College, Lancaster, Pennsylvania), Jackie Penny and Marie E. Lamoureux (American Antiquarian Society, Worcester, Massachusetts), Alan M. Stahl (Firestone Library, Princeton University), Deborah Sisum and Erin Beasley (National Portrait Gallery, Smithsonian Institution), Marianne Martin (Colonial Williamsburg Foundation), Sylvia Buchholz (Thomson Reuters), Richard Sorensen (Smithsonian American Art Museum), and Carolyn Cruthirds (Museum of Fine Arts, Boston). I also want to gratefully cite the Library of Congress Prints and Photographs Division, as well as the Open Access policies of the Dallas Museum of Arts and the National Gallery of Arts, Washington, D.C., Andrew W. Mellon Collection.

Thank-yous are also owed to Anthony Hall, Shauna Bennis, René Schallegger, and Jörg Helbig, as well as students from my graduate seminars on political iconography and on presidents as fathers. Likewise, I thank the friendly and efficient staff of the library and interlibrary loan desks at the University of Klagenfurt. At a critical stage of this project's development, I had the immense benefit of a leave of absence award from my university that allowed me to give my undivided attention to the manuscript. For this, I am indebted to Vice Rector Martin Hitz. I am also greatly indebted to the editors at McFarland, in particular David Alff, for his grace and efficiency in expediting the publishing process. To Jürgen Peper, my intellectual mentor at the University of Graz, I owe thanks for his lecture course on "Fatherless America," which kept coming back to me from a distant past as I was trying to bring the balloon of my mind into its narrow shed. Special thanks are due to my wife, Gerhild Tschachler-Nagy, who went through a lot and did a lot, and without whose steady support, wisdom, and endless patience I would have given up long ago. I'm sure she will be relieved when this book is finally in print.

Prologue:
Enter George Washington

George Washington and Political Fatherhood began in 2008, the year my father passed away. Researching the book would be an excellent way to learn about the importance of fathers, I figured soon after this sad event. My father lost his father in a World War II bomb raid when he was only seventeen years old, and simply the knowledge of that fact (for he rarely spoke of it) echoed down through his life to mine. Still, there were stories. My father saw combat at the eastern front, where he was wounded and eventually taken prisoner by the Russians. On a transport headed east, he luckily made his escape and, together with a comrade, lighted out west until, somewhere over the horizon, he saw the Stars and Stripes. The Americans treated him well. They bound up his wounds, fed him and, now that Nazi Germany had capitulated, sent him home, only to find that home no longer existed. The war experiences no doubt deeply traumatized my father, who throughout his life remained psychologically absent, and though he could be kind and sympathetic, I was never close to him. I know he loved me, but he rarely if ever showed it. He never stood up for himself, nor for me or anyone else, though unbeknownst to him he left me a valuable legacy. Over the years, I have come to call this legacy the "*possibility* of America." That possibility may have been usurped by the United States, the land where the phones and the heat work; the soulless land of tepid TV shows and, more recently, of fake news; the land littered with bottlecaps and pull-tabs and pieces of broken muffler; and the land where racism and xenophobia seem rampant, where gun nuts run amok, and where bitter partisanship divides citizens one from the other. Yet somewhere, there is still that matrix of associations and desires, attached to America's "athletic Democracy," as Walt Whitman called it, of openness, pluralism, voluntarism, individual rights, and community by contract and consent.[1] Admittedly, the two Americas are hard to reconcile, and no doubt the present book too will be found wavering between criticism and admiration.

In the fall of 2008, my daughter turned thirty, which was all the more reason for me to think about fathering and the many instances when, to my perpetual shame, I was simply dysfunctional as a father. What also fueled my interest in the many different meanings of fatherhood was the election to the presidency of Barack Obama, also in 2008, and to "Father of Year" in 2009. Barack Obama's inaugural address in January 2009 was welcomed as a "dad speech." The description would have been fitting also for his first book, *Dreams from My Father*, published as Obama was preparing to launch his political career in a campaign for the Illinois Senate, in 1995. The book was eminently topical, for in the same year a social scientist warned that some 40 percent of American children "will go to sleep in homes in which their fathers do not live."[2] This was no mere matter of demographics, but also of culture. There had been a massive father absence already in the 1940s. But that absence was war-related, ending when fathers returned home. Moreover, it had "occurred within, and was constrained by, what might be termed a culture of fatherhood." Father absence in the 1990s, in contrast, was occurring in, and fueled by, "a culture of fatherlessness."[3] If fatherlessness was a most urgent social problem in the 1990s, it has not gone away. In 2013, an estimated 17 million children in the United States were fatherless.[4]

Fatherlessness no doubt marks a most destructive societal trend, but wasn't there at least a father for all Americans, a metaphorical father, that is? To Google "Father of His Country" is to enter a boundless universe of iterations in which George Washington at times appears as uniquely great and indispensable, at other times as utterly out of place, irrelevant if not dispensable. I myself became aware of George Washington as the undisputed Father of His Country during my work on a cultural history of America's money. For modern Americans, George Washington is indelibly connected to the one-dollar bill. It is the form in which Gilbert Stuart's "Athenaeum" portrait of 1796 is seen daily. The portrait surely is the most prominent element in the bill's ritual freight. Together with other visual and verbal signs and symbols printed on it, it serves to *re-finance* the one-dollar bill from realms outside the economy, politics, religion, and the arts. Upon closer examination we realize that pictures of George Washington have been used as accompanying measures for building trust from the Revolutionary War onwards. His image was universally recognizable and who would dare to *not* accept a paper bill or coin graced by the face of the nation? Would not such a person be immediately exposed as unpatriotic?

Such questions no longer seem to interest the nation's lawmakers, who for the past thirty years or so have repeatedly attempted to replace the one-dollar bill with a coin. In the 1990s, for instance, the lawmakers' endeavors found encouragement from a special interest group called "The Coin Coalition." At the other end were the Mount Vernon Ladies' Association and, more vociferously, "Save the Greenback," an organization of Bureau of Engraving and Printing employees and paper and ink suppliers opposed to phasing out the one-dollar bill with Washington's image on it and replacing it with a coin. More recently, a dollar bill phase-out was contested by a group that called itself "Americans for George." In opposition to the COINS Act (the acronym stands for "Currency Optimization, Innovation, and National Savings Act"), which was introduced in the House of Representatives in September 2011, web postings and tweets habitually pointed to the one-dollar bill's "national symbolism, much of which dates to the founding of the nation," trumpeted the bill as a "uniquely American icon," or wanted Washington's "memory live on via the #dollarbill!"[5]

My journey to bringing all those loose ends together began in earnest once I had published *The Greenback*, in 2010, and *The Monetary Imagination of Edgar Allan Poe*, in 2013. Many of the themes in the present book resonate with my experience of America's money, not the least of which is that for as long as the one-dollar bill is still around, the characteristic portrait of George Washington performs its cultural work. It secures the bill's credibility, assuring those who handle and use it every day that it is trustworthy, as trustworthy as the country's first president, whose printed presence legitimates the notes. Borrowing from Clinton Rossiter, the doyen of American political science, we can say that the portrait re-presents the president of the United States as "the one-man distillation of the American people just as surely as the Queen is of the British people."[6] For this reason alone, Washington's portrait is truly iconic, not merely in the semiotic sense of a likeness, but in the more profound sense of symbolizing something else. An icon makes visible something absent—what a commentator called the "innermost essence" of the person portrayed—

which it preserves for posterity. Washington's portrait therefore affects people not only cognitively but also emotionally, providing an object of emotional attachment against feelings of orphanhood. "The icon acts," the French scholar Marie-José Mondzain wrote. The icon refers people back to their origins; it enables them to form a sense of identity as well as to acknowledge the legitimacy of the existing social order. Iconic portraits thus are sacred images deserving of veneration.[7]

The four properties of icons—"likeness, manifestiveness, moral stimulus, and sacredness"—have made portraits ideal vehicles of political iconography, endowing them with significance, and enabling them to perform important social functions. Through the medium of portraiture, authority becomes a sensate thing. When the rites have been performed in the name of the founder, Americans are really, and not just symbolically, in the presence of the metaphorical father (spelled with an implicit capital "*f*"), with whom they enter into a sacred union, what anthropologists call a *participation mystique*.[8] The term "*participation*" calls to mind that from the beginning of the republic, Americans have understood the nation metaphorically in family terms, with the president seen as an older male authority figure. George Washington was called "the *father* of his country," partly because he was the metaphorical progenitor who brought it into being and partly because he was seen as the legitimate head of state, which in terms of the metaphor is the head of the family, the father.[9] The present book is not therefore interested in "the real man" who, as Marcus Cunliffe wrote, "has become entombed in his own myth—a metaphorical Washington Monument that hides from us the lineaments of the real man."[10] The "real man" is of relevance rather to historians, whose legitimate business is to constantly "rediscover" or at least to "reconsider" the nation's founder and its first president. But to deny that the Washington legend exists is pushing things too far. However suspect it may be in the eyes of history, the legend does exist, as essential to acting and knowing as history itself, except that it evokes emotions, not dispassionate analysis, and so my own interest is in George Washington's cultural legacy, in the form of the metaphorical figure fatherless Americans need to believe was and would continue to be there for them.[11]

Political Fatherhood is a cultural history of a metaphorical father, arguably the most important one Americans have ever had. More so than social or political histories, which have their own respective agendas, a cultural study focuses on the ways a particular subject acquires "meanings and values" amongst "distinctive social groups and classes" and becomes expressed through and embodied in "lived traditions and practices."[12] The scope of the present book is, therefore, broad in terms of content and the amount of ground covered. It begins by bringing to mind the importance of fathers, biological as well as metaphorical ones, each in two radically different shapes, the "strict father" as opposed to the "nurturant parent." George Washington never became a parent himself, though as a metaphorical father he had any number of substitute children. Before the Revolutionary War, the English kings had been the colonists' "fathers," fathers who had a responsibility for their family. Yet fathers can fail, such as George III, who for many colonists was a "tyrant" neglecting his "children." After showing how, by an act a symbolic regicide and patricide, the exalted title of "Father of His Country" was transferred from George III to George Washington, I unfold the title's genealogy. From its origin as *pater patriae* in Roman antiquity it spread over the entire western world of letters. In the English Enlightenment, *pater patriae* was popularized as "patriot king" or rendered, in a literal translation, as "Father of His Country." In French, it became *père de la patrie*, in Spanish *Padre de la Patria*, in Italian *Padre della Patria*, and in Portuguese *Pai da Nação*. Czech people talk about an *Otec náeda* or a *Tatíček*, while

German-speaking Protestants became familiar with *des Landes Vater* through Martin Luther's Bible translations.

The Father of His Country, Marcus Cunliffe established, is one of the four guises of the "metaphorical Washington Monument," the "hero figure."[13] That image originated in the creative imaginations of the nation's cultural elites; while it has been manipulated for ideological (patriotic) purposes, manufacturing consent and establishing hegemonic rule through characteristic patterns of consumption, it also has been subject to contested readings. After Washington's death in 1799 and through the nineteenth century, reverence for him increased. His prominence reached a peak at the time of the bicentennial of his birth in 1932, when he was commemorated by almost five million activities, an average of over 16,000 per day. Then, over the next half century, his prestige seemed to be diminishing. Not only had the understanding of the presidency changed; Washington's times also had changed profoundly over the years, and few with any knowledge of history would admit to regretting the change. Worship of Washington as a hero had its price—the misery of many people exposed to the excesses of nationalism, class boundaries, and rigid stereotypes of race and gender. The fading concept of greatness, together with the diminished significance of fathers, metaphorical fathers included, precipitated Washington's descent, which was halted only with the election to the presidency of Ronald Reagan. During Reagan's presidency and in the years to follow, Washington was returned to his former glory and greatness, achieving a new significance, for the American people as much as for the nation's political leaders, who have grandiloquently exalted him as "a monumental man" (Reagan), proudly repeat the oath taken by Washington two hundred years ago (Bush father and Bill Clinton), piously retell the story of the General and his faithful soldiers huddled by dying campfires on the shores of an icy river (Barack Obama), or, like Donald J. Trump, end their own oath of office with the words, erroneously ascribed to Washington, "So help me God."

Representations of George Washington have always articulated individual and collective needs, providing scenarios that elevated, humanized, and deflated him. I discuss and analyze these scenarios, as well as the numerous attempts to establish Washington's "unique greatness" (the phrase belongs to Gordon S. Wood). Part I deals with "daddy issues," beginning, in Chapter 1, with the importance of fathers. Fathers are necessary figures in children's lives and in society. As role models, whether positive or negative ones, fathers are taken into the children's minds—internalized as objects, as psychoanalysts put it, and supplemented by mentors. George Washington was such a mentor. He also was a metaphorical father, as the nation's founder and because he was seen as the legitimate head of state, which in terms of the metaphor is the head of the national family, the father. If his presidency became the office of national "fatherhood," per his legacy it has been that to all presidents since Washington, and to all Americans, especially to those orphaned ones who can even see in Donald Trump "the father I always wanted."[14] Chapter 2 traces the transfer, by an act of symbolic regicide and patricide, of political fatherhood from the English king, George III, to George Washington. By this act of communal incorporation Washington became America's "living 'tribal' totem," hailed as the "political Father and head of a Great People" or, on the cover of an almanac published in Lancaster, Pennsylvania, in 1778, as "*Des Landes Vater*."[15] The father trope, which readily salved the feelings of orphanhood among the revolutionaries, is also a staple of poems, speeches, portraits, name-giving and, not to forget, hagiographic biographies, such as "Parson" Weems's *Life*. All these outpourings of father worship stressed Washington's "personal perfections." From them, a more perfect union was destined to follow.

Part II begins by addressing, in Chapter 3, a range of ideological and psychological problems, such as fears that the office of the presidency would lead to despotism. Political fatherhood and, by extension, Washington's role as the Father of His Country served to dispel those fears. As a delegate to the Philadelphia Convention of 1787 argued, Washington no doubt would be a father figure watching "over the whole with paternal care and affection."[16] Washington himself did everything in his power to fulfill the expectations of paternal care and affection. Already during the Revolutionary War he had been the beloved "father" of a military "family" of surrogate sons, Alexander Hamilton, the Marquis de Lafayette, Joseph Reed, John Laurens, and David Humphreys, and he also cultivated a personal bond with his other fellow officers. This doesn't mean that Washington ever laid aside the comportment and airs of a Virginia gentleman-planter. Washington may have been the head of a republic, but his republicanism was of a conservative kind, evident from his commitment to a stronger union and subordination and obedience to the federal government. But Washington also knew that national unity was to be achieved only by taking the federal government to the people. Which is what he did when he traveled through all of the thirteen states between April 1789 and July 1791. The journey was spectacularly successful, though he often cringed when the crowds responded to him as if he were their king. Other than that, the public spectacles that accompanied his journeys must have pleased one who saw himself as the protagonist in a great historical drama.

Washington's self-image as a national republican father, the focus of Chapter 4, certainly made him more calculating in gaining posthumous fame. He not only learned to screen his ambitions behind an image of republican virtue, disinterested dedication to public service, and sacrifice for his country; he also welcomed artists and writers willing to crown him as one who had won fame—"bards" like Joel Barlow, biographers like David Humphreys as well as any number of portrait artists, for whom he sat patiently. Thus arose a veritable Washington cult, powerful and inclusive enough to deflect local and regional sentiments onto a common object of veneration. If there were cracks in the polished surface, they mostly remained below the radar, in particular the laws that the alleged "man of the people" enforced. These laws also disempowered, eliminating whole categories—slaves, Native Americans, and women—from the rubric of "we, the people," thus giving the lie to Washington's ideology of unity. Even in the midst of disagreements and rising factionalism, a poem pleaded with the "Great Man without a stain" not to resign from his office: "Still, as a Father to *thy country dear*, / Regard not those who seek to wound thy peace..."[17] Political iconography provides a context for the Washington image in Chapter 5. The Father of His Country was, after all, to represent a republic. Stories told about him for instance took inspiration from British history, most notably from the consolidation of English liberties, from the time of the Magna Carta to Shaftesbury's celebration of constitutionality and beyond. Classical antiquity, too, became a powerful source. Indeed, there are many instances of depicting Washington as a Roman consul, complete with the bundle of rods, the *fasces*. Washington himself chose the upright Cato as his personal role model. Like him, Washington strove to "form himself to glory, and break the fierceness of his native temper, to copy out our father's bright example."[18] Contemporaries, mindful of his willingness to surrender power, on many occasions compared him with Cincinnatus, enshrining him, thanks to Houdon, in marble, or holding him up as the ultimate cause for the "Happiness of America": "The towns in raptures and the roads in flowers / Wher'er he pass'd!"[19]

Part III essentially treats ways of remembering George Washington. Chapter 6 begins with a discussion of portraits which, by various symbolic alliances, could be found in huts as well as in palaces and, by way of an apocryphal story, also in privies. Americans before the Civil War learned how Washington looked from the various portraits, not so much from the original paintings, but from copies that appeared in prints, as book and magazine illustrations, in almanacs, children's books and, not to forget, on coins, medals, and bank notes. Additionally, they learned what Washington was like from the orators and from Parson Weems and other biographers—Jared Sparks, John Marshall and, most notably, Washington Irving, who just before the outbreak of the Civil War reminded his readers that Washington's "precepts and example speak to us from the grave with *a paternal appeal*; and his name—by all revered—forms a universal tie of brotherhood—*a watchword of our Union*."[20] By that time, Washington's birthday and July 4 already had become annual occasions when the Father of His Country was eulogized all over the country, and public speakers found many other opportunities to recall his presence if they didn't, like the historian and geographer Emma Willard, visit Mount Vernon, "in mournful, filial pilgrimage."[21]

Washington himself hated sitting for portraits, yet he must have sensed intuitively that he had come to stand for the Union and that his portraits helped to bond people together. Central to Chapter 7 is, therefore, the thesis that the act of sitting down to a portrait artist or silhouette cutter entailed an implicit expression of consent, which is at one and the same time the foundation of constitutional government and the inviolable right of republican representation. Republican representation covered a broad spectrum, from the virtuous statesman (in Gilbert Stuart) to the gallant revolutionary (in John Trumbull) to the Father of His Country, hallowed by Roman antiquity (in Rembrandt Peale), to the visionary entrepreneur (in Edward Savage). As the century progressed, Washington came to serve different needs. Increasingly, his image buttressed the illusion of domestic happiness. Gone were the days when the Washington image was a powerful vehicle of political integration; also gone were the days when Washington was an avatar of patriarchy or the undisputed leader of the Capital venture. Faced with all kinds of disjunctions and contradictions, Rembrandt Peale spent a great deal of time and energy to defend the accuracy of his likeness of Washington as the Father of His Country. His *Patriae Pater*, he wrote, was the only portrait capable of "transmit[ing] to posterity the true and impressive image of [Washington's] countenance," of reawakening and even creating powerful sentiments about the Father of His Country and, by extension, about the republic itself.[22]

In antebellum America, the period covered in Chapter 8, personality increasingly was defined in terms of providing for oneself, the acquisition of money, and paid work. For the "self-made man," only success and failure counted. But a life in which individuals become, in the words of Alexis de Tocqueville, "strangers one to the other" (another form of orphanhood), needs some compensation, which often took the form of a broader diffusion of refinement.[23] Stories of domestic happiness, which more often than not were "haunted" by the iconic image of Washington, only pasted over the contradictions of actual families, eliding their relations to the economy, to politics, and to history, and remaining utterly oblivious to the nascent women's movement. As if to escape these conundrums, Washington's image was blown up to colossal scales, in Horatio Greenough's Jovian statue as much as in the Washington National Monument which, ironically, was begun in the 1840s but dedicated only in 1885. Until then, Americans had to salve their feelings of orphanhood—the direct result, according to a New England pastor, of "paternal neglect"[24]—through other means, such as (mostly saccharine) poetry dedicated to the Father of His Country or the collecting of various Washingtoniana, including a plethora of forged letters.

Politicians, too, came to see the importance of the Washington image. Many presidents,

John Adams, Thomas Jefferson, Andrew Jackson, Zachary Taylor, to name but a few, were only too happy to be represented as heroes in the identical molding, a few even explicitly as "new" or "second" Washingtons. And when regional tensions increased at mid-century, both sides could find in Washington's name an antidote against sectional turmoil and disunion. To Northerners, Washington was an unequivocal symbol of union, the visible embodiment of the nation. No lesser person than Oliver Wendell Holmes in 1856 asked Americans, who were soon to be orphaned by the upheavals of the Civil War, to "hear the Father's dying voice," which admonished them to "Love your country first of all!"[25] The South eventually had its own Washington, in the sense of "one of us—a slaveholder and a planter," in John C. Calhoun's words.[26] Central to Chapter 9 is the presidency of Abraham Lincoln, which was a true watershed. Less than a year after Lincoln's election to the presidency, his portraits not only outnumbered by far images of Washington but also began to compete with them for space in the American psyche, evident, for instance, in the number of books and articles published. Following Lincoln's assassination, however, there was a resurgence of tradition, with the martyred president explicitly represented as "A second Washington! / So great in every virtuous plan."[27] The pairing of the two national heroes was expressed poetically and illustrated in popular prints and lithographs, of which "Columbia's Noblest Sons" is perhaps the best known.

The Gilded Age, the subject of Chapter 10, was greatly concerned with securing citizens' allegiance and loyalty as well as cementing the legitimacy of the nation. The biggest question was how to assimilate a heterogeneous mass of people who were Americans not by birth but by immigration, and whom the elites considered as rather "*doubtful members of the national community.*"[28] In order to achieve all this, the state employed all kinds of official institutions, symbols, and practices—"invented traditions" in Eric Hobsbawm's sense—such as the rebuilding of the nation's capital, promoting a *national* flag and anthem, uniforms, maps, ceremonials like the Pledge of Allegiance or Washington's birthday and, not to forget, completing the Washington Monument and elevating Mt. Vernon and Springfield to national shrines, which "the fingers of progress" were not allowed to desecrate under any circumstances.[29] History or, rather, historiography likewise became crucial in the project of nation-building. Commissioned by the federal government, grandiose canvases like John Trumbull's *Jefferson Presenting the Declaration of Independence to John Hancock at the Continental Congress* were to teach the citizenry that the American Revolution had been an orderly one, the riot at Bowling Green and other rituals of political iconoclasm notwithstanding. Tellingly, Trumbull's painting made it on the federal currency, whereas Alexander Anderson's *Celebration of Independence* did not, was in fact largely forgotten.

For post-bellum Americans in general, George Washington no longer was the "rebel general" who had led the fight against British "tyranny." Instead, he became the avatar of Anglo-Saxonism, the leading actor in a glorious "Republican Court," too refined for the raw democracy the United States was beginning to represent. Society's highest strata crowned the Father of His Country the father of their own good taste, with Martha as a sidekick, a founding mother to go with the founding father. For those with more modest means, the new one-dollar Silver Certificates provided "an excellent picture of Martha Washington, the wife of the Father of His Country."[30] At the Centennial exhibition of 1876, relics of Washington were displayed, connecting visitors across the generations to the Father of His Country. The Centennial of Washington's inauguration in 1889 also brought with it lavish exhibitions of Washingtoniana, presenting a distinctive picture of Washington and his era, as did the Centennial celebrations. At the inaugural ceremony, national unity was reaffirmed in the name of the metaphorical father, while a parade was dedicated to "the miracle of America." Although it was not explicitly spelled out, "miracle" then meant the assimilation of successive waves of immigrants, the repetition of which was seen as increasingly difficult, if not impossible, and, for an increasing number of Americans, as simply unwanted.

Rampant nativism sets the tone in Chapter 11, which begins with a discussion of *America*, the last of D. W. Griffith's silent epics. Washington praying for guidance at Valley Forge on the evening before crossing the Delaware River on Christmas Day, 1776, is a key scene in the film, which was released in 1924. A year later, tens of thousands of Klansmen marched down Pennsylvania Avenue and held a rally at the Washington Monument, as proof of their earnest patriotism. The resurgence of the KKK in the 1920s was only the culminating act in a long history of segregating and, on occasion, excluding specific cultural, ethnic, and religious groups. However, segregation and animosity towards those groups became more poignant from the 1920s onward. Just as poignant was the resurgence of masculine ideals, a "toughening of American manhood"[31] that was accompanied by the discrediting of and attacks on women, especially independent women. Masculinity may even be said to inform the era's official nationalism on the monumental scale. Among the public buildings and monuments built "in scale" with their importance are the Union Station, the Lincoln Memorial (built to resemble a Greek temple), the Arlington Memorial Bridge, the Jefferson Memorial, and, for Washington, the 50-foot tall Princeton Battle Monument as well as his monumental head at Mount Rushmore—"patriarchy fixed in stone," in the words of art historian Albert Boime.[32]

When Mount Rushmore opened in 1941, the United States already was recovering from the Great Depression. During that time of hardship, Washington provided much-needed uplift. The more than twenty-five paintings of him created by Jean Leon Gerome Ferris were to achieve just this. Other artists, John Ward Dunsmore, Henry A. Ogden, Percy Morgan, and Howard Pyle also made a living from selling the past to the future. To an audience entranced by the romance of colonial America, the attempts, on the part of iconoclasts such as William E. Woodward or Rupert Hughes, to dismantle the prevailing filiopietism by cataloguing Washington's purported flaws must have come as a shock. Unsurprisingly, Washington's popularity was surpassed by Lincoln's, except for the period between 1925 and 1932, as the nation planned for, carried out, and reflected upon its year-long celebration of the two-hundredth anniversary of Washington's birth—the most extensive celebration ever held for a national leader, whose mythic status was most fully captured by Norman Rockwell's painting *The Guiding Influence*. Rockwell showed an earnest and well-groomed young man, an orphan of sorts, sitting at his desk. A copy of Houdon's bust is placed before him, while above him we see an image of what the all-American youth is contemplating so deeply—George Washington, in heroic pose, his outstretched left arm raised and pointed ahead.

The Iowa painter Grant Wood was no iconoclast, though in the 1930s he produced numerous paintings about the mania for all things Revolutionary. One of these paintings is *Parson Weems' Fable*, in which Wood playfully captured the moment when the self-declared parson "discovered" the story of young Washington informing his father, "I cannot tell a lie." What we learn from Wood is that the past is always mediated by representations that elevate stories like Weems's to the status of national mythology. But Wood did not seek to disparage the value of such unifying myths themselves. As he saw it, "*the preservation of our folklore is more important than generally realized.*"[33] Wood's plea was heeded when increasing numbers of Americans were being asked to leave their homes and fight, not a revolution so much as foreign military powers threatening to conquer the world. During that period, which I cover in Chapter 12, the yearning for fathers once again came to the fore. Hence the demand for mythic stories or grand narratives became more intense and the moral inspiration from even the crudest myth more deeply felt. From the 1950s, however, the fading concept of greatness, together with societal trends that diminished the significance of fathers, metaphorical fathers included, precipitated Washington's descent. Increasingly, the Father of His Country was seen as remote and distant, one of those "dead white men" who are largely irrelevant for a world that was getting ready for Civil Rights Acts or the Equal Rights Amendment. Indeed, from the 1970s a plethora of artworks and other cultural products were produced that turned the iconic image of the Father of His Country against itself, from Larry Rivers's anti-heroic *Washington Crossing the Delaware* to "I Grew Hemp" stickers to thousands of cartoons demonstrating the adaptability of Washington's myth and its instant recognition.

Far Side comics and abundant advertising may signal a growing cynicism, yet many Americans felt they still needed George Washington. "The more modern we become," Karal Ann Marling wrote, "the more desperately we cling to our Washingtons, to our old-fashioned heroes, to an imagined colonial past, to the good old days when patriots stood firm on their pedestals."[34] The "good old days" is, of course, a veiled reference to a time without political assassinations, the protests of African Americans and of the nation's youth, the Vietnam War, Watergate, the women's movement, and the gay liberation movement, all of which challenged traditional concepts of masculinity. What brings these "good old days" back is stories, compelling stories that is, not the collective "infantile phantasy" Americans had turned the Father of His Country into by the 1960s. One of the most compelling stories was told by James Thomas Flexner in a four-volume biography published between 1965 and 1972. Flexner's *George Washington* became phenomenally successful, far outselling anything written about the Father of His Country since "Parson" Weems. A three-part miniseries based on Flexner's book went on air in April 1984, two years after the 250th anniversary of Washington's birth and three years into Ronald Reagan's first term as President. As Washington rose to new prominence, America's sitting president celebrated the beginning of his second term with a round of televised balls, galas, parties, and other celebrity-packed functions, including Super Bowl XIX on January 20, 1985, during which an electrified George Washington was blinking down at his late twentieth-century children from the giant scoreboard.

Fascination with the Father of His Country came to blaze around less conspicuous campfires as well—on the website of the conservative Family Research Council, on Pat Robertson's Christian Broadcasting Network, or at the pro-gun Second Amendment Foundation. There are many more such instances, but always Washington is portrayed as a great President. The question what makes a great president has been asked from the beginning of the presidency, though from the late 1940s, polling games have gained in popularity. While answers have been sought by a variety of means, the results are usually given in a ranked order. Presidents tend to be rated in political rather than in moral terms, though sometimes, "personal qualities," "character," or "integrity" are used for evaluation, with answers expected to provide moral stimulus. Altogether, modern polls show little variation: Lincoln, Washington, and Franklin Roosevelt are consistently rated great, with Theodore Roosevelt, Eisenhower, Wilson, Jefferson, and Jackson making the list on occasion. Chapter 13 begins with an overview of contemporary scholarship, which yields almost identical results as far as presidential greatness goes. Recognition of Washington's "unique greatness" and use of him as an "appropriate symbol" against which an event, an act, or an object can be placed, are of particular importance for public events such as presidential inaugurations. Indeed, from the beginning of the republic, presidents have invoked the Father of His Country in their inaugural addresses, sometimes indirectly, sometimes directly, as when Zachary Taylor in 1849 referred to "our own beloved Washington." Altogether, the history of inaugural addresses shows some fluctuations in their genuflections to Washington, though ever since the presidency of Ronald Reagan, invoking the "monumental man: George Washington, Father of our country" has become something of a fixture. George H. W. Bush, Bill Clinton, Barack Obama and, most recently, Donald J. Trump in one way or the other made references to America's first president in their inaugural addresses.

Washington is alive also in Americans' everyday lives—on city landscapes, especially in the nation's capital, in the places named for him, in streets and businesses, in the hundreds of thousands of people that still carry his name, in the minds of people who leave "Happy Birthday" posts on the George Washington Facebook site, who bake George Washington meatloaves, or who around Father's Day 2018 disseminated on social media a Lansdownesque image of George Washington inscribed with "America, I am your father." The post drew any number of likes and comments, such as "Happy almost Father's Day to the Father of our Country," "I wish he could come back," "if you could only see your country today," or "we NEED him instead of this guy we got now." And there is Washington's iconic portrait, which endures not just on the currency, but also has become the schoolroom Washington, the TV Washington, and a staple in popular print and media imagery. Businesses too love George Washington, who sells everything from coffee to soap to baking powder to soft drinks to cigars to used cars to travels to the most unlikely places. The face on the dollar bill advertises big February sales in department stores and used-car lots and it graces all kinds of objects, including T-shirts (worn, for instance, by students at George Washington University). Altogether, then, Washington's image not only has been internalized as an object but also has been transformed into a potent visual synecdoche for the nation, its economy, and its consumerist culture.

A reconsideration of America's relationship with its first president is the subject of the final chapter. I begin with objections to Washington worship, the most vociferous of which stems from John Quincy Adams: "Democracy has no monuments," John Adams's son noted in his diary. "It strikes no medals. It bears the head of no man on a coin. Its very essence is iconoclastic."[35] The nation's sixth president targeted his wrath against the game of presidential symbol-making, which transforms each president into an icon, a stylized image of Americans' faith in themselves and in their country. But Americans' relationship with their presidents, Thomas S. Langston argues, is "dysfunctional," as it only encourages unrealistic expectations, false hopes, and willful misunderstandings.[36] This makes all "father narratives" deceptive. We need to be wary, therefore, of Diane Wakoski's claim, in a 1960s poem, on George Washington as a father. The poem is a veritable outpouring of a suppressed father hunger, a *cri de coeur* against the very real generation gap between fathers and their children, and against rising divorce rates and the ensuing fatherlessness. The 1960s saw the rise of a new women's movement, yet for many Americans in search of at least a vague sense of paternal warmth, fathers—whether real or metaphorical—then provided at least an imagined sense of permanence, continuity, and stability, relieving them, if only temporarily, from feeling orphaned.

Even the action hero presidents of films like *Independence Day* and *Air Force One* are fathers or, more inclusively, family men. Predictably in these films, the nation at large is conceived of as a family, running along smoothly, without irksome factions and parties. Their fictional presidents are, appropriately, depicted as leaders above party, representing all the people because all the people are family. George Washington, too, has been imagined and imagined himself as a leader above party. Such symbol-making, however, both immunized him against criticism and subverted ideological impetuses for further change, locking them into a "worthier" past. In that past, a patriarchal language served to legitimize political authority, at the same time as it made rebellion too daunting a task. It is no exaggeration to say, therefore, that for as long as the values, customs, beliefs, practices, and stories that constitute the way of life of the American people are alive and respected, the Father of His Country will continue to legitimate, make visible, and consecrate the stories that keep a big country and a diverse people united. Yet it is precisely those stories which make the prospect of a woman leading the United States more than merely a matter of time.

The range of transformations that America's national father has undergone over the years is quite astonishing. Surprisingly, however, no cultural history of George Washington as the Father of His Country exists, making this project an important one. "The history of America is the history of Washington," Mark Thistlethwaite wrote.[37] George Washington no doubt is at the core of America's national imaginary in which the nation has come, and continues to come, to an understanding of itself. Pictures of the nation's founder and savior testify to this—Gilbert Stuart's iconic "Athenaeum" portrait; also his "Lansdowne," which visualizes the legitimacy of a postrevolutionary, democratically elected president; the elder Peale's rendering of General Washington at Princeton; the younger Peale's *Patriae Pater*; or Emanuel Leutze's grandiose canvas of the crossing of the Delaware. Americans are familiar with these artworks from visits to the nation's museums, from prints, and other forms of reproduction. Americans are also familiar with other paintings and engravings, plaster statuary and other art objects, the poetry, fiction, and drama written about Washington, the political discourses and inaugural addresses referring to him, as well as the medals and medallions, coins and currency, postage stamps, editorial cartoons, advertisements, calendars, book and magazine covers depicting him. In addition, Americans have acquired goods of all kinds with Washington's likeness on them, paperweights, dishes, crockery and other household goods and furnishings, handkerchiefs and other textiles, bottles, belt buckles, hats, hatchet-shaped cookie cutters, ice cream molds, fans, and other objects bearing his likeness. While the cultural historian Karal Ann Marling has dismissed these outpourings as simply junk,[38] the values embedded in such traditions and practices are not without their force. They foster a sense of community. They offer a firm footing in the midst of social turmoil and economic chaos. They tender comfort and solace to those who feel orphaned, and they strengthen the bonds of union to the national community.

National communities, the historian and Washington scholar Edmund S. Morgan argued, depend for their continuation on complex fictions, such as "the people," political representation or "the consent of the governed," each requiring a "willing suspension of disbelief."[39] If nations themselves are imaginative constructions, their leadership is even more so. "Rulership of any kind," Jeff Smith wrote, "is an essentially metaphorical act, a community's projection of authority onto an individual in much the same way that love is metaphorically projected through a red rose."[40] George Washington as the Father of His Country therefore is a fiction that, in the absence of alternatives, Americans habitually believe in, even must believe in, much as in religious life they must believe in God. Demand for imaginative Washingtons has not always been at the same level; on the contrary, it varied considerably over time, continually being re-negotiated. The fiction that George Washington is the

Father of His Country, though, has proven remarkably robust. Set within the context of the nation-as-family trope, it has helped set the terms and expectations that carried the nation through many a crisis. During times of social upheaval and internal tensions the yearning for fathers generally peaked, and with it demand for representations of the metaphorical father, together with the demand for moral inspiration emanating from them.[41]

One such crisis occurred during the revolutionary period and the early republic, when republican elitism collided with loyalist sentiments, democratic radicalism, and a motley group of fractious states; then, Thomas Jefferson, though opposed to many of Washington's policies, pleaded that Washington accept another term as President, declaring that "North and South will hang together as long as they have you to hang to."[42] Also critical were the years before and during the Civil War, when Washington was seen at the same time as the guarantor of national unity (in the North) and the leader of the first American revolution, now to be followed by a second one (in the South). In the late nineteenth century, the specter of mass immigration led authorities to use Washington's hallowed memory to bring "doubtful members" of the community into the national fold. During the nativist climate of the post–World War I era, the prevailing sense of white supremacy was reinforced and male fears assuaged by "the more permanent familiarity" of Washington's presidential portrait (after Gilbert Stuart) on the currency. In the present crisis, a country divided along the rift lines of class, ethnicity, age, and gender, and stymied by congressional gridlock and a perpetual adolescent in the White House (who still doesn't know what to do with what he's been given) is seeing an increased investment in patriotic symbols and stories. The hopes and anxieties associated with Washington's successor clearly demonstrate a desire for a paternal leader, one who, as Robin Lakoff once stated in a political memorandum, is at one and the same time "a daddy, a king, a god, a hero […] a champion who will carry that lance and that sword into the field and fight for us."[43] It's the rhetoric of political *fatherhood*, not motherhood, that ameliorates, if not elides, all kinds of fears, of change, of the future, of social decline, of other people. The story of the Father of His Country thus is a gendered narrative as well as a narrative of gender. It is within such a narrative that George Washington continues to serve as a symbol of national consensus, continuity, and stability to which citizens are called upon to defer. Altogether, therefore, the metaphorical Father of His Country provides and always has provided at least a semblance of stability in periods of domestic turmoil, and of continuity and comfort in times of international crisis and decline. By tracing the story of the metaphorical Father of His Country, *George Washington and Political Fatherhood* reveals key insights into values and understandings, lived traditions and practices that add to an understanding of American culture.

I

Daddy Issues:
Presidents as Fathers

When asked about the outcome of the 2008 Presidential election, the pundits as usual were divided. While some predicted that the winner would "likely be chosen on the credibility of his plan to stabilize the economy," others swore that Americans would select, not an economist but a daddy. "Americans have always voted for a daddy," the writer Donna Leon said in an interview just before the election. "Jimmy Carter was a daddy, Ronald Reagan, even Bill Clinton was a daddy." In 2008 John McCain would have passed as a "daddy" on the strength of his looks alone. But Barack Obama? Most voters likely knew that he was the father of two fine daughters, though few would have guessed that he would be named the 2009 Father of the Year.[1] Yet why would people want a father at all for the unenviable job of getting the American economy back on track? And had not the very idea of father been discredited in the masculinity crisis of the more recent past, with its debunking of and animosity toward all "masculine models"[2]? But political and cultural headwinds notwithstanding, Barack Obama in his inaugural address of January 20, 2009, called for a "new era of responsibility." The speech generally met with much respect, often with enthusiasm throughout the world. And commentators on both sides of the Atlantic settled on a single passage as the most important one: "We remain a young nation, but in the words of Scripture, the time has come to set aside childish things." In this passage, which is from Paul's first epistle to the Corinthians, there is an austere, almost brutal analysis of the present state of the nation as being engaged in childish behavior. America must come of age, though without looking old—essentially, this was President Obama's message to his country, his call to arms as it were. It was heard. "The line about 'putting away childish things' resonated with me," a viewer said in an online exchange with Robert G. Kaiser, a *Washington Post* associate editor. Another *Washington Post* reporter observed, "I liked that it was kind of harsh—it was a Dad speech." Even the British tabloid *The Sun* caught on to this message when it showed a picture of President Obama's daughter Sasha giving her father the thumbs-up with the headline: "You're the Daddy."[3]

Barack Obama had sounded the theme of fatherhood before. "American fathers," he said in his acceptance speech on August 28, 2008, "must take more responsibility to provide love and guidance to their children."[4] The theme not only left its mark on the entire campaign. Throughout his tenure as president, Obama was an unequivocally loud champion of fatherhood. He established a variety of "responsible fatherhood" programs, following through on his 2009 Fatherhood and Healthy Families Taskforce and his Fatherhood and Mentoring Initiative created the following year. Also in 2010, he signed an Act that re-authorized funding for the National Responsible Fatherhood Clearinghouse (NRFC). But

Obama's most public confirmation of the importance of fatherhood came in a 2011 essay that was published exclusively in *People* magazine on Father's Day of that year. "I grew up without a father around," the president wrote, "I always felt his absence." Perhaps for this reason, he went on to say, "fatherhood is so important to me," adding that it was just as important for the entire nation: "There are too many young people out there who aren't reaching their potential because they don't have a father figure to guide them." By this the president meant that children don't just need fathers who are "physically present, but emotionally available."[5]

With his focus on the national fatherhood crisis, President Obama not only shifted his policies from those of his predecessor, George W. Bush, who had concentrated on marriage in his domestic policies. Obama no doubt angered some conservatives in the process. But the fact that his own father was largely missing from his childhood gave him a personal stake in the issue of fatherless families. That the issue was especially severe within the African American community doubtless also played a role in the president's decision.[6] Obama had challenged American men to act responsibly and morally and, especially, to take responsibility for their children already in a speech given in July 2007 and ominously titled "Changing the Odds for Urban America." *The Audacity of Hope*, a book published in 2006, has an entire chapter on the notion that moral education starts at home. In this connection, the future president remembers a speech on the theme "what it takes to be a full-grown man." In the speech, given one Father's Day to the members of the Salem Baptist Church on Chicago's South Side, Obama had called upon African American men to "put away their excuses for not being there for their families." He also reminded the men in the audience that "being a father meant more than fathering a child" and, finally, that "precisely because many of us didn't have fathers in the house we have to redouble our efforts to break the circle."[7] Obama knew what he was talking about. There is a touching scene in *Dreams from My Father*, in which he acts like a father to his younger half-brother Bernard, reminding him that he was "almost a man. Somebody with responsibilities. To your family. To yourself. [Thus,] you're gonna have to set some goals and follow through." There is, however, a note of sadness throughout the book that is hard to miss. *Dreams from My Father*, which was first published in 1995, chronicles the events of Barack Obama's life up until his entry into law school in 1988. Yet instead of memories of his father, loss and abandonment scream at us from almost every page.[8]

1

On Fathers, Past and Present

Fathers are important. The father, the psychoanalyst Martin Baily wrote in the year 2000, "is a necessary and not a contingent figure in the child's life and in society." The father provides his children with physical protection and help, with money and material resources. As he precedes his children by some 25 to 30 years, he also provides them with "paternal cultural transmission," contributing to the identity, character, and competence of his children.[1] The father can set an example to his children, at the same time as he is the man to chafe up against and to grapple with. He is the one to reliably maintain relations with his children during times of crisis, helping them to develop and become responsible adults. He will accept his children's partners, integrating them into the family and developing relationships with them. He creates for himself the necessary structures of life, adapting them to his needs. He pursues his own interests at the same time as he takes upon himself social duties and responsibilities. He responds to all kinds of physical, psychological, and social changes coming his way, putting up and coping with menacing situations, including illnesses and wars. He even shapes the extended period of his own aging, exploring and exploiting its potential. Finally, he passes away. This is, admittedly, an idealized picture of paternal investment, and one could easily argue that role models tend to restrict one's scope for action, "like blocks of marble … placed squarely in your path," in the words of Donald Barthelme.[2] Yet anyone who has lived to see a father following through is free to decide: This is the way I want to do things or this is the way I'll never do it. The role model imparted by the father gives children the chance either to adopt his example or to consciously distance themselves from it, building their own secure identities as men, partners, and fathers. Either way, the father is taken into the children's minds—internalized as an object, in the lingo of psychoanalysis.

Internalizing, Richard Brookhiser wrote in his book on George Washington as America's "founding father," is something everyone must do to grow up. Living as a man or woman depends on images we carry with us. Most people internalize their parents as objects, for good or for ill, supplementing them with aspects of important mentors.[3] For Brookhiser, George Washington clearly was such a mentor, though mentors might as well come from Scripture, which provides a wide range of father figures—Adam, Abraham, Isaac, Jacob, Moses, and, for the New Testament, Joseph. The impact of these "fathers" on religious life is felt to this day. For Christians, Adam is the ur-father whom God had created from clay; Abraham is the founding father of the Israelites; Isaac, Abraham's son, became the father of two sons, Esau and Jacob; Jacob, Abraham's grandson, became the founding father of the twelve tribes of Israel; and Moses delivered the Israelites from the Egyptian bondage. Muslims recognize Ismael, Abraham's son through Hagar, the maid, as their common ancestor. Catholics for their part revere Saint Joseph, spouse of the Virgin Mary, for his paternal role in the earthly family of Jesus Christ. Joseph was not the biological father, yet he assumes his fatherhood and raises the son of God, who thus redeems the promise the Lord God had made to King David: "Behold, a son shall be born to thee [...] He shall build an house for my name; and he shall be my son, and I will be his father."[4] In the Gospel according to John, the apostle Philip addresses Jesus Christ thus: "Lord, shew us the Father, and it sufficeth us." And, not to forget, in the "Lord's Prayer" God is addressed as "Our father which art in heaven…," while in Proverbs, "The fear of the Lord is the beginning of knowledge; but fools despise wisdom and instruction."[5]

God the Father is the abstract deity of Christianity. It is easy to dismiss the custom as an unwarranted lapse into anthropomorphism. As a matter of philosophical principle, it makes no more sense to imagine God as a male (the conventionally strong type) than it does to picture God with the attributes we conventionally assign to women. God, after all, is ineffable, that is, beyond human comprehension. Even the book of Genesis acknowledges this: "God created man in his own image [...] male and female created he them" (Genesis 1:27). The passage suggests that God was an androgynous being, and that the first human beings, being created in his (or her) image, were therefore likewise male and female. But it can also be read to say that there was a male Jahwe with a female goddess on his side, the unnamed one whom the Israelites worshipped in the "groves."[6] Such "idolatry" was, of course, intolerable in a society whose heavenly chieftain was a metaphysical reflection of existing patriarchal power structures. Consequently, Moses receives instruction to "cut down [the goddesses'] groves" (Exodus 34:13). Patriarchal jealousy is even more explicit in Deuteronomy: "Thou shalt not plant thee a grove of any trees near unto the altar of the Lord thy God" (Deut. 16:21). Not that the injunction was always heeded. King Manasseh had the goddess's image erected in the temple (2 Kings 21:7). It was Manasseh's grandson, King Josiah, who in the seventh century BCE took upon himself the task of radical reform: "And he brought out the grove from the house of the Lord, without Jerusalem, unto the brook Kidron, and burned it at the brook Kidron, and stamped it to small powder, and cast the powder thereof upon the graves of the children of the people" (2 Kings 23:6). Still, monotheism probably was not universal until the period of the Maccabees, that is, the second century BCE.[7]

Leaving aside philosophical principles as well as the historic rise of monotheism, it is safe to say that a heavenly father is more of a metaphorical father than a biological or sociological one. Biological fathers, for their part, belong to what Thomas Hobbes described as the state of nature, that is, a state of "no society." Sociological fathers, in contrast, are not part of the state of nature, "[f]or in the condition of meer Nature [...] it cannot be known who is the Father." Put differently, for Hobbes fatherhood belongs to, if it is not a defining characteristic of, civilization.[8] Even as radically individualistic a philosopher as John Locke linked the transition from the state of nature to civil society to the notion of fatherhood, to what in 1698 he called "the Office and Care of a Father."[9] It is not too big a step from the "Paternal Care" and "Paternal affection" in what Locke defines as the "first Society," that is, the "conjunction between Man and Wife,"[10] to the metaphorical fathers in the rest of the community, that is, in society at large. Whereas the sociological father as guardian and protector is the male link between children and the rest of the community, the metaphorical father as guardian and protector is the male link between citizens or subjects and the rest of the community.

In England from the early seventeenth century, the role of the metaphorical father fell to the king. James I believed that he had to care for his subjects "like a father." But what kind of father? In James's eyes, the king was "divine power on earth," authorized by God, and himself the ultimate authority over all earthly beings.[11] The royalist doctrine of political absolutism changed with the "Revolution Settlement" of 1688–1689, under which the king of Great Britain became a limited monarch who reigned under a constitutional framework commonly defined as a mixed government. The arrangement cemented the patriarchal and familial political ideas and attitudes voiced in the North American colonists' eagerness to acclaim their sovereign as the "Father of His Country."[12] In a speech delivered to the Massachusetts General Assembly on December 2, 1731, the Hanoverian prince George II was so called by Governor Jonathan Belcher. The honorific was no mere flattery. It carried a clear vision of the monarch's role in the preservation or restoration of a well-ordered state. Indeed, for many contemporaries the most frightful notion was that of "a *fatherless world*." Such a world, Lord Shaftesbury wrote, was a "pattern of disorder … a vast and infinite Deformity," and what could be "more melancholy, than the Thought of living in a distracted Universe"?[13] Thus, when the Reverend Samuel Davies preached on the death of George II in 1760, his subject was not the king's death but the anxieties the death arouses. Taking his text from 2 Samuel 1:19 ("How are the mighty fallen!"), Davies asked: "If the Father of a People must cease to live, shall not the People expect to die?" Davies's rhetorical question reveals a profound sense of crisis, which was assuaged only when George III ascended the throne. The king was only twenty-two years old then (born in 1738), but on him the exalted title of the people's "father" was bestowed, for instance in a petition drawn up by the Massachusetts House of Representatives on June 30, 1768.[14]

In colonial America, religious voices frequently sounded the importance of the metaphorical father. For example, in a sermon titled *Two Discourses on Liberty*, Nathaniel Niles advised, "Let us return to our father's house."[15] Niles's advice, which was first published in 1774, raised a troubling question: Which house and which father? At the time, there was more than one answer to this question. Equally important, however, is the fact that from the beginning of the republic, Americans understood the nation metaphorically in family terms, with the president seen as an older male authority figure. George Washington was called "the *father* of his country," partly because he was the metaphorical progenitor who brought it into being and partly because he was seen as the legitimate head of state, which in terms of the metaphor is the head of the family, the father. Americans still talk about their founding *fathers*, and it is not at all unreasonable for them to deploy them when in doubt about political matters.[16] Additionally, to all presidents since Washington, and to all Americans, the presidency is the office of national "*fatherhood*." When the United States goes to war, it sends its *sons* (and now also its *daughters*) into battle. A *patriot* (from the Latin *pater*, for "father") is not just a sophisticated guided missile but also someone who loves his or her *fatherland*. And following 9/11, Americans have had *homeland* security.

All these terms suggest "family." This is not coincidental. As the linguist George Lakoff has argued, we are first governed in our families, and so we grow up understanding governing institutions in terms of the governing systems of families.[17] Significantly, the "nation-as-family" metaphor provides the symbolic stage on which feelings of orphanhood, of not belonging to or even being excluded from the national family, hence of fear, are acted out. "Fearful people," the philosopher Martha Nussbaum writes in her most recent book, "want protection and care. They turn to a strong and absolute ruler."[18] Thus to see Donald Trump as "the father I always wanted" makes perfect sense.[19] In epistemological terms, the "nation-as-family" concept is one of those basic assumptions that help us make sense of our experience. For, it is easier "to understand abstract and complex concepts with the help of more concrete and understandable concepts."[20] So why is there so much divisiveness and polarization today, as if we were living in yet another period of "creedal passion," to use Samuel Huntington's phraseology? One answer is that there is more than one version of the American creed, and when people have different visions of that creed, they tend to divide into a hyperpartisan landscape. It seems that that is where America is now.[21]

Certainly as regards the "nation-as-family" creed, Americans' worldviews today are "framed" by two very different cognitive models of family life—the one may be called the "strict father" family, the other the "nurturant parent" family.[22] The "strict father" family model is epitomized in the remark, made by a John Robinson in the early seventeenth century, that "surely there is in all children … a stubbornness, and stoutness of mind … which must, in the first place, be broken and beaten down."[23] The humility and tractability ensuing from such treatment is, then, the foundation of their education, by a father who knows best. It's the father who knows right from wrong and who is the ultimate authority in making sure that children and spouse do what he says, which is taken to be what is right. When the children disobey, the father will punish them so that they will obey him. Obedience and, with it, discipline are supposed to make the children strong and able to survive in the world. These are the values of social Darwinism, the survival of the fittest in shorthand. But the strict father logic extends further, to the idea of a "natural" moral hierarchy that puts men over women, adults over children, whites over blacks or any other non-whites, man above nature, the rich above the poor, employers over employees, and, of course, the U.S. of A. above all other countries. A manichean worldview thus perceives the world as sharply divided in good v. evil. (It is hardly a coincidence that Donald Trump's victory speech was introduced by the martial-sounding Jerry Goldsmith tune from Wolfgang Petersen's 1997 movie *Air Force One*.)

Since the most striking characteristics of the strict father logic are patterns of exclusion, one is either for or against something or someone. Care, protection, and share of the spoils thus are limited, exclusively dispensed among members of an in-group, and on the premise of unconditional loyalty and obedience. Paradoxically, though the strict father logic includes a sense of belonging to a community and the desire to put its interests first, it also entails a profound self-centeredness, not just on the part of the father, but also of the children: Everyone is solely responsible for himself or herself, not for others. Arguably this patriarchal authoritarianism is the kind of frame that swept Donald Trump into the highest office in the United States and that to this very day has characterized his politics. Already in his inaugural address, Trump announced plans to "unite the civilized world against Radical Islamic Terrorism, which we will eradicate completely from the face of the Earth."[24] We hear the voice of the Old Testament God, who in his wrath sets out to destroy all humankind, the righteous Noah excepted (Gen. 6:8). And we hear God's anger at his children's disobedience: "[T]hey walked not in my statutes, neither kept my judgments to them [and] they polluted my Sabbaths," and so the Lord God says: "I would pour out my fury upon them, to accomplish my anger against them in the wilderness / And I will cause you to pass under the rod, and I will bring you into the bond of the covenant: / And I will purge out from among you the rebels, and they that transgress against me: I will bring them forth out of the country where they sojourn, and they shall not enter into the land of Israel: and ye shall know that I am the Lord" (Ezekiel 20:21, and 37–38).

While the "strict father" model links to a conception of God as authoritarian transcendence and, concomitantly, to a literal interpretation of the Fifth Commandment ("Honour thy father and mother...," Exodus 20:12), the "nurturant parent" family, in contrast, reverses this. Its first premise is that children have "something much better than obedience to give" and that they are born "with good will rather than subordination, and that they are governable, from infancy up, much more gently than we think."[25] The "nurturant parent" family, then, emphasizes, not the need to crush children's will so much as love, empathy, social ties, protection of the needy, fairness, happiness, and cooperation. Children become responsible adults through being cared for and respected, and their obedience comes from their love and respect for their parents, not out of fear of punishment. Parents are expected to explain why their decisions serve the cause of nurturance. Asking questions is seen as positive, since children need to learn why their parents do what they do and since they often have good ideas that need to be taken seriously. The principal goal is for children to be fulfilled and happy in their lives, with their potential for achievement and enjoyment fully developed. This requires respecting the children's own values and allowing them to explore the range of ideas and options that the world offers. Within the "nurturant parent" family model, the father is close and supportive, not distant and authoritarian. In the social scientist David Blankenhorn's words, he is "fatherhood with a human face."[26] Or, to use an example from Scripture, "For where two or three are gathered together in my name, there am I in the midst of them" (Matthew 18:20). Here we have Jesus Christ reversing authoritarianism and dissolving it in a community that embraces the lowliest: "Verily I say unto you, Inasmuch as ye have done it unto the least of my brethren, ye have done it unto me" (Ibid. 25:40).

Altogether, God can be seen either as a moral authority to be obeyed (within the strict father model) or as a nurturer dispensing grace (within the nurturant parent model).[27] When we talk about "the father," therefore, we at one and the same time talk about a real person and a cultural model, an "anthropomorphized composite of cultural ideas about the meaning of paternity."[28] Cultural models of paternity (what Max Weber calls ideal social types and Lakoff calls idealized cognitive models) are crucial also in politics. The idealized family models respectively of strict father and nurturant parent help us make sense of both the presidential politics of the more recent past and the hyper-partisanship of today. What we need to see is that the "nation-as-family" perspective is attached to "frames," to value-laden descriptions of reality rather than to reality itself. "Frames" are eminently powerful mental mechanisms. By selecting a segment of reality and attributing certain values to it, frames constitute order from various heterogeneous parts, allowing people to interpret, evaluate, and make sense of their experience. But frames not only create form out of seeming chaos. They also "structure what is thought," to borrow from Pierre Bourdieu.[29]

The way something is formulated influences our beliefs and preferences. Nor are all frames equal. It does make a difference whether one announces that "from this moment on, it's going to be America First" (Donald Trump in his inaugural address) or that one's policy will be to crack down on immigration, building a wall against Mexico. The spin doctors in politics are well aware of this. With the help of frames, they shift around concepts, convictions, and debates until the values contained in them are capable of gaining a majority. Altogether, then, our preferences are frame-bound rather than reality-bound. "The conservative/liberal division," George Lakoff emphasizes, "is ultimately a division between *strictness* and *nurturance* as ideals at all levels—from the family to morality to religion and, ultimately, to politics." This means that a political "father" is not per se representative of a specific political conviction or moral worldview like "liberal" or "conservative." Rather, a political "father" can be "framed" within radically different interpretive frameworks or moral belief systems, each providing constraints on human experience. Both the strict father and the nurturant parent therefore are "felt truths," not facts. It is the values attributed to "father" that influence people's everyday decisions, much as they shape political life and impact on voter behavior.[30]

Donald J. Trump, the newly elected president, is on record for saying things like "I alone can fix it" or "I'm the greatest job producer God ever created."[31] And Trump has shown by his own example of a strict and fearless authority what it means to set aside childish things and bring in discipline, authority, boundaries, law and order, and self-interest. Already the producers of *The Apprentice* had carefully crafted a Trump character who was the quintessence of steely resolve and all-knowing mastery, a hard-to-please disciplinarian who demands respect. Trump only cemented this image on the campaign trail. And supporters described their preferred candidate in directly paternal terms, chanting, "Daddy's going to win! Daddy's going to win!" Another Trump supporter told the *Boston Globe*, "He's the kind of man you would want to be your dad. He's the father I always wanted. I feel like he's protecting me."[32] Of course, the job of the POTUS is not to be anybody's dad. No president is a wizard, capable of relieving citizens of their problems and fearfulness. Still, Trump's election to the presidency cannot be separated from the fact that a significant portion of Americans were yearning for a father's authority, and it was precisely the "strict dad" image that Trump himself projected.

Yearning for a "strict father," the historian Eli Zaretsky suggested, had come out of disappointment in Barack Obama, who had promised change but had not been strong enough to shape and beneficially order the political universe. Did Obama then unconsciously reject the role of a strong leader? In fact, when he was a candidate for the presidency in 2008, the quality most frequently picked by respondents in a national survey was "strong leadership." And in a poll conducted by the Pew Research Center in March 2008, a majority of respondents said that Obama would make them feel "hopeful and proud about themselves."[33] Supporters even expected Obama to quite literally assume a paternal role. "If I help him," a supporter said then, "he's going to help me!"[34] So far, so good. But Barack Obama related his presidency (and government in general) to the nurturant parent model. In his inaugural address he proclaimed that "the faith and determination of the American people [depend on] a parent's willingness to nurture a child that finally decides our fate."[35] After his reelection in 2012, Obama told a cheering crowd in Chicago: "It doesn't matter whether you're black or white or Hispanic or Asian or Native American or young or old or rich or poor, abled, disabled, gay or straight, you can make it here in America if you're willing to try."[36] During his final days in office, President Obama seemed to have known what was coming. Wary of identification of himself with a wizardly father figure, he insisted, in his Farewell Address of January 10, 2017, that "change only happens when ordinary people get involved, and they get engaged, and they come together to demand it." He added, by way of reminder, that the notion of "We, the People" dates to the nation's founders, constituting "the great gift that our Founders gave to us." And, in an obvious bid to the nurturant parent model, he said that "the long sweep of America has been defined by [...] a constant widening of our founding creed to embrace all, not just some." Yet there was a caveat, reminiscent of his first inaugural address: The widening of America's founding creed does not happen "on its own" but depends, rather, "on each of us accepting the responsibility of citizenship."[37]

This is, in a nutshell, what George Washington gave to the nation in his Farewell Address of September 19, 1796—the lofty and dignified summons to defend self-government as the underpinning of the nation's safety, liberty, and prosperity. Washington also did not flatter his people, but rather challenged them to improve their performance as citizens. He thought he had good reasons to do so. Washington had come to see that independence of the United States as a nation was inseparable from interdependence of Americans as a people. It was the latter issue that worried him deeply. Much as the nation's union was of "immense value" to the people's "collective and individual happiness," it was still fragile and under siege from "local discriminations."[38] But when he expounds his "apprehension of danger" further, talking about "internal and external enemies," he does so in a thinly disguised poke at Jefferson's Anti-Federalists or Republicans, who had become notorious for taking inspiration from and sympathizing with the struggling French Republic.[39] Various "combinations or associations," the outgoing president warned, "are likely ... to become potent engines by which cunning, ambitious, and unprincipled men will be enabled to subvert the Power of the People."[40] Obama's conclusion echoes Washington's dire warning, even though the coding is different. Obama called upon Americans to keep believing that everyone can make a difference, if he or she is willing to hitch their wagon "to something higher than yourselves." He thus identified the honor of the presidency with the country and the people who gave it to him and whom he regarded as his offspring. But now Americans were on their own: "I am asking you to believe," Obama. "Not in my ability to bring about change—but in yours."[41]

Americans were on their own also at the end of George Washington's second term, when the country's first President referred their future conduct to the "reflections and experience" of "friends and citizens." Washington's final resignation of power becomes the more meaningful because it meant giving up his most cherished possession. This time he

President Obama proposes direct education funding, Washington, D.C., April 24, 2009 (Aude Guerrucci-Pool/Getty Images).

was not giving up power to possess it. He was a father turning out his sons and daughters to make it on their own.⁴² Hence the string of injunctions towards the end: "Promote, then ... institutions for the general diffusion of knowledge.... Cherish public credit.... Observe good faith and justice towards all nations." Hence also an almost frantic appeal: "I conjure you to believe me, fellow-citizens." To believe, that his "counsels" were dictated by "the solicitude for your welfare," and that he was offering them as "an old and affectionate friend." Thus Washington spoke to posterity.⁴³ That was more than 200 years ago, but many Americans, policy-makers in particular, are still trying to please the Father of His Country. "What would the Founding Father think?" is a question routinely asked before a decision concerning the nation is made. And when matters of importance are to be made known to the nation, we can be sure that this is being done before a portrait of George Washington.⁴⁴

It is no coincidence that President Obama poses before a picture of the eternal symbol of the Father of His Country. Americans often look to presidents for moral clarity in critical moments. When Lincoln delivered his Gettysburg Address in 1863, he sought to bring the country together by pointing to the nation's common heritage, the creation of a new nation, dedicated to the proposition that all men were created equal. A hundred years later, President Kennedy called upon Lincoln's address when he called racial segregation a "moral issue." This was not the last time a president wielded his moral authority to unite the country in the midst of a crisis. After the 9/11 terror attacks, President George W. Bush spoke at the Islamic Center of Washington, telling Muslims that he did not want them to live in fear. "Women who cover their heads in this country must feel comfortable going outside their homes," Bush said. "Moms who wear cover must not be intimidated in America. That's not the America I know." Bush's intention clearly was to model behavior, much as he wanted to provide a road map for that behavior. This is also what President Obama wanted to achieve when he spoke at the eulogy for the Reverend Clementa Pinckney, who was one of nine people killed in the shooting at the Emanuel Methodist Episcopal Church in Charleston, South Carolina, on the evening of June 17, 2015. As Barbara Perry, a presidential historian at the University of Virginia's Miller Center, said, President Obama "conflated [...] the role of consoler-in-chief, mourner-in-chief and father of the country, with a clerical vision."⁴⁵

America's 45th president, it seems, is not overly sympathetic to the idea of exercising moral leadership. "I'm not putting anybody on a moral plane," he said three days after violent clashes between white nationalists and counterprotesters in Charlottesville, Virginia, on August 12, 2017, insisting that both sides were to blame.⁴⁶ It was a clear departure from traditional remarks typically heard from presidents. But Trump also departed from traditional venerations of the Father of His Country. Already his inauguration speech was said to be "Jacksonian," according to then chief White House strategist Stephen K. Bannon, who added that it had struck the populist and patriotic tones Andrew Jackson was known for. By that time, many commentators had made the comparison between Trump and Jackson explicit, but Trump himself embraced it. A mere four days after his inauguration, he hung a portrait of Andrew Jackson in the Oval Office, as "inspiration."⁴⁷ In choosing Jackson as his personal icon, Trump communicated the idea that he's a modern-day Old Hickory, a populist outsider and scourge of Washington's elites. Unsurprisingly, the portrait of America's seventh president has been on every official photograph showing President Trump at work.

Donald J. Trump also has been the first president in a long time to visit The Hermitage, Andrew Jackson's plantation home near Nashville, Tennessee. In a speech he gave there on the occasion of Jackson's 250th birthday on March 15, 2017, Trump called Jackson "the people's president," one who "confronted and defied an arrogant elite [and] rejected authority

1. On Fathers, Past and Present

Donald Trump speaks with Russian Leader Vladimir Putin from the White House, January 28, 2017 (Reuters/Jonathan Ernst).

that looked down on the common people." No mention was made of Jackson as a slaveowner, nor of his role as the architect of Indian removal, let alone of his willful destruction of the Bank of the United States. Jackson's victory, Trump remarked to much applause, "shook the establishment like an earthquake."[48] Yet why would Trump invoke Andrew Jackson to bolster his own legitimacy? Several of his predecessors in office had extolled Jackson, including Abraham Lincoln, who hailed him as a champion of the Union. For Trump or, rather, for the Trump camp the parallels are somewhat different. They see both presidents as political newcomers, as disrupters, fighters against a political establishment that despises them, champions against "the rich and powerful" (as Jackson said in his Bank Veto in 1832), as war heroes or at least as the champions of veterans, and as staunch nationalists who unhesitatingly install protective tariffs. Yet whatever the alleged parallels, and there are many more, they are on pretty shaky grounds. While there may be continuities, assertions of identity at best reveal a tenuous relation to the "real" Jackson.[49]

Donald Trump spoke at The Hermitage on March 15, 2017. Five days later, he met with Iraqi Prime Minister Haider al-Abadi in the Oval Office. The official photograph shows the two men sitting in front of the fireplace, with a replica of Rembrandt Peale's "Porthole" portrait of a uniformed George Washington over the mantle. The portrait also was over the mantle when Barack Obama met with the president-elect in the Oval Office on November 10, 2016. That Trump left it hanging is no surprise, given his predilection for the military. The heroic qualities, the commanding presence of the revolutionary years in Peale's portrait of a still-vigorous General Washington surely appealed to Trump. What also must have appealed to him is to have flags from different rooms brought to the Oval Office—flags of the Army, the Navy, the Marine Corps, the Coast Guard—making the room "a very special place."[50]

Using the walls of the White House to assert one's political inclinations is a longstanding practice among presidential administrations. It may come as a surprise, but to hang a portrait of Jackson in the Oval Office has been done before. Ronald Reagan, Lyndon Johnson, George H. W. Bush, and Bill Clinton all put up an image of "Old Hickory."[51] There is something disturbing, however, in posing in front of Ralph E. W. Earl's 1835 portrait of a leonine Jackson, dignified in a dramatic cloak, rather than in front of Stuart's serene portrait of Washington the enlightened statesman and symbol of republican virtue. The choice suggests a continuity from the populism espoused by Andrew Jackson to that of Donald J. Trump. The continuity has been articulated, *inter alia*, in the message that the new president is "unequivocally yours." In short, then, Trump sees himself as the new Father of His Country, and as a strict one, too. As Trump said about Jackson, he was "a very tough person, but he had a big heart."[52]

So, in a sense, was George Washington, and he had a big heart, too. Let's deal with the tough person first. "The basis of our political systems," Washington wrote in his Farewell Address, "is the right of the people to make and to alter their Constitutions of Government." Yet this strict father added a caveat: "The very idea of the power and the right of the People to establish Government presupposes the duty of every Individual to *obey* the established Government." Washington would have explained that this did not spell slavish obedience but, as always, national unity, which was, he wrote, "a main Pillar in the Edifice of your real independence, the support of [...] that very Liberty which you so highly prize."[53] Now to the big heart. Washington didn't talk about bringing back jobs in his Farewell Address, let alone promise, however simplistically, to create many more and better ones.[54] Instead, he warned of the "despotism" arising from the "alternate domination of one faction over another." The "disorders and miseries" resulting from this, America's first president continued, "gradually incline the minds of men to seek security and repose in the absolute power of an Individual; and sooner or later the chief of some prevailing faction, more able or more fortunate than his competitors, turns this disposition to the purposes of his own elevation, on the ruins of Public Liberty."[55]

George Washington was known as the Father of His Country already during his lifetime. To all presidents since, and to all Americans, the presidency has been the office of "national fatherhood." As Thomas Langston remarked, "whatever his actual qualities as a person, [the president] stands as the preeminent symbol of national identity. As the symbol of the nation, the president embodies the beliefs and values of the American people and fulfills emotional and psychological needs among the population."[56] Langston's remarks were published in 2004. Today, it is difficult to see Donald J. Trump as "the preeminent symbol of national identity," especially in light of what he said on January 20, 2017:

> Today we are not merely transferring power from one Administration to another, or from one party to another—but we are transferring power from Washington, D.C. and giving it back to you, the American People. [...] because this moment is your moment: it belongs to you. It belongs to everyone gathered here today and everyone watching all across America. This is your day. This is your celebration. And this, the United States of America, is your country.[57]

Such words make it difficult to imagine that George Washington would have been "gladdened by this day," to borrow George H. W. Bush's words of 1989. Instead, one is tempted to invoke Karl Marx who, adding to Hegel's dictum, wrote: "All great historic facts and personages recur twice ... once as tragedy, and again as farce."[58] Closer to home, one is reminded of Will Rogers, who midway through the disastrous presidency of Herbert Hoover quipped that George Washington "would sue us for calling him 'father.'"[59] On a more serious note, one can hardly escape the question, raised recently by the legal scholar Cass Sunstein, whether it can happen here, "it" being the "despotism" George Washington had warned against in his Farewell Address. Trump's resentment toward government, repeated ad nauseam in his inauguration speech, indeed is quite the opposite of Washington's conservative republicanism. For Washington, a government "by the people" was simply anathema. America's first president could never bring himself to accept the notion that all the people were equally endowed with political virtue and disinterestedness. Some people, he thought, were clearly more virtuous than others and could more safely be entrusted with the affairs of government.[60]

Donald J. Trump's inaugural address had little in common with the one by the nation's founder. Instead, his lines resonated with the sentiment Richard Nixon expressed in his second inaugural address of 1973: "We have lived too long with the consequences of attempting to gather all power and responsibility in Washington. [...] Abroad and at home, the time has come to turn away from the condescending policies of paternalism—of 'Washington knows best.'"[61] Trump has taken Nixonian sentiment one step further. His resentment against the federal government borders on, or even embraces, hatred. And it was heard. Lest I be misunderstood, I am not saying that Trump—or, for that matter, the people who voted for him—hate their country. Throughout his campaign, Trump professed to be a true patriot. His inaugural speech, too, has a deep root of patriotism. It is in Trump's declared "new vision"—that "from this moment on, it's going to be America First." And it is in his promise that "the bedrock of our politics will be a total allegiance to the United States of America." Thus, he suggested, "It is time to remember that old wisdom our soldiers will never forget: that whether we are black or brown or white, we all bleed the same red blood of patriots, we all enjoy the same glorious freedoms, and we all salute the same great American Flag."[62]

Trump did not specifically refer to the nation's founders in his inaugural address, though his avowed patriotism nicely fits the wish to restore the old American republic that is being entertained among pro–Trump conservatives. Especially associates of the Claremont Institute, a right-wing think tank based in California, have for years been discussing the Federalist Papers, the dangers of progressivism, and the wisdom of Leo Strauss, a German exile and political philosopher who taught for decades at the University of Chicago, exposing several generations of students to an amalgam of natural rights, natural law, human nature (humans are by nature evil, therefore they are in need of dominion), the possible coexistence of freedom and excellence, and the policy implications of all this. A "permissive egalitarianism," Strauss pontificated in the 1960s, had debased contemporary American society. Strauss's was not a lone voice in the wilderness. Thomas G. West (a former student of Strauss and a former teacher at Claremont) in a new book, *The Political Theory of the American Founding*, argues that the Founding Fathers had created a uniquely virtuous republic whose greatness derived from biblical religion and classical philosophy—that is, from ancient as opposed to modern principles.[63]

The question remains how Trump and his followers can love the country and its founders, at the same time as they appear to resent and hate the government? We can trace that resentment to the "strict father" model. In that model, the mature children are on their own. They sink or swim by themselves. And, having attained self-reliance and responsibility through iron discipline, they resent any parental meddling or interference. By extension, they know what is good for them better than their government. For them, a good government "does not meddle or interfere in their lives. Any governmental meddling or interfering is strongly resented."[64] Clearly, then, spurred by Trump's promises to "Make America great again" and to put "America first," many Americans have become "patriots" again, turning to Trump as an all-powerful father who will at one and the same time protect them and tell them that they are ok as they are. This is a gesture that once again makes these people feel at home, not in their mother country but quite literally in a fatherland.

This brings us back full circle to Barack Obama's inaugural address of 2009, the "dad speech." Obama's message was the exact opposite of Trump's—you have to change yourself! No doubt to do so is difficult, while it is much more comforting to find someone who understands (or says he understands) your quirks and eccentricities, even your weaknesses and vices. People are easily enchanted by magicians, and political magicians, once they gain their hearts have them at their beck and call. Obama, in contrast, is not known to have told people that they are ok as they are, not in his inaugural address, and also not in an earlier speech, in which he set out to drive home the point that fatherhood is not just a function of men's procreative capacity but rather of their courage to raise children and to accept responsibility for them: "It makes a difference when a father realizes that responsibility does not end at conception; when he understands that what makes you a man is not the ability to have a child, but the courage to raise one."[65]

That's easier said than done. Many men may be completely unsuitable, with their talents lying elsewhere. Others may feel simply overburdened by the role assigned to them, while still others may find different reasons for not accepting their responsibilities. Moreover, even those men who try often feel that the cards are stacked against them, as in custody battles in divorce proceedings. To his credit, Barack Obama did not simply demand the seemingly impossible, he also considers possible causes. What about those men who never saw their own father in the house? Or else, what if they lost their fathers at an early age? Given such conditions, how can they possibly be responsible? The answer, Obama said in the Father's Day speech he gave in Chicago's Salem Baptist Church, is to redouble one's efforts: "[P]recisely because many of us didn't have fathers in the house we have to redouble our efforts to break the circle."[66]

Breaking the circle had been on the agenda already of the Clinton administration. In July 1994, Vice President Al Gore spoke about fatherhood as "the most important role that any of us will ever play in life," admonishing men who wanted little or no part of that role after becoming fathers.[67] Thus he set about to push employers in the direction of enabling employees to spend more time with their kids, he launched a "Father to Father" program, and he encouraged Fathernet, an Internet forum for fathers to communicate with each other and share ideas. One of the strongest advocates of these and other initiatives was Al Gore's boss, President Bill Clinton, who in the public imagination became the most well-known American dad of the late 1990s, and a truly "national dad" for that matter.[68] But as justified as all these initiatives were, they were not nearly enough to stop what the social scientist David Blankenhorn in 1995 called "the most destructive trend of our generation."[69] Almost twenty years later, Stephen Marche put on the table the "brute facts: The number of American families without fathers has grown from 10.3 percent in 1970 to 24.6 percent in 2013." With over 17 million children fatherless in the United States, Marche has few illusions left. "There is no cure for fatherlessness," he wrote in *Esquire* magazine in 2014.[70]

If not even a redoubling of efforts seems sufficient to solve the fatherhood crisis, it might make more sense to put one's trust in God. To do so would, at any rate, be in keeping with the nation's self-understanding. As of the 1950s, the United States no longer has been simply "one nation," but "one nation, under God," and the call to trust in God has become a daily reminder to the people who still handle dollar bills. Alternatively, fathers then could be met on television, as in the series *Father Knows Best*. The series began in 1949 as an NBC radio broadcast and became instantly popular. Its popularity only increased when it was taken over by television in 1954. Many stations broadcast the series through 1964. Its popularity no doubt rested on the family values at its core. *Father Knows Best* reflects the cultural climate of the postwar era. Like other sit-coms of the time, it reconstituted and resocialized the American family after World War II. It linked real (chiefly white middle-class) families with the paternalistic imagined community of the nation, substituting imaginary social relations for real ones, and masking social contradictions. Hence the idealized figure of the show's title, an extraordinarily patient, wise, and warm-hearted father, the breadwinner who assumes a role of paternal authority and thus becomes the solid emotional basis for all members of the family, the homemaker mother as well as the growing children, all placed within the domestic space of the suburban home.[71]

The enthusiastic embrace, among post-war Americans, of the traditional values of family life began as soon as fathers came "marching home."[72] Millions of American children had experienced what social scientists had called the primary social problem caused by World War II—war-induced fatherlessness. This "mass-deprivation," as one scholar called it, was temporary for some; for others, it permanently disrupted their lives, as soldier-fathers were killed in combat or returning fathers proved unable to establish good relationships with their children. But the idyll of domestic containment, heavily defined as it was by consumption, leisure, and suburbanization, often was just as disappointing. Following the War's end, women were forced from their positions as skilled labor; men not only became the breadwinners again but were also expected to brave the storms of economic growth and the concentration of business, an impossible burden. It does not come as a surprise that many children found that they did not like their fathers very much, including Jim, Judy, and Plato, the three main characters in the 1955 movie *Rebel without a Cause*, who all have dysfunctional fathers—either absent, overbearing and strict, or impossible to command any respect. Similarly, for the young hero in J. D. Salinger's *The Catcher in the Rye*, fathers—as well as adults in general—are just "phoney," determined only to make children "play it according to the rules."[73]

Doubtless there were such fathers in the 1950s. But Salinger's Holden Caulfield, lost, directionless, with nothing to hold on to or to break away from, is pretty much an unreliable narrator and, Blankenhorn contends, as a group, "the fathers of the 1950s did rather well by their children, at least compared to the fathers who preceded and followed them. They got and stayed married. [If] these fathers sometimes fell asleep while reading the paper or watching TV, they did so partly because their work made them tired." Importantly, they "spent more time with their children than their own fathers had with them, and also more than their sons, living in a divorce culture, would later spend with *their* children." Altogether, the fathers of the 1950s were "the most domesticated generation of fathers in modern American history."[74] There may be a good deal of idealizing in Blankenhorn's account here, though a look at the parents' advice literature of the 1950s supports it. The culturally dominant ideas governing the father-child relationship of the 1950s were values like emotional closeness, participation, and physical affection.[75] Significantly, these values also governed contemporary characterizations of George Washington. Howard Swiggett's 1953 Washington, for instance, is a compound of "goodness and charity, troubles and woe ... believing in dignity and decorum but able to laugh at or discard them." Two years later, Saul K. Padover characterizes the Father of His Country as a "passionate, sensitive, earthy, deeply feeling human being."[76]

Understanding paternity, including metaphorical paternity, in terms of emotional closeness, participation, and physical affection has not gone away. If anything, it has become intensified, extending to the presidency. To be a good president, it seems, you have to like or at least give the appearance of liking kids. John F. Kennedy was a master of this, as he consistently used to put himself and his family in position to be photographed. Contemporary celebration of involved presidential fatherhood was scripted, for instance, into the immensely popular NBC series *The West Wing*, which ran from September 1999 through May 2006.[77] The fictional Chief Executive in *The West Wing*, who is played by Martin Sheen, is truly an involved parent, who lovingly attends to his daughter even amid political crises. (He even accepts the fact that his daughter is dating a black youth, who works in the White House as an intern.) "President Josiah (Jed) Bartlet" also keeps his staff out of mischief, most notably Josh Lyman, in the very first episode, and he consistently pronounces what is the case. Unsurprisingly, the White House Press Secretary, J.C., in Episode 6 calls him "a very protective father." Lest anyone misses the connection to the "wise man" people can trust, there are many shots that show the fictional POTUS in front of Stuart's "Athenaeum" portrait of George Washington.[78] *The West Wing* received much acclaim from critics, as well as praise from political scientists. Yet its popularity was chiefly among higher-income viewers.[79] Critics also found that the series was unjustifiably optimistic, sentimental, and forgetful of the dirty realities of politics—it was, in short, "feel-good" television marred by "pseudo-politics."[80]

After the election of George W. Bush in November 2000, the show continued to appeal to a broad audience of both Democrats and Republicans. Change came with the fictional 2006 election and the real-life 2008 United States presidential election. Suddenly the show was labeled "Left 'Wing'" because of its portrayal of an ideal liberal administration.[81] As much as conservatives may have tolerated a revisionist look at the Clinton presidency, the Obama presidency was a clear no-go. This view seems most pronounced among Republicans. An American Values Survey in 2016 found that roughly two-thirds of Republicans prefer America as it was in the 1950s.[82] Perhaps they remembered (or had been told about) the shreds of fatherhood, as head of the family and as breadwinner, that could be found in that era. As Daniel Yankelovich wrote in 1994, "until the late 1960s, being a real man meant being a good provider for the family. No other conception of what it means to be a real man came even close." But Yankelovich is careful to add that even that diminished definition of a real man was gone by the 1970s and was continuing to erode through the 1990s.[83] If fatherhood was diminished, it also was devalued. From the 1970s, fathers were simply not very important. A generation later, however, fathers are returning home again, including metaphorical fathers. George Washington's rankings for instance have improved dramatically, much as numerous "Georgers" have rallied against the phasing out of the one-dollar bill with his likeness on it. As for real fathers, the *Economic Report of the President* of the year 2000 has over 30 pages on them.[84] The report was published during the administration of George W. Bush, always a champion of fatherhood (and "family values" in general). Seventeen years later, even as autocratic a president as Donald Trump habitually showcases his children to make the case that his leadership style would prove inspiring rather than alienating to Americans (or at least to those who voted him into office).

2

George Washington Becomes the Father of His Country

When Samuel Davies reminded the British, in January 1761, that "George was our father, too," he was referring to George II, the English King, who had died in October the year before. In 1774, Nathaniel Niles still values that veneration, this time reserved for George III: "[L]et the world see that their king is dearer to the Americans than their blood."[1] At the time of the first Continental Congress, several delegates clung to the pleasing fiction that a benevolent George III was under the evil spell of a tyrannical ministry, and they implored the king as their "loving father" to employ his royal prerogative to rescue his colonial subjects. Two years later, the hope that "the horrors of civil discord [could be] prevented" had given way to a furious disillusionment. George III no longer figured as the Father of His Country but had become a "tyrant" neglecting his "children." This was the rage of unfulfilled expectations, a willful denial and suppression of a much-valued family connection. The "expected father of his people" had looked on "the violation of American rights […] with a most unfatherly calmness."[2] The charge was a severe one. First raised in this form during a meeting of the Congress, it found its way into one of America's most sacred documents. "A Prince whose character is thus marked by every act which may define a Tyrant," the Declaration of Independence concludes, "is unfit to be the ruler of a free people."[3] As a piece of secular Scripture, the Declaration of Independence holds a special place in the political and cultural history of the United States. Yet what many colonists felt about the sovereign in far-away London was also articulated through more profane documents—pamphlets, newspaper articles, editorials, broadsides, songs and poems, prints, cartoons, and speeches, sermons, letters, plays, fiction, and, as we will see presently, pieces of paper money and coins.[4]

Thomas Jefferson had used a good deal of anti–British rhetoric already in *A Summary View of the Rights of British America*, and with George III as his real opponent: "But can his Majesty thus put down all law under his feet?" Jefferson asked in 1774, and he answers the question with a direct attack on the king: "[L]et him remember that force cannot give right." Elsewhere in the pamphlet Jefferson talks about "arbitrary measures," "designs of despotism," "the hand of oppression," and "exercises of usurped power," thus transforming the English monarch into an alien presence and loyalty to him into an unnational act.[5] But the "first catalyst of change," at least in the form of literature, was Thomas Paine's *Common Sense*. While many colonists clung to the myth of George III as a benign father in thrall to treacherous ministers, for Paine, the king of England becomes the acknowledged enemy. Thus, he bluntly attacks the king as the "Royal Brute of Great Britain," whose rule is to be replaced by "a continental form of government" in which "the law is king." Only God, Paine writes, reigns above this new creation as "the King of America."[6] *Common Sense* was published in Philadelphia on January 10, 1776. Its success was phenomenal. The pamphlet ran through one hundred and twenty thousand copies in three months. It also has become "the one pamphlet from the period that still captures the imagination of the American reader," thus living as literature today. Yet at the time the "natural and intended audience" of Paine's invective was "the American mob," to use Robert Ferguson's words. *Common Sense* indeed appropriates the language of the mob, embracing it in a collective union through the ever-present "we," and empowering people to action through its unbridled anger. Both the pamphlet's language and its tone distinguish it—as well as publications by other writers whose rhetoric had been liberated by Paine's immediacy—from the more formal prose of John Dickinson's *Letters from a Farmer in Pennsylvania* or Jefferson's *Summary View*, which were restrained by a decorum of loyalty that owed a good deal to fears of inflaming the populace.[7]

Paine's *Common Sense* is not the only exception to the rhetoric of restrained feelings; another one is a Maryland bank note from July 1775, which repeats Paine's invective through pictorial language. The note, which was produced by the woodcutter Thomas Sparrow and the printer Frederick Green, constitutes a veritable revolutionary tableau, advertising the identity and merits of the colonial fraternity.

An allegory of Britannia is shown receiving a congressional petition (abbreviated as "CONG PETI") from a female figure representing America. America is trampling on a scroll marked "SLAVERY" and holding a liberty cap in front of American troops gathered under a flag inscribed with "LIB" (for "LIBERTY"). As for the metaphorical father, George III is depicted trampling on a scroll marked "M.[AGNA] CHARTA" as he is about to set fire to a city (Annapolis or Baltimore) under attack by a British fleet. Even the frame of the bill is trimmed with patriotic propaganda. At left is a Latin motto, "PRO ARIS ET FOCIS" ("FOR ALTARS AND HEARTHS"), at left a few words in English that reveal the urgency of the cause, "AN APPEAL TO HEAVEN."[8] The purpose of the issue, which was done without the British government's approval, that is, illegally, was to finance the acquisition of

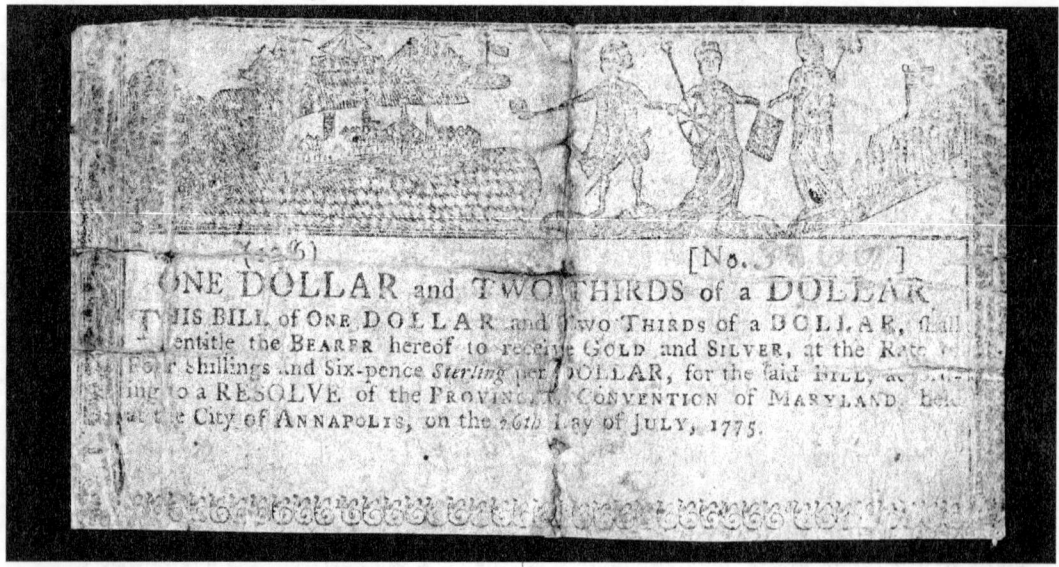

Maryland issue, 1 and ⅔ Dollars, July 26, 1775, front (2.75 × 3.6 in.) (Division of Work and Industry, National Museum of American History, Smithsonian Institution).

gunpowder (hence the colloquialism "gunpowder notes"). The bills were redeemable against Spanish silver dollars until January 1, 1786, to the generous rate of 4s and 6d to the dollar. The liberty cap (also known as Phrygian cap or *pileus*) recalls the Roman tradition. It was worn by former slaves on the day of their manumission. The tradition was revived in eighteenth-century France, when the cap came to symbolize liberation from tyrannical rule. Unsurprisingly, it became tremendously popular with the Jacobins. In the aftermath of the battles of Lexington and Concord in April 1775 American "patriots" too adopted the cap as a symbol of liberation from tyrannical rule and, as well, of republican government.

The Maryland notes visibly communicate the decline in the colonists' faith in their sovereign and a preparedness for rebellion, together with liberty and republican rule as the only form of government that is fit for America. Yet the back of the notes is much more low-key, even conciliatory, as if the inflammatory pictorial rhetoric of the front had to be somehow constrained. We see Britannia and America joining hands; the olive branch between them symbolizes peace. The message is reinforced through another Latin motto suggesting that peace was still more desirable than war—"PAX TRIUMPHIS POTIOR."[9] The Maryland notes are from July 1775. A little over a year later, the iconography on some Virginia notes is much more drastic, the mood openly furious, furious enough to act against England. An allegorical figure—Virtue, with spear in hand—is seen standing with her foot on the prostrate form of Tyranny, whose crown lies nearby. The motto too could not have been more direct: "*SIC SEMPER TYRANNUS.*" "Tyrannus" is, of course, grammatically incorrect. It was set right in the 1778 issue. Henceforth it read "SIC SEMPER TYRANNIS" ("Thus always to Tyrants")—and can be read on the flag of the State of Virginia to this very day.[10]

The outcome of the conflict between the English mother country and the United Colonies is well known. Less well known is that the revolutionaries faced a deeply divided people. Thus, their assumed task was "to extract consensus at all costs," to appeal to what Thomas Jefferson in 1825 called "harmonizing sentiments."[11] These sentiments were imaginatively recast in the trope of "a more perfect union" (in the Preamble to the Federal Constitution) as well as in the national motto, "E Pluribus Unum" (adopted for the second Continental Congress in 1782). The two phrases suggest that the newly forming national identity had no place for apocalyptic conflict. Even controversy was to be avoided as much as possible. Many Americans, for instance, were hostile to the notion of a national federal republic in 1787, so the Constitution, in creating one, never mentions the words "national," "federal," or "republic." The "limits and forms of the sayable," to borrow from Foucault,[12]

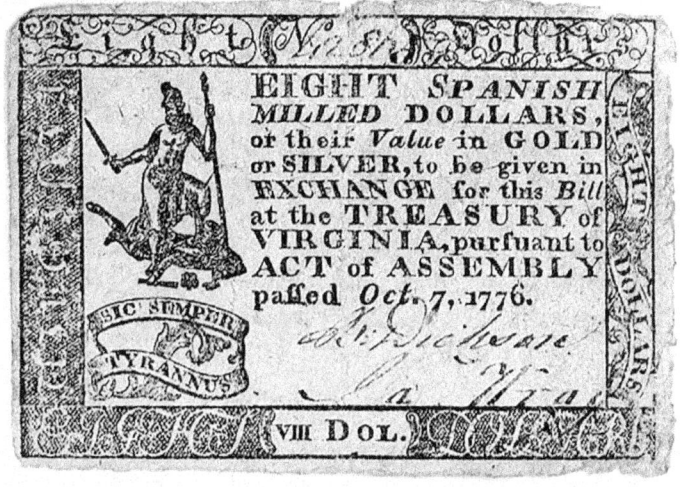

Virginia issue, October 7, 1776, front (3.5 × 2.7 in.) (Princeton University Numismatic Collection, Department of Rare Books and Special Collections, Firestone Library, Princeton University).

were transcended by other means, though, chiefly by the personification of public virtue. Construed thus, the separation from England was seen as a natural movement toward the control of one's own destiny. Often, however, it implied a deeply traumatic experience, the irreparable loss of the orphan. The distinction, Robert Ferguson suggests, depends at least in part on assumptions about the maturation process in America. "Only children can be orphans." And, one might add, only children can be expected to cast together their completed or at least stilled angers in the role of founding fathers.[13] Among the founders, the austere and commanding figure of Washington became the undisputed symbol of authority, and, since George III was destroyed as a symbolic entity, the exalted title of "Father of His Country" was transferred onto him.[14]

The identification of George Washington with the newly forming nation constituted an act of communal incorporation, much as it constituted a basic act of mutual recognition between leaders and led. In these acts, leaders—the "gods of the clan," in Émile Durkheim's words—are deemed superior in dignity and power, that is to say, "sacred," not because of any inherent qualities so much as because they symbolize something greater than themselves—the moral authority of society or nation.[15] George Washington became the moral authority of the American nation when the second Continental Congress appointed the Virginian commander in chief of the Continental Army, then gathered in Cambridge, Massachusetts. At this point Washington may not have been ready for America, but America was ready for him. As of June 19, 1775, he was America's "living 'tribal' totem."[16] His name became the signal for unlimited panegyric in prose and verse. He was the pride and glory of America. In his hands was put "the sword of liberty … by the unanimous voice of his country."[17] In January 1776, Levi Allen, younger brother of Ethan Allen, hailed Washington as "Our political Father and head of a Great People."[18] And just over a year later, Brigadier General Henry Knox, possibly drawing from his vast reading in the writers of classical Rome, wrote, "the People of America look up to you as their Father, and into your hands they entrust their *all*."[19]

These early manifestations of Washington worship clearly answered to the incipient nation's need to articulate and concretize the fervent beliefs and emotions of its citizens and the intangible virtues of the patriots' cause. It does not really matter, therefore, who first explicitly referred to Washington as the Father of His Country. In the interest of historical accuracy, however, it is worth noting that the appellation was first used in print on the cover of an almanac published in Lancaster, Pennsylvania, in 1778. As the yearbook was published in German, the paean read "*Des Landes Vater*," and Washington, who was a mere forty-six at the time, was spelled "*Waschington*." The cover depicts a winged figure of Fame holding a suspended portrait of Washington; from the figure's trumpet the words "*Des Landes Vater*" are blasted forth. The unknown artist was also the first to represent Washington in a medallion portrait, the first to crown him with a laurel wreath, and the first to depict him together with the trumpeting figure of Fame, a motif that was then associated with the Cincinnatus legend.[20]

The likeness, in the almanac's illustration, to the historic person is negligible; Washington rather resembles a generic folk-art figure, in striking contrast to Charles Wilson Peale's portrait of 1772. The painting, which also marks the first visualization of Washington, shows him in the uniform of a Colonel in the Virginia Militia. Since Washington had retired from soldiering in 1758, the serene painting seemingly offers a nostalgic backward glimpse to the former warrior. The red uniform suggests pride in being a member of the British empire, fighting the French; but with an Order of March protruding from Washington's fob pocket, the painting is also truly prophetic, suggesting that an armed conflict with England was no longer unthinkable.²¹ Still, the images in the Pennsylvania almanac for 1779 constitute the first pictorial renderings that explicitly link Washington to the newly forming nation. Identification of George Washington with the nation also speaks from another foreign-language document from October 1783, in the form of a poem composed in Washington's honor and sent to him by a "Lady in Holland," the Dutch poetess Lucretia Wilhelmina van Winter of Leyden. The poem uses the exact phrase of "the Father of his Country" at the end of its twenty-some stanzas:

> Et que votre Statue, au Conseil etablie,
> Soit par le grand Congres de ces nots honoré.
> Contemplez Washington, Père de la Patrie,
> Defenseur de la Liberté.²²

The two phrases—"The Father of his Country, the Protector of Liberty"—are telling. They constitute Washington both as a metaphorical father and as a warrior. Increasingly, however, the warrior frame was left behind, while the father frame prevailed, becoming dominant in the end. On the eve of the Federal Convention in Philadelphia Henry Knox wrote Washington to consider revisions to the Articles of Confederation. Knox urged Washington to attend the Convention, suggesting that his "signature" would "doubly entitle you to the glorious republican epithet—The Father of Your Country."²³ Washington also needed some prodding to accept the presidency. To sway him to run, Gouverneur Morris on December 6, 1788, slyly alluded to his childless state: "You will become a Father to more than three Millions of Children."²⁴ By the time of Washington's inauguration, use of the title had become even more common. During Washington's journey to New York City, a Pennsylvania paper reported: "Every countenance seeked to say, Long live George Washington, the Father of the People."²⁵ Similar rhetoric met Washington upon his arrival in New York: "All ranks and profession," a contemporary observer recorded, "expressed their feelings, in loud acclamations, and with rapture hailed the arrival of the Father of his Country." Officials and legislators from New York, Connecticut, and Massachusetts, as well as various correspondents, addressed Washington with similar titles, including the "Father of our Country," the "Saviour of Your Country," and the "Great Father of thy People."²⁶

Petitions from veteran soldiers as well as praises from children also kept pouring in. And in a poem published in Philadelphia in 1789 and titled "Inscribed to the Father of His Country" an "untutor'd muse, with feeble lays" brings together several aspects of Washington's exemplary character—his leadership in war, at the same time heroic, inspiring, and caring, his public virtue, his Cincinnatus-like willingness to resign power, and, as the nation's first president, his paternal care in protecting his children's liberties against external and internal enemies. The poem closes with the earnest wish that "future ages still applaud thy fame, / And tyrants only shudder at thy name."²⁷ The extravagance of figure and gesture of "Inscribed" was typical of the neoclassical poetry of the Revolutionary and Early National periods. Poetry of this kind was widely produced and just as widely consumed, though more often than not in a thoroughly anonymous print culture. That quintessentially republican print culture, Max Cavitch argued, "put a premium on fellow feeling as an index of social coherence."²⁸ The same can be said about public oratory. A good example is an Independence Day oration delivered by the youthful William Munford, the first American translator of Homer, in Williamsburg, Virginia, in 1793:

> Immortal Washington! Thou shield of the wide-spread states of America! Revered by thy enemies—beloved as a father by those who followed thy steps to glory—why shall we find thy parallel?—Shall

the annals of Greece and Rome be ransacked for this purpose? ... Let Trenton—let Princeton—let our native York bear witness to thy matchless vigilance and glory....[29]

Personal correspondence was not subject to the authorial anonymity that characterized republican print culture and oratory, though a rather impersonal discourse likewise was a condition of generalized fellow feeling. In the same year as "Inscribed" was published in Philadelphia, John Bell, Revolutionary soldier, statesman, and Washington's first biographer, wrote to a friend in Europe that Washington's name "will command the veneration of the latest posterity."[30] Also in 1779, the Supreme Executive Council of Pennsylvania recognized the importance of Washington's image and commissioned Charles Wilson Peale to document an early Revolutionary War triumph in *George Washington at Princeton*, intended by the council to "excite others to tread in the same glorious and disinterested steps which lead to public happiness and private honor." Certainly that was the intention of David Rittenhouse with the Pennsylvania almanac for 1779, which for the first time pronounced Washington as the "Father of His Country." In 1795, a Philadelphia magazine also hailed the "Father of His Country." James Hardie's commemorative book of the same year eulogized Washington as "the father of his country and the friend of mankind." Ten years later, Hardie's short paragraph had swollen to twenty-five pages. The tenor had not changed, though. Of Washington's 1783 journey back to Mount Vernon—Washington had resigned his commission as commander in chief—Hardie wrote, "[H]e was every where received with all possible demonstrations of respect, and universally hailed as the father, the deliverer of his country."[31]

By the time of his death in 1799, Washington had been the subject of eight separate biographical accounts, and the exalted title Father of His Country had entered the public consciousness. "The dearest and best of all appellations, '*The father of his country*,' was the natural fruit of that benevolence which he so carefully cultivated through life." These are the words of Mason Locke Weems. Weems's *The Life of Washington*, first published in 1800, became an instant bestseller, establishing its author, who usually referred to himself as Parson Weems, as Washington's first hagiographer.[32] Although Weems uses the exact phrase "father of his country" only twice, allusions to Washington as a nurturant parent abound. In Weems's account, General Washington is in tears when he takes leave from his soldiers, for "nature stirred all the father within him." As president, he "with a father's joy ... could look around on the thick-settled country." And even after he had passed away, Washington remained "a shepherd father [to the] sons and daughters of Columbia." Weems's biography is no mere narration of Washington's public career; rather, the book describes Washington's "private virtues" for the "humble imitation" of his "example."[33] Washington's goodness is not, however, merely a moral model for others to emulate but also serves to legitimate the new political order. Washington's "private virtues" shelter the new nation against any lingering partisan claims, cementing the link between his—and therefore the nation's—civic and moral identity. By representing Washington in this way, Washington becomes truly representative of the republic.

While Weems fashioned Washington to the needs of a fledgling nation, the title Father of His Country was in vogue also abroad. The poem composed in Washington's honor and sent to him by a "Lady in Holland" in 1783 has been mentioned. Another instance is the recommendation, by David Steuart Erskine, eleventh Earl of Buchan, to constantly remember "the moral and political Maxims conveyed to [America's] citizens by the Father and Founder of the United States."[34] Parson Weems, too, calls attention to the fact that the idea, if not the exact phrase of "Father of His Country" was also used by foreign travelers to the United States. He notes that the Chevalier de Chastellux, upon his visit to Washington's Continental Army headquarters during the Revolutionary war, had admitted to being quite "astonished and delighted to see this great American living among his officers and men as a father among his children, who at once revered and loved him with a filial tenderness." And, Weems claims, a French journalist who visited Mount Vernon in 1788 had assured his readers that "throughout the continent, everybody spoke of Washington as of a father."[35]

To modern readers, Weems's saccharine style seems unmistakably Rousseauvian, especially when he tests our patience with his references to Washington as a father figure. Rousseau had expanded on the "sweet sentiment [of] paternal love" in the first of his *Discourses*.[36] The idea of paternal love seems to have caught on especially in America, where the stern, authoritarian father of the traditional patriarchal family was, if not replaced, at least coexistent with more affectionate relationships between father and children. These relationships prepared children for independence and moral self-sufficiency, a combination that, in Jay Fliegelman's opinion, "easily extended to an argument for colonial rights." When the colonists' rationale needed materialization, it found one in Washington, "Father, Friend, and Guardian." Washington thus was "the embodiment of the new understanding of paternity." The reconstituted father made it possible for the colonists to transfer both their filial affections and the exalted title of Father of His Country from King George to President George Washington. Washington's idealization as *patriae pater*, Fliegelman concludes, "served to complete the transformation of the antipatriarchal ideology into a national dogma."[37]

Fliegelman's interpretation has come under attack as a neo–Freudian aberration, though the idea that the emergence of democracy in America went hand in hand with the reconstitution of fatherhood already can be found in Alexis de Tocqueville. As this famous French visitor saw the new relation of father and children, it was "more intimate and affectionate; rules and authority are less talked of; confidence and tenderness are oftentimes increased, and it would seem that the natural bond is drawn closer."[38] Tocqueville was a precise observer, who did not fail to notice that the era in which public deeds were the measure of a man's character had given way to a more sentimental and evangelical age in which private virtue became paramount and citizens hoped to know their leaders as flesh-and-blood human beings. It was the American Revolution that fueled this shift by a series of social and ideological changes. The War had in its wake a growing sense of female importance and autonomy and a reconstitution of women's traditional roles. And with the colonial woman becoming the republican mother entrusted with the education of children, especially sons, to proper republican adulthood, motherhood was highly politicized; on the flip side, fatherhood was marginalized in real life. The shift would reverberate for years to come, and it was all the more reason to elevate metaphorical fathers, George Washington as the Father of His Country more than anyone else.[39]

It is no surprise, in light of the changing conceptions of paternity, that Weems's biography went through nine printings between 1800 and 1806, when it was extensively expanded; this edition, called the fifth, is the first to contain the cherry-tree story. Another story, that a Quaker named Potts found Washington praying aloud in the woods at Valley Forge, was added in 1808. While no more changes seem to have been added thereafter, the book's popularity remained unflagging. By the time of Weems's death in 1825, it had run to forty editions, to fifty-nine by 1850, and to eighty by 1932, the year of the two-hundredth anniversary of Washington's birthday. Weems's biography is the first and most successful example of a genre that treats biography at the same time as history and myth, the sacred story of the divine man at the foundation of the republic. Its very ambiguity, which edits out its subject's more turbulent, unruly emotions, reveals the deep structure of America's collective unconscious during the first half of the nineteenth century—the longing for a metaphorical father or, if you will, a charismatic leader, from another time and another place, one "treated as endowed with supernatural, superhuman, or at least specifically exceptional powers or qualities."[40]

Overall, the idolization of Washington as a national father figure was an instant success. By the end of the War of Independence Washington had become the darling also of portrait artists, sculptors, printmakers, copper and steel engravers, silhouette cutters, and manufacturers of household furnishings. Already during his lifetime, some twenty-seven artists did the "father's" portrait, chief among them Charles Wilson Peale. Peale, who had served in the Continental Army, completed no fewer than seven portraits, including what is most likely the best known, *George Washington at Princeton*. Statues and busts by Jean-Antoine Houdon, Giuseppe Ceracchi, and Joseph Wright also appeared during Washington's lifetime, though demand for sculptural representations was modest then. Citizens yearning for patriotic images rather sought the more plentiful and affordable engraved prints or, as upscale versions, mezzotints made after paintings by artists such as Peale, John Trumbull, Edward Savage, and Gilbert Stuart, whose patriarchal "Athenaeum" likeness of 1796 was in particular demand.

The desire for images of Washington was also satisfied by a record number of goods of all kinds—medallions, paperweights, plaster statuary and other art objects, books, magazines, almanacs, calendars, and sheet music, mugs, dishes, crockery and other household goods and furnishings, snuff boxes and whiskey flasks, handkerchiefs and other textiles, mostly imported from England, and, not to forget, coins, and currency. As the writer and critic Henry Tuckerman observed in his memoirs, "All over the land, at the close of the war, [Washington's] beloved image was substituted on banner, seal, parlor wall, journal, and bank note, for royal physiognomies; and Rip Van Winkle was not the only conservative absentee, who incredulously rubbed his eyes at the appearance of our republican chief on the tavern sign so long radiant with a kingly visage."[41]

Tuckerman's claim that Washington's "endeared and hallowed countenance" is capable of reforming "by its silent monition," perfectly fits the nurturant parent model. It also constitutes an imprimatur to the iconic character of the Washington image. Icons, we have seen, act, as if they wanted to establish contact with the viewer. And icons affect viewers emotionally, enrapturing them. Iconicity aptly describes Cornelius Tiebout's 1798 printed image *Sacred to Patriotism*. The image depicts General Washington in a pose reminiscent of ancient sculpture, standing on a pedestal set between a pair of neoclassical obelisks identified as Liberty and Independence. Another pedestal, the one that had supported an equestrian statue of George III in New York's Bowling Green Park before patriots pulled it down in 1776, stands empty in the background. In the distance is a scene of the departure of British navy vessels from New York harbor in November 1783. "A more inspirational view of Washington," Barbara Mitnick remarked, "could hardly be imagined; it remains both a tour de force of iconic imagery and a counterpart to the laudatory descriptions published in the literature of the day."[42]

Laudatory descriptions also came to be stamped on the many commemorative medals struck in Washington's honor. One of these medals even bore the inscription "PROVIDENCE LEFT HIM CHILDLESS THAT THE NATION MIGHT CALL HIM FATHER." That Washington was not a biological father no doubt made it easier for him to be established as the metaphorical father of the nation. It was divine providence, contemporaries felt, that had preserved him in an immaculate state to become the Father of His Country. Listing the arguments for electing Washington as president, a Massachusetts paper wrote in March 1788: "As having no son—and therefore not exposing us to the danger of an hereditary successor." The fear was plausible, as dynastic marriages were quite common among monarchs at the time. To John Adams, Washington's childless state was a veritable boon, as it posed no danger of subverting the new republican government: "If general Washington had a daughter," he wrote to Thomas Jefferson, "I firmly believe she would be demanded in marriage by one of the royal families of France or England, perhaps by both; or, if he had a son, he would be invited to come a courting to Europe."[43] To Gouverneur Morris, Washington's childlessness was God's tacit way of protecting America. As he stated in his eulogy, "AMERICANS! He had no child BUT YOU and HE WAS ALL YOUR OWN."[44]

"HE WAS ALL YOUR OWN." Many Americans took this literally, and so a popular form of worshipping Washington was to name babies for him, or else, to have mothers or nurses take infants to go look at America's first President. Washington also received honorary degrees from universities and colleges, including one from Washington College, renamed in his honor in Chestertown, Maryland, in 1782. Fort Washington and Washington Heights appeared in Manhattan in 1776. Veterans from the Revolutionary war made up most of the settlers in Washington, Kentucky, founded in 1786. Over time, there have been other instances of this anthroponymous name-giving, as hundreds of counties, townships, and villages, mountains, streams, and lakes, and, not least, the nation's capital, were named for him. At least nine colleges appropriated his name. So did numerous banks and similar institutions, which also used the face of the nation on coins, paper bills, checks, stamps, and similar documents. Americans celebrated Washington's birthday long before it became an official holiday in Massachusetts in 1856 and a federal holiday in 1879. Also from early on, Washington's name was preached from pulpits and, unsurprisingly, some clergymen wanted to insert his farewell address into the Bible as an epilogue.[45] Washington's death was followed by an outpouring of remembrance, tribute, and visual portrayal. There were remembrance cards printed with Washington's portrait and life dates. In Boston, the engraver and goldsmith Jacob Perkins designed a funeral medal bearing Washington's likeness and inscribed with "He in Glory, The World in Tears." In Philadelphia, the music publisher Benjamin Carr advertised the forthcoming publication of the *Dead March and Monody*, composed by himself and to be performed as part of a memorial service for the late president.

These outpourings took two basic forms: In the one, Washington was represented as a religious hero, a saint ascending to heaven; in the other, Washington was represented as a secular hero, mourned as the Father of His Country. An example of the latter is a print produced by Enoch S. Gridley in 1800. Titled *Pater Patriae*, the print features a medallion of Washington on a tomb with the inscription "Sacred to the memory of the truly Illustrious GEORGE WASHINGTON ... a GREAT and GOOD MAN." Above the medallion is the figure of Fame, wings expanded, holding in her left hand a wreath, enclosing the "Pater Patriae." The print was made under the patronage of the Sons of Columbia in Boston, who had stated in a broadside that "posterity may see [Washington's] effigies, as well as hear the great and noble Deeds of the Father of His Country."[46]

For Parson Weems, in contrast, it was clear that "Swift on Angels' wings, the brightening Saint ascended; while voices more than human were heard ... warbling through the happy regions, and hymning the great procession towards the gates of heaven."[47] Weems's account of Washington's entry into heaven was plausible to many Americans. Artists of the time only lent the image greater clarity. "Mourning pictures" constituted one type of symbolic memorials; they usually showed weeping figures before the remains or a symbol of the hero. The scenes were often set in imaginary landscapes graced by allegorical architectural forms and populated by allegorical figures, all reflecting the classicist spirit of the Federal period.[48] Another type of pictures treating Washington's death were true apotheoses featuring an ascendant hero. A popular print that adorned American homes at the turn of the century showed the departed hero rising to heaven on a thick cloud and caught in a shaft of celestial light. Washington is decked out in white robes, an arm outstretched, as a winged angel is about to crown him with a laurel wreath and two fallen generals from the War of Independence bid him welcome.[49] More openly antiquish was *The Apotheosis of Washington*, which an H. Weishaupt produced after an illustration by Samuel Moore about the same time. It shows Washington on his way to heaven, while Columbia and fifteen allegories representing the states are mourning below.[50]

The Irish émigré artist John James Barralet produced his own version of the *Apotheosis of Washington*. In his stipple engraving from 1802, Washington is raised from the tomb by Father Time (identified by Barralet as "the spiritual and temporal Genius"), lifted heavenward by an angel and Immortality, and wept over by America holding the staff with the liberty cap, as well as, on the opposite side, an Indian crouched in sorrow. In the background are three other allegorical females, Faith, Hope, and Charity, copied from European renderings of the Crucifixion, Deposition, and Lamentation of Christ.[51] Barralet's allegory, which blends the official rhetoric of the early Republic with traditional European iconographies, was instantly reproduced in media ranging from Chinese reverse painting on glass to Liverpool ceramic pitchers. As different as *Apotheosis of Washington* is from Barralet's commemoration of Washington's resignation as commander in chief, done only a year before, when Washington was still alive, it is an indication of America's emerging creed, which imbued the nation and its highest representative with religious meaning. It also bridged two periods in Washington imagery and in American cultural history—the republican era in which public deeds were the measure of a man's character; and a coming sentimental and evangelical age in which private virtue became paramount and citizens hoped to know their leaders as flesh-and-blood human beings.[52]

In this new era of sentimentalism and evangelicalism, graphic evidence of the deification of the Father of His Country could be found everywhere: "No cottage should be without his likeness, no mansion without his picture ... [so] that rich and poor ... may have him always before their eyes, and copy, each according to their own station, the public and private virtues of Washington." This was written in 1836. A European visitor had become alerted to the Washington cult as early as 1811. He noted, somewhat sarcastically, that to have Washington's picture in the household was something of a patriotic duty within America's civil religion: "Every American considers it his sacred duty to have a likeness of Washington in his home, just as we have images of God's saints."[53] The visitor was a Russian diplomat, who no doubt had personally encountered religious icons in his home country. His remark aptly explains the functions of pictorial renderings of George Washington at the time: The first president's face was to at once make outwardly visible and legitimate the foundational values and the essence of the American nation. As a *visual* symbol of national unity, Washington became a "crucial means of establishing and perpetuating an American identity," an identity that was inseparably tied to political sovereignty, republican values, and, through the ritual forms incorporated into veneration of him, a civil religion.[54]

Altogether, images of the metaphorical father were not, therefore, illusionistic images of George Washington as he appeared at the time so much as public representations of an idealized self. Still, these representations could not quite obliterate some deep-seated ideological and psychological problems. These problems stemmed from the new republic's difficulties to live up to its own ideals. Americans, the historian Lawrence Friedman explains, tried hard to realize a more perfect union and find a secure place within it, but then, how does one progress and remain in place at the same time? To ameliorate, if not elide, this dilemma was the function of what Friedman calls "the mythical Washington." If Washington's contemporaries found him to be a model of perfection, it was because a flawless hero was "helpful to patriots who fretted over the American experience in nation making." A more perfect union followed from Washington's "personal perfection." In elevating Washington, Friedman concludes, Americans found a model that reconciled their own striving towards perfection with serene stability and a sense of place.[55]

There is hardly a better example of Washington's elevation than the words spoken by "THE GENIUS OF AMERICA," to which readers of the *Pennsylvania Gazette* were treated in March 1791. Importantly, when "THE GENIUS OF AMERICA" talks about Washington as "unanimously elected the Sovereign of an enlightened, a free, and a jealous people, without opposition, without distrust, and without envy,"[56] he or she speaks, not to a state but to a nation. A nation is a community with a territorial affinity, that is, a well-bounded group of people with shared values and understandings and a common allegiance. In contrast, a state is the formal institution of power and coercion that has a monopoly of sovereignty over a particular territory. The relationship between nation and state can be problematic. Some states (such as Britain or the former Austro-Hungarian Empire) have more than one nation and certain nations (the Kurds, for example, or the Slovenes in Austria) are not represented by a state. In contrast, the United States is almost unique because, apart from the Native American population, there is a high degree of congruence between nation and state. Since the Civil War, there have been no separatist movements of note and even groups who consider themselves a distinct nation (such as the Nation of Islam) had, and still have, no territorial affinity that can be considered separate. In the United States, therefore, the geographical construction of the state has been bound up with the territorial imagination of the nation.

In America, the hegemonic trope of an imagined community (the term is Benedict Anderson's) first developed around a number of complex fictions, such as "the people," along with related concepts like political representation and "the consent of the governed." To be successful, governments require the acceptance of these fictions, require "the willing suspension of disbelief."[57] What greatly contributed to this success was the image of the metaphorical father, George Washington. With the help of his image, the fledgling republic—conceived of as a family—legitimated itself against a powerful monarchic tradition. Volker Depkat, an American Studies scholar from the University of Regensburg, Germany, has described the transition in terms of a historic rupture. The nation's founding, Depkat emphasizes, was not merely a question of drafting a constitution and setting up institutional procedures, of structuring decision-making and legal processes, or of organizing political parties and elections. Just as crucial was the creation of a political *culture*, that is, of an ensemble of cultural values and practices that frame political institutions, define the normative ideas on which a rule of law is based, and generally provide for meaning and orientation. For, political orders can raise a claim to legitimacy and are able to achieve political hegemony only when they can fall back on normative ideas of their own. Importantly also, political orders need to make these claims visible to produce general acceptance and following of cultural norms and values, as well as of the interpretational jurisdiction over political sovereignty. The need to make these claims visible seems particularly strong under the conditions of popular sovereignty. Popular sovereignty, Depkat argues, requires that *all* members of a community be convinced of the legitimacy of the new order.[58]

"Sacred" documents like the Declaration of Independence and the Constitution were crucial for America's imagined community, lending legitimacy, value, and authority to the new institutions. But these foundational documents target knowledge or cognition; Washington's human face, in contrast, was both the incarnation of the nation's ideas, values, and norms, and had the ability to move people's emotions, to stir their passions, and even to shape public perception of what was happening throughout the country. Thus, the image of the Father of His Country articulated the accomplishment of a *common* mission, "the work of many heads and many hands," as James Madison wrote in 1834. Commonness is the source of all agreement, securing the achievement in time and place. While this was true of the Constitution (as Madison modestly but accurately said), which became the ultimate source of definition in the culture, a new collective symbol would bind the elements of their faith in a human center, "a man—a farmer, a soldier, and, at least metaphorically, a father."[59] Other nations' founders mostly were legendary heroes, mythic figures, even messengers or emissaries from the gods.[60] But into the image constructed of Washington, contemporaries poured values like freedom, liberty, or political unity, values that at the same time accompanied their first steps toward nationhood. Identification of Washington with the newly forming nation thus represented an act of communal incorporation, much as it constituted a basic act of mutual recognition between leaders and led. By identifying with Washington, Barry Schwartz wrote, "Americans could articulate their own stake in the war and justify their personal sacrifice [...] Through him, they expressed their common attachment to a new political unity."[61]

Washington's renown initially followed his revolutionary fervor during the War of Independence. In a number of instances, American Protestantism even heralded Washington as the nation's savior for delivering America from the bondage of Britain, in analogy to Moses leading the Israelites from the Egyptian bondage. In an undated engraving, for example, Washington is represented as giving the laws, that is, the sacred text of the Constitution, to America.[62] In the public clamor for him to become president, Washington was again cast less as the leader of a revolution than as a figure of stability, a moral leader, a bulwark against fragile and quarrelsome states as well as against rebellious locals, economic depression and hyperinflation, and a guarantee against a reversion to monarchy. A popular engraving by Amos Doolittle in 1788–1789 showed him in civilian garb within a circle of interlocked rings, each displaying a state seal. Versifiers praised him as the one capable of stemming the threat of anarchy:

> At his approach vile Faction stands aghast,
> And civil Discord breathes, in pangs, her last;
> Paper emissions, too, at his command,
> With legal tenders, fly this happy land.[63]

During the late 1780s, the search for a collective symbol was to compensate for the weakness of the Confederation. But the manufacturing of consent had been a matter of survival from the beginning of the Revolutionary War. *E Pluribus Unum*, taken from the first volume of the English *Gentlemen's Magazine* of 1731, had furnished a catch phrase for the wartime need of the whole community when it was first selected by the Continental Congress for an official seal in 1776; by the time the United States Congress adopted it as official motto, it already signified how "the many" had dissolved into "one." The distinction is central also to Thomas Paine's pamphlet *American Crisis*: "Our great title," he wrote in 1783, "is AMERICANS—our inferior one varies with the place." Local interests must yield to a newly forming national identity. The goal, Paine argued, was to "conciliate the affections, unite the interests, and draw and keep the mind of the country together." Forming a national identity would, of course, take time, as Paine had known from the beginning. The patriots' cause was "posterity," not "the concern of a day, a year, or an age," Paine wrote as early as January 1776.[64]

George Washington certainly embodied the values of the new nation, fulfilling the role of a "symbol of union. As the nation's highest representative, he also bestowed legitimacy to the new system, sanctifying it," in Barry Schwartz's words, "not by controlling it but simply by identifying with it. Correspondingly, loyalty to Washington the individual held the government together until the people could learn to be loyal to the government itself."[65] Strong religious convictions only reinforced allegiance to Washington. During the War of Independence many of the calls to serve in the Continental Army were voiced in a decidedly religious vocabulary. Additionally, the conviction that God's punishment of war-mongers was intended only for the English allowed only one outcome of the conflict—American victory. The battle of Monmouth would have been lost, Washington wrote his brother John Augustine, but for "that bountiful Providence which has never failed us in the hour of distress." His General Orders after Yorktown called for religious services to recognize the "reiterated and astonishing interpositions of Providence." The prevailing belief in providential intervention not only rendered every battle a manifestation of the divine plan; it later sanctified the new political system itself. Washington himself devoted a large part of his first Inaugural Address to a discussion of the "providential agency" at work in the nation's founding.[66] And in a pseudonymously published "Anniversary Ode, for July 4th, 1789," Columbia is praised for having aroused her "CHIEFTAIN... Who, aided by Heaven, defeated our foes."[67]

Official iconography, too, legitimated political power theologically. "ANNUIT COEPTIS" reads the inscription above the pyramid on the United States seal, "He [God] has favored our undertakings." The grammatical form of the unfinished past suggests that God has already approved of the undertaking, *annuit coeptis*, and he will continue to do so, hence that there is indeed hope. The origin of the phrase in Virgil's *Georgica* (1.38–42), in contrast, uses the simple subjunctive, *adnue coeptis*, "may the gods approve of the building [of the Roman Empire]," which expresses a wish. The Seal of the United States thus bears the mark of God's approval of what Americans had undertaken but what had been bestowed by God's grace or, in the diction of the time, through God's providence.[68] Official iconography thus seems to vindicate Carl Becker's argument, so controversial when it was first advanced, that the Enlightenment had dethroned Christianity only to reinstate it "with more up-to-date-materials."[69] With the sacred smuggled so blatantly into what purported to be secular institutions, it is no surprise that Americans of religious persuasion saw George Washington as the executor of God's plan. This is suggested, for instance, by the inscription on a commemorative medal struck in his honor, that "Providence" had left him childless so that the nation might call him "Father." A funeral oration even proclaimed that Washington was a "Gift from God," raised up from youth "for the salvation of his country." In 1814, the youthful Ralph Waldo Emerson conceived the idea in the following way: "The God of Israel heard our groans and cries / And bade to life a WASHINGTON arise." It was not only Northerners who were consistent on this point; many Southerners too came to see Washington as "the man designed by heaven" to follow through.[70]

If Washington came to stand for everything Americans held dear, he at the same time was all that they had in the way of a national symbol. Washington was the man of destiny, "indispensable," as James Thomas Flexner rendered it in the title of his magisterial biography. Of course, Washington could not be all things to all people, as he often was required to be, but he could be a metaphorical father. No man, female educator Emma Willard asserted, could offer a more important service to his country than in leaving, "to future sons his great and good example." While other heroes were praised for their love of glory, Willard noted, the "true, and distinguishing praise of Washington is, that he was above the love of glory."[71] Clearly, the words of this nineteenth-century woman are as untouched by the nascent women's movement as can be. They are nevertheless important in that they indicate two rhetorical levels for the metaphorical father to speak to his charges. On a cognitive level, he defines the spiritual power and the fundamental moral values of the nascent nation by embodying it in tangible form. But Washington then was and still is not only "good for thinking." He also is "good for feeling." When, for instance, Pennsylvania's Supreme Executive Council resolved in 1779 to request Washington to sit for his portrait to Charles Wilson Peale, it justified its commission with the need to "excite in others to tread in the same glorious & disinterested Steps which lead to public happiness and private honor." Five years later, the *Boston Magazine* wrote that Americans might be "agitated" to contemplate "a WASHINGTON ... saluted as the Deliverer of his country."[72] The "deliverer," in a conflicted society, provides a fixed point with which people can identify. On this second, emotional level, the metaphorical father appeals to ("excites," "agitates") the affective elements of people's consciousness and relationships, elements that the cultural critic Raymond Williams defined as a "'structure' ... a set, with specific, internal relations, at once interlocking and in tension."[73]

Few Americans at the time knew Washington's personality, and fewer still knew him personally, yet many had an impression of his physique and character. Poems and songs of the war had popularized his image, both as a "hero" and as the embodiment of "the highest existent patriotism."[74] Washington also was visually well known to the American public, not so much through the great paintings we know from museums, which at the time most people would not have seen, but thanks to the many paintings commissioned by legislative bodies and, especially, thanks to the many engraved prints, lithographs, and other material objects published to satisfy those who were, as Benjamin West said to Charles Wilson Peale in June 1783, "curious to see the true likeness of that phenomenon among men."[75] Functionally, the image of Washington served to stabilize the political order, much as it served as a moral model for American citizens. It projected a sense of national identity, a pride in common history, and an active political awareness among the people. Chronology is important here, if only for analytical purposes. For, the Father of His Country is not at first a material image that can be experienced but rather an immaterial or mental image. Immaterial or mental images are spectral, virtual; they emerge from conceptual spaces and are inscribed with meanings in those spaces before they are transformed into material images.

It is easy to recognize a picture of America's first president, such as Gilbert Stuart's "Lansdowne Portrait," named after its longtime owner, the Marquis of Lansdowne, for whom it was commissioned by William Bingham, United States Senator from Pennsylvania and one of the wealthiest men in the United States. The "Lansdowne" was a gift to thank the Englishman for his role in the negotiations that led to the Jay Treaty that put an end to disputes with England. Once it reached London, the picture very much pleased its recipient, who thought that it was "in every way worthy of the original" and gave it a place of honor in his library. Since 1968, the painting has been on permanent display at the Smithsonian's

National Portrait Gallery where, after an eighteen-month restoration, it now is the centerpiece of the reopened "America's Presidents" exhibition. Full-color replica prints are available from the Smithsonian's online gift shop, allowing modern viewers to own a substitute for the original "Lansdowne," if only at one-fourth its size. A copy of the painting graces the East Room of the White House, where the original hung before its removal to the Smithsonian. Stuart, who is often called the "Father of American Portraiture," painted the "Lansdowne" in 1797 and made several copies of it afterwards. Numerous prints were also made of it, most notably by George Graham in 1801 and Charles Goodman and Robert Piggot in 1818. John Vanderlyn's 1834 Washington portrait shares many compositional elements with Stuart's original, such as the formal clothing and pose; the paper-filled desk; and the open view in the back left corner.[76]

The White House copy of the "Lansdowne" has been said to serve as a memento of republican virtues to Washington's successors to the presidency. In a general sense, every portrait is more than a mere mirror of someone's physiognomy; it also re-presents something, that is, it makes something visible. Put differently, a portrait always contains an absence, which it strives to bring to mind. A portrait ideally visualizes the invisible and preserves it for posterity, which in the case of the "Lansdowne" is the good and morally sound character of George Washington as the democratically elected head of state and chief of government. Stuart's painting thus is in no way an illusionistic image of George Washington as he appeared at the time but a public representation of an idealized self that helped secure Americans' achievements—independence, new nation, republic—in time and space. Cast in the role as the nation's founder, Washington was not only the personification of public virtue but also responded to anxieties that the hard-won liberties were not secure.[77] The "Lansdowne" depicts the nation's first president as frozen in midgesture, his right arm outstretched, palm up. Contemporaries would have identified this as the *ad locutio* gesture, a proper pose for statesmen and heroes. Here was Washington in a truly oratorical manner as if he was addressing an audience. Indeed, Stuart painted his president as the man was preparing for his departure from public life.

If the figure in the portrait is giving a speech, Washington in life was working on one, his farewell address to the nation. He never read the speech, in which he sought to explain his decision to decline a third term, to an audience, but that only cemented the pairing of the portrait and the speech. Another striking feature of the "Lansdowne" is the dress sword in Washington's left hand, which he holds pointing downwards to the floor. The sword thus only hints at the General's military career, as does the rainbow in the upper right corner, which implies the storms through which he had led the new nation. Overall, however, heroic fervor is clearly subordinate to the civilian authority of the presidency and the constitutional order Washington presides over. The emblems of that order are the various books—under the table, the *General Orders*, *American Revolution*, and *Constitution & Laws of the United States*, and on the table, the *Federalist Papers* and the *Journals of Congress*. The books look used. Washington appears to have been working with them, which is underscored by documents on the table, the inkwell, and a quill pen. President Washington is personally working to lead the nation.

The "Lansdowne" was a private portrait and thus not an official state portrait. Still, it has customarily been seen as the epitome of republican state portraiture. Washington's clothes are certainly fitting. The unadorned black suit, discreet and sober, distinguished and of high quality, but not lavish or glamorous. A formal black hat, which is lying on the table, has replaced the king's crown. Additionally, the democratically elected president no longer

Gilbert Stuart, *George Washington (Lansdowne Portrait)*, 1796, oil on canvas, 97½ × 62½ in. (National Portrait Gallery, Smithsonian Institution; acquired as a gift to the nation through the generosity of the Donald W. Reynolds Foundation).

stands upon a dais but on the floor. Ruler and ruled are no longer separated; the President of the United States of America is approachable, an integral element of the society that elected him into office, and even while he is in office he continues to be a member of it. Yet there are still echoes of the monarchical-aristocratic tradition of painting nobility. Take, for instance, the interior, framed, setting—the richly adorned neoclassical furniture, the gold armchair with red upholstery, the Turkish rug in the foreground, the colonnaded background. The composition's formalism, too, betrays its debt to earlier portraits, by Hyacinthe Rigaud, for instance, and, more importantly, to British state portraiture—the portrait's full-length type with one arm or hand resting on a piece of furniture, standing before an ornate, thronelike chair, the table leg inspired by the Roman fasces, a symbol of power. Add to this the background of massive doors, high ceilings, heavy drapes, and pillars, signifying the dignity and power of the office. Already the state portraits of Elizabeth I made use of the same props to convey to the viewer the awesome power of the ruler.[78]

King George III (studio of Allan Ramsay), oil on canvas, based on a work of 1761–1762, 58 × 42 in. (1473 × 1067 mm) (National Portrait Gallery, London).

Stuart also borrowed from or at least was inspired by an official British state portrait, Allan Ramsay's coronation portrait of George III. Like the British King, America's first president is placed at the center of the painting. Washington stands erect, a pillar of stability, slightly bent to the left, his head turned to left of the canvas. He does not look directly at the viewer but beyond. Although his face is based on Stuart's own "Athenaeum" portrait, its symmetry and even its proportions are reminiscent of Ramsay's George III of 1761. So are Washington's godlike features, at the same time suggestive of classical statuary and, in the physiognomic tradition, of a beautiful mind. Just as the inkstand bears the Washington family coat of arms, the coat of arms in Ramsay's portrait underscores the dynastic principle, alluding to "blood" as one of the two sources of a monarch's authority (the second one being divine grace, bestowed in the act of coronation).[79]

Stuart was not the only artist to exploit monarchical conventions for the purpose of creating a new, republican icon. Noël Le Mire's *Le Général Washington* (1780), an engraving after Jean-Baptiste Le Paon, shows the general in front of an oriental-looking field marquee, one hand in his waistcoat, the founding documents of the nation in the other. Behind

Washington stands his black valet, caring for his horse. The outdoor scene echoes Anthony Van Dyck's portrait of Charles I (*Le Roi à la chasse*, c. 1635, now in the Louvre). Even less "republican" is John Norman's etching *The True Portraiture of His Excellency George Washington Esq.* (c. 1783). Washington's head is based on a portrait by Charles Wilson Peale, and the inscription speaks of Washington "in the Roman dress." Strangely, however, the full-length portrait shows the alleged man of the people in sixteenth-century European field armor. Norman had copied the ancient garb from John Guillim's *Display of Heraldry* (1611), which he knew from a later edition, though the finished work also shows a strong resemblance to the armored prince in Robert Pollard's portrait of *George the IIId* (1778).[80]

II

Political Sovereignty and Metaphorical Fathers

As willingly as the North American colonists had seen Britain as "the revered parent," and America as "the dutiful child," with the outbreak of the Revolution, disillusioned colonists suddenly repudiated all that. "Almost at a stroke," Gordon Wood wrote, "the Revolution destroyed all the earlier talk of paternal … government."[1] But patriarchal language as such persisted. On the eve of the American Revolution, Simeon Howard preached a sermon to an artillery company in Boston, in which he observed that a father was bound to his children "by the common tie of nature" and thus felt it his duty to defend them. Indeed, a father's willingness to risk his life in defense of his children, a 1772 essay pronounced, "will make him venerable and beloved while he lives, be lamented and honored if he falls in so glorious a cause, and transmit his name and immortal renown to his latest posterity."[2] Even talk of paternal government came back to stay after the Revolution. For, the creation of the new nation, a republic of laws, generated any number of fears—of disunion, of anarchy, of mob rule. Consequently, there were numerous attempts to revive and legitimize authority by restoring the image of political leaders as trustworthy civic fathers. In 1774, for instance, a Gad Hitchcock addressed public officials as "honored fathers" and "civic fathers." Similarly in 1778, Phillips Payson referred to them as "civil fathers." And in 1780, Samuel Cooper described the framers of the Articles of Confederation as "fathers of their country" filled with "paternal tenderness."[3] During the constitutional debates, federalists used the language of political fatherhood to dispel fears that the office of the presidency would lead to despotism. While Samuel Langdon pronounced public leaders as "fathers of a large family," James Wilson, a delegate to the Philadelphia Convention of 1787, argued that the future president would be a father figure who would "watch over the whole with paternal care and affection."[4]

Federalists were fortunate that the first president was to be George Washington, America's greatest father figure, who was hailed as "THE FATHER OF HIS COUNTRY" by the "Ladies of Trenton" in 1789, given the "the august title—Father of his Country" by Judith Sargent Murray in 1794, called "our political father" by Zephania Swift Moore in 1802, and "the Great Father of his country" by Alexander Addison in 1800.[5] All this is to say that when the exalted title of "Father of His Country" was transferred from George III to George Washington, the colonists' traditional, patriarchal, and familial political ideals were left intact, together with the language of political fatherhood. Thus, the framers were referred to in terms of "fathers of their country," "fathers and guardians of their people," and "fathers, guides, and guardians." At the same time, the nation's political "fathers" were told by Israel Evans that citizens would "be their political children as long as they are good parents," while

Timothy Stone enjoined officials to be true "civil fathers" who treated citizens with the "tender care of natural parents."[6]

The appearance of a new "Father of His Country" not only affected public rhetoric but reinforced the patriarchal structures in the society at large.[7] In that society, fathers were the undisputed heads of a hierarchical social order in which, as in the colonial era, authority and reverence, governance and submission were carefully balanced. Each part had, in equal measure, rights as well as duties and responsibilities. Fathers, however, had the ultimate responsibility for the care and well-being of their children, they would administer rewards as well as punishments, as it was deserved and always for the good of their charges. Throughout the eighteenth century, David Blankenhorn has shown, child-rearing manuals were generally addressed to fathers, not mothers. Until the early nineteenth century, in almost all cases of divorce, custody of children was customarily awarded to fathers. Fathers, not mothers, were the chief correspondents with children who lived far away from home. Most important, fathers were primarily responsible for the moral and religious education of the young. Thus, societal praise or blame for a child's outcome was usually bestowed not on the mother but on the father, the personification of a transcendent "natural" order.[8]

3

Strict Father Washington?

Thomas Jefferson, who was ten years younger than George Washington, too came to view the Father of His Country as the personification of a transcendent "natural" order. Thus in August 1799, he described Washington as a tough, unbending man, "a hard master, very severe, a hard husband, a hard father, a hard governor."[1] Jefferson's characterization was clearly influenced by policy differences and what he saw as Washington's preferment of Hamilton. Yet employers and, as well, slave owners too believed that they were obliged to watch over their charges, much as Congressional and other "guardians" had, at least in theory, responsibilities towards the indigenous population, that is, their "wards." White young men, too, often put themselves under the protection of a "patron" (the word "patron" is etymologically related to "pater," father) if they wanted to get on in the world. Washington himself was such a "patron," who saw himself as the primary and irreplaceable caregiver. As commander in chief, he often referred to his staff as his "family." To do so had been common practice among colonial officers, who were faithfully following the English tradition, but for Washington it was not mere rhetoric. The military "family" shaped him, much as he shaped its members, transforming them.

General Washington was the beloved "father" of a military "family" of surrogate sons, Alexander Hamilton, the Marquis de Lafayette, Joseph Reed, John Laurens, and David Humphreys.[2] For Lafayette, Washington had a special fondness, which may well have expressed some buried longing for paternal intimacy. When Washington learned, in 1779, that Lafayette's American exploits had been recognized by the French king, he purportedly "blushed like a fond father whose child is being praised," saying "'I do not know a nobler, finer soul, and I love him as my own son.'"[3] The feeling was reciprocal. For Lafayette, Washington was "my adoptive father." About to return to America in 1783, Lafayette enthusiastically wrote to Washington, "Happy, ten times Happy will I Be in Embracing My dear General, *My father*, My Best friend Whom I love with an Affection and a Respect Which I too well feel, Not to know it is impossible for me to Express it."[4] Washington also cultivated a personal bond with his other fellow officers, at one point describing himself as their "constant companion and witness of [their] distress."[5] Washington spoke these words at a meeting with rebellious officers at Newburgh on March 15, 1783. He followed it up with letters to Congress, warning about yet another "storm." Luckily, Congress delivered and granted the officers a generous payment. Moderation, not confrontation had achieved victory. Washington's strong leadership at Newburgh signified that patriotic sacrifice, not the will to grasp power, would prevail. Those who were of his own class, detected in him not merely "the strong feelings of the patriot" but, especially, "*the father* as well as the commander of his soldiers."[6] Newburgh indeed effected a change in Washington's general attitude to the soldiers under his command. Ron Chernow thus points, rightly I think, to the two people that for most of his career "seemed to coexist inside Washington's breast." One was the devoted patriot, steeped in a militant republicanism. The other was the soldier steeped in the British military system, who believed in strict discipline and the importance of rank.[7]

Patriotism and the British military tradition fit Washington well. His republicanism, after all, was of the conservative kind. While he was ready for a government "of the people" as well as "for the people," a government "by the people" was anathema to him. Washington could never bring himself to accept the notion, so central to Lincoln's model of democratic government, that all the people were equally endowed with political virtue and disinterestedness. For the Father of His Country, some people were clearly more virtuous than others and could more safely be entrusted with the affairs of government. One of the best illustrations of Washington's conservative republicanism can be seen in his relationship with his troops. In Washington's opinion, the true criteria for an office (in the military) were "a just pretension to the character of a Gentleman, a proper Sense of Honor, & some Reputation to lose." In other words, men like Washington himself, "the Virginia planter who felt little in common with the scruffy plebeians around him."[8] So the question was, "Could this elitist southerner with aristocratic inclinations fathom and embody the hopes of revolutionary Americans and of reformers around the world?"[9]

Not all those who admired and respected him would have dreamed that he could, James McGregor Burns and Susan Dunn argue. Certainly not Thomas Jefferson, who in 1799 described Washington as "a hard master," though in 1814 he rather thought of him as a fellow Virginia planter: Washington's "person, you know, was fine, his stature exactly what one would wish, his deportment easy, erect and noble; the best horseman of his age, and the most graceful figure that could be seen on horseback."[10] Already the poetry of the Revolutionary period had readily depicted Washington as a warrior. As early as June or July 1775, Philip Freneau (who eventually came to fiercely criticize the president in the *National Gazette*) hailed Washington as one who is "Bold in the fight, whose actions have aw'd / A Roman hero, or a Grecian God." Unsurprisingly, revolutionary ballads struck a similar tone, summoning, in Jonathan Mitchell Sewall's "War and Washington," Americans to "shout, and shout America! And conquering Washington."[11] In 1780, David Humphreys, one of Washington's aides, wrote, "I go where'er the battle bleeds: / To-morrow—(brief then be my story)—I go to Washington and glory." In 1795, Richard Snowden's poem on the American war saw Washington's "courage rise as the flowing tide." Epic poetry, too, came to celebrate Washington as a warlike hero, the country's "greatest son, in that young martial frame, / From yon lost field begins the life of fame."[12]

In the antebellum period, Washington Irving explained the "*beau ideal*" of the Father of His Country's existence as the direct outcome of "the aristocratical days of Virginia."[13] Of course, Irving also injected a goodly dose of republicanism into the Virginia gentleman, though the British tradition is unmistakably there—a timely concession to Southern sentiments at a time when regional tensions were heating up fast. Irving not only offered a common heritage to both sides. His image of Washington as a Cincinnatus who, "gladly, when he had won the cause, hung up his sword never again to take it down," likewise would not have been offensive to anyone.[14] Pictorial representations of Washington also popularized the dramatic flair of Washington as a gallant revolutionary. Painting the Father of His Country as a soldier began with John Trumbull in the 1790s, to include such well-known artworks as *Washington at Verplanck's Point*, *General Washington at Trenton*, and *The Death of General Mercer at the Battle of Princeton*, which depicts him as an impetuous man of action. The general on horseback also dominates numerous renderings

Nathaniel Currier, *General George Washington, The Father of His Country*, hand-colored lithograph, between 1835 and 1856 (Library of Congress Prints and Photographs Division).

of Washington's epic crossing of the Delaware River on Christmas night, 1776, en route to the Americans' victory over the British forces at Trenton. The daring crossing helped boost American morale at the start of the Revolutionary War, and as numerous versions of the subject indicate, the theme became a particularly popular one for nineteenth-century American painters and engravers. A lithograph by Nathaniel Currier appeared almost contemporaneously with Washington's Irving's description of the Virginia gentleman in *Life of Washington*.

Somewhat earlier is an engraving of the crossing by George S. Lang. The engraving originated from Thomas Sully's well-known painting of 1819, *Washington at the Passage of the Delaware*, now at the Museum of Fine Arts, Boston. The engraving probably would be forgotten today, had it not been for Edward Hicks, who, like many folk painters, often took inspiration from the prints or paintings of other artists. *Washington at the Delaware*, painted around 1849, the year of Hicks's death, was based on Lang's engraving. Washington did not take part in the signing of the Declaration of Independence, though the folk painter Edward Hicks recognized that the general's military victories secured the freedoms proclaimed in that historic document in Philadelphia on July 4, 1776.[15]

What neither pictorial nor verbal descriptions show is that Washington, though always punctilious about the distinction between officers and the rank and file, over time became much more "affectionate," as one sergeant recalled, eventually seeing farmers, shoemakers, weavers, and carpenters as intimate comrades-in-arms. He took great care that officers provided music for their corps, as "Nothing is more agreeable, and ornamental, than good music." This does not mean that Washington ever abandoned his belief in hierarchical distinctions, especially between officers and their men, but the war was gradually molding him into a far more egalitarian figure.[16] Especially his sharing in the hardship and inconveniences of Valley Forge proved an experience that transformed him into a commander of truly paternal dimensions. "The people of America look up to you as their father," Henry Knox told him in 1777, "and into your hands they entrust their *all*, fully confident of every exertion on your part for their security and happiness."[17] Washington's nurturant parent qualities are also evident from ordering, in April 1783, his quartermaster general to collect discharges so he could begin sending soldiers home. In a wonderful tribute to his men, he personally signed thousands of these documents. This fatherly gesture, Ron Chernow notes, "spoke volumes about the affection and empathy he had developed for them."[18] An equally telling instance of affection and empathy occurred at New York's Fraunces Tavern, where on December 4, 1783, Washington bid a final farewell to his officers. When the glasses were lifted, the departing general said, with tears in his eyes, "I cannot come to each of you, but shall be obliged if each of you will come and take me by the hand." The moment was legendary, not for any feat of oratory, but for the simple heartfelt emotion palpable in Washington's words. Unsurprisingly, the Fraunces Tavern farewell became a popular subject of biographies and artworks.[19]

Washington had demonstrated his paternal qualities already in June of 1783, when he addressed the problems facing the fledgling nation. In the "Circular to State Governments," the departed commander in chief envisions a glorious future for America's citizens, now "the sole Lords and Proprietors of a vast Tract of Continent [and, as well,] acknowledged to be possessed of absolute freedom and Independency." And, he adds, Americans now were living in an age "when the rights of mankind were better understood and more clearly defined, than at any former period." Thus, by no means should Americans forfeit the "political happiness" they were enjoying.[20] As Washington's last communication as a public character, the "Circular," which became known also as "Washington's Legacy," for all intents and purposes is a veritable "dad speech," telling the children who they are and with whom they belong. The document was reprinted in countless newspapers and later excerpted in numerous schoolbooks, gaining a wide readership and reaching out to the citizenry at large. In the "Circular," the Father of His Country also issued a warning, a warning that is so blunt that it is almost a rebuke. "At this auspicious period," Washington writes after a long, stem-winding warm-up, "the United States came into existence as a Nation, and if their Citizens should not be completely free and happy, the fault will be entirely their own."[21]

The sentence must have come as a shock, not only for its style, which seems terse, almost curt, but especially for its thought. With so many blessings, why should Americans fail? Easily enough, Washington says; see that you don't. Richard Brookhiser has pronounced, justly I think, the sentence as "one of the most sobering moments in any major American speech—even more sobering than the bleak mysticism of Lincoln's Second Inaugural."[22] Washington is saying that America's political success is problematic: This is the time, he writes, of Americans' "political probation ... the moment to establish or ruin their national Character forever." At this moment, Washington is a father turning out his sons and daughters to make it on their own. For, "it is yet to be decided whether the Revolution must ultimately be considered as a blessing or a curse," that is to say, whether the United States "will stand or fall."[23]

The moment of decision came four years later, at the Constitutional Convention, when the goals of the "Circular to State Governments" came to dominate the discussion in Philadelphia. In the "Circular," as well as later, Washington urged a stronger union, a commitment to public justice, a thorough attention to the public defense and, lastly, a spirit of subordination and obedience to the federal government in the sacrifice of local prejudices and rivalries to the community at large. Although in the "Circular" he called for "an indissoluble Union of the States under one Federal Head,"[24] in his first Inaugural Address he was much more cautious, speaking of the "Republican model of Government" in its American form as an "experiment."[25] If Washington was uncertain, in 1789, that the United States would work, when he distributed the "Circular" he nevertheless had believed that his task as a founder and father of his country had been done. It turned out to be less than half done. But even when it was finished, it was only all he could do. The rest was up to the "Citizens of America."[26] Perhaps Washington remembered what he once had copied as his forty-fourth "Rule of Civility": "When a man does all he can though it Succeed not well blame not him that did it."[27] Perhaps this is also why in closing the "Circular," Washington abruptly abandons the discourse of the Enlightenment, assuming instead the pastoral tone of a father advising his flock. The ending rises to the fervor of a benediction:

> I now make it my earnest prayer, that God would have you, and the State over which you preside, in his holy protection, that he would incline the hearts of the Citizens to cultivate a spirit of subordination and obedience to Government, to entertain a brotherly affection and love for one another, for their fellow Citizens of the United States at large, and particularly for their brethren who have served in the Field.[28]

By time of the "Circular," the United States was still in the making, as Americans were still waiting for the definitive peace treaty. Just over a year later, Washington received alarming news from a trusted friend, General Nathanael Greene: "Many people," the former brother in arms warned, "secretly wish that every state should be completely independent; and that as soon as our public debts are liquidated that Congress should be no more."[29] The news only added fuel to Washington's fears about America's future: "We are either a United people under one head," he wrote in a letter, "or we are thirteen independent Sovereignties, eternally counteracting each other."[30] Winning independence in 1783 had been crucial, but it did not guarantee the success of the republican experiment. Only a strong central government, Washington believed, was a strong enough bulwark against disorder and anarchy. In advocating enlarged powers for Congress, Washington two years later argued that "we never shall establish a National character, or be considered on a respectable footing by the powers of Europe," unless this was accomplished.[31]

In 1785, Washington was still reluctant to give up his serene Mount Vernon retirement, though in the fall of that year the outbreak of violence in rural Massachusetts finally shattered his comforting fantasy. Shays's Rebellion not only crystallized for Washington the need to overhaul the Articles of Confederation; it also prompted him to come out of retirement and attend the Constitutional Convention in Philadelphia.[32] On May 25, 1787, the convention reached its seven-state quorum and began to meet officially. Washington was nominated and chosen as its president. The role was nonpartisan and nonspeaking and thus ideal for his temperament, yet his mere presence reassured Americans that the delegates were acting in their behalf, striving for the public good. As the *Pennsylvania Gazette* intoned, "we behold [George Washington] at the head of a chosen band of patriots and heroes, arresting the progress of American anarchy."[33]

President Washington would compromise on means, but not on ends. He established clear rules, another sure sign of his extraordinary leadership qualities. Thus, he won Independence; thus also, he steered the Constitutional Convention to its successful conclusion, learned to avoid the Senate on treaty drafts, appointed ten Supreme Court justices, built institutions to cement the fledgling nation, strengthened the federal government, helped create the Bank of the United States, saved the union from foreign entanglements, factionalism, and a feuding cabinet, and vanquished rebellions. Just as important for Washington's leadership was that he surrounded himself with individuals who were strong leaders themselves. This is especially true of his cabinet—Hamilton again, Jefferson, Henry Knox, Edmund Randolph, James Madison, and John Adams (who never took part in cabinet meetings) formed "a group of luminaries without equal in American history."[34] Not that it was always easy to orchestrate these bright, strong personalities. Washington habitually invited all members of his cabinet to submit opinions, which often produced collisions of interest and bad feelings, Still, Washington's "relational" leadership style gave him a full spectrum of opinion, saving his administration from monolithic uniformity. For Garry Wills, therefore, Washington became the embodiment of Rousseau's ideal legislator, who "shall not use either force or argument," but "resort to another kind of authority entirely, an ability to lead without compelling and persuade without proving."[35]

Washington's leadership reached beyond the inner circles of the cabinet, as he chose to reach out directly to the people, monitoring public opinion. This may be seen as a profoundly republican impulse, though underlying it was the realization that most Americans were still emotionally attached to their states, while attachment to the new nation was at best tenuous. Only by taking the federal government to the people, Washington was convinced, would he be able to give life to the abstract idea, laid down in the Constitution, of national unity, be able to inspire Americans with feelings of belonging, love of country, and a shared sense of national destiny. This rationale, T. H. Breen argues in *George Washington's Journey*, motivated Washington's decision to undertake his presidential journeys throughout the country, covering all of the thirteen states between April 1789 and July 1791.[36] The journeys were hugely successful, accompanied by public spectacles no one had ever seen before. People organized parades complete with floats and marching militia; they built triumphal arches and colonnades and even, in Boston, a colossal statue; they fired cannons and displayed special flags in honor of the nation's first president; at night, they often illuminated their entire city; and they gave speeches and held elaborate dinners. At these events, toasts were given, first by Washington and then by the local organizers. Toasts had had a long tradition, but in this instance they became, in Breen's words, "an important vehicle for political communication, linking local groups to the head of the new federal government."[37] With George Washington in their town or city, local dignitaries would pass over their provincial interests and respond to him by expressing the national concerns that he expected.

The toasts offered to George Washington affirmed a vision of the Union that the Father of His Country wholeheartedly endorsed. He also felt highly flattered by the words inscribed on the arch in Boston: "TO THE MAN WHO UNITES ALL HEARTS" and "TO COLUMBIA'S FAVORITE SON."[38] He was less enthusiastic about the behavior of the crowds, though, who often responded as if he were their king, sometimes belting out the song that the English had greeted George II with sixty years earlier: "He comes! He comes! The HERO Comes! Sound, sound your trumpets, beat, beat your drums."[39] Some people even treated him as if he were a god, having turned out to see "the man! *Columbia's* son! … the godlike WASHINGTON!" People addressed him with a variety of titles, among them bizarre ones such as "His Most Patriotic Majesty" or familiar ones such as "the beloved Father of the great American Family," "the political father and savior of his country," "the glorious father of the glorious age," or "the great father of the people."[40] Unsurprisingly, the success of Washington's journey is also remembered in nineteenth-century history books. In 1836, for instance, Jesse Olney put it in this way: "Never was a *king* received with such unfeigned applause and sincere affection. Multitudes traveled many miles to enjoy the luxury of seeing the man whom all acknowledged to be the *father* of his country."[41]

Henry Knox's suggestion to bestow on Washington the "glorious republican epithet—The Father of Your Country"—dates from March 1787. Knox was a former bookseller from Boston. It is quite possible, therefore, that he may have encountered the epithet in his vast reading, for it had been bestowed, *inter alia*, on Cicero in 63 BCE, for uncovering, during his consulship, the Catiline conspiracy.[42] James Hardie, the author of the commemorative book of 1795, may have drawn from similar sources, as in early 1792 he sent a copy of his Latin grammar to Washington, offering it as a testimony of his "respect for one, who on account of his many & superior virtues, is by all deservedly named *the Father of His Country*."[43] Roman antiquity doubtless was the premier supplier of cultural values and traditions to the fledgling United States, though the genealogy for "father of his country" is much more diversified. When in 1760 Samuel Davies offered to the British that "George was our father, too," he did not directly borrow from the classical tradition of bestowing "*patriae pater*" to the ruler.[44] Rather, he tapped into a British view of the role of kings in the preservation and, if necessary, restoration of a well-ordered state. The British view had evolved among a diverse group of English political writers in the second quarter of the eighteenth century.

Collectively called the "Country Party," these thinkers among the landed gentry were convinced that the hallowed English liberties were endangered by the "corrupt" politics of the age, in particular by Robert Walpole's, the "prime minister's," ministerial system of government. "Country Party" thinkers saw in England the same tendencies that had ruined the "virtuous" Roman republic, despite the efforts of patriots like Cicero or Cato, the hero of Joseph Addison's much-admired tragedy.[45] *Cato's Letters* by John Trenchard and Thomas Gordon, as well as Henry St John, 1st Viscount Bolingbroke's extended essay *The Idea of a Patriot King* (1738, 1749) and his *Letters on the Spirit of Patriotism* (1749) are the key texts in which these sentiments were expressed, though there were many more works of a similar bent (by Swift, Pope, John Gay, Johnson, Fielding, Lord Chesterfield, among others).[46] Importantly, these writings were the lens through which American radicals, too, scrutinized English politics.

By the mid–1750s, the "Country" tradition had begun to shape colonial thinking about the institution of monarchy and colonial attitudes towards their sovereign. Significantly, "Country Party" texts, both imported by colonial booksellers and in colonial editions, could be found in the library of Daniel Parke Custis, which George Washington inherited when he married Custis's widow, Martha Custis, in 1759. Washington had already begun reading about English history and politics while still in his teens. Bolingbroke's rather more fictional "Patriot King" thus not only served as a model for the future George III but also looms large in the political education of George Washington. The belief, among Bolingbroke and other "Country Party" thinkers, that their hard-won liberties were in jeopardy only bolstered the suspicion, among Washington and other disgruntled colonists, that "corrupt" English politics was to reduce them to "slavery."[47] Washington owned a complete set of Bolingbroke's early journal named *The Craftsman*. From it he gleaned the idea of a politics of fatherhood. "A good King … is the *Father of his People*," he would read there, and as such the king, owing his country "a Duty," would be required to act as a check to corrupt ministries. In his later book, *The Idea of a Patriot King*, Bolingbroke not only wrote about checks and balances as a way of curbing factions but developed the fantasy of politics without factions at all. Only a "patriot king," who would "begin to govern as soon as he begins to reign" and would "espouse no party, but … govern like the common father of his people," could be the proper bulwark against "universal corruption," Bolingbroke fantasized.[48] American colonists readily absorbed Bolingbroke's doctrine, and they were also receptive to his idea that the "true image of a free people, governed by a PATRIOT KING, is that of a patriarchal family, where the head and all the members are united by one common interest, and animated by one common spirit."[49]

Bolingbroke's "PATRIOT KING" had no equivalent in the real life of eighteenth-century England. George I was too inept to qualify, while his son, the Prince of Wales, was too eaten up by hatred for his father to have much interest in governing. This brings us all the way to George III and to the American patriots. George III ascended the throne in 1760. By that time, "The Idea of a Patriot King" had become a commonplace in colonial rhetoric, so much so that it was employed without reference to its author and, in some instances, without direct knowledge of Bolingbroke's doctrines. Unsurprisingly, it was also employed to celebrate the accession of George III. On him, colonists focused great expectations. Especially the idea that the English king would restore America's liberties had a compelling force then, as many colonists blamed the British Parliament for unlawfully usurping the "father's" prerogatives. Never mind that this interpretation of the roles played by king, ministers, and the Parliament in London was largely mythological. George III throughout his reign obeyed his perceived duty to uphold the British constitution and accordingly felt obliged to take a firm stand against the American colonies because Parliament had so decided. The king thus may have been curbed in his intentions by the British constitution and so was a "limited" monarch against his own will or even against his better judgment. Such finesses were beyond the colonists' grasp, though. "No British king," William Liddle wrote, "ever enjoyed the prestige, popularity, and influence in America that George III possessed in 1766."[50]

It was only when George III disappointed the American colonists that their dreams were transferred to Washington. Then patriots no longer sang "God Save the King" but, to the same tune, "GOD save great WASHINGTON":

> Crush all the tyrant's crew,
> Dogs that our lives pursue;
> WASHINGTON them subdue—
> Conquer them all.[51]

Patriots came to their condemnation of George III as a "tyrant" only reluctantly and rather belatedly. John Dickinson, for instance, detested and vehemently opposed inflammatory measures. Rather, he wrote in *Letters from a Farmer in Pennsylvania*, the colonists must be "dutiful children," even though they "have received unmerited blowes from a beloved parent." But not even Dickinson, the American pamphleteer who reached the largest audience in the colonies prior to Independence (Washington himself purchased a copy), could ignore the Townshend Acts of 1767, which slapped import duties on glass, paper, paint, and tea. This most moderate of colonial protesters therefore argued that the British Parliament cannot tax the colonies. What helped was Dickinson's education at the London Inns of Court, which ultimately translated into the celebrated cry in Letter VII of his *Letters*: "*We are taxed* without our own consent, expressed by ourselves or our representatives. *We* are therefore—*SLAVES*."[52]

Pamphleteering in the service of a revolution was one thing; the construction of governmental institutions was quite another. Thus, they reflect the most troubling question at time: Who will rule at home? Should that role be retained for the British king? It was the challenge facing the framers of the Constitution. Their solution, I will show presently, was a republicanized version of Bolingbroke's patriot king, a public persona displaying humility, self-restraint or what the age called "virtue."[53] George Washington was that "great and good man, governed by superior motives," that the Founders wanted.[54] A poem published just before Washington's inauguration claimed that neither "Alexander's mad career" nor "Caesar's dictatorial reign" would tempt America's first president.[55] Yet would his proven, virtuous leadership be sufficient proof against a cabal or, worse, against caesarian ambitions leading towards a military dictatorship? Over this question the founders were divided. Franklin found in Washington reason enough to believe that America would always produce selfless and virtuous leaders, at least a few, in any given era. Antifederalists put the odds much lower, at one or two in a century after Washington. This meant that nine out of ten presidencies would be marked by political corruption and worse. Another antifederalist was even more pessimistic, putting the odds of a virtuous president at one in a hundred million. This "Old Whig," as he called himself, therefore foresaw only scenes of horror and confusion as the country descended into military dictatorship.

Unsurprisingly, Thomas Jefferson, who was then United States minister to France, too had misgivings: "Our jealousy is only put to sleep by the unlimited confidence we all repose in the person to whom we all look as our president. After him inferior characters may perhaps succeed and awaken us to the danger which his merit has led us into."[56] The emotional appeal of the antifederalists offended and worried their opponents, Alexander Hamilton in particular. Taking up the pen of "Publius," Hamilton therefore accused the antifederalists of willfully spinning "extravagant" tales in order to make their audience "tremble" and "blush." A limited term, Hamilton said, would be sufficient to swallow up any president's ambitions. And, in contrast to the millions-to-one odds laid against the presidency by the antifederalists, Hamilton insisted on the "constant probability of seeing [the presidency] filled by characters pre-eminent for ability and virtue."[57]

More than two centuries on, it is questionable whether the supply of ability and virtue has really been as "constant" as Hamilton predicted. Still, Hamilton had in mind George Washington, whose comportment made people trust him, and so the honorific "Father of His Country" or, for that matter, "*des Landes Vater*" was bestowed on him as a matter of course. It was the almanac published in Lancaster, Pennsylvania, in 1778 that first bestowed on George Washington the exalted title "*des Landes Vater*." Pious Germans in the area, including the Amish, would have been familiar with the paean from Martin Luther's Bible translations. In Luther's version of Genesis, for instance, the Egyptian pharaoh has Joseph proclaimed as the father of the country ("*Der ist des Landes Vater*," Gen. 41:43). In the final authorized version of 1545, Luther added a commentary explaining that "*des Landes Vater*" was his rendering of the original Hebrew word "*abrech*."[58] As pithy as Luther's language is, he does not say why he translated "*abrech*" as "*des Landes Vater*."[59] Luther's motives may well have been political. Faced with persecution, excommunication, and even death after the publication of his Ninety-Five Theses at Wittenberg in 1517, Luther became the protégé of Prince Frederick III, Elector of Saxony. It is not improbable, therefore, that Luther's rendering of "*abrech*" is an oblique homage to the prince who had him escorted to the security of Wartburg Castle at Eisenach. Moreover, Luther had raised political authorities to the status of fathers ("*ynn den vater stand*") already in his catechism of 1529, and applying the title of "*des Landes Vater*" to political rulers had become common usage in Protestant countries a century after Luther.[60]

In 1653, a German Bible commentary referred to the Egyptian pharaoh as "*patriae pater deß Landes Vater*," thus merging Luther's German with the tradition of classical Rome. Closer to home is a political pamphlet of 1681 that urged rulers to prove themselves fathers of their country ("*deß Landes Väter*"). Forty years later, Christian Wolff decreed that rulers behave towards their subjects as fathers to their children ("*Regierende Personen verhalten sich zu Unterthanen wie Väter zu den Kindern*"). By the time of the American Revolution, the exalted title was a fixture of political discourse in German. Johann Karl August Musäus put it in the form of a rhetorical question: "Who doesn't know that ... certain rulers deserve to be called fathers of their country?" ("*Wem ist unbekannt, daß ... mancher Fürst des Landes Vater zu heißen verdienet?*") In 1778, Justus Möser found the title fitting for King Ernst August II of Hanover (the younger brother of Britain's George I), whom he called "one of the good fathers of their countries" ("*einer von den guten Landesvätern*").[61] Similar ideas about the sovereign's role seem to have circulated in eighteenth-century Russia. For instance, Tsar Peter the Great was acclaimed as "Father of His Country" in 1721; a biography of this archetypal reforming autocrat was published in England in 1758 under the title *The Father of His Country*.[62]

Given the ubiquity of "*des Landes Vater*" or "Father of His Country" in Europe, one should not be surprised that in 1783 the Dutch poetess Lucretia Wilhelmina van Winter of Leyden, the "Lady in Holland," sent George Washington a poem that she had composed in his honor and that uses the exact phrase, rendered in French. The exalted title can be found also in the works of Friedrich von Schiller, most notably in *Wilhelm Tell*. In that historical play of 1804, Ulric von Rudenz, nephew and heir to the Baron von Attinghausen, proudly proclaims: "I count myself amongst the Country's Fathers, / And their first duty's to protect her children."[63] Rudenz's lines, in William Peter's translation, reveal the transformation, in republican terms, of the German tradition of glorifying sovereigns as fathers of their country. In this capacity, sovereigns were expected to protect their countries' liberties and sovereignty. But the duty to also protect the country's "children" was a true innovation, extending the metaphorical father's duties to all citizens, independent of birth and status, and, even more importantly, passing on his paternal qualities to his "children," thus enabling them to emulate their father.[64] Schiller, like Lessing, Klopstock, Herder, Goethe, and numerous other German writers of the time often expressed a keen and sympathetic interest in the country that had become a shining symbol of freedom. It is quite probable, therefore, that in *Wilhelm Tell*—a play that was particularly popular in the American South—the German dramatist not only gave expression to his political message in the cloak of Swiss republican fervor but had reimported the republicanized concept of the metaphorical father from the fledgling new nation across the Atlantic.[65]

Newborns need fathers, the great historian Seymour Lipset once claimed. George Washington was revered both as the Father of His Country and as the Protector of Her Children. Being childless, Washington's hagiographers hinted, he took on paternity for all America. As John Adams famously said in 1785, Washington was the "exemplification of the American character."[66] Though it was impossible to reach his level of perfection, emulation was something of a patriotic duty. Washington not only exemplified the virtues which Americans dreamed of living up to. His childless status also had removed any temptation to consider the presidency as a hereditary office entrusted to the Washington family. This was fortunate for the young nation. On the other hand, the very idea that Washington *was* a superior surrogate for George III implied that the presidency itself was a semi-regal office. Washington's way of conducting it, with levees, official birthdays, and "royal" progresses to various regions of the United States, aroused the suspicion of men like Maclay and Benjamin Franklin Bache that the transition to republicanism was incomplete, and reversible. It was therefore the more necessary, after Washington's retirement in 1797, and still more after his death in 1799, to insist on the gulf between him and George III. The need to define a separate national identity demanded that America's first president be absolutely differentiated from her last king. Washington must be exalted as George III was execrated.

The difference between the abuse that George III received both during his lifetime and thereafter and the vast admiration George Washington received—as a soldier, patriot, and president—could not be greater.[67] In broad terms, the contrast stands as the difference "between a corrupt and vainglorious monarchical system and an honest, modest, competent republicanism."[68] Phrased differently, an old order was juxtaposed to the new order of the ages. Within this trope, George III for most Americans was a symbol of the bad old days; in contrast, George Washington came to symbolize the good new days, superseding the old order. "How different is power when derived from its only just source, viz. THE PEOPLE, from that which is derived from ... hereditary sucession," sounded "The Trenton Ladies's Sonata," continuing, "The first magistrates of the nations of Europe assume the title of Gods, and treat their subjects like an inferior race of animals. Our beloved magistrate delights to show, upon all occasions, that he is a man—and instead of assuming the pomp of master, acts as if he considered himself the FATHER—the FRIEND—and the SERVANT of the PEOPLE."[69]

The "Sonata" was written as Washington was on his way to his inauguration in New York City where, later, the base of a destroyed statue of George III was used to accommodate one of George Washington. Both the success and the rapidity of the transfer is illustrated by Washington Irving's tale "Rip Van Winkle" (1820). The first thing that Rip notices as he wakes up from his "nap" is the changed sign on the village tavern—instead of the ruby face of King George he now sees the head of George Washington decorated with a cocked hat. But it is Irving himself who testifies to the fast and willing acceptance of George Washington. Born in 1783, Irving was given the name of the nation's hero—"a citizen, first in war, first in peace, first in the hearts of his countrymen," as Henry Lee famously wrote in a speech to Congress after Washington's death.[70] Washington surely would have been moved by Lee's eulogy, but to be first in the hearts of his countrymen was not enough for him. There was also in him an "underlying hunger for posthumous glory," and to secure for himself a place in history's pantheon was never far from his mind. Given his almost excessive concern for maintaining appearances, he had begun to tend his own image already as a youth, when in 1747 he copied out over a hundred maxims from *The Rules of Civility and Decent Behavior in Company and Conversation*, a humorless guidebook of etiquette that traced its origins to a French Jesuit work of the sixteenth century.[71] Washington's sensitivity to what the public thought of him has been noticed by all his biographers. Born with a thirst for public respect of a special kind, his self-fashioning became more pronounced when he first became a public figure in Virginia in his early twenties. Then, he did everything in his power to show courage when leading the Virginia militia against the French, or else to be the most graceful dancer, or the finest horseman.

4

Inventing George Washington

In July 1771, Washington placed an order with Robert Cary & Company of London, asking for "a Topaz or some other handsome Stone fixed in the gold Sockt [socket] Sent, wt. the Washington arms neatly engraved thereon." A London jeweler by the name of Benjamin Gurden accordingly engraved a suitably stone and mounted it on Washington's gold frame or socket. A few months later the completed seal, one and a half inches tall, arrived at Mount Vernon. In 1776, Charles Wilson Peale made it a detail in his portrait of Washington as commander in chief of the Continental Army (the seal is seen hanging from Washington's watch chain); today, the seal is on view at the Art Museums of Colonial Williamsburg.[1] To say that documents of this kind reveal Washington's class consciousness and status-based ostentatiousness is not to make any new claim. If anything, they magnify the fact that George Washington did not invent himself by himself. He was also a construct fashioned by a society that had few illusions left concerning human nature. Human nature therefore must be held in check, by a hierarchical system in which everyone has his or her place as much as by self-mastery. Washington's invention of himself thus seems like a case of nature imitating art, of making life conform to the perfection of character and conduct that he had absorbed as his ideal.

Over time, Washington also became more calculating in gaining posthumous fame. For one thing, he had learned to screen a "burning ambition" behind an image of republican virtue, dedication to public service and sacrifice for his country.[2] For another, he had come to believe that the task of artists and writers was to crown those who had won fame. As much as he hated sitting for portraits, some twenty-seven artists immortalized the Father of His Country during his lifetime. As for writers, Washington had convinced himself that poets make heroes. "Alexander the Great is said to have been enraptured with the Poems of Homer and to have lamented that he had not a rival muse to celebrate his actions." To do as Alexander the Great had done, Washington wrote to the Marquis de Lafayette in 1788, was "no vulgar function." So who was there to celebrate Washington's actions? It would have to be one whose works must not be "inferior to the rest of the world."[3] Would that illustrious poet be Joel Barlow, who in 1787 published his epic poem *The Vision of Columbus* (it grew into the much more expansive *Columbiad* by 1807)? Barlow, too, put the extravagance of figure and gesture in his poetry to serve morality and politics. And Barlow, who had lavishly praised the Father of His Country in an Independence Day oration at Hartford in 1787, was, as Washington wrote to the Marquis de Lafayette, "one of those Bards who hold the keys of the gate by which Patriots, Sages, and Heroes are admitted to immortality."[4]

In the end, Washington, who willingly extended his patronage to a considerable number of writers, artists, and composers, managed to attract greater talents than Barlow's, since for all his professions of modesty, he never was backward in putting himself forward. He patiently sat for portraitists, knowing full well that engravers would reproduce or borrow from them in engravings, prints, almanacs, broadsides, schoolbooks, magazines, and virtually every other sort of publications, not to mention coins, medals, and bank notes. He also profusely thanked Joseph Hopkinson for his "favourable sentiments" that had come with his "Pamphlet and Song"—the "patriotic song adapted to 'The Presidents March'" that Hopkinson wrote in April 1798 and that became known as the spectacularly popular "Hail Columbia."[5] For painters as for public appearances, Washington always chose the clothing most appropriate to his desired or current national role: He attended the Continental Congress in his old military uniform when that body was considering whom to appoint as commander in chief of its army; he appeared at presidential levees in the black suit of American manufacture that Gilbert Stuart captured in the "Lansdowne" portrait. Washington's presidential tours of the country, respectively in 1789 and 1791, likewise reflected his keen sense of public performance.

Washington not only wanted to establish the respectability and stability of the office of the presidency and the fledgling nation. He was similarly concerned about his afterlife. Thus, he left detailed instructions for preserving his wartime papers. With the approval of Congress, he had the papers unsealed, and William Gordon, a minister from Massachusetts and a loyal supporter of the cause of American independence, went to work on them in June 1784.[6] When Gordon's multivolume history appeared in 1788, Washington bought two sets for himself and urged friends to buy it. It is perhaps significant that he also declared that now it was "time for the age of Knight-Errantry and Mad-heroism to be at an end."[7] Washington's hunger for military fame had been satisfied. The year after Dr. Gordon's stint with the wartime correspondence, the Father of His Country agreed to have his biography written. The task fell to David Humphreys, who had served as Washington's aide late in the War of Independence. Humphreys came to Mount Vernon in the summer of 1786, eventually producing an admiring narrative of Washington's life, though a manuscript copy of several early chapters is all that has survived.[8] Yet in the process of writing "Life of General Washington," Humphreys also became a kind of surrogate son, like Tobias Lear, who became Washington's personal secretary in January 1786, the beginning of a personal and professional relationship that lasted until the end of Washington's life.

By the time of his death, Washington's status as the Father of His Country was secure. His birthday became an unofficial holiday second only to Independence Day. Yet the emerging hagiography of him all but eclipsed the historic George Washington, the "real man" as it were. That man, Henry Lee famously eulogized, had been "first in war, first in peace, first in the hearts of his countrymen." Lee's ordering, Stephen Brumwell maintains, is "revealing" insofar as it draws attention not to the solemn Father of His Country, the model of republican virtue, simplicity, and dignity, so much as to the soldier who, when he heard the "bullets whistle" for the first time believed there was "something charming in the sound."[9] In May 1779, he even described himself as a "warrior."[10] In 1779, Washington *was* a warrior, the commander in chief of the Continental Army, who always made a point of distancing himself from the revolutionary movement's political leaders while at the same time emphasizing that there were some matters about which he would not speak, "because they belong to Congress, and not to us warriors."[11]

Contrary to what is frequently said, Washington was not among the signers of the Declaration of Independence, but it was his final victory as the revolutionaries' premier soldier that led to his roles as president of the Constitutional Convention and, ultimately, as the first president of the new United States of America. And it was as a soldier above all that he expected, and wished, to be remembered. Why else would he instruct, on his deathbed, his personal secretary Tobias Lear to "arrange & record all my late Military letters and papers"[12]? It was largely Washington's exploits as a soldier that bestowed on him not only the "approbation of all America," as John Adams put it, but also the international prestige that brought him the admiration even of the English monarch, George III, who in 1799 called him the "greatest character of the age."[13] Military fame may well have been Washington's "ruling passion," in the words of a British officer from 1778.[14] It is also safe to say that Washington's martial side paved the way for everything else, the presidency included, yet this side was often unappreciated by Americans at the time. Leaving aside patriotic spasms over battles won, Washington's contemporaries developed a curious propensity to charge him with indecisiveness and timidity, calling him, quite unflatteringly, "the *American Fabius*."[15]

Washington himself was deeply disturbed by these charges, the more so since at times he had no more than 3,000 "much broken and dispirited" men under his command, becoming more painfully aware, from day to day, of the circumstances that forced him to grind down his opponent by a cautiously defensive "war of posts"—circumstances like shamefully short supplies, short-term enlistments instead of a permanent army, desertions, congressional directives that all major decisions be made in a war council, the ill-fated congressional decision to defend New York. The list could easily be extended.[16] Yet as much as he was hamstrung by forces outside of his control, Washington lost more battles than he won, and he botched several through strategic blunders, as at Long Island in the summer of 1776, or at Brandywine in September 1777, which led to the loss of Philadelphia to the British.[17]

A "self-cultivated nobility"[18] had led Washington to resign his commission as commander in chief, though the shock of Shays's Rebellion drew him back into public life. The Rebellion was an armed uprising in Massachusetts, led by Revolutionary War veteran Daniel Shays who, like other farmers, had lost his land in foreclosure. The uprising prompted Washington to emotional outbursts such as "We are fast verging to anarchy & confusion!" or "Are your people getting mad?" It also put a deep dent into his view of human nature: "What, gracious God, is man!" an exasperated Washington wrote to David Humphreys, "that there should be such inconsistency and perfidiousness in this conduct?"[19] The rebels' march, in 1787, against the United States armory at Springfield, not only struck the law-abiding Washington with horror but also convinced him that it was time to go to Philadelphia.

Under the Articles of Confederation the executive consisted only of a feeble committee that was part of Congress. For Washington, in contrast, the reins of government should be "braced and held with a steady hand." It was a message he pounded home over and over again.[20] It also convinced enough lawmakers that the Articles of Confederation, then the nation's governing document, were in dire need of reform. Spurred by the events in Massachusetts, the Constitutional Convention thoroughly reshaped the government. Under the Constitution, George Washington seemed the obvious candidate for the presidency. Only he was known, respected, and trusted in all the states, and only he had the requisite charisma, glory, and prestige demanded for the office. Once elected president, Washington instantly dealt with the depreciated currency. He supported Hamilton's plans of the assumption of state debts by the federal government as well as the creation of the Bank of the United States, a kind of national bank. The Assumption Bill brought prosperity to the new nation, and together with the B.U.S. solidly established the credit of the United States at home and abroad.[21]

President Washington not only dealt effectively with public credit and the banking system. He also took care of revenue for the federal government, the vast majority of which then came from tariffs. In 1791, therefore, the government introduced an excise tax on spirits. The measure, which was to increase the size of the regular army and to reform the militia in order to fight Indian tribes, led to massive protests, the Whiskey Rebellion, which Washington, like a stern parent, threatened to crush with 15,000 militia. The term rebellion is hyperbole, as resistance was not widespread, yet it shows that one's purse is one's most sensitive organ. On the political level, Washington saw the rebellion as an attack on the legacy of the Revolution, all the more serious because it mimicked its arguments. The Revolution had been provoked by various taxes and fees; the Rebellion was provoked by an excise tax on whiskey. But the first measures had been passed by the Parliament in London; the tax on whiskey came from the United States government, representing the American people. Washington's decisive action thus only strengthened the national government, demonstrating its resolve and ability to enforce the nation's laws. The immediate cause of the collapse of the rebellion, however, had been the force of Washington's presence. "WASHINGTON IS EVER TRIUMPHANT," read a sign that greeted him in one of the villages. One soldier even wrote about him as "THE MAN OF THE PEOPLE [who,] with a mien intrepid as that of Hector, yet graceful as that of Paris, moved slowly onward with his attending officers, nor once turned his eagle eye…."[22]

The laws that the alleged "man of the people" enforced also disempowered, eliminating whole categories from the rubric of "we, the people," thus giving the lie to Washington's ideology of unity. Articles 1 and 4 of the Constitution, for instance, perpetuated the institution of slavery and reduced all individuals who were not "free" to three-fifths of a person. And in 1792, Washington signed into law the Fugitive Slave Act, over and above his own misgivings about the institution of slavery.[23] Again in Article 1, Native Americans were excluded from representation, while Congress was given an exclusive power in commerce over them. Washington himself was ambivalent about the indigenous population. Once he had overcome his youthful prejudices against Indians, he became well-intentioned, even envisioning their integration into the society of white settlers. As president, he, together with Henry Knox, sought to balance the continuing and inescapable expansion of the nation onto Indian land and a legal and ethical policy in dealing with Native American tribes and nations. His "Address to the Cherokee Nation," issued in his last year in office, attempted to define a way of harmonious coexistence. Yet as warm and friendly as the speech was in its tone, it was unrealistic to ask Native Americans to simply abandon their traditional ways of life. And there was an unspoken threat. If the Cherokees flouted his advice, harm would follow. As it soon did, for Washington—upon whom the Seneca Chief Cornplanter in 1790 had bestowed the title "Town Destroyer"—dealt remorselessly with Indians who menaced white settlers at the frontiers.[24]

As regards women, the New Jersey Constitution of 1776 gave women the vote—until 1807, when the constitution was amended. The federal Constitution, in contrast, avoids all mention of them, one half of the population. All pronouns referring to gender are in the masculine form. Women's suffrage had been defeated already in the Constitutional Convention. Washington himself took no public position on women's rights during his administration. He seemed content with their role, in the political iconography of the time, as figurative symbols of liberty and republican virtue. The reduction of women to political symbols only underscores the expectation of their passivity in public life. Their alleged purity of status and their presumed innocence of experience all required masculine protection, at the same time as they precluded independent female action, not least in the political arena. This is no surprise, as the illustrious body of the Constitutional Convention was all male, as was

Washington's cabinet and all appointments to federal office. Only briefly were women freed from the clutch of white males who dominated society and political life of the early republic. That was during the "Long Farewell" following George Washington's death. Other than that, there simply was no place for "black swans," as active or independent-minded women were called, in what John Adams, writing to his wife Abigail Adams on the eve of the American Revolution, had self-confidently called "our Masculine systems."[25]

The patriarchal structures of the early republic will be treated at some length in the following chapter. At this point, it should be made clear that whatever George Washington and the Founders did not do, what they did was what mattered—and still does.[26] Such as Washington's success at keeping the country at peace. When France declared war on Britain, Spain, and Holland in 1793, Washington shepherded his cabinet towards the Proclamation of Neutrality, even though this was contrary to the Franco-American Treaty of 1778. The Proclamation started a pamphlet war between Hamilton and Madison, who deemed it a capitulation to the "cause of Anglomany."[27] The pamphlet war shows that the cabinet was fast becoming a political battleground. This was "the spirit of party and faction," as Madison had come to call it, realizing that political parties were normal in any civilized nation. Washington appears to have been temperamentally unable to see that parties might help clarify choices for the electorate, organize opinion, and draw people into the political process. For him, parties were the expression of parochial self-interest, a blight on the still fragile republic. By 1792 his cabinet was split down the middle. Washington was deeply distressed by the contentions and often wished that they would simply go away. "My earnest wish, and my fondest hope therefore is," he wrote Jefferson in the summer of 1792, "that instead of wounding suspicions, & irritable charges, there may be liberal allowances—mutual forbearances—and temporizing yieldings on *all* sides."[28]

As naïve as Washington's wishes were, they flowed from his policy. Thus it was both the contentions in his official family and his fears that without him the union might not last that finally convinced him to undergo the ordeal of a second term in office.[29] Even Thomas Jefferson, though opposed to many of Washington's policies, pleaded that he accept another term as President, declaring that "North and South will hang together as long as they have you to hang to."[30] A poem by St. George Tucker, a lawyer from Virginia and friend of Philip Freneau, as well as a harsh critic of Washington's politics, also pleaded with the "Great Man without a stain" not to resign from his office:

> Still, as a Father to *thy country dear*, / Regard not those who seek to wound thy peace, / Nor to their impious falsehoods lend an ear, / Who would persuade Thee *her* regards can cease. / Still at the helm go on our Bark to steer, / Nor quit it, *till thou leave thine Equal There*.[31]

The poem is a good example of the prevailing Washington cult, which by the time was powerful and inclusive enough to deflect local and regional sentiments onto a common object of veneration. That was quite sufficient to unanimously reelect him in the Electoral College in 1792. Yet once that was done, Washington was no longer exempt from direct criticism. Freneau publicly accused him of aping royalty in his presidential behavior. Not much later, this poet laureate, who in 1783 had praised Washington as Cincinnatus, heaped abuse on the festivities, in Philadelphia, on the occasion of Washington's birthday, branding it a "monarchical farce." Perhaps, Freneau and other Republicans suggested, it was more appropriate to celebrate the nation's birthday on July 4 than to honor the Father, Washington, on *his* birthday, as if he were a semidivine figure and something of a king.[32] For anyone even vaguely familiar with the opulence of Versailles, Windsor Castle, or imperial Vienna, accusations of aping royalty would have seemed wildly overblown.[33]

Worries about a return to monarchism were perhaps understandable after a war against royal absolutism. Yet in the aftermath of the Jay Treaty, Washington's enemies not only disparaged his presidency but also blackened his wartime reputation. Benjamin Franklin Bache, grandson of old Ben and Washington's arch nemesis, even purported to show—through reprinting fake letters that when they first appeared had been dismissed as a joke—that Washington had pocketed bribes from the British and was a double agent for the Crown.[34] Thomas Paine, who in *Common Sense* had attacked George III as the "Royal Brute of Great Britain," also turned his wrath on George Washington. General Washington had been merely a figurehead during the Revolutionary War, Paine now said, sleeping away his time in the field until he could start his new career. As president, Washington was leaning monarchically towards Britain, at the same time as he was being unduly hostile to republican France. In short, George Washington was a man without principles, whose typical behavior was a "chameleon-colored thing." So savage were the diatribes against Washington that his popularity towards the end of his second term in office sank to such depths that some Democratic-Republican critics even spoke of him as a "political hypocrite," not the Father but the "Step-Father" of his country.[35]

For Washington's political allies, these assumptions of hostile intrigues were the articulations, not of those Republicans who disagreed with the Federalists over policy but of a political minority, the "French Party in the United States," for whom Washington's retirement was, as one Federalist reported, "a cause of sincere, open, and indecent rejoicing." In contrast, the "real friends of this country ... considered the loss of Washington's personal influence a public calamity."[36] So much for the lethal political atmosphere—what Richard Hofstadter called "the paranoid style" in American politics—at the end of Washington's presidency.[37] Today, different toxins prevail, while the bitter partisan feuding of Washington's time seems forgotten. George Washington is, with Lincoln, the most frequently featured president in portraiture and sculpture. And in a recent book ranking American Presidents by performance, Washington comes in second place, trailing Lincoln by just two points. Had Washington scored better for his domestic programs (he is ranked 15th, with Martin Van Buren), the Father of His Country might easily have topped the list as America's greatest president.[38]

All this goes to show that there is no "true" Washington outside historic and social contexts. The Father of His Country cannot be confined to his biography, he cannot authenticate himself. His credibility depends on representing him as such. It is a function of his role within the culture, which marks the horizon for citizens turning towards him or away from him. Dixon Wecter, writing in the 1940s, had other purposes. His interest was rather in comparing Washington's actual characteristics, as established by modern biographical research, with some of the traits popularly attributed to him.[39] Yet Wecter, as well as those who also wanted to reveal the "true" Washington, was unable to or did not want to acknowledge what economists call the "halo effect" in stories about the Father of His Country.[40] These stories are mostly success stories. They come easily to mind, with no contradictions and no competing scenarios; additionally, they are about key events and memorable moments, not about time passing. Washington had been identified with the nation through an act of communal incorporation, an act that constitutes mutual recognition between leaders and led. In this act, leaders are deemed superior in dignity and power not because of any inherent qualities so much as because they symbolize something greater than themselves: the moral authority of society or nation.

George Washington passed away on December 14, 1799. The Senate address to President

John Adams indicated that "our country mourns a father." And Samuel Dexter, Senator from Massachusetts, promptly called upon Americans to "consecrate the memory of the heroic General, the patriotic Statesman and the virtuous Sage; let them teach these children never to forget that the fruit of his labors and his example are their inheritance."[41] Yet how do people commemorate? How can commemoration become a stimulus to moral behavior? And should it? As word of Washington's death spread from Mount Vernon, selectmen or councilmen ordered bells to be tolled and guns to be fired, requested churches to drape their pulpits and altars in black cloth, and called town meetings to draw up plans for appropriate funeral ceremonies. Eventually, funeral rites and commemorative observances were held in various forms all over the nation, so that the Father of His Country almost literally had "a tomb on every hill and in every valley of his bewailing country."[42] Funeral processions were attended by thousands of people, some 6,000 in Boston alone, with more at the state funeral held in Washington City on December 26, 1799. Popular feelings were also articulated through all kinds of pictures, from mourning pictures to true apotheoses, as well as through verse, odes, hymns, sonnets, even prose poems, some brief, some running over hundreds of lines. At least one of these works was written in German, by a Pennsylvania farmer named Christian Jacob Hütter, in whose *Washingtons Ankunft in Elisium* the departed hero strolls around heaven chatting with Brutus, Columbus, Franklin, and William Penn. Another oddity was a fictitious "Lady Washington's Lamentation for the Death of her Husband." All of these products were not only circulated in a variety of print media—pamphlets, broadsides, and periodicals—but also spoken or sung at civic processions, religious services, and commercial theatricals all across the nation. Fellow feeling was fueled by words and expressions like "general grief," "general sorrow," "the People's grief," or "the country's woe," as well as from generalized titles like "Columbia's Distress" or "America in Mourning."[43]

The poetry of public mourning for the most part showed all the characteristics of neoclassical poetry—extravagance of figure and gesture, authorial anonymity, and depersonalized sentiments as the condition of establishing grief as a national affect. Neoclassicist conventions already had shaped the elegies American colonists had written a generation earlier for King George II.[44] But grief in a republic ought to be different. Americans "seemed to realize intuitively that there could be no liberty without union," Barry Schwartz explains, "and when they expressed praise of Washington, the benefits of union were often affirmed in their next breath." "When WASHINGTON lived," one of his mourning countrymen recalled, "we had one common mind—one common head—one common heart—we were united—we were safe."[45] In death, the nation once again rallied around Washington. Putting aside party and other animosities, Federalists and Democratic-Republicans, northerners and southerners, men and women, mourned the passing of their first president. For all their differences, eulogies generally emphasized Washington's sacrifices and achievements in the service of his country. Many of the eulogists also took the long view, envisioning how his sacrifices and achievements would be viewed by posterity. "To Americans his name will be ever dear," wrote the Reverend Dr. Timothy Dwight, president of Yale College, "a savor of sweet incense, descending to every succeeding generation. The things which he has done are too great, too interesting, ever to be forgotten." The general peace, liberty, religion, safety, prosperity, Dwight continued, therefore will have every American "naturally, and almost necessarily, say, 'To Washington it is owing, under God, that we are here.'"[46]

The insertion, in Dr. Dwight's eulogy, of "under God," is telling. For the clergy of practically all denominations, Washington's death was seen as a divine sign, calling Americans to humiliation and repentance. Accordingly, countless memorial services across the entire nation adopted the style of the puritan jeremiad, at the same time as the worthy clergymen often had difficulties "proving" beyond doubt that Washington actually was a "Christian."[47] In contrast, eulogists had no difficulty whatsoever defining Washington's legacy in the terms stated by Congressman Henry Lee—"first in war, first in peace, first in the hearts of his countrymen," that is to say, as commander in chief ("in war"), as president of the constitutional convention and the country's first president ("in peace"), and as America's ultimate hero ("in the hearts"). Washington had left an indelible mark on the face of the new nation, and veneration of the nation's hero also brought unity to a diversified society. No longer reviled as the first Federalist, Washington again assumed his place as the Father of His Country. "What solemn sounds the ear invade, / What wraps this land in sorrow's shade, / From herein the awful mandate flies, / The Father of His Country dies," wrote Jacob French in his "Mount Vernon Hymn."[48]

The *George-Town and Washington Advertiser* announced that, on December 18, 1799, the "mortal part of … the Father of His Country … was consigned to the tomb." Indeed, stories about his death and national mourning for him "filled the black-bordered columns of the nation's newspapers" from the day of his death through the national day of mourning on February 22, 1800, the day Americans would have celebrated Washington's sixty-eighth birthday.[49] Congressional Representatives too experienced a brief respite from political bickering and partisanship when they were debating about a proper memorial for the deceased president. Tellingly in this debate, which took place in December 1800, Representative Clairborne stated his preference for "a statue to mausoleum, because the former, from representing the form and features [of George Washington] would inspire the beholder with more lively emotions than a mass of stones formed into a pyramid."[50] Perhaps for the worthy representative, a statue would have been less of a "monarchical" practice. Representative Clairborne may even have remembered the suggestion that Washington become America's first monarch. The suggestion had been brought to Washington's attention in 1782 and indignantly repudiated. Ideas of a kingship, Washington wrote, "I must view with abhorrence, and reprehend with severety," and he added that a return to a monarchy would be "the greatest mischief that can befall my country."[51]

Washington's fears and apprehensions did not go away any time soon.[52] Washington also strained at James Wilson's move, in debates of the Constitutional Convention, that "the Executive consist of a single person." At the time, this was difficult to swallow for men like Washington, Franklin, or Madison, who were convinced that Americans had just won their independence from an autocratic monarch, and who so feared one-man rule that they flirted with the idea of a double executive (based on the ancient Roman consulship) or even a legislative council. After a summer of deliberations, the framers of the Constitution had made up their minds. A single chief executive, the "president," would be more impeachable, in contrast to fixing responsibility on members of a team or council. The president would be appointed by Congress to serve for seven years. He could not be reelected, and his powers were tightly constrained. He could neither negotiate treaties nor appoint Supreme Court justices and ambassadors. The Senate would do all that. The final document is profoundly different, however, thanks largely to the political savvy of Gouverneur Morris.[53]

Just how explosive the topic of massing power in the executive was, is evident also from the controversies about the correct forms of addressing the president or, rather, the President.[54] These controversies (and there were others, too) always were precarious balancing acts between republican aspirations and demands and European monarchical traditions.[55] Washington's position was unwavering. Although it was important to him to

4. Inventing George Washington

Nathaniel Currier, *Washington's Reception by the Ladies, on Passing the Bridge at Trenton, New Jersey, April 1789, on his Way to New York to be Inaugurated first President of the United States*, hand-colored lithograph, New York: N. Currier, c. 1845 (photograph Library of Congress).

maintain "the dignity & respect which was due to the first Magistrate," he did not want the office of the president to become "an ostentatious imitation, or mimicry or Royalty."[56] He was adamant, therefore, that he not be addressed as "His Mightiness," "His Elective Majesty," or "His Highness the President of the United States, and Protector of their Liberties."[57] That his journey to New York, in the spring of 1789, took on the air of a royal procession was beyond his control, though. Washington everywhere was saluted by cannon, triumphal arches, and illuminations, and greeted by enthusiastic crowds shouting, "Long, long live GEORGE WASHINGTON, THE FATHER OF THE PEOPLE!" All this only confirmed what James McHenry had already told him before he left Mount Vernon: "You are now a king, under a different name."[58]

When on April 30, 1789, New York chancellor Robert R. Livingstone administered the oath of office to Washington, he followed it up by intoning "Long live George Washington, President of the United States." The spectators under the balcony of Federal Hall responded with huzzas and chants of "God bless our Washington! Long live our beloved President!" This may sound odd, but they celebrated in the only way they knew, as if welcoming a new monarch with the customary cry of "Long Live the King!"[59] Washington was visibly moved by the ceremony, including seeing his own portrait exhibited as a transparency in Broad-Street, though in his inaugural address, delivered in the Senate chamber, he gave expression to altogether different convictions: "[T]he preservation of the sacred fire of liberty, and the destiny of the Republican model of Government, are justly considered as *deeply*, perhaps as *finally* staked, on the experiment entrusted to the hands of the American people."[60] Less visibly, Washington also had refused coat buttons engraved with his portrait or his name. Instead, he chose metal buttons that had the heraldic eagle of the republic chased upon them.[61] Other buttons and memorabilia came with simple inscriptions such as "Long Live the President," "Memorable Era," or "Remember March Fourth, 1789." Of course, medals with Washington's portrait did circulate, though they were privately produced, as were, later, cent trials struck by a Robert Birch, which carried a brief reverse legend, "G*W Pt"— for "George Washington President," the final gasp of the movement to honor the nation's first chief executive on its coinage.[62]

5

Representing the Republic

Wary of the quasi-mythological status accorded to the presidency, Congress made sure that veneration of the person was separated from the prestige and authority of the office of President. At the end of the day the lawmakers agreed on two visual symbols—an allegorical representation of liberty and an eagle. Selecting an eagle for the nation's iconography was somewhat odd, as the bird was customarily associated with military and imperial might rather than with the ideals of independence and republicanism. To establish that fit, the eagle was said to be "the symbol of supreme power and authority and signifies the Congress."[1] Liberty and the eagle thus epitomized what had been obtained so dearly—political sovereignty, based on a free people and later also embodied in a glorified individual. The ideals of political sovereignty and the rights of free citizens are visible also in iconographic details such as the liberty cap and the motto "AMERICA INIMICA TYRANNIS" ("America, Enemy of Tyrants"), which had been stamped on a pattern coin as early as 1785. The use of symbols from republican Rome also is proof that there was no real rupture in the political iconography of the post-revolutionary era. Rather there was a slow and complex process of reformulating and adapting earlier traditions. More precisely, the new nation's symbolic constitution was achieved by going back to submerged origins.[2]

While many patriots turned to classical history for inspiration, America's cultural elites also ransacked British history. Representations of liberty are good examples of this tendency. Lady Liberty, an amply draped female carrying the *pileus* on a pole, seems to have grown quite naturally out of the seated Britannia on British coins. There are, in addition, other associations to British history. In November 1765, crowds in Boston hung in effigy a supporter of the Stamp Act. Paul Revere's engraving pictures him on Boston's Liberty Tree while a dragon, symbolizing the hated Act, threatens the Magna Carta—the *Magna Carta Libertatum* from 1215, the sacred document that chartered the concessions won from the English king by a rebellious aristocracy.[3] In 1775, Maryland notes depicted a tyrannical George III trampling on the Magna Carta, that is, on the chartered rights of his "children." Massachusetts notes issued in December of the same year show a rebellious colonist with a scroll of the Magna Carta in his arm.

When American patriots opposed the English king, the notion of liberty already had taken on attributes of political sovereignty and other ideas that traditionally had been the prerogatives of the king. Already the Puritans who came to America in order to escape King Charles I and Archbishop Laud had believed that civil government was established, not by God's grace but upon a contract between the ruler and the ruled. (Puritan divines, including Governor Winthrop, were of a different opinion: They believed that civil magistrates had their authority from God, but by and large their belief was not perceived as too much of a threat to people's liberties and property.) The Glorious Revolution in England confirmed the idea of a contract, at the same time as it sparked vigorous debates over political responsibility in New England, eventually limiting the magistrates' authority. By the 1730s it was widely believed that magistrates were responsible to those who had chosen them. The American Revolutionaries, who were mostly not Puritans, carried on these political traditions.[4]

The Revolutionaries' political convictions were also fueled by a book by Lord Shaftesbury, *Characteristicks of Men, Manners, Opinions, Times*, first published in 1711. On the title page of the second volume, *Virtue*, there is an allegorical depiction of Liberty in the form of a crowned female figure on a war chariot drawn by two royal lions. The caption beneath reads "Triumph of Liberty." In the second edition of 1714 the caption was substituted by a page reference directing readers to a description of liberty as the power "which sets us free from so many inborn Tyrannys." The passage, from a 1709 treatise on moral philosophy, is not very revealing. More revealing is Shaftesbury's treatise on liberty, also from 1709, as well as a fictive letter to an author from 1710. In the letter, Shaftesbury points to the lack of a public in absolutist regimes which legitimize their rule as God-given. Such legitimation, Shaftesbury contends, is merely the trademark of "tyranny." By contrast, in England there are a public and, importantly, chartered rights and liberties, in short, "a CONSTITUTION."[5] Shaftesbury continues these ideas in the miscellanies in volume three (1714), arguing that people have a "country" only when there is a constitution guaranteeing freedom and independence. Those who are "held together by Force," however,

> are not properly united: Nor does such a body make a People. 'Tis the social Ligue, Confederacy, and mutual Consent, founded in some common Good or Interest, which joins the Members of a Community, and makes a People ONE. Absolute Power annuls the Publick: And where there is no Publick, or Constitution, there is in reality no Mother-COUNTRY, or NATION.[6]

For the political iconography of the fledgling United States, the Roman and the British tradition were equally important. From ancient Rome came the idea of a republic, together with corresponding symbols and, not to forget, exemplary characters like Cato and Cincinnatus. The British tradition contributed the abstract notion of liberty, from the Magna Charta through Shaftesbury. Washington's understanding of self-government rested on his understanding of these liberties, which he had formed before the Revolution. In 1769, he wrote George Mason about the importance of "maintain[ing] the liberty which we have derived from our Ancestors." Washington gravitated towards rebellion because he believed that his inherited liberties were being violated by the mother country. And for Washington as well as the other Founders, English liberty became an immutable principle of statehood that would provide ideological ammunition for years to come.[7] Ideas are not the same as visual representations, though, which follow artistic conventions. These conventions are often divided along the lines of gender. Consider, for instance, the division between realism and classicism: Realist iconography is largely a male domain, whereas allegories are usually female, especially when they are used to represent nations. The fusion of liberty, in the form of a female allegory, both with the origin, the Roman republic, and with the newly formed United States, reduces Liberty to a "spectacle of nationhood," a mere decorative attachment to the male subject, the vehicle of *his* message. As the conveyor of the "father's" truth, her role is merely to endorse male dominion over the household. Phrased differently, the female Liberty helps maintain a male or patriarchal culture. Liberty's countenance thus registers memory of the real "mother," who during the formative years of the United States became the mediator of republican ideology, the metaphorical lap for the new citizens.

A good example of Liberty proclaiming America's political independence is a popular print titled *Liberty and Washington* (ca. 1800–1810). Liberty is swathed in Graeco-Roman robes and surrounded by the emblems of the new nation—stars and stripes, a bald eagle, the liberty cap and pole, and a laurel-wreathed bust of George Washington. The British crown lies trampled under her foot. On the bust's base is engraved Henry Lee's famous eulogy, "first in war, first in peace, and first in the hearts of his countrymen."[8] In the aftermath of the American Revolution, Americans understandably became more and more reluctant to ransack British history for heroes, with many patriots turning to classical history for inspiration. John Norman's etching *The True Portraiture of his Excellency George Washington Esq.* (c. 1783) has been mentioned. George Washington in a full suit of sixteenth-century European field armor may seem preposterous, especially since the inscription speaks of him as "represented in the Roman dress, holding a truncheon in his right hand, and his head encircled with a laurel wreath"—a reference to a congressional resolution of 1783 proposing a bronze equestrian statue of Washington. (The commission eventually went to Joseph Wright, who at his Rocky Hill, New Jersey, headquarters, did an oil painting and a life mask of the president-to-be.)

Ancient Rome in its republican phase provided uplifting examples also for banknote designers. In the late 1820s, for instance, Asher Durand designed notes for the National Bank of New York on which Washington is depicted as a Roman consul, donning a toga and carrying the fasces, a bundle of rods enfolding an ax.

Washington's powdered wig was, of course, a stylistic incongruity that raised quite a few eyebrows. In Richard Doty's irreverent comment Washington is making his escape from a village bathhouse.[9] But would a laurel wreath have been more desirable? Laurel wreaths were the prerogatives of the caesars; a Washington adorned with such a wreath no doubt would have been even less fitting. The bundle of twelve rods enfolding an ax posed less of a problem. A symbol of sovereign virtues as well as a badge of authority from early on, it was first borne by kings, later by office holders in the republic and, finally, by victorious military commanders. The bundle (*fasces*) was usually carried by minor officials (*lictores*) marching up front and clearing the way for the consuls, magistrates, and other authorities. Washington himself had identified with the stern code of honor and duty in ancient Rome so fully that a visitor from England felt compelled to comment on his "Roman face," expressive "of

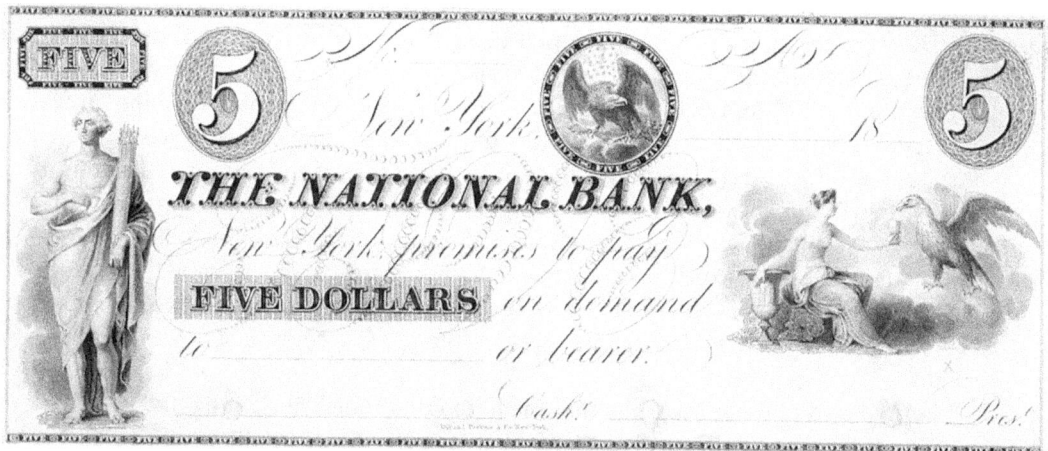

$5 note, National Bank of New York, c. 1829 (Division of Work and Industry, National Museum of American History, Smithsonian Institution).

Sagacity, of Prudence, and of Moderation."[10] Later, when Washington reluctantly agreed to attend the constitutional convention, his decision to do so was taken as proof of his "zeal for the public interest."[11] Republicanism as defining character and behavior contributed greatly to the Washington image, much as Washington himself seemed the embodiment of republican ideals, of benevolence, disinterestedness, restraint, rationality, a capacity for compromise, and patriotism. Even so, the dignified nobility attributed to Washington was not given to him in his cradle but was the product of life-long self-cultivation. As inspiration Washington took two popular works by or about Romans, filtered through English sensibility: *Seneca's Morals*, which he acquired in his teens in a translation by the English pamphleteer Roger L'Estrange, and Joseph Addison's *Cato*. The tragedy, written in 1712 and first performed in 1713, was Washington's favorite play and, the Bible excepting, there is no literary text that he quoted from more frequently.[12]

The upright Cato not only became Washington's personal role model—"Transplanting, one by one, into my life / His bright perfections, 'till I shine like him." It's been said that he also had *Cato* performed for the Continental Army while they were encamped at Valley Forge. The evidence for this is questionable, though. What is beyond doubt is that Marcus Portius Cato became a martyr to republicans for all time when he took his own life rather than submit to the tyranny of Julius Caesar. Beyond that, Cato's personal struggle to hold to his beliefs served as a kind of private parable for the Father of His Country. Cato, David Leverenz points out, "mastered all personal passions to achieve lasting honor through dedication to public duty."[13] By adopting Cato's classical republicanism, Washington found the perfect solution to a personal problem, that of the charismatic leader. Not that Washington renounced power altogether. On the contrary, he perfected power politics by giving away power, first by resigning his commission as commander in chief and then by subjecting his presidency to the Constitution he had been sworn in on. Ultimately, the republican code of conduct that shaped and determined Washington's life (at least his public life) crystallized in the implicit summons from the Father of His Country to his "children"—"To copy out our father's bright example."[14]

Contemporaries were all too familiar with the link between Washington's code of conduct and the Roman republic. The broad picture of him as a soldier, landowner, and statesman all in one is decidedly Roman. And there is something Roman also in Washington's family situation, his unfailing attachment to Mount Vernon, his dutiful concern for his mother, and his constant attention to the well-being of his extended family. Duty no doubt is a Roman clue to Washington. As John Marshall, Chief Justice of the U.S. Supreme Court and an old friend of Washington, remarked at the end of his biography, Washington was "a real republican, devoted to the constitution of his country, and to that system of equal political rights on which it is founded." But duty, in the sense of a cluster of obligations, is a *social* virtue. Personality is different. Washington's "temper was humane, benevolent, and conciliatory," Marshall wrote, "but there was a quickness in his sensibility to anything apparently offensive, which experience had taught him to correct."[15] Once again, the parallels to Addison's *Cato* are too obvious to be overlooked: "With how much Care he forms himself to Glory, / And breaks the Fierceness of his Native Temper / To copy out our Father's bright Example."

Marshall also praised Washington's "unaffected and indescribable dignity."[16] The eulogy at the same time points to the core problem of neo-classicist political art: How, if at all, can republican simplicity be represented? How, if at all, can "unaffected" dignity be dramatized into "greatness"? By portraying Washington in the style of a Roman military hero, emphasized by the close-cropped locks with thick short curls and dressed in a toga? This was done by the Italian sculptor Giuseppe Ceracchi, for whom Washington sat in 1795. Ceracchi's marble bust was the darling of Thomas Jefferson.[17] In 1816, when the North Carolina legislature decided that a Washington monument was appropriate for the state capitol, Jefferson, now a former president, recommended that Ceracchi's idealized likeness be used as a model. The artist chosen for the task was Antonio Canovo, again by Jefferson's recommendation. Canovo sculptured Washington as a seated Caesar writing on a tablet, and wearing antique garb, sandals included.[18] The verbal equivalent of dressing the Father of His Country in a toga and sandals is Francis Glass's *Georgii Washingtonii, Americae Septentrionalis Civitatum Foederatarum Praesidis Primi, Vita*, a "Life of George Washington in Latin Prose" modeled after Plutarch's first-century *Lives* of Greek and Roman heroes. Glass composed *Georgii Washingtoni* in 1822, though it was not published until 1835, almost cotemporaneous with the unveiling of Horatio Greenough's monumental statue. Glass's book brims over with soaring encomiums and hero-depicting descriptions of Washington. The idea seems to be that if the Father of His Country was to be a monument, not a living person, the story of his life might as well be written in a dead language too.[19]

Contemporary painters too made use of attributes that connoted Roman antiquity. It is impossible not to see the Roman taste in John Trumbull's *General George Washington Resigning His Commission*. Trumbull was a contemporary, who had joined Washington's army in Cambridge, Massachusetts, in 1775. Following his return from England in 1789, he had numerous occasions to portray his former commanding officer. In 1817, Congress commissioned him to create four paintings. The fourth and final one, *General George Washington Resigning His Commission*, was painted between 1822 and 1824 and placed in the Capitol Rotunda in 1826. It depicts the scene on December 23, 1783, in the Maryland State House in Annapolis when Washington resigned to the assembled Congress his commission as commander in chief of the Continental Army. The action was highly significant, as it established civilian authority over the military, a fundamental principle of republican rule. Washington, illuminated by the light falling into the room, stands in uniform before the president of the Continental Congress, Thomas Mifflin, and the delegates, among whom is Thomas Jefferson. Behind Washington are his aides-de-camp, Colonel Benjamin Walker and Colonel David Humphreys, and spectators. The delegates and spectators direct their attention to Washington as he extends his right hand to return his commission. The empty chair draped in a cloak, suggestive as it is of a throne covered with a king's robe, symbolizes Washington's act of retiring from his position of power.[20]

On the occasion of Washington's refusal of a third term as President, John James Barralet reimagined the resignation scene in the Annapolis Statehouse in an "emblematical" painting in 1797. In 1799, "General Washington's Resignation" appeared as a frontispiece in the *Philadelphia Magazine and Review*, relating Washington's resignation as commander in chief in 1783 to his retirement in 1797. The explanation described the piece as an "emblem of the American Cincinnatus retiring from public office." It depicts a uniformed Washington, his epaulets removed, standing before the goddess of Peace who represents America. At her feet are placed Washington's helmet and sword, instruments of military power. America, situated atop marble steps, holds a letter (presumably his resignation) as Washington gestures back toward Mount Vernon. An American eagle holding the shield is placed in the foreground, together with symbols of prosperity that come with peace, an olive branch and a cornucopia. In the background, an altar burning incense signifies the country's gratitude. In depicting the glory of Washington's resignation, Barralet emphasizes not only the greater glory of America but America's supremacy, reinforcing this republican ideal by the fact that Washington appears alone before her.[21]

A different approach to the representation of republican simplicity was a form of minimalism or, more precisely, the "stripping-away" of insignia.[22] Certainly Gilbert Stuart attempted this in his sober, almost grim "Athenaeum" portrait of 1796. The "Athenaeum" (named after the Boston library that acquired the portrait after Stuart's death) depicts the 64-year-old Washington as an elder statesman, fatherly, without the glorifying insignia of general, president, or hero, and against an empty background—there are no pillars, no drapery, no richly adorned furniture, no symbols of political authority. While the portrait still captures Washington's aristocratic grandeur, the man somehow seems to float in a timeless realm, projecting the image of benevolent paternity and offering assurances to the citizens of the new nation that as heirs to Roman republican virtues they would prosper both materially and morally. Contemporaries who had become familiar with the face of the nation either through meeting Washington in person or through other media would have noticed that Stuart had taken great pains to rectify the distortions that public life, partisan strife and, not to forget, time had visited upon Washington.[23]

At the time, most people would not have seen the original "Athenaeum." Instead, they would have seen miniatures and reproductions of it, on almanacs, broadsides or, as upscale versions, on mezzotints. Still, the "Athenaeum" soon became the favorite Washington portrait and eventually dominated America's visual conception of the Father of His Country, whose accomplishments were no longer seen as the work of a single human being but as the destiny of a new nation. Aesthetics alone does not therefore explain the portrait's vast appeal. The "Athenaeum" became America's most cherished icon because, following Barry Schwartz, "it did credit to its subject by reducing rather than enlarging him, by placing him among the people rather than above them. The new republic's admiration for restraint and its disdain for ostentation were captured in this most popular image of its representative man."[24]

Stuart's mode of portraiture—reducing rather than enlarging—had been attempted before. Portraits done by Christian Gullager (1789), Edward Savage (1793), and Adolph Ulrich Wertmuller (c. 1794) reveal a similar tendency toward restraint and republican simplicity.[25] It is not known whether Stuart consciously imitated their works. We do know, however, that he closely studied the bust and life mask the French artist and sculptor Jean-Antoine Houdon had derived from his two-week visit to Mount Vernon in 1785. Houdon's bust was a commercial success. Numerous replicas circulated before his Virginia statue was completed, and countless busts were produced "after Houdon," including one issued in 1876 as part of the centennial celebration that showed Washington dressed in a Roman toga. Of Houdon's original, Asher Durand did an engraving, and Thomas Crawford was inspired by it for his idealized 1848 bust. Crawford also imitated Houdon's marketing strategy: Replicas of his bust procured a steady stream of orders, for plaster casts or marble varieties, depending on the buyer's budget.[26]

The Smithsonian Institution's Inventory of American Sculpture, for instance, lists more than 290 examples of statues and busts of the Father of His Country, and that list is by no means exclusive. Although interpretations range from revered exemplar to ordinary citizen and back to model citizen and patriot, the statues and busts show a considerable consistency. This, H. Nichols Clark argues, is mainly due to the profound impact Houdon's likenesses had on later sculptors.[27] Houdon's bust of Washington was part of the artist's preparation for a full-length statue commissioned by the Virginia General Assembly for the State House in Richmond. As for the bust, Houdon refused the temptations of heroic exaggeration also for the statue, which he completed after his return to Paris. Already the statue's scale is an instance of "stripping-away." The sculptor's first major decision was to limit—at Washington's own request—the statue to life-size. Houdon also did without a pedestal. In its present home, the State Capitol of Richmond, the statue *is* standing on a pedestal, but this was the decision of later generations. Presumably, they had become disabused of the idea, going back to the Roman republic, to represent Washington as a citizen among citizens. A pedestal creates distance and exaggeration, contradicting the republican ideal of the principal equality of all citizens.

Another distancing effect would have been to represent Washington dressed in a Roman tunic or toga. Houdon, on Benjamin West's advice, discarded the idea, a decision that Washington, upon learning of the advice, somewhat reluctantly endorsed.[28] (Two years after sitting for Houdon, Washington rebuffed the portraitist Joseph Wright's request that he don a toga.[29] In 1840, Horatio Greenough created a colossal statue that finally did show Washington in a toga, breast exposed.) Yet even without the Roman garb, Houdon's marble Washington retains references to classical antiquity: Washington's left hand is resting on the bundle of fasces, though the old symbol of civilian or military power and justice is now topped by his riding cape. And although Washington is still dressed in his general's uniform, he has exchanged his sword (which is shown hanging from the fasces) for the civilian's cane. Behind him is a plowshare, the visible expression of his wish, now that he has finished his military and political duties, to return to his former life as a gentleman farmer—a clear and unmistakable allusion to the Cincinnatus legend.[30]

George Washington (the "Athenaeum" portrait), by Gilbert Stuart, oil on canvas, 1796 (48 × 37 in.) (National Portrait Gallery, Smithsonian Institution; owned jointly with the Museum of Fine Arts, Boston).

By the time Houdon received his commission—he had been selected by no lesser persons than Benjamin Franklin and Thomas Jefferson—the Cincinnatus legend had reached the highest circles in American society.[31] In 1783, the Society of the Cincinnati had been founded by officers of the Continental Army, with Washington a natural president-general. The proposed name of the society seemed particularly appropriate, because the officers were looking forward to returning to their plows following victory in the War of Independence, much like Cincinnatus had done a long time before in republican Rome. Even so, critics feared that the society would develop into a military aristocracy in America. One of those critics was Thomas Jefferson, who was especially concerned about the society's plans to grant hereditary memberships. In light of these fears, there is a good deal of irony in Jefferson's recommendation that Houdon was "resorted to for the statues of most of the sovereigns of Europe."[32] Who else would Houdon work for if not for European aristocracy? This is not to disparage Houdon's Richmond statue, which is rightly famous and renowned. Houdon managed no less than to pack a statue of a single man with dramatic action—by showing Washington in a moment of transition, metamorphosing from soldier to gentleman farmer. Of course, Washington is wearing his general's garb, though he has already shed both his riding coat and his sword. Additionally, Houdon has stripped away all insignia of political power. What we see is a George Washington returning to the self-chosen civilian world, symbolized by the walking stick, customarily carried by gentleman farmers. Washington is quite literally standing (or rather, he *was* standing before the pedestal was added) on *his* land, looking around himself. It was Houdon's republican-inspired stripping-away of the emblems of officialdom that helped define Washington as a liminal figure, an incarnation of Cincinnatus.[33]

Memory of Lucius Quinctius Cincinnatus is shaped by the Roman's refusal of military rule, however tempting it might have been. But what made the fifth-century BCE Roman statesman such a salient model for Americans was the distinction they drew between private and public life. Most Americans at the time, Barry Schwartz noted, "pursued their interests, satisfied their needs, and derived their status from the land." Thus, "the public arena was regarded by them as a place of temporary involvement, to be entered reluctantly and left joyfully."[34] Washington's own words testify to this. "When we assumed the Soldier, we did not lay aside the Citizen," he offered to the New York Provincial Congress on June 26, 1775, "& we shall most sincerely rejoice with you in that happy Hour, when the establishment of American Liberty on the most firm, and solid Foundations, shall enable us to return to our private Stations in the bosom of a free, peaceful, & happy Country."[35]

Houdon was not the only artist to depict Washington as a born-again Cincinnatus. On the contrary, Houdon connected to and continued a neo-classicist iconography that in America had begun with Trumbull and the elder Peale. Each had done portraits which showed Washington as Cincinnatus. The portraits have been lost, though a bust that Giuseppe Ceracchi executed around 1786 has been preserved.[36] Other examples abound, not least beyond official sculpture. For instance, on his way home from New York, where he had bid a final farewell to his officers at Fraunces Tavern, Washington had to pass through Philadelphia. There, a triumphal wooden arch had been constructed in the classical style; suspended in the center was a huge transparency of Cincinnatus, returning to his plow, his brow crowned with laurels. And lest anyone missed the allusion, the Pennsylvania legislature, which had ordered the arch, said the "countenance of Cincinnatus is [to be] a striking resemblance of General Washington."[37] Philip Freneau, sometimes called the poet of the American Revolution, dedicated some seventeen stanzas to Washington's arrival in Philadelphia, with the thirteenth containing an allusion to Cincinnatus: "Now hurrying from the busy scene.... He who Rome's proud legions sway'd, / Return'd and sought his sylvan shade."

On March 26, 1785, readers of the *Virginia Gazette* were treated to Washington "abandoning the delights of peace, the enjoyment of affluence, and the pleasures of domestic felicity" when called upon to defend his country. In the following year, on Independence Day of 1786, the New York *Daily Advertiser* published a toast praising Washington as the "great Cincinnatus," praise of whose merits is even beyond the power of art: "Great CINCINNATUS, first and best, / Thy merits ne'er can be exprest, / Though every Muse attends."[38] The effusions continued, aptly summarized in David Humphreys's "Poem on the Happiness of America": "The towns in raptures and the roads in flowers / Wher'er he pass'd! What monarch ever knew / Such acclamations, bursts of joy so true?"[39] Yet when Washington was to assume the presidency, he left his home with reluctance, for, in Samuel Low's words, "when recall'd from Vernon's peaceful shade, / The matchless man his country's call obey'd!" Though the author's patriotism far surpassed his poetic gifts, he revels in comparing Washington to Cincinnatus: "With God-like port our Cincinnatus stood; / Awful in virtue, firm in rectitude." Even Washington's presumed biographer Mason Weems cautiously alluded to Cincinnatus in praising the "grand republican virtue" of George Washington, that "illustrious patriot."[40]

These examples show that Rome not simply "belonged to every educated man," as Peter Gay has written.[41] In America, Rome also belonged to the semi-educated, who learned from newspapers, prints, almanacs, broadsides, and biographies, shared the classical associations of the elites, understood the symbolic references, and drew appropriate conclusions. Altogether, Marcus Cunliffe argues, George Washington's America was "in a way more truly 'Roman' than the mother country."[42] If it had not been, men like Washington would not have been able to create a new nation on the republican model. The lessons of the classical past suggested that an extensive republic was a working possibility. Even George Gordon, Lord Byron saw it in this way, when on April 10, 1814, amid rumors of the abdication and exile of the emperor Napoleon (which in fact occurred the next day), he wrote and copied his *Ode to Napoléon Buonaparte*. While Byron had much admiration for Napoleon as a charismatic leader and military genius, he was repelled by the Frenchman's ruthlessness and authoritarianism, his descent into "all evil spirit." Thus, Byron's unreserved praise is bestowed on George Washington, whom in the final stanza he celebrates as "the first—the last—the best—/ The Cincinnatus of the West, / Whom envy dared not hate."[43]

III

One Whom Memory Oft Recalls

"The evil of the time," the editor, writer, politician, and diplomat Charles Francis Adams remarked in *Hunt's Merchants' Magazine* for December 1839, "is a great want of confidence."[1] The ominous remark by President John Quincy Adams's son and President John Adams's grandson was prompted by the various paper bills from private banks. Americans in the antebellum period indeed had every reason to closely watch the currency. The absence of paper money issued and controlled by the federal government in particular contributed to a situation in which whoever was wealthy yesterday could be poor today, and vice versa. A stranger could also spell trouble, especially if he was arriving at a bank's door with a bulging carpetbag in hand, demanding specie to the full value of the many different notes he presented for payment. The currency was not the only problem, though. People trying to create a new town tried to drive up real estate values on land they owned. Often enough they sold sections of land they knew were worthless. Others paid for purchases in counterfeit bills. Still others sold useless patent medicine, watered-down whiskey, phony lottery tickets, stolen horses and cattle and, at least in fiction, forged letters and delivered them to rich people, asking them to pay postage themselves.

The latter scheme, of the "sham-post," forms an episode in the revised version of Edgar Allan Poe's story "The Business Man," which appeared in the *Broadway Journal* of August 2, 1845. The story's central character, tellingly named Peter Proffit, discloses without compunction, "Nobody hesitates at paying for a letter—especially for a double one—people are *such* fools—and it was no trouble to get round a corner before there was time to open the epistles."[2] Peter Proffit no doubt answers to the contemporary ideal of the self-made man, an ideal that Poe set out to deconstruct, emptying out its meaningfulness as a mere social construct. Proffit's operations to defraud other people, however, are all on a small scale—like those of a diddler, who might, for instance, accept a genuine fifty-dollar bill as a reward for handing over a pocket book he had allegedly found, though the "large amount" of money in the book is later seen to be merely "'a counterfeit presentment,' and the whole thing a capital diddle." Activities of this kind, and there are many more in the satirical sketch Poe published in the *Broadway Journal* of September 13, 1845, are said to be different only in scale from what true "financiers" then were doing by way of "magnificent speculation." Accordingly, a diddler (the verb "diddle" means "defraud") may be regarded as "a banker *in petto*—a financial 'operation,' as a diddle in Brobdingnag. The one is to the other, as Homer to 'Flaccus'—as a Mastodon to a mouse—as the tail of a comet to that of a pig."[3]

What conclusions can we draw from Poe's irreverent language? "Diddling," like "The Business Man," does not require much explication; straightforward accounts of frauds are simply entertaining. And they were extremely popular at the time, both in the form of fictitious magazine items fleshed out by narrative illustrations and of life stories peddled about by impostors—of Poe's fictitious diddler as much as of that celebrated Connecticut Yankee showman, P. T. Barnum, whose chief personal aim was "to put money in his coffers."[4] Barnum first tried to achieve his goal in Connecticut, but when lotteries were banned there in 1834, cutting off his main income, he moved to New York City. It took him less than a year to begin as a showman, with his purchase (from another showman by the name of R. W. Lindsay) and exhibition of a blind and almost completely paralyzed slave woman, Joice Heth. Heth, Barnum claimed, was now 161 years old and thus the nation's sole living connection to the Father of His Country, whose nurse she had been. When Joice Heth died in February 1836, a public autopsy revealed that she could not have been more than seventy-five or eighty years old. Barnum was unperturbed. He anonymously fed stories to the press that emphasized his "Yankee ingenuity" by earning a small fortune in the course of playing a rich practical joke on the American people.[5]

In putting over his joke, if only for a little while, Barnum had made the Father of His Country come alive. Washington in the flesh had gone, but thanks to Barnum the entire nation could cling to his memory and identify with his image. The impression given by Barnum's hoax was reinforced in other media and, importantly, by portraits. "The name of Washington is constantly on our lips," Walt Whitman remarked in 1858, adding that "His portrait hangs on every wall and he is almost canonized in the affections of our people."[6] Whitman's remark was no exaggeration. Portraits of Washington could be found in huts and palaces and, per a story about Ethan Allan that Abraham Lincoln liked to tell, also in privies.[7] In Thomas Jefferson's Monticello, for instance, visitors could admire at least four portraits as well as any number of busts. Ralph Waldo Emerson had a portrait hung in his dining room and simply could not, as he admitted, get enough of it. And Nathaniel Hawthorne, traveling abroad, wrote in his notebook that he "was proud to see that noblest face and figure here in England; the picture of a man beside whom ... any English nobleman would look like common beef or clay."[8]

6

Symbolic Alliances

The Ethan Allan story is apocryphal, and the picture of Washington the British allegedly put into the outhouse also has not been specified. In contrast, we do know which Washington portrait Hawthorne saw in England—a copy of one of Gilbert Stuart's portraits. The picture here serves as a good illustration of the symbolic alliance in venerating the Father of His Country. Americans before the Civil War learned how Washington looked from the various portraits, not so much from the original paintings, but from copies that appeared as engraved prints or lithographs, as book and magazine illustrations, in almanacs, children's books and, not to forget, on coins, medals, and bank notes. Additionally, they learned what Washington was like from the orators and from Parson Weems and other biographers. The importance of Washingtoniana lies in their impact on the American people, including those who wrote and read biographies, stories, and poems concerning Washington, spent currency notes with his portrait or, following the historian and geographer Emma Willard, visited Mount Vernon, "in mournful, filial pilgrimage." Washington's birthday and July 4 became annual occasions when the Father of His Country was sure to be eulogized all over the country, and public speakers found many other opportunities to recall his presence. Ministers, lawyers, educators, members of Congress, state governors and other public officials, lecturers, even humorists such as Artemus Ward found in George Washington an excellent subject.[1]

Washington "had no Boswell," William Alfred Bryan ruefully notes, even though between 1800 and 1860 alone, at least four hundred books, essays, short sketches, and character studies appeared; some, including John Bell's of 1775, were published already during Washington's lifetime.[2] All these efforts contributed to consolidating Washington's god-like status, though none as fully as Mason Locke Weems's. Begun before Washington's death and published as a 90-page pamphlet in 1800, Weems's biography became the most widely circulated life of Washington through the Civil War. His argument that Washington's status was due to "his Great Virtues" tapped into the sentimental and ethical mentality of the time. Schoolbook writers repeated and disseminated Weems's anecdotes, however apocryphal (the cherry-tree story was added only in 1806), far beyond their original publication.[3] In contrast, John Marshall's reverential five-volume *Life of Washington* (1804–1807) was not well received, certainly for its Federalist bias but also for its heavy style and, importantly, because it had too much of background and of the facts of Washington's public career and achievements, while it was almost completely silent on personal traits and circumstances, including his marriage to Martha Washington. As John Adams quipped, Marshall's *Life* "is a Mausoleum, 100 feet square at the base, and 200 feet high."[4]

Biographies published in the centennial year, 1832, as well as Jared Sparks's (1839) and Washington Irving's (5 volumes, 1855–1859) proliferated throughout the antebellum period.

While they offered more details of Washington's private character, they retained the tendency, characteristic of earlier biographies, to keep Washington at arm's length. The idea seemed to be that to place him in a more prosaic or pedestrian story might deflate the flawless hero or cut him down to size. Sparks's *Life*, which essentially was the same work as the first volume of *The Writings of George Washington* (1834), created a Washington that is as perfect as could be, blending the Jovian Washington of neoclassicism with Weems's priggishness, and continuing a theme of the persecution of the saint that had been popular with Marshall. Today, Sparks's work is remembered for the author's cavalierly tampering with Washington's language, omitting passages, and adding some of his own.[5] Irving had planned to write a Washington biography for many years, yet the first volume of his *Life* did not appear until 1855, the fifth and last only in 1859. Offers to write a biography were made in the 1820s, prompting Irving to collect materials, and by 1829 he had definite plans for the work that would be his "crowning labor," about the man for whom he was named. Irving worked hard to present a living man rather than a marble statue, using simple language and avoiding the pompousness and grandiose style of his predecessors. Still, it is a matter of debate whether he was successful in this, in particular since he—like his predecessors—fabricated speeches, conversations, and thoughts that he either had no way of knowing about or were based on dubious childhood memories. Moreover, Irving could not rid himself of hero-worship. Towards the end of the final volume, for instance, he describes Washington as possessing "fewer inequalities and a rarer union of virtues than perhaps ever fell to the lot of one man: prudence, firmness, sagacity, moderation, and overruling judgment, an immovable justice, courage that never faltered, patience that never wearied, truth that disdained all artifice, magnanimity without alloy."[6]

Irving was, however, the first writer to include a chapter on the Washington family in England. He also had to be mindful of the growing sectionalism, and thus was extremely careful to create a Washington that would offend neither Northern nor Southern sentiments. His Washington appears as a true gentleman in the British tradition, thus offering a common heritage to both sides. Nor would any side have objected to seeing Washington as a Cincinnatus who, "gladly, when he had won the cause, hung up his sword never again to take it down."[7] Irving also included in his biography a chapter on "the aristocratical days of Virginia," some fifteen pages in length, in which he raves about the "*beau ideal*" of Washington's existence.[8] When Irving wrote this, the squirearchy of Washington's time was as remote from many Americans in the 1850s as it is today. It did persist in the South, though, in somewhat attenuated form, until the Civil War when it, too, expired, resurrected off and on in fiction and film. When Douglas Southall Freeman was at work on his biography of Washington, these "outposts of the English aristocracy" had faded away even further into a remote past, prompting Freeman to devote more than one hundred pages on Virginia's past. Freeman's motives were those of the historian, to show what the past was like. Irving had a different purpose. A conservative from temperament, he wanted to stem the obliteration of America's past, the Father of His Country included. As Donald A. Ringe argued, for Irving, change and progress always resulted in the destruction of order and stability; thus, Irving fervently believed, "important values are lost when men prefer change to stability."[9]

But for Irving, who after his death was characterized as all sweetness and light, a "gentle humorist" in Longfellow's memorable words, George Washington was quite literally "usable." Building his argument carefully, Irving writes that his hero was "like a parent" to his adopted children, while in a later volume he emphasizes the "paternal spirit with which [Washington] watched over the army."[10] Then in the final volume, published only two years before the beginning of the Civil War, Irving writes that the Father of His Country "knew no divided fidelity, no separate obligation; his most sacred duty to himself was his highest duty to his country and his God." The climax comes on the final page of the biography: "With us, [Washington's] memory remains *a national property* […] his precepts and example speak to us from the grave with *a paternal appeal*; and his name—by all revered—forms a universal tie of brotherhood—*a watchword of our Union*." It is no exaggeration to say, as Mary Bowden did, that Irving's *Life of Washington* was "a five-volume plea that the Union be preserved."[11]

Irving's *Life* was tremendously successful. George P. Putnam published it in six varying formats, including a Popular Edition, an octavo or Subscribers' Edition, and an ambitious "Illustrated Edition" in 68 folio parts. Altogether, Irving's biography had a great appeal to educated middle-class readers and advanced students, for whom it became standard. It was even considered for schoolchildren, by John Fiske in 1887.[12] Yet for Americans who with elders and children would gather at the fireside for a winter's evening tale, Weems's book remained more appealing.[13] So did lighter and more popular biographies by, *inter alia*, James Kirke Paulding (1835) or Caroline Matilda Kirkland (1857). Paulding's two-volume *Life of Washington* was written for use in schools and expressly dedicated to the "pious, retired, domestic Mothers" of America. Although Paulding points his moral at least as obviously as Weems, the book received much praise from Edgar Allan Poe in the *Southern Literary Messenger*.[14]

Poe's praise is somewhat surprising, as he was usually most discriminating in his reviews. In this instance, however, this fatherless poor-devil of a writer may well have found in Paulding's Washington the surrogate father he'd been looking for, a father who would look benignly down on him from "an elevation which is never attained by mortal man. A few have approached it, and none nearer than Washington."[15] Poe also had much good to say about the talents of Kirkland, whose *Memoirs of Washington* set out to portray the Father of His Country in private life and was targeted to reach younger readers or, rather, younger women readers. By the 1850s women readers had become a sizable and important group of readers in America, one who would eagerly snap up any frothy anecdote of Washington's alleged love affairs.[16] Poets and novelists, too, could not possibly bypass Washington.[17] For poems written to or for Washington, William Alfred Bryan's verdict is as devastating as it is short: "Much verse has been written about Washington, but very little poetry."[18] An ode by Phillis Wheatley, Philip Frenau's verses about the glorious struggle for freedom, the anonymous "Inscribed to the Father of His Country," or Joel Barlow's verse epics are typical of a verbal art not bound to originality so much as to didacticism and, specifically, to neoclassical forms of hero worship. There is no need to repeat the profusion of literary memorials to the deceased Father of His Country. Much more interesting than all these "effusions," as Bryan calls these versifications, are the Revolutionary War ballads. One such ballad, by Jonathan Mitchell Sewall, not only heaped praise upon "Godlike Washington," but also summoned Americans to "shout, and shout America! And conquering Washington."[19]

A figure of Washington's stature would also be portrayed in fiction and drama, some intended for the stage and some in the form of closet dramas. Washington made his first appearance as a dramatic character in *The Fall of British Tyranny* (1776). In 1789, William Dunlap wrote an interlude in verse, "Darby's Return," in which an Irish soldier goes back to Ireland and describes his adventures in America. Washington himself witnessed the first performance and heard the line "*They love him like a father…*" During the Revolution and later, actors sometimes spoke from the stage a tribute to Washington in the form of epilogue or prologue, usually in verse. One example is the epilogue written by Jonathan Mitchell for a production of Addison's *Cato* in 1778.[20] As the Civil War was approaching, Washington became *the* man for a time of national confusion and conflict. In an anonymous work, *America: a Dramatic Poem*, published in New York in 1863, an appeal to Washington as the "Great Father of thy country" is followed by a rhetorical question: "[P]roved thy tomb / Too narrow also, when its walls received / The tumult of our strife?" Altogether, there is little actual characterization of Washington in plays through 1865. The Father of His Country was simply put on stage, suitably made up (almost always as General Washington) and provided with a few patriotic and rhetorical lines. The preconceptions of the audience would do the rest.[21]

In early nineteenth-century fiction, the Father of His Country appeared both as a character and spoken of by other characters or a narrator. When used as the main protagonist, Washington again is mostly presented as commander in chief. As, for instance, in James Cooper's novel *The Spy* (1821), in which he—appearing until near the end as Mr. Harper—is cast as a character straight out of classical mythology, an impeccable man radiating stability and calm, whose "whole appearance was so impressive and decidedly that of a gentleman, that ... the ladies arose from their seats...."[22] About four fifths into the novel, Washington alias Mr. Harper, in parting, sounds a well-known theme: "God has denied to me children, young lady; but ... all who dwell in this broad land are my children, and my care...."[23] The passage marks somewhat of a literary about-turn, from historic romance back to the novel of sentiment and, thus, to Weems's precedent, which served as inspiration to numerous narratives best labeled "juvenile," plus to a plethora of fictional works depicting Washington as a secondary character. Among the latter, James McHenry's *The Wilderness* (1823) according to Bryan is probably "the most prolonged and ambitious of early attempts to treat Washington in fiction."[24]

By and large, however, nineteenth-century novelists despaired over using Washington as a character. The Father of His Country may have been a fit subject for eulogies, but not for novels. Voicing his praise in sonorous verses could pass as somewhat of a national habit, but to portray him in fiction seemed somehow irreverent. James Kirke Paulding wrote a biography, yet he refrained from presenting Washington as a character in one of his romances: "Washington was no hero of romance, and his name associates but illy with fiction. It is too sacred for such profanation."[25] William Makepeace Thackeray was the only one bold enough to devise a believable Washington in his novel *The Virginians*, yet he was beset by doubts: "Tell me," he asked John Pendleton Kennedy, "was he a fussy old gentleman in a wig? Did he take snuff and spill it down his shirt front?"[26] *The Virginians* was published, contemporaneously with its publication in Britain, in serialized form in *Harper's Monthly Magazine* from 1857 to 1859. After only eight chapters had appeared, Thackeray was warned in the *Southern Literary Messenger* that it was a dangerous undertaking "to involve Washington in the machinery of a work of fiction," for he was in no way a fit subject for satire. Cornelius C. Felton, a classical scholar and educator, attacked Thackeray on much the same grounds: "Washington was not like other men," Felton wrote in the *North American Review* of October 1860, "and to bring this lofty character down to the level of the vulgar passions of common life, is to give the lie to the grandest chapter in the uninspired annals of the human race."[27]

Realistic treatment of George Washington was a no-go as long as America's cultural elites ruled that "Washington's character has come to us spotless ... pure and white as you see him in Houdon's statue."[28] This was too much for a nay-sayer like Nathaniel Hawthorne, who brashly exercised his imagination on cultural practices that stripped Washington of his humanity and made him a god. Hawthorne had found Stuart's "Athenaeum" portrait extremely irksome and he wrote a few pages on the issue for a magazine in 1836. But it was Greenough's statue of Washington as a barechested Jove with a Gilbert Stuart head that finally became the straw to break the camel's back. Toying with the idea of a nude statue of Washington, Hawthorne facetiously mused whether anyone had ever seen the Father of His Country nude. It was, Hawthorne decided in June 1858, "inconceivable. [Washington] has no nakedness, but I imagine was born with his clothes on and his hair powdered, and made a stately bow on his first appearance in the world."[29] Hawthorne here targets the notorious rigidity of Washington's public persona, which made imagining Washington's character a true challenge for the novelist, not just for Cooper or Thackeray but also for, *inter alia*, Marjorie Bowen, Gertrude Stein, Howard Fast, Gore Vidal, and Thomas Pynchon. Their attempts demonstrate the need for a Washington who seems close, visible, and idiosyncratic instead of merely flat.[30]

The need for a Washington that is good for feeling is an important factor also in the at best lukewarm response to characterizations of him in fiction and drama. Readers as well as theater-goers always already have drawn in their minds their own image of Washington, and the last thing they want is to have that image shattered, least of all the image of him as the Father of His Country. Therefore, any portrayal of Washington that is not in sync with the preconceived notion of him as the metaphorical father must be false.[31] One way out of the dilemma is offered by Susan Warner's *The Wide, Wide World*, in which Washington makes an appearance not as an actual character but rather in an indirect way. In what became the first best-selling novel of the 1850s, the young heroine Ellen Montgomery receives Weems's biography as a New Year's gift and cannot put it down. Washington soon becomes her hero, not least for his moral virtues: "Washington was great and good both."[32] Even enslaved African Americans could find something useful in Washington's words and example. The most extreme example, perhaps, is Frederick Douglass's only work of fiction, the serialized novel *The Heroic Slave* (1853), whose protagonist Madison Washington, a name "ominous of greatness," had led the 1841 mutiny aboard the slave ship *Creole*. This revolutionary Washington symbolized the revolutionary potential, not of white planters such as John C. Calhoun, for whom Washington was "one of us—a slaveholder and a planter," but of enslaved black southerners.[33]

In Harriet Beecher Stowe's novel *Uncle Tom's Cabin* (1852), revolutionary potential is at best implied. Among the adornments in the eponymous hero's slave cabin are illustrations from the Bible as well as a remarkable version of a mid-century household staple, "a portrait of General Washington, drawn and colored in a manner which would certainly have astonished that hero, if he ever had happened to meet with its like."[34] While Ms. Stowe acknowledges the quasi-religious connotations associated with Washington, she left open the question of the portrait's authorship. At the time, her readers would have been able to fill in the gap with an overwhelming number and variety of examples, an abundance that in 1842 had amazed a visiting Charles Dickens. Today, we may reasonably assume that the cabin's wall was adorned with one of the inexpensive images that had become available with the invention of lithography and the rise of printmaking firms such as E. B. and E. C. Kellogg, Nathaniel Currier, and, starting in the late 1850s, Currier and Ives. The Currier and Ives catalogue raisonné lists dozens of prints bearing depictions of Washington, the vast majority of them derived from Stuart's "Athenaeum" portrait, and these and similar images sold by other companies were practically everywhere. In 1836, *American Magazine* reported that "prints of Washington, dark with smoke are pasted over the hearths of so many American houses—And long may he live there!"[35]

At the beginning of the American Revolution, almost any fictitious image could pass as a portrait of George Washington, at the same time as printmakers clamored for accurate likenesses of the Father of His Country. They soon found these likenesses in numerous paintings. Already during Washington's lifetime, some twenty-seven artists had done portraits, following all kinds of techniques and artistic conventions. If the art of the time was, in Hugh Howard's apt phrase, truly "Washington-centric," it was in the form of engravings and other mass-produced imagery, many of which owed their existence to a newly invented drawing machine called the *physiognotrace*, together with copies and studies by other artists, folk art, and compositions in new circumstances, including banknote vignettes, coins, and medals that Washington's likeness was quite literally brought into the hands of viewers, privatizing their experience. As for style, portrait artists in the Antebellum period increasingly concentrated on Washington's domestic character, echoing the private virtues that characterized the "self-made man" in an era dominated by evangelical Christianity and capitalist expansion.

When Harriet Beecher Stowe claims that the manner of drawing and coloring "would certainly have astonished" Washington, it is because from the early 1800s, images of Washington were no longer iconic so much as inspirational, encouraging viewers "to think of him as similar to themselves and therefore someone they could aspire to emulate."[36] Certainly this is the mood in *Barroom Dancing*, an 1820 watercolor by the genre painter John Lewis Krimmel, which shows a room in a country tavern, with people frolicking under a print taken from Stuart's "Athenaeum" portrait.[37]

While citizens in the antebellum period may have wished to experience the Father of His Country as a flesh-and-blood human being and thus as an object of emotional attachment, during Washington's lifetime, when public deeds were the measure of a leader's character, artists had rooted their vision rather in republican ideology and Augustan iconography. Possibly the first artist to do a portrait of George Washington was John Singleton Copley, for whom Washington is said to have sat in Boston in 1756. A certain John Wollaston likely was second, in the same year. By far the best known of the early portraitists, however, is Charles Wilson Peale, a veteran of the Continental Army. Beginning in 1772, Peale altogether completed seven portraits, all commissioned by private subscribers, of which one—a 1776 painting done for John Hancock, president of the Continental Congress—was immediately mass-produced. Copies of Peale's portrait gave to people across the North American colonies a common icon. Reproduced in books, magazines, children's primers, broadsides, sheet music, and currency notes, the portrait brought the liberator of Boston (visible in the background) to the presence of people who would never otherwise have been able to see him in person.[38]

Doubtless the best-known of the elder Peale's paintings of Washington is *George Washington at Princeton* (1779), which shows the victorious general after the battle of Princeton. In this full-length portrait, a high point in Peale's artistic career, Washington is posed casually, legs crossed, one arm akimbo, the other resting on the barrel of a cannon. Hessian standards captured earlier at Trenton lie unfurled at his feet; Nassau Hall can be seen in the background. Washington stands tall and imposing, the magnetic personality that so enthralled his contemporaries. Contemporaries would have been delighted also by the change in the uniform colors, from the British scarlet to the American buff and blue.[39]

The symbolic value invested in the change in the uniform colors notwithstanding,

John Lewis Krimmel, *[Barroom Dancing]*, ca. 1820, drawing, watercolor, 20.8 × 27.9 cm. (Library of Congress, Prints and Photographs Division).

something else had not changed, though the painting veils rather than reveals this. Already during his time in the Virginia Regiment, in the 1750s, Washington was never squeamish about meting out harsh punishment, from applying lashes to deserters to having them hanged. Washington's methods, Ron Chernow explains, though "seemingly cruel to modern eyes, were standard practice in the British Army of his day." The future Father of His Country embraced this practice, referring to "Subordination & Discipline" as "the Life and Soul of an Army." He encouraged military discipline even in private matters, frowning on camaraderie.[40] It is not without a certain historic irony that Washington's regime is owed to his close reading of two British military manuals, Humphrey Bland's *Treatise of Military Discipline*, first published in 1727, and the *Regulations* of 1764, which went through no fewer than twenty-six North American imprints between 1766 and 1780. Even John Adams was impressed. Discipline, he wrote in 1776, "in time brought our troops to a capacity of contending with British veterans, and a rivalry with the best troops of France."[41] Discipline and subordination remained Washington's watchwords as commander in chief of the Continental Army. During the Revolution, the fair treatment of civilians formed an essential part of the war effort. When in October 1778 American troops sacked houses under the pretext that the owners were Tories, Washington did not hesitate to have the offenders hanged.[42]

Drunkenness among officers was another evil Washington was bent on eradicating. While he contented himself with a glass or two of Madeira in good company, such temperance was unusual, particularly among military men. "I would beg leave," Washington

Charles Wilson Peale, *George Washington at Princeton*, 1779, oil on canvas (93 × 58½ in.), Acc. No. 1943.16.2 (courtesy the Pennsylvania Academy of the Fine Arts, Philadelphia; gift of Maria McKean Allen and Phebe Warren Downes through the bequest of their mother, Elizabeth Wharton McKean).

wrote as early as 1756, "to represent the great nuisance the number of tippling-houses in Winchester are to the soldiers, who by this means, in despite of the utmost care and vigilance, are, so long as their pay holds good, incessantly drunk, and unfit for service."[43] This was a hard-drinking age. It's thought that the average person back then inhaled around six gallons of alcohol a year, compared to today's average of two. Hot ale flips, warming wassails and planter's punches were consumed in such alarming quantities that Benjamin Franklin published over two hundred expressions for being tipsy in the *Pennsylvania Gazette* on January 6, 1737, among them "oil'd," "fuzl'd," and "half way to Concord."[44] As Dr. Benjamin Rush wrote to John Adams on October 31, 1777, officers were penalized for drinking "more than one quart of whiskey, or [got] drunk more than once in 24 hours."[45]

Mutiny among the military was a different matter, for which Washington had zero tolerance. When on New Year's Day 1781 some thirteen hundred troops from the Pennsylvania Line mutinied and killed several officers, General Washington, bent on setting an example, approved of Brigadier General Anthony Wayne's decision to have twelve of the ringleaders lined up before firing squads made up of their fellow soldiers. "Sudden and exemplary Punishments were certainly necessary upon the new Appearance of that daring and mutinous Spirit which convulsed the Line last Winter," he later told Wayne.[46] A "sudden and exemplary punishment" had been meted out also in October 1780, when Major John André went to the gallows as a Tory spy. André had been captured with papers handed to him by Major General Benedict Arnold, who was bent on handing over the garrison of West Point to the British. Washington did not relish hanging André, whose accomplishments and gallantry as an officer he respected, though he felt he had to mete out punishment for a heinous crime that might have given the Revolutionary cause "a deadly wound, if not a fatal stab." As he told the Count de Rochambeau, commander of the French expeditionary force, "policy required a sacrifice."[47]

"Policy" must have required a "sacrifice" also from Charles Wilson Peale. Though Peale had actually fought under Washington's command during the Trenton-Princeton campaign of 1776–1777, there is little of the General's heroic and military character in his *Washington at Princeton*, no hint of the steely resolution and fiery spirit of the "gentleman warrior." The overall mood of the painting is languid: Peale could have painted the general urging on his men to the attack, as eyewitnesses said he did. Instead, he faithfully followed Augustan iconography, depicting Washington as essentially passive, calm and dignified, not as the man of action that he no doubt was.[48] Peale, the elder Peale, that is, had begun work on *George Washington at Princeton* at Valley Forge early in 1778, but it was interrupted because of continuous fighting in New Jersey and was not completed until 1779. Peale had been commissioned to do the full-length portrait of the Commander in Chief by the Pennsylvania Council of State. The painting was then hung in the Pennsylvania State House in Philadelphia, and so can pass at least as semi-official. It was vandalized in 1781, though fortunately Peale had made a first copy for Nassau Hall, Princeton College, where it still hangs. The *Princeton* also was widely reproduced for people to get an idea of Washington as a leader.[49]

By the time *Washington at Princeton* was finished, Peale had already become a kind of court painter of the Washingtons.[50] George Washington's first sitting for him took place on May 20, 1772, per Washington's diary entry. The first sketch was finished ten days later. The price tag was 18 Pounds and 4 Shillings, to which were added 13 Pounds each for miniatures done of Martha Washington and her two children.[51] Peale customarily did three-quarters or full-length portraits; an early head-and-shoulders portrait remained unfinished and Peale kept it for himself. The full-length, life-size portrait, in contrast, shows Washington in the uniform of a youthful Colonel in the Virginia Regiment before the American Revolution. Sword and gorget were standard pieces of equipment of a colonial officer then, though the rifle over Washington's shoulder was not. Possibly, Peale wanted to signify the importance of firearms in colonial America for all men; possibly also, he wanted to lend a distinctive frontier flavor to the painting. Don Higginbotham even suggested that the portrait exemplified "a colonial military tradition distinct from the professional tradition of the mother country."[52] If this was Peale's true intent, it may well explain Washington's fondness of the painting, which remained the principal showpiece in the parlor at Mount Vernon as long as Martha Washington lived. Martha Washington also approved of it, in contrast to the 1779 portraiture of Washington as General—the "Goldsborough" portrait—, which she considered inadequate.[53]

Peale himself was unperturbed by Martha Washington's disapproval. He already had used the original Princeton piece as the prototype of at least nineteen copies, which differ in many details of Washington's dress and of background. In addition, in 1780 Peale pulled from the original Princeton piece a signed mezzotint engraving. The prints, 14 × 10 inches in size, sold for $2 a piece or £6 per dozen; they had a very large sale and, as they were mostly intended for export, distribution. Demand for engravings and prints of the "rebel general" was especially high in England. A certain G. Shepard of London had issued the earliest pictures of Washington offered for public sale, on September 9, 1775. One of these, a mezzotint, showed Washington on horseback, purportedly from a drawing, from life, by one Alexander Campbell of Williamsburg, Virginia. No such painter is known to exist, and when a copy of the Shepard mezzotint was sent to Martha Washington, George Washington responded that to his knowledge he had never seen Campbell although, the General added, the artist "has made a very formidable figure of the Commander in Chief, giving him a sufficient portion of Terror in his Countenance."[54]

If Washington meant what he said, the fraudulent Campbell prints must be considered a success. The outward projection of a subject's inner world then was rated as the ultimate goal not only of portraiture but of painting in general. Most contemporary portraits of George Washington would fall short of the axiom, though, as very few of them permit any conclusions to character. Some artists simply may not have seen anything; others lacked the technical sophistication to transfer onto the canvas what they saw; still others thought that Washington's features were too inconspicuous for an unmistakable portrait; and finally, the republican ethos simply did not allow for heroic poses, in contrast to the political romanticism of later years. All these conditions and circumstances may help explain Washington's patience when sitting for his portraitists. "In for a penny, in for a pound," he said while sitting for Robert Edge Pine in 1785.[55] The "pound" most likely was an understatement, as Washington thereafter sat for at least a dozen more artists, not counting any number of silhouette cutters. Washington did want to have his likeness preserved for posterity. Yet no matter how carefully he protected his image, the Washingtons resulting from the efforts of his portraitists are strikingly different one from the other. There are differences even in fundamentals such as the form of the head or the jaws. As a contemporary observer smugly remarked, "His hair, eyes, complexion, apparently partook of each individual color of the rainbow."[56]

There were other mishaps too. A portrait done in 1786 shows Washington in the uniform of a general. The colors are somewhat accurate, though the epaulettes are of a fashion Washington would never use—unequivocally European. The portrait in question was done by Joseph Wright. Wright had studied at the London Royal Academy, then left for Paris, where he caught the attention of Thomas Jefferson. Back in the United States, the Congress commissioned him to do an equestrian statue of Washington. (The congressional resolution is referred to in John Norman's etching *The True Portraiture of his Excellency George Washington Esq.*) Thanks to a letter of recommendation from Benjamin Franklin, Wright gained access to Washington himself. One result is a 14 × 12 inches half-length portrait. Jefferson first took it to Paris; later it graced his home in Monticello. Today it is owned by the Historical Society of Pennsylvania, on view at the Philadelphia History Museum at the Atwater Kent.[57] Jefferson thought it was more felicitous than Peale's full-length portrait (of which he owned a copy). He was especially enthusiastic about the "faithful likeness" in Wright's portrait; his only regret was that it was rather unflattering as it showed the general "in the moments of his gravest difficulties."[58]

Nevertheless—or possibly because of this—Wright's portrait gave rise to numerous copies, engravings, medallions, and medals. Bushrod Washington, George Washington's nephew, also approved of Wright's portrait, seeing in it "the most literal similitude" to his famous relative.[59] Washington himself had conceded that the portrait was "a better likeness of me, than any other painter has done."[60] Perhaps as a token of his appreciation, he designated Wright as chief engraver for the United States Mint.[61] (Wright died of yellow fever before taking office, and so the statue he had been commissioned for also was never completed.) Even so, at one point Washington had enough of all the buzzle and hullabaloo. In a letter of July 1792, he thanks the sender for recommending a painter by the name of William Joseph Williams. The worthy painter might well be "a luminary of the first magnitude," yet he, Washington, had become so tired of such attentions that he had not sat for anybody in two years. Not only had he found the sittings extremely boring and "irksome"; above all, it hurt his sense of justice that the portraits were being copied or engraved—usually badly—and subsequently "hawked about or advertised for Sale."[62]

7

Expressions of Consent

As much as Washington hated sitting for portraits, he must have realized that the act of sitting down to a portrait artist or silhouette cutter amounted to a willing entry into a "presentation of self," a process in which artist and sitter generally colluded. The collusion, Wendy Bellion argues, "entailed an implicit expression of *consent*, the category of agency that political philosophers from Locke onward identified as the foundation of constitutional government and the inviolable right of republican representation."[1] In other words, Washington must have sensed intuitively that he had come to stand for the Union and that his portraits helped to bond people together. (He also knew that, like poems and biographies, they would add to his posthumous fame.) He therefore complied again—as when a portrait was publicly commissioned or when he could not say no for other good reasons.[2] Thus, he bowed to the wishes of his Alexandria lodge and sat for a portrait by William Joseph Williams that depicted him in his Masonic outfit. Another reason to comply was Martha Washington. At her behest, Washington had sat for an Irish portrait artist in October of 1789. The result, a miniature on ivory which shows Washington in uniform adorned by the badge of the Society of the Cincinnati, was a disappointment. So was the cameo miniature done by the Marquise de Bréhan around the same time, to which Washington had agreed out of respect for the French minister.[3]

Martha Washington's instincts appear to have been more felicitous. She had heard of an artist by the name of Gilbert Stuart. Stuart's family was loyalist, conservative supporters of George III, but what led him to leave America, in 1771, was a keen desire to study art. He soon established himself as a reasonably successful portraitist in London and then in Dublin. When Stuart returned to America, it was not so much because he thought it politically safe to do so; nor was it entirely because, as he admitted in a letter of November 1794, he was absorbed by the idea of portraying Washington, President Washington, that is. Stuart had returned to America, at least in part, because he was deeply in debt. Still, a letter of recommendation from John Jay, one of the signers of the Declaration of Independence, gave him the opportunity to get near the object of his desire. Stuart was deeply impressed by the president, though he later complained that once a sitting started Washington instantly assumed a rigid indifference and that he found it next to impossible to paint the president's empty face. Stuart employed a trick: He engaged Washington in a conversation about the Revolution and the War of Independence. In this way, Stuart believed, he would be able to awaken "the heroic spirit in him." The opening gambit backfired. "Now, sir," Stuart instructed his sitter, "you must let me forget that you are General Washington and that I am Stuart, the painter." To which Washington responded rather ungraciously, "I'll not forget that I am president, don't you forget you are a painter." Washington's displeasure only mounted, and Stuart could continue only because of Martha Washington's friendly persuasion. Three portraits can be attributed to Stuart with a measure of certainty. The first one, measuring 24 × 30 inches, stems from 1795. The original (or, possibly, a copy of it) was purchased by an Englishman named Samuel Vaughan.[4]

Charles Henry Hart, who for years devoted himself to studying portraits of Washington, thought that the "Vaughan" portrait was the most felicitous of all. This is somewhat surprising, as the unfinished "Athenaeum" portrait is generally considered as the most authentic representation of Washington, as *the* standard portrait. Stuart infused into the Athenaeum "an amplitude and grandeur that were never the attribute of Washington's face." Instead, an English guest at Mount Vernon had noticed in Washington's face a "compression of the mouth and [an] indentation of the brow ... suggesting habitual conflict with and mastery over passion." Certainly that was the conclusion of Johann Caspar Lavater, who ended the 1789 English edition of his *Essays on Physiognomy* with a discussion of Washington's character as revealed in portrait prints. While Lavater, who had never seen Washington in the flesh, observed that everything in the general's face "announces the good man, a man upright, of simple manners, sincere, firm, reflecting and generous," he nevertheless thought that the eyes possessed "neither that benevolence, nor prudence, nor heroic force, which are inseparable from true greatness." Seen in this light, Stuart's attempt to preserve what Sir Joshua Reynolds had called "the general effect of the countenance" could not quite obliterate the inner person, visible, whether intentional or not, in Washington's eyes, his wary, penetrating gaze and hooded lids, as if he had noticed something hard and suspicious.[5]

Such subtlety was beyond the artistry of John Trumbull, even though no one else had so many opportunities to portray the Father of His Country. Trumbull had joined Washington's army in Cambridge, Massachusetts, in 1775. Aged nineteen, Trumbull had already distinguished himself as a topographer. The distinction came to Washington's attention and the general made him his aide-de-camp. In 1777, Trumbull left for England to study art with John Singleton Copley and Benjamin West. In 1780, the two teachers got him out of jail, where he had been imprisoned as a citizen of an enemy country. During his stay in England, Trumbull wrote an ode on "The Genius of America," in which he glorified the stirring events of the Revolution, most notably the battles of Trenton and Princeton. He also painted scenes from Revolutionary history, as well as a full-length portrait of George Washington, who is shown standing on the banks of the Hudson River, the village of West Point in the background. Trumbull painted the portrait from memory. Completed in 1780, it is the first authoritative representation of George Washington done in Europe.[6]

Trumbull returned to the United States in 1789. In New York, he resumed work on a painting about the signing of the Declaration of Independence. In January and February 1790, Washington granted Trumbull about a dozen sessions. At one point the artist requested that the President put on his general's uniform. The two men went for a ride on horseback, with Trumbull making sketches. One result of Trumbull's moving the setting from indoors to out—*Washington and the Departure of the British Garrison from New York City*—today hangs in the Governor's Room in the City Hall in New York. The painting (108 × 72 inches) shows a towering Washington in his full military uniform, standing by his horse; in the background are the ruins of Broadway, the old fort at its end, also British battleships and other vessels, as well as Staten Island.[7] Also in City Hall hangs a similar painting, smaller and with a different background. The painting—*Washington at Verplanck's Point*—also was done in 1790, for Martha Washington. Today it hangs in the Winterthur Museum, Winterthur, Delaware. Perhaps because Trumbull situated Washington in historical settings, the President wrote admiringly of the "greatness of the design," and the artist's

Washington at Verplanck's Point by John Trumbull, 1790, New York, New York, oil paint, canvas (20.125 × 30.125 in.) (courtesy Winterthur Museum, Winterthur, Delaware, Gift of Henry Francis du Pont, 1964.2201).

"masterly execution" and "capacious mind," and never displayed toward him any of the petulance or impatience he did toward Gilbert Stuart.[8]

Washington at Verplanck's Point belongs to a distinct genre of portraits, of posturing generals. Nothing distracts from the victorious general. There is, however, no cheap triumph in Washington's gestures; moreover, Washington is dressed in the uniform of a citizen general, without military insignia, once again a reminder of Cincinnatus—the Roman citizen soldier whom Houdon had immortalized in his marble statue.

As much as the *Verplanck* painting was and still is admired, the Cincinnatus pose does raise questions. True, Washington himself cultivated it, but in Trumbull's painting the function is to neutralize an ingrained dislike, even antipathy, from the colonial era, of paid *professional* soldiers. The dislike was rooted in fears of the threat posed by a strong standing army, the kind of army that Washington, shaped by British military organization, wanted to establish. Washington had no patience for the idea of a selfless amateur militia that many of his contemporaries admired. His "ruling passion," a British officer who had served with Washington during the French and Indian War remarked in 1778, was "military fame."[9] Thus it is doubtful whether Washington was entirely happy with the characterization of the calm, dignified leader the Chevalier de Chastellux, major general in the French expeditionary force led by the Comte de Rochambeau, came away with from his visit, in 1781, to the Continental Army headquarters. Chastellux was deeply impressed with Washington's character, and wrote admiringly about the "perfect harmony ... between the physical and moral qualities." Such balance extended to the future president's "mild and agreeable" face, with "neither a grave nor familiar air."[10]

George Washington no doubt would have appreciated Trumbull's *General George Washington at Trenton*. Commissioned from the artist by the city of Charleston, South Carolina, in 1792, the painting breathes a blend of heroism and nobility, showing Washington's generalship "in the most sublime moment of its exertion." The painting's visual rhetoric unmistakably resembles Ramsay's *George III*, though the latter's ceremonial pomp has been replaced by a cannon and the arms of the defeated British. Still, Charleston refused to accept the artwork on the grounds that they preferred a more amiable and peaceful image. Trumbull produced another likeness, this time with the city in the background, which Charleston accepted. One wonders what the city's officials would have said of Trumbull's *The Death of General Mercer at the Battle of Princeton, January 3, 1777*. There is nothing "mild and agreeable" in the Washington on horseback that Trumbull depicts in this later painting. Although Washington was not anywhere near Mercer when he was killed, Trumbull intended the painting as an homage to the "wisdom, activity, and energy of one great mind." This was not the patriotic *amateur* soldier but the "gentleman warrior," in Brumwell's apt words, whom Trumbull painted at center, in the middle distance, where the battle rages. In life, too, an exultant Washington had galloped after the running enemy troops, urging on his own men by shouting: "It's a fine fox chase, my boys!" These words have been reported at second hand, but, given Washington's formative years among English-born gentility in Virginia, they sound characteristic enough to be credible. As one of his officers observed: "Such was the impetuosity of [Washington's] character, when he gave rein to his sensibilities."[11]

Washington's "colossal status," Stephen Brumwell argues, "rested upon the twin pillars of his character, the gentleman and the warrior."[12] Yet *Death of General Mercer* is said to be one of the few paintings that show Washington in a battlefield (normally, a commander in chief did not see battles up close).[13] Unsurprisingly, it is also Brumwell's favorite image of George Washington (a detail of the painting graces the dust jacket of his book). And throughout his monograph, Brumwell is at great pains to breathe life into the incarnation of Washington as a "pugnacious fighting man," the creation of eighteenth-century military culture. It was British models of military organization and a gentlemanly code of honor that shaped Washington's distinctive style of leadership. These influences, Brumwell contends, have been "curiously neglected."[14] This seems to be pushed too far. Until his inauguration as President in 1789, Washington's identity and status were customarily signified through military accouterments. It is true that later portraits no longer show him as military officer, yet this shifting emphasis, Catherine Kelly argues, not only reflected a new, romantic style of portraiture. It also coincided with the emerging market economy: "[I]t was far less labor intensive—and therefore less expensive—for a painter or engraver to render a head than a full figure posed against an elaborate background." The simpler format also owed much to the "absence of an established set of presidential props. Monarchs, soldiers, sea captains, and even ordinary gentlemen had their defining garments and other material accoutrements. But [...] with no comparable signatures for republican statesmen, engravers and printmakers generally avoided the issue altogether by focusing on the bust."[15] Or, if they did attempt a full-length portrait, they had to arduously adapt and transform earlier monarchical or aristocratic conventions—as Stuart did in the "Lansdowne" portrait.

Outside the realm of art, many citizens saw Washington's election to the presidency as an appropriate token of gratitude for his military accomplishments. As president, he was customarily referred to as *General* Washington, and sometimes welcomed to cities to the tune of "Hail the Conquering Hero Comes." Even at his death, virtually all funeral processions had a distinctive military tone, while eulogies would be dedicated to "*General* Washington." In Samuel MacWhorther's funeral sermon, for instance, Washington appears as a "man of war from his youth [...] the most eminent, the most prosperous, and the most honored general in modern times."[16] And contrary to Brumwell's lament, the image of Washington as a warrior *was* preserved in the portraits and engravings that showed him in military attire. A mezzotint engraving by Charles Wilson Peale bears this out. The engraving was issued in September 1787 at a crucial time in the Constitutional Convention, over which Washington presided. (He had sat for the original portrait before attending the Convention's morning sessions.) The Father of His Country must have been pleased, for a framed print given to him by Peale hung in the music room at Mount Vernon until his death.

Until at least the Civil War, the image of Washington as a warrior, uniformed, with sword drawn or on horseback, was never completely replaced by decidedly unmilitary images of him, such as Stuart's "Athenaeum" or "Lansdowne" portraits, even though the latter were embraced as iconic as soon as they appeared. If republican virtue and civil moderation became part of the collective consciousness, so did military zeal and political passion. Gilbert Stuart himself reconciled these two tendencies in *Washington at Dorchester Heights*. In this painting of 1806, a president's head is attached to a general's body.[17] Sculpture, too, gave expression to Washington's military leadership and bravery, reinforced, especially on the equestrian statues by Thomas Crawford (in Richmond, Virginia) or Henry Kirke Brown (in New York's Union Square), by Washington's emphatic gesture, as though he was leading a charge. Even more of a superhuman hero is connoted by an equestrian statuette executed by Daniel Chester French around 1897. French's statuette depicts the moment Washington took command of the Continental Army; it shows him seated erect on his charger, gazing skyward, holding a sword aloft. Subsequently numerous casts were made of the statuette, to commemorate the centennial of Washington's death in 1899.[18] By that time, film had arrived, and Washington's image as a "warrior" or military leader was given fuller scope. The vast majority of films including him, from one of the first, *Washington Under the American Flag* (1909), until the most recent, *The Patriot* (2000), show Washington as a military leader. He appears either as a participant or in flashbacks in films about various wars, and almost always standing upright, frequently in profile shot, or seated on his white horse, leading troops (stunningly created through digital photography in *The Patriot*).[19] Washington's image as a "warrior" was also cultivated in drama. In 1924, Belle Willey Gue published her play *George Washington*; four years later, it was republished as *Washington the Warrior*.[20]

In the interest of space, I have discussed only a few selected portraits of George Washington, those that reached a wide audience and became important to America's collective memory. I also did not do full justice to the numerous copies, prints, or engravings made from the portraits or done without an original. Charles Henry Hart's invaluable catalog lists about 880 such pictures, including mass-produced, immediately recognizable portraits, mostly in the form of lithographic reproductions of early oil paintings, which were also engraved for banknote vignettes or stamped on medals and coins. Already during the Revolutionary War, Washington had become a celebrated national hero and the subject of a proliferation of images, from grand neo-classical marbles to schoolgirl samplers, from prints to almanacs and broadside cuts and, not to forget, book and magazine illustrations. Even children opening their primers and schoolbooks were confronted with likenesses respectively of "General Washington," "President of the United States," or "the American Hero"—all titles for a 1780 relief cut attributed to Paul Revere, after Charles Wilson Peale.[21] Primers also served as vehicles for alphabet cuts. During the years 1799–1800, for instance, instead of the traditional whale illustrating the letter "W," a miniature stick figure was substituted in a number of primers (such as *The New England Primer Improved*, published by Naphtali Judah in New York), accompanied by an appropriate verse, such as "By Washington, Great deeds were done." Schoolchildren thus were to see George Washington not only as a military leader or president, but also as an exemplar of moral conduct for all to emulate.[22]

One of the most widely reproduced images originated from a crude copper engraving a John Roberts executed in 1789 from a Charles Wilson Peale image. Roberts gave one of the mezzotints to the woodcutter Alexander Anderson. In 1791, Anderson did a Washington likeness in letter metal. The work became one of the best-known images of America's hero, serving as it did as frontispiece to the 14th edition of Noah Webster's *American Spelling Book*. No other book was ever as popular as Webster's, which went through numerous editions, selling more than 100 million copies.[23] It was popular art such as Anderson's that, through the mid-nineteenth century, brought home visual representations of the metaphorical father to the majority of Americans. These usually were people who had neither the means nor use for an expensive portrait done in oil. American folk artists of the early republic too produced works that were affordable to people of more modest means. Unlike book illustrators, they brought their subjects into correspondence with visual norms and conventions that were those of a well-bounded group rather than the largely European-influenced fine-arts tradition. In the early nineteenth century, for instance, in Greenville, Green County, New York, a farm woman named Mary Ann Wilson made a watercolor titled *George Washington on a Horse*. The piece shows Washington all by himself, resembling a cardboard figure on a cardboard horse. Sprightly dots and dashes brighten saddle blanket and harness. A small circle of smoke from a pistol's barrel indicates that it is being fired, while squiggles of color in the background set the figure in space. What makes the watercolor unique is that unlike in other renderings of Washington on horseback, there is no background whatsoever. The ensemble evokes the ghostly rider, a motif, as readers of Washington Irving's "The Legend of Sleepy Hollow" recall, still popular among the Dutch of the Hudson River Valley in the early nineteenth century and, Klaus Lubbers has found, among Germans in Pennsylvania.[24]

Folk artists, it has been said, may have lacked the ability to describe, but they certainly had the ability to express. Thus they perceived the nation's official icons, not in the abstractions of nation or state but in the community and, even more tangibly, in the family. Since the folk's "sense of identity proceeded from hearth and home to garden and gate, to fields and horizon," folk art renderings of Washington show him "in his down-to-earth-roles of soldier and tiller of the soil" rather than as the founder or elder statesman.[25] A small watercolor titled *Exselenc Georg General Waschingdon and Lady Waschingdon* bears this out. The drawing, rendered about 1780 in the *fraktur* style, is attributed to a Pennsylvania-German artist, most likely from Lebanon or Lancaster County, whose work has been complimented for its sureness, precision, and strict symmetry. The aesthetics rests on the formal effect of balanced arrangement; the thematic effect derives from the harmonious juxtaposition of male and female, who are of exactly the same height, while the emphasis on the vertical axis underlines the notion of concord or twosomeness. Several details drive home the idea of a spiritual bond between the General and his Lady: Martha Washington's left arm is on George Washington's back, while the husband is holding up lilies (or tulips, which botanically are lilies), symbols of spiritual love in the biblical Song of Solomon.

The emphasis, in *Exselenc Georg General Waschingdon and Lady Waschingdon*, on the couple, not on the individual, renders the figures as representative, not as accurate likenesses. This is what the watercolor tells us: George Washington surely was a great general, the Father of His Country, but he was also a married man, blessed with a wife of equal splendor. For the folk artist it was therefore entirely appropriate to depict him *together* with her, as a couple, as newlyweds about to found a family. There is a most striking difference to fine-art depictions of George Washington, which are almost always *without* her. Gilbert Stuart never showed the couple on a single canvas, nor did Trumbull, or the two Peales. As if *his* greatness would not suffer the proximity of even his wife. Savage did show George and Martha on a single canvas, but the union of husband and wife is not its defining characteristic. By choosing a marriage motif for the watercolor, then, the artist has embedded the Father of His Country in folk culture, in which there is no dearth of depictions of couples. In this instance, the very clumsiness of the title, which renders the names of the Washingtons phonetically, echoes the speechways of Pennsylvania-Germans.[26]

Exselenc Georg General Washingdon and Lady Washingdon has become quite a favorite in books on American folk art, though at the time it was not an object that was considered useful for mass distribution.[27] Mass distribution was the domain of all kinds of engravings from fine-art appropriations of the face of the nation, as well as medallions, copies of miniatures, and silhouettes. A number of silhouettes were produced already during Washington's lifetime, including by Washington's adopted grandchild, Eleanor Parke Custis, who was only seventeen when she did some in 1796.[28] Charles de Saint-Mémin, who ran a thriving business first in New York and, as of 1798, in Philadelphia, attracted a large clientele that included political and civil luminaries, military men, and French refugees. In 1798 he produced the last portrait to be executed during Washington's lifetime, a drawing, in pink chalk on paper, that subsequently was used for a myriad of engravings. Upon Washington's death in December 1799, Saint-Mémin's portrait was mounted, in miniaturized form and under glass, on a number of gold rings. Simon Chaudron, a goldsmith and jeweler from Philadelphia, placed the following advertisement in the daily press: "Mourning Rings, With an elegant Portrait of the late illustrious General Washington. To be had at S. Chaudron, No. 12, South 3d Street."²⁹

Saint-Mémin's chalkboard drawing is the last portrait done during Washington's lifetime. What came after is simply not known. It seems impossible to do full justice to the number of visual representations of the Father of His Country. Of course, there is no dearth of books and catalogs on the topic. Hart's *Catalogue of Engraved Portraits* (1904) has been mentioned. Also noteworthy is an earlier catalog, William S. Baker's *The Engraved Portraits of Washington* (1880), which lists over 400 items, including silhouettes, memorial designs, and fictitious portraits. Engravings in turn spawned any number of prints, from book illustrations incorporated into school primers, histories and biographies to stand-alone images, suitable for framing or pasting into scrapbooks.³⁰

Exselenc Georg General Washingdon and Lady Washingdon by The Sussel-Washington Artist, probably Lebanon or Lancaster County, Pennsylvania, circa 1780, watercolor and ink laid on paper (*The Colonial Williamsburg Foundation. Museum Purchase*).

Baker compiled his catalog "simply as a Text-book for the Washington collector." Thus he prefaced it with the obligatory paean to the nation's "father," whose likenesses conveyed "the nobility of his character, the dignity of his manhood, his truth and patriotism." Given the book's purpose, Baker has little to say about the artistic merits of the original portraits, let alone the engravings. Baker's "Washingtons," Catherine Kelly concludes, "were valued not as art but as Americana."³¹ In contrast, Gustavus Eisen's three-volume study, *Portraits of Washington*, published in 1932, the year of the bicentennial of Washington's birth, does treat the portraits as art, through the end of the nineteenth century. Eisen's summary is revealing: Pictorial representations of George Washington mostly focus on his accomplishment as Commander in Chief during the Revolutionary War, as president of the constitutional convention, and as first President of the United States. But there was one role left for him. In his retirement, Washington became a national symbol, his likeness representing the whole country.

An etched and engraved print Amos Doolittle created between 1788 and 1789 conflates all of these roles into one image. Doolittle's picture, titled *Display of the United States of America*, features a medallion profile portrait of Washington (after Joseph Wright) framed by fourteen interlocking rings signifying the union of the states. Within each ring appears a state's seal; the fourteenth ring includes the seal of the United States.³² Doolittle's print is of considerable historic interest, as are the notes from the Washington Bank in Westerly, Rhode Island, for which Doolittle did the plates, thus creating the first paper money with a portrait of George Washington on it. In Eisen's catalog, however, historic interest is trumped by artistic merit, and so Rembrandt Peale's "*Patriae Pater*" portrait of 1824 is singled out. The style of *Patriae Pater* clearly shows the influence of French neo-classicism. Peale surrounded the portrait with an illusionary stone arch replete with allegorical signs. The garland of oak leaves, for instance, symbolizes faith, virtue, and endurance in the face of adversity. Above the arch, the keystone mask of Jupiter, the Roman king of the gods, suggests not only Washington's godlike status in the hearts of many Americans but also the classical principles on which the nation was founded. Peale's aspiration to neoclassicism is further emphasized by Washington's elegant black cloak and ruffled shirt, the Olympian clouds and shadows beyond his head and, not to forget, the painting's title, *Patriae Pater* (Latin for "father of his country").

Patriae Pater was an honorary title conferred by the Roman Senate, though it may have originated with Romulus. During the republican period, the title was in common use. It was bestowed on Cicero in 63 BCE, during his consulship, for discovering Catalina's conspiracy. As Cicero wrote in *Republic* (I, vii): "For there is really no other occupation in which human virtue approaches more closely that august function of the gods than that of founding new states or preserving those already in existence."³³ Peale's painting no doubt recalls the passage, as he deliberately emphasizes the Father of His Country as a *moral* exemplar. The difference also had not escaped Chief Justice John Marshall, who in his obituary on Washington remarked that Julius Caesar too had been referred to as "pater patriae." (Under Caesar and Augustus, *patriae pater* increasingly became more of a political concept; Augustus's successors even had coins minted with the impression *patriae pater*.) Some three years after Peale had finished his portrait, the church divine William Ellery Channing remarked that moral and ethical standards distinguished George Washington from Napoleon Bonaparte. "By an instinct which is unerring we call Washington, with grateful reverence,—THE FATHER OF HIS COUNTRY."³⁴

Remarks of this kind illustrate that once fashionable, the title Father of his Country appeared everywhere. By the same token, it is safe to say that the younger Peale was not just interested in art for art's sake but also and importantly in matters moral and political. For the renowned artist, it was self-evident that portraiture had to serve the nation's moral and ethical standards. Thus, the exemplary character of a subject had to be made visible in the face, in this instance, George Washington's "mild, thoughtful & dignified, yet firm and energetic Countenance."³⁵ Rembrandt Peale likely adopted from Leonardo da Vinci the axiom that a likeness was not a more or less accurate representation of an individual's face but a map of character. Additionally, he learned from his own father, Charles Wilson Peale, who as early as 1787 advertised a mezzotint portrait of "His Excellency General Washington," as "the best likeness that has been executed in print."³⁶

Rembrandt Peale was only eighteen years old when in the company of his father, Charles Wilson Peale, he did his first portrait of Washington. The result, done in 1795, he found utterly disappointing, though. It showed an aging Washington, worn down by the presidency, not the inspiring, grandiose image of Washington he had wanted to present. The experience left Peale determined to create a likeness that would transcend representational accuracy, conveying the heroic qualities that Washington produced in the minds of many Americans. In 1823, he decided to make one last effort to create an image that would, he hoped, become the "standard likeness" of the first president, unseating Gilbert Stuart's enormously popular "Athenaeum" portrait in the process.[37] Inspiration for *Patriae Pater* came to Rembrandt Peale from many different sources, including the works of Stuart, Trumbull, his own father and, most notably, the sculptural portrait by Houdon. What the younger Peale created, however, was something quite different, an image of Washington that, by transcending representational accuracy to convey the idea or general effect of the Father of His Country, was as much icon as likeness. The composition represents Washington in a highly symbolic manner, blending portraiture with history painting. Within the large format (roughly twice the size of conventional portraits), he painted a strikingly illusionistic stone oval window—the "porthole," as it was soon dubbed—that frames the bust-length figure of the Father of His Country, giving Washington the permanence of stone. The result is an undeniably forceful presence, not Washington exactly, but a posthumous reinvention that resonates with dignity and venerable nobility.

Rembrandt Peale, *George Washington, Patriae Pater*, "Porthole Portrait," 1824, oil on canvas (72¼ × 54¼ in.), Acc. No. 1912.14.4 (courtesy the Pennsylvania Academy of the Fine Arts, Philadelphia; bequest of Mrs. Sarah Harrison [The Joseph Harrison, Jr. Collection]).

Rembrandt's father, Charles Wilson Peale, studied the portrait on the easel. "You have it now," he eventually said, approvingly clapping his son on the shoulder, "this is indeed Washington."[38] Visitors to Peale's studio, too, instantly swore to the remarkably faithful likeness. This was not nearly enough for the artist, who was anxious to solicit the opinions of individuals who had actually known Washington and soon collected more than twenty testimonials, which in 1824 he published in an advertising brochure titled *Portrait of Washington*. The younger Peale followed the pamphlet up with an 1834 letter in which he claims that the "Porthole" portrait was the most authentic Washington portrait of all times, "the most exact representation of the original," "the only faithful likeness," "the best and most faithful portrait of the great Father of his Country," "the most accurate likeness," and "more Washington himself than any [other] portrait."[39]

The letter had been prompted by heated debates, among America's lawmakers, about the most correct likeness of George Washington. The question arose in 1832, the centennial year of Washington's birth. Then, the United State Senate purchased *Patriae Pater* for the princely sum of $2,000, while the House commissioned John Vanderlyn to do a full-length portrait with the head based on Stuart's Washington. The problem, of course, was how to determine "most accurate likeness" or "correctness" in the absence of photographic records. The decision—in the end, Stuart's portrait won over Peale's—was, not aesthetic but political.[40] Peale did not like this, but Stuart had painted from life, whereas Peale did not have any certification of authenticity, not anyone in authority saying "Yes, this was the way Washington looked." Hence Peale's efforts to solicit opinions from those who had known Washington. Hence also Peale's continued efforts to promote and defend his portrait. It should also be noted that from 1824 until his death in 1860, he painted no fewer than seventy-nine idealized depictions of Washington, many of them oil replicas of the original porthole portrait. Peale justified the many replicas by claiming that, because he was the last living artist to have painted Washington from life, "the reduplication of … [my] work, by … [my] own hand, should be esteemed the most reliable."[41]

Personal acquaintance with Washington certainly distinguished the younger Peale from painters of a later generation, who could lay claim to the authenticity of their works at best performatively. The final qualification Peale claimed in his favor was that he, "born on Washington's birthday, was annually, from infancy, excited to greater admiration of his character."[42] It is not entirely clear whether Peale's entrepreneurial activities were motivated by self-interest or the public good, though his claims engaged the attention of his contemporaries for more than three decades. In 1835, Edward Everett, then a member of the House, had come to Peale's support by claiming that the present generation was better able to do justice to Washington's character than that in which he lived.[43] Still, in view of the diversity and heterogeneity of depictions of Washington, the question which likeness was to be authenticated could not be resolved on aesthetic grounds. "We know the history of the man, and the impression he made upon contemporaries," Henry Tuckerman resignedly wrote at mid-century, "and are prepared to authenticate his likeness, though we have never seen his living face."[44]

Viewing habits that had been shaped by a republican ethos of egalitarianism, virtue, and civic responsibility likewise were not conducive to portraying Washington in a heroic pose. Nor do simple dignity and ethical nobility per se inspire picturesque or dramatic effects. Washington was, an obviously clueless Tuckerman wrote, too complete, too perfect, so that no depiction was to ever do justice to him.[45] The—real or merely asserted—impossibility of adequately depicting George Washington raised the stakes for the authenticity of portraits of the Father of His Country. It is no surprise that Rembrandt Peale used all available means to enforce the claim to exclusive authenticity for his *Patriae Pater*. About the sheer power of Washington's face he wrote: "Nothing can more powerfully carry back the mind to the glorious period which gave birth to this nation, nothing can be found more capable of exciting the noblest feelings of emulation and patriotism." Peale's advertising brochure was more than self-aggrandizement. For him, as for other artists who had painted Washington from life, preoccupation with authenticity went beyond a workmanlike desire to meet contemporary standards for accurate and pleasing "likenesses." An authentic portrait of Washington had to "transmit to posterity the true and impressive image of that countenance," be capable of reawakening and even creating powerful sentiments about the Father of His Country and, by extension, about the republic itself.[46]

Once more, the younger Peale seems to have learned from his father, Charles Wilson Peale, who had said that portraits of "worthies" were portraits of virtuous characters who therefore were worthy of emulation.[47] The patriotic glory of *Patriae Pater* and other portraits—be they oil paintings, busts, or mass-produced reproductions—constituted a moral and political act, providing guidance and reference for a society that was in dire need of unifying sentiments not least because of its size and the diversity and heterogeneity of its members. Modern societies necessarily are culturally differentiated and plagued by conflicting interests. The notion was well-known among nineteenth-century intellectuals, as was the power of unifying symbols to make up for the loss of primary social relations and to restore a form of solidarity among members. In *The Elementary Forms of the Religious Life*, Émile Durkheim argued that unifying symbols, by becoming attached to a concrete object would overcome both the remoteness of political centers and the non-binding nature and vagueness of moral and ethical standards circulating in modern societies. Unifying symbols, Durkheim concluded, "are necessary if society is to become conscious of itself, and no less indispensable for assuring the continuation of this consciousness."[48]

8

The Father of the Fatherless

There was a strong demand for unifying symbols already during the War of Independence and the early republic. Symbols are powerful vehicles of political integration, yet nothing represents a political community's ideals and values quite so well as an actual person. Until the War of Independence, the colonies' aims, continuity, and destiny had been made intelligible through the English monarch. The symbolic regicide and patricide—when George III was discarded as the father of the country—left those born after truly "orphaned," until George Washington became the new Father of His Country. Americans of the nineteenth century were again "fatherless," albeit for different reasons. Now they were confronting an unfettered capitalism and an economic logic based on entrepreneurial competition. Capitalism, Marx and Engels wrote in 1848, "has left remaining no other nexus between man and man than naked self-interest." Not only will social cohesion fall apart, and solidarity be trampled underfoot. Family ties, too, are unraveling: "The bourgeoisie has torn away from the family its sentimental veil, and has reduced the family relation to a mere money relation." Ultimately, even respect for fathers is drowned "in the icy water of egotistical calculation."[1]

Several scholars have tried to explain the crisis of fatherhood in nineteenth-century America in fairly general terms as a result of modernization.[2] Such explanations are euphemistic at best, and certainly unhistorical. Phases of modernization and the social changes accompanying them can be found in various historical periods. What was truly unique in nineteenth-century America, however, was the free and unimpeded expansion of industrial capitalism. From its beginnings in the northern states, industrial capitalism reshaped the entire nation in the course of a half century. This was not a marginal change, but a fundamental one. First, industrialization and the modern economy led to the physical separation of home and work, thus gradually nudging fathers from their central role in family life. Cotemporaneous with these economic instabilities and insecurities (including the devastating consequences of notes issued by private banks), radically new notions of self and subjectivity emerged, which marginalized and made irrelevant traditional forms of male identity construction, those based on the mere possession of property. The historian Jay Fliegelman has seen in this development a wholesome "rebellion against the fathers."[3] This view seems one-sided. The rapid changes of course brought with them enlightened sensibilities that extended to new styles of fatherhood, new inventions as well as improvements in science and medicine that would, overall, benefit humankind. Yet these changes would, at the same time, disconnect individuals from family and true community as people left their farms for the cities, to work in dismal factories and to live in overcrowded and miserable slums breathing in bad air, the kind of life that Marx and Engels were observing with horror in England. It was no lesser person than Thomas Jefferson who viewed the prospect with both anticipation and alarm, hoping that an "agrarian" United States could delay for as long as possible arriving at that final stage of development.[4]

Jefferson's hopes were in vain, though. Nor would the dismantling of traditional forms of identity constructions have stopped short of George Washington. Edward Savage's painting *The Washington Family* casts Washington and his family as pioneers of venture capitalism, thus advancing a new vision of property ownership. Begun in 1789 and first exhibited in 1796 in Savage's Columbian Gallery of New York, then the nation's capital, the painting became the most familiar rendering of the Washingtons at home, copied and adapted by engravers, lithographers, and amateur artists in genres ranging from engraving to needlework, often altering the composition to suit contemporary tastes. Indeed, throughout the nineteenth century, Americans came to know the domestic Washington largely as Savage had pictured the president and his family.[5]

The Washington Family effectively exploits the blending of public and private life. In doing so, the artwork not only captures the spirit of the time but also celebrates it as exemplary. The painting is loaded with symbolic meaning. On one hand, there is Savage's vision of the Washingtons as America's national family. The scene depicts a bourgeois household, dominated by a rigid order that includes hierarchized gender roles. Each family member is in his or her proper place, each performing a normative social role of early republican domestic life. There is Martha Washington, dressed in sartorial silk and brocade, together with the two grandchildren from her first marriage, and the liveried domestic servant, whose skin color captures the white supremacist underpinnings of society much as it indicates Washington's origin in Virginia's planter elite (the baroquish scene suggests Mount Vernon, though the Washingtons posed for Savage in New York). George Washington, the paterfamilias, is depicted almost in life size. His general's uniform, the spurs on his boots and the set jaws dutifully evoke the revolutionary hero, while the black hat, dress sword, and the various papers on the table speak of "President Washington," ready to leave home at a moment's notice.[6]

Republican domestic life is only one aspect of Savage's painting. *The Washington Family* also depicts the Washingtons as a family of economic visionaries.[7] Most tellingly, the group—the unnamed black slave excepted—are seated around a table on which is spread out Andrew Ellicott's plan of the new national capital, then known as Federal City. By having the Washingtons focus on Ellicott's plan, Savage represents them as a family of entrepreneurs, a body of far-sighted schemers, with George Washington as the undisputed leader of the capital venture.[8] Seated in an ornate chair, George Washington has his left arm on a copy of the street plan, gazing into the future as if he were engaged in calculating forecasting, perhaps envisioning "the grand avenue," now known as Pennsylvania Avenue, the future location of the White House.[9] *The Washington Family* thus affirms the capital venture and its long-term viability. At the same time, it advances a new vision of property ownership, one that was no longer tied to familial land inherited and passed on to the following generation, thus to the mere possession (the basis of feudal relations in which customary rules govern use and material production, reproduction, and consumption), but one that is keyed to the priorities of the emergent market economy, such as fungible properties like real estate, all volatile and fluid, held for sale, for mortgaging or loaning, for yielding appropriate returns.[10]

Aligning George Washington and Washington family with the economic ideals and the speculative ethos of American capitalism, Edward Savage effected a profound change from past social ideals. Those ideals had been rooted within a relatively small but homogeneous colonial elite composed of well-to-do merchants, lawyers, and landowners. It was a

Edward Savage, *The Washington Family*, 1796, oil on canvas (84 × 112 in.) (National Gallery of Arts, Washington, D.C., Andrew W. Mellon Collection).

society in which little changed, but everything differed, a society that had been formed, directly or indirectly, by ideals of English gentility. George Washington's prolonged exposure to the English-born members of the Fairfax dynasty contributed an essential strand to his character—the conduct, bearing, and outlook that led his contemporaries to see him as a "complete gentleman." As one of the Count de Rochambeau's aristocratic aides observed in 1781, Washington's "manners are those of one perfectly accustomed to society, quite a rare thing certainly in America."[11]

In keeping with the ideals of English nobility, America's colonial elite relied on the family as a force of cohesion. George Washington left no direct comments about his marriage, though he left too many "peans to domestic felicity" as to leave any doubt of his contentment with Martha. George Washington and Martha Dandridge Custis were married on January 6, 1759. Martha was a widow then, who brought two children into the marriage, John Parke Custis aka "Jacky" and Martha Parke Custis aka "Patsy," both of whom George Washington adopted. In 1781, he also adopted the two children left behind by Jacky's death, Eleanor, called "Nelly," and George Washington, called "Washy."[12] But what was he like as a father? Abigail Adams's comment, upon Washington's arrival in Boston in 1775, that the commander in chief "has a dignity which forbids familiarity, mixed with an easy affability which creates love and reverence" is insightful. Her words also bear upon the patterns of emotional style, tone, and preference within the Washington family, suggesting a mixture of admiration, love, respect, as well as the slightest touch of fear. As Nelly Custis recalled,

George Washington's own near relatives "feared to speak or laugh before him, not from his severity," but out of "awe and respect."[13] It is also no surprise that more often than not, Washington's formal presence would freeze the children's jollity. Even to the second set of children, with whom he was much more tolerant and relaxed than with Jacky and Patsy, he was sometimes a grandly remote figure. "He was a silent thoughtful man," Nelly said years later. "He spoke little generally, never of himself."[14]

The absence of strong visible emotions was typical of the time. Patriarchal fatherhood, E. Anthony Rotundo argues, rested on the "belief that too much affection would lead to parental indulgence, which would in turn ruin a child's character."[15] George Washington's role as the "family disciplinarian" bears this out. That role was normal by eighteenth-century standards, though as Ron Chernow reminds us, it often was a "thankless task," as when Washington felt uneasy about chastising the rather profligate Jacky lest he antagonize the more indulgent Martha. George Washington had a most solemn sense of responsibility, and he took seriously his duties towards the children. On closer examination, however, Washington was quite capable of deep emotions. One only has to think of his outpouring of grief by Patsy's deathbed.[16] Yet is a gesture of this kind enough to consider, as Jay Fliegelman does, the Washingtons as an emblem of an antipatriarchal family? Perhaps George Washington did embody a new understanding of paternity, but the makeup of his family needs to be traced to the culture he represented. From the few materials that are available, we may reasonably assume that among colonial fathers the rein over affection towards daughters was much looser than towards sons.[17] Still, artistic conventions would bar depictions of George Washington at Patsy's death, in 1773, when she was only seventeen years old; and Washington himself, fiercely private man that he was, would never allow to make intimacy and affection a public spectacle. He also did not make a public spectacle of Jacky's death, in 1781, though he was "uncommonly affected" by it and unhesitatingly decided, with Martha, to informally adopt the two youngest children, Eleanor Parke Custis, then two years old and like her mother called "Nelly," and George Washington Parke Custis, seven months old, called "Washy." The two stepgrandchildren called him "papa" and sometime during the 1790s Nelly wrote to George Washington of how she looked up to him "with grateful affection as a parent to myself and family."[18]

While it is too far-fetched to trace the culture that George Washington represented to the makeup of the family, it is nevertheless possible to say that within the typical patriarchal family, love and affection, respect and loyalty spread outward from the family, which thus was the state in microcosm. Indeed, when David Ramsay in 1789 called on Americans to honor "the men who with their own hands maintain their families, and raise up children who are inured to toil, and capable of defending their country," he effectively summarized the founders' association of family men with stable citizenship. By the same token, the Massachusetts Cincinnati called for "illustrious Washington" to be perpetually remembered as "the patriot, the hero and citizen combined."[19] In the political discourse of the time, tropes such as "common interest" and "common good" were dominant, much as in the patriarchal family "the head and all the members are united by one common interest, and animated by one common spirit." This, the Viscount Bolingbroke thought, was the "true image of a free people."[20]

Bolingbroke mentioned the "patriarchal spirit" only in passing, and Washington's contemporaries often bestowed the title "patriarch" on the nation's founder, in an equally casual way. But, as Richard Brookhiser argues, the word "patriarch"—whether applied to fathers or rulers—"could be very precise indeed."[21] As Brookhiser has shown, patriarchy's main defender in the English-speaking world was, not Bolingbroke but Sir Robert Filmer, a country gentleman of the early seventeenth century, who in 1632 unsuccessfully tried to publish a "Discourse … in praise of Royalty." The discourse was finally published almost fifty years later (and nearly thirty years after Filmer's death), under the title *Patriarcha*. Filmer's model for fathers was "the lordship which Adam by creation had over the whole world, and [which] by right descending from him the patriarchs did enjoy." The patriarchs of the Bible were the forefathers of Israel and its twelve tribes, and throughout the eighteenth century the word was often used as a metaphor, making of Washington a kind of "crossover" between a Roman *pater familias* and an Old Testament "patriarch."[22] But for Filmer the patriarch was real. Born in 1588, Filmer lived under James I who, following Queen Elizabeth on the throne in 1603, became the first of the English monarchs to conflate the patriarchal functions of God, king, and father. Not only did James I compare himself to God but also, by extension, to the "Fathers of families, for a King is truly *Parens patriae*, the politique father of his people."[23] For Filmer, the first nation was Adam's family, a true "commonwealth." Following Adam's precept, every subsequent nation should be ruled by fatherly command, as there was something of a "natural right of a supreme father over every multitude."[24]

Filmer's ideas received a devastating blow from John Locke, who asked why God had created so many petty monarchies if he had really wanted a true patriarchal order. And, Locke continued, who is to succeed the *pater familias* upon his death? Locke's answer was that it was up to the consent of individuals who was to rule and in what form.[25] Thanks to Locke's critique, Filmer's ideas never became as popular as Bolingbroke's, yet they had a strange afterlife in the North American colonies. This was most notable in Virginia. A number of Filmer's neighbors and peers were involved in founding the Virginia Company in 1606. Filmer's younger brother, Edward, moved to Virginia, as did one of his sons, whose widow, Mary Filmer, became related by a second marriage to most of the founding families of the colony. These families would honor the King, but they wanted government to leave them alone and to run their neighborhoods and their families as they saw fit. In the words of Richard Brookhiser, they were "patriarchs of the private sector."[26]

The "patriarchs of the private sector" shared Filmer's mindset. They were at once civic and acquisitive, men who, like George Washington himself, were chronically cash poor and would therefore ground personality in "real" values such as ownership of land, buildings, and other fixed goods. It is important to remember that land, buildings, and other fixed goods were not merely de facto possessions, but de jure possessions over which owners had documented claims on the basis of which they could be sold, mortgaged, or loaned with a view of appropriate returns. Among the possessions over which owners had documented claims (land, buildings, and other fixed goods), land had the most prestige by far.[27] That is to say, land not held de facto merely, but de jure, which meant working it in order to secure one's property. George Washington, like other landowning farmers of his time, had to acquaint himself with the process of selling for the express purpose of repaying his debts. In more general terms, land held by documented claims made their owners behave like debtors, for even as debtors, property owners had to remain net creditors by holding on to a surplus of assets over liabilities.[28]

In eighteenth-century America, moreover, working one's own land was the basis of civic virtue, a patrician reflex against the have-nots, and a central element in the belief in strict hierarchy as a "natural" (or "God-given") way of things. That hierarchy put men over women, adults over children, and whites over people of color. A typical "racial" patriarch then ruled over families that included a wife, concubines, children, domestic servants, and slaves.²⁹ Concubines excepting, the description fits George Washington's Mount Vernon, which was a typical a southern plantation of several thousand acres, with some two hundred slaves managed by hard-driving overseers, directed from near or afar by entrepreneurs computing profit and loss, sales and expenses, and the buying and selling of slaves as chattel property. The Father of His Country was the undisputed master of Mount Vernon's slaves, yet he was utterly dependent on them, in a hierarchical community. It was the "profit from their toil," the historian Fritz Hirschfeld noted, "that resulted in the creation of the luxury and great beauty … that made Washington's ancestral home a magnificent showplace during much of his lifetime."³⁰

More generous to Washington's memory was Richard Allen, the minister of the African Methodist Episcopal Church of Philadelphia. Following Washington's death, Allen (a real clergyman, unlike the self-declared "Parson" Weems) delivered a widely reprinted prose eulogy in which he described Washington's posthumous emancipation of his slaves as an act of fathering: "If he who broke the yoke of British burdens 'from the neck of the people' of this land, was hailed the country's deliverer, by what name shall we call him who secretly and almost unknown emancipated his 'bondmen and bondwomen'—became to them a father, and gave them an inheritance!"³¹ Allen's language not only demonstrates the flexibility of the paternal convention but also suggests the ambiguousness ("by what name," "secretly and unknown") of Washington's national legacy for African Americans. Of course, to accept chattel slavery almost without questioning was one thing. But as Edmund Burke remarked to the British Parliament in 1775, the patriarchs in the South were attached to liberty "with a higher and more stubborn spirit" than those of the North.³²

Southern slave owners knew what bondage meant and thus valued their own freedom, including the freedom to oppress others, much more strongly. "Such will be all masters of slaves, who are not slaves themselves," Burke reflected. "In such a people, the haughtiness of domination combines with the spirit of freedom, fortifies it, and renders it invincible."³³ George Washington was of that South, where ideals of liberty reinforced and were reinforced by a culture of buying, owning, and selling human beings. Furious that Britain was taxing the colonies without their consent, he had urged resistance. "No power upon earth can compel us to do otherwise," he wrote to Bryan Fairfax in August 1774, "till they have first reduced us to the most abject state of Slavery, that was ever designed for Mankind."³⁴ Among the founders, only Thomas Jefferson was worse off financially than Washington, yet upon his return to Monticello in 1793, he described himself as "the most blessed of the patriarchs" nonetheless.³⁵ The role Jefferson fashioned for himself as a republican patriarch clearly influenced his conduct as he moved through the world as a plantation master, father, grandfather, revolutionary, public figure, and finally elder statesman. At his home in Monticello Jefferson made the most of being a patriarch, ruling autocratically over his extended family, including his hundreds of slaves, because, as Annette Gordon-Reed and Peter S. Onuf have shown, that was where he seemed most in control of the world.³⁶

For Washington as much as for Jefferson and other patriarchs, a well-governed family was the foundation of republican self-government. Understanding the nation metaphorically in terms of a patriarchal family reminds us that Washington's America was not an egalitarian society. It was, in John G. A. Pocock's words, a society "consisting of an elite and a nonelite, in which the nonelite regard the elite, without too much resentment, as being of a superior status and culture to their own, and consider elite leadership in political matters to be something normal and natural."³⁷ In America, the colonial elite of merchants, lawyers, and landed gentry depended, not merely on slave labor and the exclusion of women from public life but also on a much larger class of artisanal producers, whose key values were personal independence, pride in their craft, and a measure of republican civic virtue. These values did not always square with the patricians' demand for respect and deference, but by and large this did not put too much strain on social harmony.[38] Only with the rise of the so-called "middle classes" did serious conflicts emerge. For, the "middle classes" or, rather, middle-class men, increasingly defined personality in terms of providing for oneself, the acquisition of money, and work. In fact, this meant a random switching between often monotonous jobs, depending on the market, and a continuous search for a direct way to happiness. It also meant fewer privileges, as relations between humans became more egalitarian. However, with money the only criterion to establish difference, these relations were neutralized, so that individuals became, in the words of Alexis de Tocqueville, "strangers one to the other."[39]

The rise of the middle classes marked a true sea change, one that not only put an end to a patrician world of aristocratic assumptions, heroic leadership, and powdered wigs and knee britches, but also increased the number of those in competition against each other. For these "self-made men," as they came to be identified, only success and failure counted.[40] The loss of fellow-feeling among members of the most commercially ridden society history has ever known correlated closely with two distinct phenomena: a surge of the homicide rate, both within the family and among unrelated adults (friends, acquaintances, and strangers), and the unraveling of family relations. "Fatherhood," regardless whether in terms of strictness or nurturance, whether patriarchal or more modern in style, no longer had a solid foundation to rest on. In the traditional patriarchal family, the father had assumed paternal authority. He was charged with the moral and spiritual growth of children; his orders may be disobeyed, but his advice was nevertheless held to be the most authoritative. With the rise of the middle classes, paternal authority was attenuated, "if not destroyed, [it was] at least impaired" because, following Tocqueville again, "the ties of filial obedience are relaxed day by day."[41] Of course, the relaxing of ties was the logical consequence of the decreasing presence of middle-class fathers in the house as the family ceased to be an economic unit. Increasingly, therefore, it was the mother, *not* the father, who molded the children's character. With the father away from home, the feelings of intimacy bred by the everyday give-and-take fell irrevocably by the wayside, leaving fathers outside the currents of feeling and establishing the mother as the emotional core of the family.[42]

These changes can be gleaned from private diaries and other historical records. The way the new middle-classes saw themselves and wanted others to see them was profoundly different, though. One only needs to take a look at Erastus Salisbury Field's painting *Joseph Moore and His Family* (c. 1839). Joseph Moore and his wife are shown nearly life-size, seated in gaily painted chairs and surrounded by four attentive children, their looks like little elves, with pointy ears and stubby fingers. The figures are stringently balanced, as are the features of the room, and yet the arrangement seems more companionate, the entire scene more sentimental. The difference from earlier, more patriarchal family arrangements (as, for instance, in Savage's *The Washington Family*) cannot be overlooked. Middle class also speaks from the sparse furniture, the absence of brocade and expensive draperies, and the prominence of the down-home carpet. Joseph Moore was a part-time traveling dentist and hatter, one of the beneficiaries of the market revolution, like other merchants, farmers, and professionals, including Field himself, who as an artisan-entrepreneur linked to artisans and craft production rather than to genius and the romantic conception of the artist.[43]

Field's painting stands out for representing the family as a figure of social cohesion. But

8. The Father of the Fatherless

Erastus Salisbury Field, *Joseph Moore and His Family* (about 1839), oil on canvas, 82⅜ × 93⅜ in. (Museum of Fine Arts, Boston, Gift of Maxim Karolik for the M. and M. Karolik Collection of American Paintings, 1815–1865, accession number 58.25).

the story of domestic happiness was, as Anne McClintock argues, a master narrative that pasted over the contradictions of actual families, erasing their relations to the "commodity market," to "politics," and even to "history proper."[44] In antebellum America, "the family" even became a metaphor that immunized masculinity against the threats of disempowerment by posing the image of former patriarchal glory as a microcosm of the nation. Field does this by arranging both his figures and the features of the rooms in a stringent balance. Photographers also worked with articulations of family and nation. And, in the words of Laura Wexler, they were "haunted" by the iconic image of George Washington.[45] In a daguerreotype by Gabriel Harrison, for instance, the artist's son, George Washington Harrison, embraces a Houdonesque bust of the Father of His Country. The boy, Pygmalion-like, and George Washington "commune across the generations in a physical relation that reflects both the fact of their shared names and the appearance of similar facial expressions around the mouth and eyes."[46] Two other early daguerreotypists, Albert Sands Southworth and Josiah Johnson Hawes also articulated the idea of the nation as filiation. In this instance, it is

Stuart's portrait of George Washington that is the focus of a child's attention, and the child is a girl, not a boy. As a girl, she does not inherit the metaphorical father's name, but as an American she stands on his level, an adopted child, and indeed is a reflection of the sainted ancestor, nonetheless. The viewer scans the expressions of the old and new Americans and compares them as one does the generations in a family portrait. And the intensity of the relation of these children to the metaphorical father shows that no matter what the actual configurations of the family—whether in the early national period or in the present—were like, the paradigm itself was already set.[47]

On closer examination, actual family configurations were much less idyllic than the diverse narratives: A "good father" in antebellum America was one who strictly guided his family based on the principles of "Christian living" and, as the following poem illustrates, held a great deal of paternal authority:

> The father gives his kind command.
> The mother joins, approves;
> The children will attentive stand.
> Then each obedient moves.[48]

Clearly in this poem from 1844 the father's chief responsibility within the family is that of a benevolent moral compass. What the poem does not say is that the Industrial Revolution radically altered the father's role, which became primarily defined as breadwinner. To a degree, fathers still offered moral guidance and possessed considerable authority, but that was not their first order of business any more. More often than not, economic logic and the mechanisms of industrial production limited a father's role to that of a supervisor or the ultimate dispenser of discipline. When the occupational ties between father and offspring became severed, children (especially sons), in order to become their own masters, began to claim their independence as a kind of natural right. And with the power and authority of fathers becoming disposable, fathers and sons became competitors, with far-reaching consequences: Whenever personal identity is defined in terms of success or failure, personal survival becomes a matter of minimizing loss. This includes minimizing the loss of the father. Even those who survived the merciless competitive pressures were unfit to be fathers. "Paternal neglect," a New England pastor warned in 1842, was causing "the ruin of many families."[49]

What also undermined patriarchal authority was the extraordinary number of first or second-generation Americans. For many, a farewell to the old country spelled a farewell to fathers as representatives of "the old." Indeed "the old" often was a liability. For the children of immigrants, a father's accent (or his total lack of English) made it more difficult for them to become integrated into society. Phrased differently, fathers (less so mothers) ceased to be useful role models for life in the outside. The diminished importance of fathers was not restricted to immigrants and their children. The new economy and new ideas of individuality generally led to a sharp contraction of fatherhood as a social role, a shrinking of paternal requirements. For children, this meant that an identifiable stage in their personal development from childhood to adulthood was missing. (What, for example, do we know about Natty Bumppo's parentage or, for that matter, that of Herman Melville's Ishmael? As if to compensate for the absence, "initiation novels" would later flourish, from Dreiser to Salinger, with Sinclair Lewis's Babbitt a prime example of a man who's not had any youth.[50])

"I have no father—nor mother," Edgar Allan Poe is quoted as saying as early as 1829. Six years later, Poe bemoans the fact that he has never known parental love: "I [...] never knew [my mother]—and never knew the affection of a father."[51] There can be no doubt that

8. The Father of the Fatherless

both the early death of his mother and the absence of a father left traces in Poe's psyche, much as they impacted on his writings. There are, for instance, no fathers in Poe's major works; nor are there mothers, or parents. Such figures are conspicuously absent, expunged, perhaps even denied. One can only speculate but it is not improbable that Poe's perceived fatherlessness drew him to orphan imagery, much as it may have prompted him to praise James Kirke Paulding's saccharine version of George Washington's life in the *Southern Literary Messenger*. Poe certainly was much less enthusiastic about J. T. Headley's *Washington and His Generals* (1847), which was all about the romantic aspects of warfare, though he might have been drawn to what Horatio Hastings Weld had written in his preface to the *Pictorial Life of George Washington* (1845): "The first word of infancy should be mother, the second father, and the third WASHINGTON."[52]

Paternal neglect no doubt helped to revive the memory of the Father of His Country, who became a veritable "father of the fatherless."[53] Indeed, fatherlessness spawned a pressing desire for permanence, continuity, and stability—qualities that speak from every ounce of Horatio Greenough's 12-ton marble statue of George Washington, commissioned in 1832, the year of the centennial of the founder's birth. Greenough wanted the statue to represent Washington as an exemplar of the classical ideals of liberty, democracy, and knowledge. Installed in the Capitol Rotunda after its completion in 1840, the gigantic statue, which depicts the Father of His Country wearing a tunic and a chest-bearing pleated toga, sits atop a granite pedestal and base. Greenough had modeled his Washington on the classic statuary of ancient Greece, specifically on Phidias's statue of Zeus in Olympia, a reminder that Greece was the cradle of democracy. Carvings on the sides depict the Greek god Apollo and an infant Hercules. Small flanking figures of an American Indian and Christopher Columbus represent the New and the Old World. The most striking symbol, however, is the sword in Washington's outstretched left hand. It calls to mind the fact that after he led the country to victory in the War of Independence, Washington selflessly gave back his power.

Horatio Greenough, George Washington Sculpture, 136 × 102 × 82½ in., 1840 (Smithsonian American Art Museum, transfer from the U.S. Capitol).

Altogether, the statue's style, the attributes of toga and tunic, plus the allusion to the Cincinnatus legend evoke the classical heroism that embodied Washington's presidency and that had found a lasting articulation in the sculptures of Jean-Antoine Houdon (Greenough's commission specified that he must use Houdon's bust likeness as a model), though in this instance we may justifiably see the last gasp of neoclassicist art. Unsurprisingly, therefore, the statue was embroiled in controversy from the beginning. While many visitors admired the "loftiness" of Greenough's vision, others were scandalized by the rendering of a semi-nude Father of His Country. A New York politician by the name of Philip Hone, for instance, attacked the artist for depicting Washington "undressed, with a napkin lying in his lap." A tourist even found that "some heathen had taken the pains to climb up and insert a large 'plantation' cigar between the lips of the *pater patriae*.... I could not help thinking ... that if Washington had looked less like the Olympic Jove, and more like himself, not even the vagabond who perpetrated the trick of the cigar would have dared or dreamed of such a desecration." Unsurprisingly, one of Greenough's friends noted: "This magnificent production of genius does not seem to be appreciated at its full value in this metropolis."[54]

Mimicry of the ancient classics—together with a penchant for gigantism—persisted as a mode of depiction, though. A year after the centennial of Washington's birth, President James Madison, Chief Justice John Marshall and others founded the Washington National Monument Society for the purpose of building a monument to the nation's first president that would be "unparalleled in the world."[55] "Unparalleled" it became in many instances. The monument was never built. Nor were Washington's remains removed from Mount Vernon to Richmond, where, in putting into effect the congressional resolution of 1799, a suitable mausoleum was to be erected in 1816.[56] The project of removing the remains was debated again by Congress in 1832. This time, the Father of His Country was to be interred in Washington, D.C., with appropriate ceremonies on the hundredth anniversary of his birth. When Congress finally attempted to take action, it was blocked by Washington's relatives. Nor was Congress alone in debating various motions; citizens at large also made suggestions. In 1816 a contributor to the *North American Review* considered the possibilities of an arch, a pyramid, and other architectural forms, but decided that a column was the proper memorial for George Washington, because only in that form could America surpass the whole world. The proposal too came to nothing.[57]

What we call the Washington Monument was designed by architect Robert Mills, who also designed the Treasury Building and the General Post Office in Washington, D.C. Mills's original plan provided for a 600-foot Egyptian-style obelisk ringed by thirty 100-foot columns to enclose a rotunda, intended to serve as a pantheon of the nation's heroes. A figure of George Washington in a triumphal chariot was to sit atop the obelisk. As Mills also hoped that Washington's remains be transferred to the monument, a crypt was reserved for Washington's tomb. Mills also submitted a second, more modest design. Neither design was ultimately used. In 1845, a final design was agreed upon, and the cornerstone was laid on July 4, 1848, with President James Polk and other dignitaries attending. As on previous occasions, the Society solicited donations, this time from banks, because that's where they thought the money was. They were mistaken, and construction stopped again in 1854. With only one third of the structure completed, the architect died in 1855. In 1859, the Washington National Monument Society went bankrupt after much squabbling. During the second phase of building, 1876–84, Congress appropriated funding, though on a more modest scale. The Monument was finally dedicated on February 21, 1885, just one day before Washington's birthday. The speech made at the dedication was by Robert C. Winthrop, who had also made the speech in 1848. At just over 555 feet, the Washington Monument became the tallest building in the world—until the Eiffel Tower was completed a mere four months later.[58]

The long history of the Washington Monument no doubt kept the hero's memory green for successive generations, though in itself the Monument is a mere abstraction, which does nothing to bring George Washington closer to the people. Today, visitors can at least see a statue of Washington, which was added in 1994, and they can assume the place of the Father of His Country and, from the summit, survey the whole scenery of national grandeur spread out below them. Or else, they can stand in naïve awe before the Monument, like Jefferson Smith in Frank Capra's *Mr. Smith Goes to Washington* (1939), released in the year of the 150th anniversary of Washington's inauguration. In the antebellum period, the Washington Monument was still unfinished, and Americans had to look elsewhere to salve their longing for permanence, continuity, and stability. Henry Wadsworth Longfellow, for instance, wrote about the colonial mansion that Washington used for his Continental Army headquarters at Cambridge, Massachusetts, early in the Revolutionary war:

> Once, ah, once within these walls,
> One whom memory oft recalls,
> The Father of his country dwelt.[59]

Longfellow's lines of 1845 are dripping wet with nostalgia, though his motives were primarily didactic. Insight was to be gained into Washington's noble character by means of the written word. Such a usage of poetry was the perfect response to Thomas Carlyle's disparaging remark, in one of his lectures on heroes, that Washington was a "no very immeasurable man" who "prefers planting cabbages."[60] Just as didactic as Longfellow's lines are visual images, such as Francis William Edmond's *The Image Peddler* (1844), where a man points to a cheap plaster bust of Washington for the edification of a child. The attitude of setting Washington up as a moral example also is embodied in an illustration in John Frost's *Pictorial Life of George Washington* (1844), where a child pays homage to the national ancestor by hugging a bust of the "Father of His Country." Frost's eminently popular book likely provided the source for the first photographs that Americans came to see in the 1840s, by Gabriel Harrison, as well as by Albert Sands Southworth and Josiah Johnson Hawes, all representing Washington as the Father of His Country, with the nation as his "family."[61] This view disregarded the contradictions of actual families, yet it was characteristic of mid-century cultural ideas about the meaning of paternity. Fathers, the historian Stephen M. Frank found, "were being urged by the 1850s to abandon an authoritarian posture in the family in favor of tender ties with children."[62] The so-called Christian Fatherhood Movement, too, at the time propagated the belief that "fathers owed their children more than material support."[63]

Unsurprisingly, all kinds of private and public organizations made use of Washington's name and likeness to advance their causes, faithfully following the admonition from the Book of Proverbs: "[E]nter not into the fields of the fatherless ... [f]or their redeemer is mighty; he shall plead their cause with thee" (Prov. 23:10–11). The leading temperance society of the 1840s called itself the Washingtonians, linking the Father of His Country to the crusade against intoxicating liquors. Evangelical Christians deployed the image of Washington praying in the snow at Valley Forge. George Lippard likewise used the iconic image in one of the fourteen "legends" collected in *Washington and His Men* (1849), an odd mixture of heroic action and mystic miracle working. Lippard will be remembered also for imagining, in *Paul Ardenheim, the Monk of Wissahikon* (1848), Washington's consecration, in the first hours of the year 1774, as the nation's deliverer. The episode is set in a half-ruined monastery near Philadelphia, where an ancient preacher has Washington kneel before an altar to receive his "mission," while his daughter places a "crown of fadeless laurel" on his head and her brother buckles a sword on his side.[64]

In 1854, *Graham's Magazine* began its serial of a Washington biography and could immediately boast of a host of new subscriptions. Artists and writers too began to domesticate the Father of His Country, rendering his family life as noteworthy as his public deeds. In 1851, Junius Brutus Stearns completed his *Washington as a Farmer, at Mount Vernon*, which marks the beginning of a long interest in the estate which culminated in its purchase by the Mount Vernon Ladies' Association in 1858. Stearns's composition depicts Washington tending to the management of his land, representing the Father of His Country as "first farmer of his country." But what a farmer! Stearns's Washington is a well-dressed planter with a tricorn, striking a "domestic Lansdowne" pose as he speaks to his overseer. Nearby, slaves are seen harvesting wheat or resting. A small girl and a boy, Washington's adopted children, complete the handsome group. The family mansion and the Potomac River are seen in the background.[65] Perhaps in response to Stearns's work, Nathaniel Currier in in 1852 published a color lithograph titled *Washington at Mount Vernon*.[66] Currier's scene is more rustic than Stearns's, with a Washington on horseback inspecting his holdings. But as in Stearns's painting, slaves are part of an arrangement that in the border of the work is described as "the most healthy, the most useful and the most noble employment of man." The words are actually Washington's, the patriarch's, but they have an even stranger ring when read in the context of George Fitzhugh's assertion, in an 1856 book, of the moralism of the slaveholder: "His whole life is spent in providing for the minutest wants of others.... Hence he is the least selfish of men ... is not the head of a large family almost always kind and benevolent? And is not the slaveholder the head of the largest family?"[67]

Pro-slavery advocates often used such rhetoric in the 1850s and 1860s in justifying the "peculiar institution," emphasizing, by way of evidence, Washington's status as slave-owner. Certainly this was not the intention of Lambert Sachs, who in 1854 painted *General Washington at Prayer in Valley Forge*, an idealistic work that added foliage to the naked tree of winter in order to conceal from Washington an observer who accidentally passes by. The work appeared as a lithograph by Peter Kramer in the same year. Between 1849 and 1856, Junius Brutus Stearns produced a cycle of scenes from Washington's life, which included military scenes (*Washington as a Captain in the French and Indian War*), but also *The Marriage of Washington to Martha Custis* and *Washington on His Deathbed*. Stearns's cycle of paintings was widely engraved for home display, its sentimental poses especially of women, together with the utterly unheroic scene of a nuptial ceremony, appealing to a public feeding on the popular monthly *Godey's Lady's Book*. In order to present George and Martha Washington as the ideal Christian couple, Stearns set the wedding not at the Custis residence in New Kent County (where it had taken place) but in a church. Even Washington's mother was drawn into the "cult of domesticity." Manuals for young mothers held her up as the ideal to be attained, even if they were more or less silent about her child-raising practices or her strained relationship with her son. And in Margaret C. Conkling's best-selling *Memoirs of Mother and Wife of Washington* (1850), both Mary and Martha are offered as staples of popular culture—as was George, on a whole range of commercial products, from printing textiles and crockery to razors and buttons, kidney oil, chewing tobacco, even apples as well as other healthy and nourishing food, advertised, for instance, by Kellogg Company in the mid–1840s.[68] To modern eyes, such practices seem strange, even alien. It is true that few of these antebellum productions truly humanized George Washington. But they only replaced one ideal (the Federalist citizen soldier and republican statesman-cum-entrepreneur) with another (the Christian family of the antebellum era).

IV

From the Civil War through the Bicentennial of 1932

During the antebellum period, literary prospectors like Weems, Lippard, and their imitators, Robert Spring and his ilk, painters like Stearns, orators and advertisers—they all supplied a demand for Washingtoniana, which both reflected and reinforced a sense of national identity, a pride in common history, and an active political awareness among the people. The latter was blatantly exploited, for instance, by *The Dollar Weekly Times*. The paper, which was published in Cincinnati, Ohio, in the 1850s championed the American Party, popularly known as the Know Nothing Party. In a column under a portrait of Washington, the editor in March 1855 proclaimed the nation's first president as "the first Know Nothing." He also printed Washington's portrait with the party's electoral ticket in the presidential elections of 1856.[1] In the elections, the American Party's nominee, Millard Fillmore, lost against Democrat James Buchanan, as did Republican candidate John C. Frémont. But politicians had tried to make people happy by invoking the Washington image long before that. The Whig Party of the 1830s and 1840s, for instance, claimed Washington's mantle for its presidential candidates. Whigs, successors of sorts to the defunct Federalists, claimed to espouse nonpartisan politics, embodied by candidates like General William Henry Harrison, the pro-slavery governor of the Indiana Territory who in 1809 negotiated the Treaty of Fort Wayne and who in 1840 would be elected President of the United States.

To Democrats, George Washington had much less appeal; Democrats preferred to liken their candidates of the 1840s and 1850s to Andrew Jackson. Washington's appeal resurged when regional tensions increased at mid-century, and both sides agreed in using Washington's name "as a charm against sectional turmoil and disunion."[2] During the congressional debates over the legislation that would emerge as the Compromise of 1850, for instance, Henry Clay proposed that Congress purchase the manuscript of the Farewell Address. Contemporary Americans, Clay argued, could learn from Washington's words "amid the discordance and ungrateful sounds of disunion and discord which assail our ears in every part of this country and in both halls of Congress." As Clay interpreted the Address, the Father of His Country had warned his children "to beware of sectional division, to beware of demagogues, to beware of the consequences of indulging a spirit of disunion." Clay's famous opponent in the debate, John C. Calhoun, summoned his own Washington, as "one of us—a slaveholder and a planter. We have studied his history, and find nothing in it to justify submission to wrong."[3] Northerners were unconvinced. Perhaps Calhoun and his allies had gotten Washington's history all wrong. But how to prove it? Best, to let Washington speak for himself.

In an article titled "Washington's Vision," published by one Wesley Bradshaw (a pseudonym for Charles Wesley Alexander) in the *Philadelphia Inquirer* on June 24, 1861, the Father of His Country was made to do just this. Bradshaw claimed that this important "incident of Washington's life" had come from an old veteran, whom he had encountered on Philadelphia's Independence Square two years before. According to the story, Washington, busy writing letters at his desk, at once saw a "singularly beautiful female" standing in the room, ordering the "Son of the Republic" to "look and learn." Washington did as told and saw a celestial being wearing a crown emblazoned "Union" and slamming a flag bearing the words "Remember, ye are brethren!" into the ground. A truly apocalyptic scenario follows, at the end of which the angel booms an admonition: "Let every child of the Republic learn to live for his God, his Land, and Union!" Washington was convinced that he "had been shown the birth, progress, and destiny of the Republic of the United States. In Union she will have her strength, in Disunion her destruction."[4] Unsurprisingly, "Washington's Vision" was followed by *Jeff. Davis' Confession* and, in February 1862, by another episode of Washington's ghostly adventures, in which the founder gives his blessing to General Sherman that he may confound and finally defeat the Confederates. None of these visions had ever happened, of course, but Northern newspapers reprinted them several times. In 1864, "Washington's Vision" appeared in pamphlet form, with a promotional blurb by Edward Everett. Nor did its popularity end with the conclusion of the Civil War. It was reprinted in 1871, in 1877, and again in 1880, this time with a variation on Washington's final words: the warning about disunion was omitted.[5]

9

North and South

Disunion was still topical in 1856, when Oliver Wendell Holmes asked Americans to "hear the Father's dying voice," which admonished them to "'Love your country first of all! / Listen not to idle questions / If its bands may be untied; / Doubt the patriot whose suggestions / Strive a nation to divide!'"[1] Holmes's ode was expressly written for "Washington's Birthday." A year later, Henry T. Tuckerman suggested that the day become a national holiday, as such a day might induce "a unanimity of feeling and of rites, which shall fuse and mold into one pervasive emotion the divided hearts of the country."[2] Americans had celebrated Washington's birthday long before it became a federal holiday in 1879. The centennial of his birth in 1832 had seen festivities all across the nation, and Congress established a joint committee to arrange for the occasion. The committee at first invited Chief Justice John Marshall to deliver an oration. The seventy-seven-year-old Marshall—too frail to physically speak—declined "the honor proposed," regretting his inability to mark "that great event." In his stead, Senator Daniel Webster at a public dinner in New York spoke of the new age that had begun with America's Independence, and Washington standing "at the commencement of a new era, as well as at the head of the New World."[3]

A generation and the nullification movement in South Carolina later, there was renewed urgency. Webster's expounding of the principles Washington had laid down in his Farewell Address (about half of Webster's speech was concerned with that document, culminating in the admonition that "the Union was the great object of [Washington's] thoughts") had not had the desired effect. Nor had his warning, delivered in an 1850 speech, that "there can be no such thing as a peaceable secession," been heeded. Henry Tuckerman likewise had wasted his breath with his suggestion that Washington's birthday be made a national holiday. But a year into the Civil War, a memorial from the mayor and citizens of Philadelphia prompted the House and Senate to commemorate Washington's birthday by reading aloud the Farewell Address in a joint session.[4] In other instances, too, use of Washington's name and image reflected the two regions' different self-images.

To Northerners, Washington was an unequivocal symbol of union, the visible embodiment of the nation. In 1855, Rufus Griswold described Washington at the Constitutional Convention: "He is the central attractive figure, and wields a mighty moral influence over these statesmen, not unlike in its effects that which he exercised over the officers of the army. *He binds them into union.*"[5] Griswold's words were probably known by Junius Brutus Stearns, who in 1856 completed a painting, *Washington as Statesman, at the Constitutional Convention*, an appropriate symbol at a time when growing sectionalism threatened the fabric of the republic.[6] Equally appropriate is an 1860 lithograph by E. Deschaux, which shows Washington in his general's uniform hovering over Mount Vernon and his tomb, and below the U.S. Capitol, as the symbol of national unity.[7] The year before, the *Cosmopolitan*

Art Journal had as its frontispiece for the June issue an engraving titled *The American Eagle. Guarding the Spirit of Washington*. The print, which was dedicated to the Mount Vernon Ladies' Association, shows a recumbent profile of Washington silhouetted against a radiant sun; the American Eagle watches from up among the clouds.[8]

The year 1861 began with the Union disintegrating. The wrenching experience gave rise to artistic responses unmatched in presidential iconography. The firm of Middleton, Strobridge & Co. of Cincinnati, Ohio, for instance, in January 1861 published a print titled "The American Union," which is truly unique for bringing together the symbolism of the presidency, the Union, and the American nation. In the center of the design, the portrait of George Washington, the first president, is surrounded by portraits of his successors, including Lincoln, who was as yet to be inaugurated. Around the presidents, a cordon of shields bearing the arms of all states affirms the unity of the presidency and the states. The flags and shield above the presidential display underline the symbolism with the word "Union," while angels are holding the banner of "Peace" and the national eagle spreads its protective wings. Below, Columbia stands over the continent of North America, her shield emblazoned "The American Union Forever," a prospect of harmony reinforced by depictions of peaceful Indians and frontier settlers. The City of Washington with the Capitol and the Washington Monument reaching skyward completes the peaceful panorama, which only the preservation of the Union could preserve.

Northerners bent on the contemporary notion of Washington's spirit animating the nation also would quote from overly Federalist portions of the Farewell Address and point to Washington's stand against the spread of slavery in the Northwest Territory. Anything that alluded to Washington's "Southernness" was dutifully avoided, even expunged, such as any hints at his origin from Virginia's planter aristocracy, which necessarily would have suggested chattel slavery. In reproductions of Edward Savage's *The Washington Family*, for instance, the liveried servant, who was an African American, was simply painted out of the picture, a gesture that no doubt was intended to placate abolitionists.[9] Equally sanitized was the Washington disseminated in public lectures, which customarily presented him as a powerful example and stimulus to moral reform. "There is a Virtue in the looks of a Great Man," Rembrandt Peale said at the beginning of the lecture with which he toured the country in 1857 to 1858.[10] Peale's tour coincided with a tour by Massachusetts orator Edward Everett. Everett's oration on "The Character of Washington" became hugely successful; he gave it no fewer than 137 times from March 1856 until the spring of 1861, most spectacularly on February 22, 1856, when seven thousand people waited inside New York City's Academy of Music to listen, eventually filling the aisles and part of the stage so as to share in the great event.

In the lecture, Washington is presented as a hero for *all* Americans, "the beacon of light which guided the country through that broken and stormy sea" of the Revolutionary War. This had been "an age of great men and great events," but "the star of Washington shines the brightest and in the highest sphere," full of "a latent power we have not measured, a mysterious beauty of character [and] a moral fascination." Altogether, memory of Washington, that "model of a patriot President," is "founded upon a life of services to his country and mankind, without a parallel in history." To show respect to his memory is a sacred duty of all "citizens of America." The oration thus ends with a plea that North and South cling together in memory of Washington and his principles, especially the exhortations he had included in his Farewell Address, to not let the Union break down. The disintegration of the Union, Everett warns, is a "great woe to our beloved country, [a] catastrophe for the cause

The American Union. Lithograph, 28 × 22 in., published by Middleton, Strobridge & Co. of Cincinnati, Ohio, January 1861 (Library of Congress Prints and Photographs Division).

of national freedom." Should it happen, the bells of the ships passing Mount Vernon "will strike the requiem of constitutional liberty for us," though at the time, 1856, Everett was still hopeful that "that sorrow and shame shall never be."[11]

If Everett hoped that memory of George Washington might help stave off the impending sectional conflict, he was wrong. Nor did Everett see that in the naming of the Father of His Country also was the strength and beauty of a successful revolution. Many Southerners, John C. Calhoun included, saw the Revolution of 1776 as the first step towards the second American revolution, the secession from the Union. The view that the South must rebel against Northern oppression even as Washington had done against the British was to lend legitimacy to this momentous event—both morally and under international law. John Richter Jones, author of *Slavery Sanctioned by the Bible*, produced in 1858 a Revolutionary romance in which Washington is called "rebel" at least on four occasions. An anonymous piece of newspaper verse, titled "Rebels" and published shortly after hostilities had begun, presents the conviction that Washington belonged to the South particularly well: "Rebels! 'tis our family name—/ Our father, Washington, / Was the arch-rebel in the fight / And gave the name to us—a right / Of father unto son."[12]

Everett's hopes for a peaceful solution to the conflict may have failed, though his endeavors helped to raise funds for the rescue and purchase of Mount Vernon, which by the time was rapidly deteriorating. In 1858, the estate became the property of a new organization, the Mount Vernon Ladies' Association of the Union. Founded by Ann Pamela Cunningham, a South Carolinian, it had started as "a Southern affair altogether," but financial necessity soon made it more inclusive. During the Civil War, therefore, Mount Vernon was considered "neutral territory." Washington's home was too sacred to be used as a war-trophy for either side. Its new owners even insisted that soldiers cover their uniforms and leave their weapons outside the grounds. Over the years, and in time for the Centennial Exposition of 1876, Mount Vernon acquired the warmth and personality of a colonial home. It became a popular and much-visited resort, a wholesome contrast to the nearby capital city, as the protagonists of Henry Adams's novel *Democracy* would find.[13]

In itself Mount Vernon was only the wooden house of a gentleman farmer, but the knowledge that George Washington had lived and died there transformed the place into a shrine of national patriotism, a true *lieu de memoire* in Pierre Nora's sense, the subject of numerous paintings and engravings, and the place where Ms. Cunningham's plea to resist progress (that "one spot, in this grand country of ours, be saved from change") was read at every annual meeting of the Mount Vernon Ladies' Association of the Union. The Association still owns the place and continues its work of preservation and restoration, including building on its impressive collections for research on Washington, as well as holding symposia and lectures. (The website attracts millions of hits every year.) From 1999 onwards, the organization was also raising funds for a museum that was to significantly cover Washington's public life.[14] In their original fundraising efforts, the Association had featured another famous orator of the time, William Lowndes Yancey. Yancey presented Washington as the southern patriot in much the same terms as Calhoun had done. And while Everett in 1860 became the vice-presidential candidate of the Constitutional Union party, Yancey became a fire-eating secessionist. Washington's "true legacy," the one-time congressman from Alabama thundered, was not "fealty to government" but that "immortal, new-born, American principle," that governments are made for the benefit of the governed, and that it was not merely the people's right but even their duty to overthrow a government that fails to fulfill its purpose.[15]

The eventual dismemberment of the Union did not happen overnight but was the culminating act in a long drama. There had been considerable social and cultural differences between North and South from the beginning of settlement, differences that did not disappear with the foundation of the United States. The breakup of the Union thus can be seen as an intensification and radicalization of existing differences. Even so, the conventional image of a "progressive" North pitted against a "backward" South, distanced from modern society and the world scene, is too simplistic. The South championed slavery, and it did so before the world, yet it was championing a backward system. That coerced laborers lack any incentive to improve performance had been known at least since Adam Smith's *The Wealth of Nations* (1776). The knowledge may help explain why the South also built a euphemistic defense of its society by fabricating cultural myths about its alleged superiority to the North. Slavery was no longer presented as a "necessary evil" but became a powerful argument for the South's superiority over the system of industrial capitalism in the North, an argument that was buttressed by all kinds of philosophical, sociological, and theological refinements.

The perceived cultural divide eventually became so great that some leading southerners said that the Civil War was not about slavery but about radically different peoples. "The people of the North and those of the South are distinct and separate," a southern correspondent for the *New York Herald*, the nation's most widely read newspaper, wrote. "They think differently; they spring from a different stock; they are different every way; they cannot coalesce." How could they, when the various abolitionist movements in their religious or moral fervor did not or did not want to see that the North's industrial progress had been largely financed by Southern capital. Southern leaders gloated that many of the ships used in the international slave trade were built in the North, and that even abolitionists sometimes participated, as in the case of a slave ship run by someone who was the owner of an abolition newspaper in Bangor, Maine. Politically, too, the South had been dominant from the beginning of the republic. Slave owners occupied the presidency for about three quarters of the nation's first sixty-four years. And two longserving chief justices of the Supreme Court, John Marshall and Roger Taney, likewise were slave owners. It is no surprise that in the Southern view the North was hypocritical, fanatical, and suffering from a loss of memory.[16]

There had been neither hypocrisy nor historical amnesia in Abraham Lincoln's ruminations, in 1855, on the moral wrong of slavery. Lincoln began by recalling the time "when we were the political slaves of King George, and wanted to be free."[17] His comment that the "self evident truth" that "'all men are created equal'" had become a "'self-evident lie'" is, of course, to the point. It was Lincoln's aim, as President, of halting the spread of slavery that led to the South's secession and the outbreak of war. The North did not confine itself to various forms of religious and moral upgrading, though. There also emerged a new economic self-confidence that no longer relied on Southern capital and, ultimately, an industrial production that would prove essential for the war effort (raw iron, rifles, guns, and cannon, ammunition, fabrics, clothes, etc.). At the outbreak of the Civil War, the North's material and technological superiority was breathtaking.[18] Nonetheless, once the first shots had been fired at Fort Sumter on April 12, 1861, each side was in desperate need for money for the war effort. Less than a year after Lincoln's election to the presidency, his portrait was printed on Northern currency notes—on 14 million of them, outnumbering by far images of Washington. The new notes were typical for war times—they demonstrated the North's sovereignty, internally as well as externally. The message the notes, in denomination of $10, conveyed was utterly unambiguous—the master in the house is Abraham Lincoln.

The Confederacy responded by printing on the currency a portrait of its president, Jefferson Davis. They did not forget the nation's founder, though. George Washington was eminently present at the swearing-in of the Confederate administration in 1862. Not only did the ceremony take place in Richmond, Virginia, on Washington's birthday, February 22. It also took place on Capitol Square, under the Washington Monument of which Thomas

Crawford's colossal equestrian statue is the centerpiece. For the statue's inauguration, Alfred Mitchell wrote an epic poem in couplets, concluding in these words: "Princeton was thy jewel—Monmouth was thy crown; / But what completes thy glory, is thy battle at Yorktown!"[19] Verse written by James Barron Hope and John R. Thompson was also written for the occasion. Thompson, an editor of the *Southern Literary Messenger*, even made a plea for national unity. Asking what the purpose of the ceremony was, he answered: "'T is that we here in gratitude renew / The patriot-vows to country ever due, / And on this holy altar firmly swear / The blessed compact never to impair."[20] And Virginia Governor John Wise, speaking the name of Washington, exclaimed at the ceremony: "Magic name! If none other under Heaven can draw us to each other, that talisman can touch the chords of unison, and clasp us hand to hand, and bind us heart to heart, in the kindred heirship of one Patriot Father ... for, in the very naming of that name, there is ... the strength and beauty of *National Union*."[21]

Another reverential naming occurs in the pages of Morrison Heady's book *The Farmer Boy, and How He Became Commander-In-Chief*. In a crucial scene the book's protagonist, Uncle Juvinell, removes from the wall a dusty old picture of the nation's first President, announcing to a gathering of his young wards: "This, my cherubs ... is the portrait of the good and great Washington, who is called the Father of our Country." After silently studying the picture for some moments, the children speak, identifying Washington's farewell address to the army, his sword, his impressive height and stature, his charger, even his tomb at Mount Vernon. A young girl of seven has the last word: "How kind and good he looks out of his eyes, just like father!" Heady's usage of the Washington picture (which according to Mark Thistlethwaite cannot be identified) is a good illustration of the role art played in perpetuating the real and mythic image of George Washington, who at the height of the Civil War is cast as "Father of His Country," which of course signifies union. As we learn from the introduction to Heady's book, which was published in Boston in 1864:

> In this period of mighty struggles and issues, when our nation is groaning and travailing in pain to bring forth a future of surpassing renown and grandeur, it is important to inspire the hearts of American youth by the noblest examples of patriotism and virtue. And such is WASHINGTON, the "Father of His Country." It is best that the young of this battling age should study his character and emulate his deeds.[22]

The nation that emerged from the crucible of the Civil War, however, had less need for an awesome, remote, and largely unreal Father as its symbol of nationality or national unity. Instead, images of Abraham Lincoln began to occupy a larger space in the American psyche. This is evident, for instance, in the number of books and articles published. Baker's *Bibliotheca Washingtoniana* lists ninety-eight for the 1850s, thirty-nine for the 1860s, and just over thirty for the 1870s and 1880s. Reverence for Lincoln already set in during the presidential campaign, when he was hailed as "our Prairie King." The title "King" would have been impossible for Washington, the icon of republicanism, but for Lincoln it spelt natural nobility and leadership. Lincoln was seen as a man of the people, "No gentleman, like Washington," as the poet Richard Henry Stoddard would later write. Following Lincoln's assassination in 1865, however, there was a resurgence of tradition, with the martyred president explicitly represented as a "A second Washington! / So great in every virtuous plan."[23] Elevated to the role of Savior of His Country, Lincoln was expected to "affirm and reassert the principles of Washington." Praise of the Father of His Country was somewhat disingenuous, as it effectively broke Washington's unique hold on the nation's affections. "Mt. Vernon and Springfield will henceforth be kindred shrines," one eulogist declared.[24]

Bringing into the world a second national shrine also was symptomatic of the rapid transformation of American society in the post-bellum era. The transformation weakened or destroyed the social patterns for which "old" traditions had been designed, producing new ones to which they were not applicable. So large and rapid were the changes on the demand or the supply side of traditions that it seems perfectly legitimate to speak, with Eric Hobsbawm, of a "particular assiduity" in the business of "inventing" traditions during the post–Civil War period. Hobsbawm distinguishes three types of invented traditions, which overlap: (a) those that establish or symbolize social cohesion or the membership of groups, real or artificial communities; (b) those that establish or legitimize institutions, status, or relations of authority; (c) those whose main purpose is socialization, the inculcation of beliefs, value systems, and conventions of behavior.[25] Clearly portraits of the nation's presidents and other public symbols, from the heraldic Eagle to Liberty and Columbia, but also verbal symbols such as the phrase "United States of America" belong to type (a) as they establish or symbolize social cohesion or group membership. A walk through the Rotunda of the Capitol has a similar effect. Gazing upward to the dome, visitors see George Washington floating far overhead, a life-sized and heavenly vision that makes it possible to look up to the Father of His Country figuratively as well as quite literally.

Constantino Brumidi's *The Apotheosis of George Washington* unites the founder of the United States with the deities of ancient Rome. The old General and first President sits in majesty, like Greenough's Zeus, except that he is wearing the attire of his own period. He is flanked on the right by the Goddess of Liberty and on the left by a winged figure of Victory sounding a trumpet and holding a palm frond aloft in a symbol of victory. Thirteen female figures stand in a semi-circle around the nation's founder, representing the thirteen original states. On the outer ring of the canopy, six allegorical groupings surround him, representing Agriculture, Arts and Sciences, Commerce, War, Mechanics, and Marine, classical images that triumphantly illustrate American values.[26] In post-bellum America, Brumidi's "apotheosis" fresco, which dates from 1865, served as a powerful symbol of the immortalization of the country's hero. Both the majestic scale and the work's public placement were intended as a measure of the esteem in which Washington was held. (The Brumidi fresco was also a deliberate counterpoint to the modest scale of "apotheosis" compositions engraved in the aftermath of Washington's death. Indeed, Brumidi's figure of the hero is based on Greenough's colossal statue executed two decades earlier.) Paintings and sculptures of Washington's celestial rise were soon to be found in living rooms and civic halls across the country. Ironically, a portrait of Washington also hung in the box in Ford's Theater in which Lincoln was assassinated. The martyred president was also instantly apotheosized, rising to an equal footing with America's first president.

When Lincoln joined Washington as a talisman of American virtue, his image began to attract its own apocryphal elements which reinforced America's ideas about itself. Yet Washington's myth was not diminished. If Lincoln was placed next to Washington in the pantheon of great American leaders, the latter was frequently invoked to validate the canonization of the former, and the two leaders were viewed as natural compatriots, even complements: The figure of Lincoln addressed the issues of race and equality and better contained the frontier mythos than could that of Washington, who rather encompassed conceptions of "liberty," even as Washington might still have suggested to both North and South a unity and commonality in *spirit* that Lincoln had only helped effect in physical and political terms.[27] In the following illustration, Currier and Ives picture Washington and Lincoln standing before the glowing flame of liberty on a monument adorned with the

Washington and Lincoln. The Father and the Saviour of Our Country. **Hand-colored lithograph. Currier & Ives, 1865 (Library of Congress Prints and Photographs Division).**

American eagle and the shield of union. Standing slightly taller than Lincoln, Washington is shown shaking Lincoln's hand, while raising his left hand in a gesture of blessing. The rolled document in Lincoln's left hand may be presumed to be the Emancipation Proclamation. Thus, the lithograph documents both Washington's critical role in establishing the nation and Lincoln's struggle to preserve it.[28]

Abraham Lincoln was not only seen as the nation's savior but also, most famously in Richard Henry Stoddard's "Horatian Ode" of 1865, as his "country's father," a title that until then had been Washington's alone. Stoddard was one of the first to articulate an essential contrast in the popular images of Washington and Lincoln when he speaks of "The People of whom he was one: / No gentleman, like Washington, / (Whose bones, methinks, make room, / To have him in their tomb!)"[29] The acceptance of Lincoln as Washington's peer marks the end of what the German historian Michael Butter has termed the "Washington-Code," that is, representation of George Washington as a *republican* hero. That model began with Washington's heroization, in response to the needs of a newly independent nation. Until the Civil War, many presidents were represented as heroes in the identical molding, a few even explicitly as "new" or "second" Washingtons. Both John Adams and Thomas Jefferson, Washington's immediate successors, were hailed as "Worthy of him who laid the high-souled band / Which wrought deliverance for this wide-spread land, / Immortal WASHINGTON!" After the War of 1812, Washington-style hero worship was reserved for presidents who had distinguished themselves militarily, such as, most notably, Andrew Jackson, the hero of New Orleans and, equally important, the self-styled modern Cincinnatus. "When smiling Peace check'd War's fell rage / He sought the tranquil Hermitage," a pro–Jackson poem proclaimed in the campaign of 1828. And in "The Battle of New Orleans" (1825), Jackson is even described as "Like WASHINGTON, thron'd in the heart of the nation, / The same in his virtues, the same in his station."[30]

The Whig Party, formed in the early 1830s in opposition to Jackson, had it its own hero candidates. Generals William Henry Harrison and Zachary Taylor, who became presidents respectively in 1840 and 1848, were new Washingtons and, according to the new zeitgeist, men of the people, the former content with "a barrel of hard cider," the latter ready to "faithfully serve 'The *whole* Nation.'" And while Harrison was hailed as being "born very near to the same spot of earth / That gave the illustrious Washington birth," Taylor became "the very one / God chose to train a Washington." Altogether, from John Adams onwards, the values and characteristics that originally were associated with or ascribed to Washington became projected onto or, in a process of auto-heroization, were claimed by his successors. Until, that is, Lincoln arrived, whose heroic status required different forms.[31] From about 1812 onward, collective portraits of American presidents became popular. Their purpose was to convey both national political unity and the succession of Washington. Sometimes, these collective portraits had quite outlandish names, such as "American Kings" (a series of lithographs from the 1820s, with all the portraits after Gilbert Stuart), "National Galaxy" (a poster from 1840 that contained portraits of the presidents though Van Buren), or "Family Monument" (an 1858 engraving done by a German immigrant, which lines up the presidents on a huge rock in the center of the picture). By that time, portraits of American presidents had long been associated with the theme of the Union, whose future seemed no longer a certainty. Fears for the Union's survival continued until it was restored in 1865. For all their differences in style and artistry, however, collective portraits of American presidents have one compositional element in common—George Washington's portrait usually occupies a place of honor in the center of the artwork.[32]

Washington also occupied a place of honor in the rhetoric of Abraham Lincoln. The arguments of Calhoun, Yancey, and other secessionists drew from him rebuttals referring to Washington. On the occasion of his first debate against Stephen Douglas, on August 21, 1858, Lincoln stated that in his party's stand against slavery it was only following Washington's principles. In the Cooper Institute speech of February 27, 1860, he quoted Washington's warnings against sectionalism. Lincoln also alluded to Washington after his election and before his inauguration. In early 1862, he recommended that the people of the United States assemble "for public solemnities" on the occasion of Washington's birthday, adding that his "immortal Farewell Address" be read out then. On another occasion, Lincoln again cited Washington as a truly paternal example: "General Washington himself endured greater physical hardships than if he had remained a British subject, yet he was a happy man because he was engaged in benefiting his race, in doing something for the children of his neighbors, having none of his own." And in the same year Lincoln mentioned Washington in an order for the Army and Navy, reverentially quoting from "the first general order issued by the Father of his Country after the Declaration of Independence."[33]

Lincoln's words reveal the nostalgia for an idealized Old Republic in the days of the Founders. Their war, unlike the present one, seemed unequivocally noble, heroic, and right. Their world seemed simpler, purer, better somehow. Yet it was vanishing. As the Reverend Elias Brewster Hillard wrote in 1864, "Our own are the last eyes that will look on men who looked on Washington; our ears the last that will hear the living voices of those who heard his words."[34] Hillard's book, *The Last Men of the Revolution*, was a compilation of biographies and photographs of the survivors of Washington's Continental Army, accompanied by interviews with the few remaining worthies. The role of eyewitnesses to a rapidly receding past was crucial in that pre-electronic age; they were the only link to the substance of firsthand experience. When they were gone, memory took their place.

Following the tragic event in Ford's Theater of April 14, 1865, Abraham Lincoln became "A second Washington! / So great in every virtuous plan," and destined to "affirm and reassert the principles of Washington."[35] Much more frequently, however, we hear religious overtones in the eulogies. A Christian martyr, a Moses, even a Jesus Christ were used as sources for Lincoln imagery. In one instance, Lincoln is shown in heaven, embraced by Washington, who is about to crown the martyred president's head with a laurel wreath.[36] If Lincoln was established as the North's new heroic martyr, he was also, more generally, seen as a figure of pathos and humanity. (For white southerners, Robert E. Lee became the parallel icon, visible for instance in a statue dedicated in Charlottesville, Virginia, in 1924; the planned removal of the Lee statue was the pretext for the "Unite the Right" rally there in August 2017.) George Washington, in contrast, became rather more an object of nostalgia. When the Ohio representative Rutherford B. Hayes visited Mount Vernon in 1866, the Father of His Country appeared to him as "formal, statue-like, a figure for exhibition."[37]

10

National Myths

In the year of the nation's centennial, 1876, Erastus Salisbury Field finally completed his epic painting *Historical Monument of the American Republic*. Field, a self-taught folk artist, had decided to create an artwork that would embody the history of America from the first British settlement in Jamestown in 1607 to the end of the Civil War. The result, on a canvas nine feet tall and thirteen feet long, is a fantastic metropolis of ten huge towers that all but overwhelms by its "eclectic architectural grotesquerie." Scenes from American history drawn from famous history paintings—John Trumbull's *Signing of the Declaration of Independence* and *The Surrender of Lord Cornwallis at Yorktown*, and Benjamin West's *Penn's Treaty with the Indians*—appear on these buildings as sculptural reliefs, as do copies of landscape paintings, especially those of Thomas Cole—the five-painting cycle of *The Course of Empire* (1836) and *The Architects Dream* (1840). On the central tower Field depicted Lincoln's assassination and ascension to heaven. Field reworked his canvas in 1876, in honor of the nation's centennial celebration, which thus became a backdrop to the nation's most cherished ideals and their potent role in constituting a site for the production of symbols of national identity and for the memorialization of popular myths. Fundamentally, however, Field's reading of history was apocalyptic, and so his exaggerated monumentalism and the random arrangement of historical moments at the same time suggest the vulnerability of the moral republic. Perhaps for that reason the canvas was not exhibited at the Centennial Exhibition in Philadelphia, nor did it travel through the U.S.[1]

Also in 1876, the United States Congress appropriated funding for the Washington National Monument, which upon its dedication in 1885, just one day before Washington's birthday, became a much less ambiguous site for the production of symbols of national identity and for the memorialization of popular myths. Ten years later, the United States Treasury released a new issue of Silver Certificates, in denominations of 1, 2, and 5 Dollars. (Silver Certificates were authorized by Acts of Congress respectively in 1878 and 1886.) The notes are generally considered the most historical and artistically designed of all issues of United States currency. The $1 Silver Certificate had on its back the dignified portraits respectively of George and Martha Washington. The bill's front, designed by Will H. Low and engraved by Charles Schlecht, is known as "History Instructing Youth." An allegorical figure of History is pointing out to an equally allegorical Youth the principal sights of Washington, D.C.—the Washington Monument and the Capitol—and presumably telling the narratives behind them, including the story of the United States Constitution, which appears at right.

The Silver Certificates of the series of 1896 have become sought-for collector's items because of their superb engraving. But the bills also comprise the so-called "Educational Set," a designation that unfolds its meaning in an entirely different context, not of the self-representation of America's cultural elites so much as of the mass immigration of the time. The United States after the Civil War indeed was facing a paradox. Although the country was then the most democratic and, both territorially and constitutionally, one of the most clearly defined nations, the basic political problem, once secession had been averted, was how to assimilate a heterogeneous mass of people who were Americans not by birth but by immigration. In Eric Hobsbawm's estimation, immigrants provided a body of rather "*doubtful members of the national community*; all the more doubtful because [...] they could actually be classified as foreigners."[2] Immigrants in the late nineteenth century thus were encouraged to recite the "Pledge of Allegiance," originally composed by Colonel George Balch in 1887 and revised by Francis Bellamy in 1892, and to accept rituals commemorating the history of the nation—the Revolution and its Founding Fathers (July 4), and the Protestant Anglo-Saxon tradition (Forefathers Day, Thanksgiving Day)—as indeed they did, since these now became holidays and occasions for public and private festivity within America's civil religion.[3]

The educational system too was transformed into a machine for political socialization by such devices as the worship of the flag, which, as a daily ritual in the country's schools, spread from the 1880s onwards. When the New York publishers Appleton and Company started a "Great Commanders" series, they gave the Washington volume to Bradley Tyler Johnson, a veteran of the Confederate Army and author of a book on *General Washington*. Patriotic hereditary societies, most notably the Daughters of the American Revolution, prepared lectures in American history and government to be delivered in foreign languages to young males who would soon be voting. In their efforts, the women of the D.A.R. faithfully followed President William McKinley, who in his inaugural address of March 4, 1897, urged "the spread of knowledge and free education" as a royal road to "a safer, a better, and a higher citizenship." Promotion of these, McKinley said, must be undertaken "with the zeal of our forefathers."[4] Overall, the elites' mood was optimistic. "Education," a New York high school principal declared in 1902, "will solve every problem of our national life, even that of assimilating our foreign element." The principal's rhetoric reveals that immigrants were to become members of what nationalists from all social strata considered an ethnically united community.[5]

More than anything, authorities in the Gilded Age relied on the mass immersion in nationalistic iconography to mold people's identity and their perceived destiny, much as they expressed explicit commands to them. The Silver Certificates of the series of 1896 were no exception in this regard. They too were employed in the manufacturing of consent. Possessing the notes could make one an American, much as the notes identified the holder as an American. Patriotism was even more glaring on another type of post–Civil War currency, the National Bank Notes. In March 1863, Lincoln's Treasury Secretary, Salmon P. Chase, invited banknote designs that would be "national in their character." The new notes were emitted from December 1863. Their designs were hailed as conveying, in Senator John Sherman's words, "a sentiment of nationality."[6] Altogether, the new notes were truly emblematic of the consolidation of the state's authority following the North's victory in the Civil War. The notes still displayed features that retained for them a measure of the local and regional. A measure, but not too much. They might proclaim that they were from New York, or North Carolina—or the Nevada Territory, in time. But they all looked alike. They all displayed the same scenes and, from by the beginning of the 1880s, they were all coming from a single printer, the Bureau of Engraving and Printing in Washington, D.C.

On March 28, Treasury Secretary Chase received a letter from his chief clerk, Spencer M. Clark, concerning the role of currency design. The new notes, Clark explained, ideally would use panoramic scenes extending across their faces, each scene providing a patriotic, uplifting imagery. "The advantage of such a currency," the letter said,

> would be that a series properly selected, with their subject titles imprinted on the notes, would tend to teach the masses the prominent periods in our country's history. The laboring man who should receive every Saturday night, a copy of the "Surrender of Burgoyne" for his weekly wages, would soon inquire who General Burgoyne was, and to whom he surrendered. His curiosity would be aroused and he would learn the facts from a fellow laborer or from his employer. The same would be true of other National pictures, and in time many would be taught leading incidents in our country's history, so that they would soon be familiar to those who would never read them in books, teaching them history and imbuing them with a National feeling.[7]

Secretary Chase's chief clerk not only speaks to anti–British sentiments in his reference to General John Burgoyne.[8] He also identifies two central points about the potential power of imagery on paper currency in constructing a collective national identity. First, because of the pervasiveness of paper currency in the kind of market economy that was spreading across the American continent, images on paper money were guaranteed a much larger audience than images carried by other media. These images were particularly effective in conveying messages to the poor and illiterate with whom the state had difficulty communicating through other means such as newspapers or schooling. Second, images on paper currency were considered particularly effective tools of propaganda because people could not avoid encountering them in their daily transactions. By providing a frequent reminder to people that they were members of a common, homogeneous community, the currency could be expected to work as a much more effective vehicle of nationalist messages than even flags or anthems. The National Monetary Commission, upon reviewing Secretary Chase's proposal of the national banking act, came to just such conclusions. While they listed the economic benefits of the proposed currency, they found particularly attractive its ideological surplus value—"the stimulation of the patriotism of the people which would arise from the closer touch with national affairs…."[9]

Among the signal moments of American history that came to be printed on National Bank notes (and on the National Gold Bank notes of California) was a number of artworks from the Rotunda of the United States Capitol. Lawmakers in Congress saw the originals at regular intervals and it is safe to assume that off and on they even heeded them—John G. Chapman's *Baptism of Pocahontas* (engraved by Charles Burt for the back of the $20 note), Robert W. Weir's *Embarkation of the Pilgrims* (engraved by W. W. Rice for the back of the $50 note), Peter Frederick Rothermel's *Landing of the Pilgrims* (engraved by Charles Burt for the back of the $1 note), John Trumbull's *Washington Crossing the Delaware* (on the face of the $50 note, with a vignette of Washington at Valley Forge at right), and his *Jefferson presenting the Declaration of Independence to John Hancock at the Continental Congress* (on the back of the $100 note, in John Girsch's rendering).[10]

Trumbull's rendering of the scene in Congress is a perfect example of visualizing the new political order in the spirit of the Enlightenment. The way in which the delegates are gathered together suggests that the revolution obtained legitimacy and authority through rational argumentation. Yet Trumbull's artwork is a post-hoc construction. There were other ways for the American revolution to advance. One such way is captured by Alexander Anderson's engraving titled *Celebration of Independence*. The engraving was used, *inter alia*, as illustration in a popular history book, John Warner Barber's *Interesting Events in the History of the United States* (1830). In Anderson's engraving, the revolution does not advance in an orderly and civilized way; instead, a tumultuous mob is shown toppling the equestrian

Alexander Anderson, *Celebration of Independence*, engraving, reproduced in John Warner Barber's *Interesting Events in the History of the United States* (1830) (courtesy American Antiquarian Society).

statue of George III from its pedestal. The gilded lead statue, which showed the king in the garb of a Roman emperor, had been put up in August 1770 following the repeal of the hated Townshend Acts earlier that year. Then the statue was a suitable symbol of the easing of tensions and, as well, an articulation of the Englishness of New Yorkers. A mere six years later, the statue was torn down and decapitated; the head was paraded around the town to the beat of the fifes and drums of George Washington's soldiers and sailors, who had joined the jubilant crowd of civilians.

Anderson's engraving represents various disenfranchised groups expressing their political views through a tort action of political iconoclasm or image-wrecking. Historically, the toppling of the statue was only one among a number of similar actions. Several liberty poles were raised and subsequently destroyed, and a marble statue of the British parliamentarian William Pitt the Elder was likewise decapitated. Other symbolic assaults included the destruction of royal portraits or the removal by angry crowds of the King's coat of arms from courthouses, churches, taverns (lovingly recorded for posterity by Washington Irving in "Rip Van Winkle"), and shops.[11] Bowling Green had quite literally been a fashionable place for bowling but, following the Stamp Act it became a place of radical political protest well before the statue of George III went off on its pedestal and came down in 1776. Moreover, the ritual that happened in Bowling Green in 1776 was quintessentially English. It followed a cultural script that reproduced English rituals of iconoclasm, such as the attack, in Newcastle in 1689, on an equestrian statue of James II. At Bowling Green, bringing the statue down was preceded by reading out the Declaration of Independence, ratified just five days before. The king's likeness was desecrated as if it were a real human body: It was decapitated (recalling the fate of Charles I), and parts were dragged through the streets; most of the statue was carted away to a military depot in Connecticut, where it was melted down to make musket bullets for the Continental Army. (A few pieces were saved and eventually found their way into New York collections.) The pedestal was left standing, evolving into a memorial of the American Revolution itself. In Cornelius Tiebout's 1798 printed image *Sacred to Patriotism*, the pedestal still stands empty in the background. In 1792, however, William Sullivan's wooden replica of George Washington was presented to the public—atop the pedestal that once supported the statue of the English sovereign, which led some critics to refer to America's first president as George IV.

Functionally, the perpetual destruction of the king's likeness constituted an act of *damnatio memoriae* ("condemnation of memory"), that is, of the complete erasure of memory. It was a reenactment of a form of dishonor that could be passed by the Roman Senate upon traitors or others who brought discredit to the Roman state. And it was followed by the ultimate malediction: "God bless Great Washington; God damn the King."[12] The *damnatio memoriae* of 1776 was not the end of the story. In the nineteenth century, painters and printmakers created some nineteen or so representations of the statue's destruction.[13] The act also was restaged and written about; as late as 1909, it became a vital creation story in a civic pageant in the City of New York, remaking an English ritual of protest into a thoroughly American story. Further reenactments followed, respectively in 1932 and in 1976. Millennial Americans now have a new way to experience the Bowling Green iconoclasm, courtesy of the New-York Historical Society. Visitors to the society's premises at the corner of 77th Street and Central Park West can trigger sensors that activate an image of the event, with the drama culminating with the statue crashing to the ground in a bizarre echo of the toppling of a statue of Saddam Hussein in Firdos Square in Baghdad on April 9, 2003, shortly after the Iraq War invasion.[14]

A comparison between Trumbull's and Anderson's visualization of the American Revolution demonstrates the use of pictures as visual arguments in attempts to define social and political goals and ideals. In these processes, pictures are always arguments directed against other pictures circulating in society. Whereas Trumbull visualized the glorified image of a revolution guided by reason, Anderson staged the founders' nightmare, the extremes of political fervor, what the founders conceived of as democracy's shadow. To George Washington, ever the strict father, the tort action of political iconoclasm at Bowling Green had "much the appearance of riot, and want of order, in the Army, that he disapproves the manner."[15] Washington wanted this revolution to be an orderly one, and he refused to condone even the desecration of the king's statue. He, like other revolutionary leaders such as John Adams or Alexander Hamilton, also strained at the rabble-rousing spirit unleashed by figures like Thomas Paine. Washington stuck by his convictions. As late as 1787 he wrote, "It is among the evils, and perhaps is not the smallest, of democratical governments that the People must *feel* before they will *see*."[16] Washington's words, directed to Henry Knox, show that he feared nothing so much as "anarchy and confusion." The phrase is ubiquitous in Washington's correspondence. One example, among twenty or so, is from a letter to James Madison, prompted by the uprising in Massachusetts: "We are fast verging to anarchy & confusion!"[17]

The political ideas Washington expressed in his correspondence can be traced back to Plato and Aristotle. Both Plato's writings and a commentary on Aristotle were part of Washington's library. It is also no secret that Washington was obsessed with subjecting his own passions to reason, much as he resolutely committed himself to what he saw as the public good. It is safe to say, therefore, that he formed himself into the republican citizen-soldier who does not go to war for private glory or territorial expansion, but solely for liberty. In the course of the nineteenth century, Washington's self-image achieved the status of memory and myth. Consider but accounts of his role in the French and Indian wars. Understood as the result of the competition between Britain and France, these accounts glorified "Young Washington" as "prudent and brave," and as someone who "could be relied on."[18] Patriotic accounts of the French and Indian War also served to legitimize the American Revolution as a political necessity, the combined result of the destructiveness of the colonial powers and the long tradition of American self-defense. Indeed, British politics was seen as the prime cause of uniting the colonies. As a history book from the 1820s expresses the point, British politics gave the colonists "one heart and one mind, firmly to oppose every invasion of their liberty."[19]

That there were considerable ideological controversies, social tensions, or divergent interests, did not matter for the historiographers. What did matter were the encounters in Lexington and Concord in April 1775, which were used as the beginning of the Revolution, creating the first martyrs. Even the battle of Bunker Hill, which the Americans lost, was re-interpreted as a victory, as British losses had been substantial. Washington's distinguishing himself at the battles of Trenton in December 1776, and of Princeton in early January 1777, gave rise to further glorification, again by Olney: "The bold and successful movements of Washington excited the admiration of both Europe and America. Joy and hope now began to revive the drooping spirits of the nation. The people everywhere hailed Washington as the *Savior* of his country."[20]

Clearly, the romantic view of Washington as the heroic savior of his country also speaks from Emanuel Gottlieb Leutze's monumental oil painting *Washington Crossing the Delaware*. The hero's apotheosis is evident from his resolute pose, erect, with one foot solidly planted on the boat's rim, metaphorically anchoring the cause of the American Revolution. If the boat provides a visual analogy to the ark of the covenant, the general's gazing onto the distant shore underscores his resolution and optimism, at the same time as it symbolizes the strength and glorious future of "these United States," read, territorial expansion under the aegis of manifest destiny. The painting's performative function as "visual ideology" is heightened by the still unfurled flag which, together with the figure of the general, is both centrally placed on the canvas and gloriously backlit, creating a unifying and centering symbol, both visually and metaphorically. Altogether, therefore, Leutze's canvas works not only as a visual embodiment of the energy and drive as well as the ideals of an America on the go, but also mediates the disjunctions and contradictions of a nation teetering on the brink of civil strife and the break-up of the Union.[21]

It will be hard to find a better-known picture in antebellum America than Leutze's ennobling history painting. Leutze began work on it in Düsseldorf, Germany, in 1850. A copy of it was placed on exhibition in New York during October 1851, to reviews that were uniformly superlative and exclusively nationalistic in tone. The *New York Evening Mirror* of November 7, 1851, called it "the most effective painting ever exhibited in America." The artist had originally intended his work for the United States Capitol. However, Congress refused to purchase it, possibly because the worthy lawmakers were unaware of or lukewarm to the artist's intentions. Leutze sought to embody a sense of the spiritual fraternity between German liberals (especially Ferdinand Freiligrath) and their struggles in the Revolution of 1848 and the mid-century democratizing impulse that was heir to American revolutionary ideals. Thus, Leutze's Washington is not the avatar of stability from the early republic so much as a romantic revolutionary.[22]

Emanuel Gottlieb Leutze, *Washington Crossing the Delaware*, 1851, oil on canvas, original size 149 × 255 in. (Metropolitan Museum of Art, New York, Gift of John Stewart Kennedy, 1897).

Leutze's painting now hangs in the Metropolitan Museum of Art, New York, an exhibition context which, by activating a premier public space, bestows on the painting the imprimatur of an officially certified visual argument. As part of America's cultural memory, the painting accomplishes nothing less than the apotheosis of Washington in a key event in the history of the United States. The image of the crossing of the Delaware River on December 25, 1776, prior to the Americans' attack on the Hessians at Trenton, is, in David Hackett Fischer's words, "one of the folk-memories that most Americans share."[23] Over the years, *Washington Crossing the Delaware* became the most famous of all American paintings, a true site of memory, as Karsten Fitz maintains.[24] At one point, the artwork even traveled through the country. (It also traveled through Europe.) Engravings, embroiderings, copies by other artists, and studies also contributed to the painting's popularity, as did reinterpretations. Not all of these reinterpretations proved successful. George Caleb Bingham's version, for instance, took many years to complete (1856–1871), but the scene he depicted remained utterly static. Bingham's Washington stands at the apex of a pyramid of figures, on horseback, with the actors rather resembling the figures of his better known frontier paintings such as *Daniel Boone Leading the Settlers* (1851).[25]

Compositions of Leutze's picture in new circumstances range from a tableau ending the first act of John Brougham's *The Miller of New Jersey* (1856) to a dramatic scene in the silent film *Janice Meredith* (1924), an adaptation of Paul Leicester Ford's bestselling novel of the same title (1899), or Howard Fast's novel *The Crossing* (1971), which became the basis for an historical TV film that went on air in January 2000.[26] Leutze's masterpiece also inspired more serious artists in the twentieth century. In 1932, Grant Wood placed three Daughters of the American Revolution in front of Leutze's painting to show how far these matrons had strayed from its spirit. Larry Rivers's *Washington Crossing the Delaware* in 1953 featured a blurred Washington and an anxious soldier, a perfect fit for a period when heroism seemed unfashionable. Equally unheroic was Peter Saul's pop-art-inspired *Washington Crossing the Delaware* (1975), in which a dazed-looking general holds up a comically small flag while he is riding his charger into the river. Other contemporary artworks include Edward Sorel's satirical drawing *Nixon Crossing the Delaware* (1973) or Robert Colescott's *George Washington Carver Crossing the Delaware* (1973), which altogether dispenses with the hero in a powerful comment on American racism.

In contrast to these modern and postmodern examples of questioning fixed or transcendent categories of meaning, Washington's heroic crossing persists in any number of recreations, usually done by schoolboys, though the annual event on the Pennsylvania side of the Delaware River has gone on under the title of an "officially recognized Bicentennial project" sine 1976. The bicentennial of Washington's birth in 1932 likewise provided an opportunity to recycle Leutze's masterpiece, this time on a set of twelve commemorative plates. The plates were rather flat, too flat to hold any quantity of Liebig's Extract of Beef, which in the late nineteenth century was advertised with a rendering of Leutze's painting. The message on the advertisement was clear: Liebig's Extract of Beef was an example of scientific achievement comparable, in its own realm, to Washington's river passage. The Inaugural Centennial also paid tribute to the fame of Leutze's picture, in the form of a huge float for the Civil Parade held in New York on May 1, 1889, in the presence of President Benjamin Harrison.[27]

All these events and artifacts reveal a profound nostalgia for the time when the Founder was alive. Such nostalgia was no Gilded Age invention; Americans had bemoaned the passing of the founders' generation and their supposedly selfless commitment to public virtue ever since the 1820s. But the quickening pace of capitalist expansion after the Civil War intensified the attachment many Americans felt to what they believed was a simpler past. Thus the 1870s saw the beginning of the revival of the Society of the Cincinnati, an illustrious organization of former officers of the War of Independence which flourished during the early republic but had become practically defunct by 1812. Washington had been a member of the society and its first president-general. Nostalgia also had set the tone in Ann Pamela Cunningham's farewell address to the Mount Vernon Ladies' Association in 1874, which summoned the audience to not allow "the fingers of progress" to desecrate Washington's home but, instead, to "care for the Home of our Hero!"[28]

Ann Pamela Cunningham's personal concern had been to refurbish the Mount Vernon mansion, so that visitors could get a sense of Washington's daily life. Other people found more attractive the trappings of aristocracy and Britishness they associated with the colonial period. For them—some of whom of distinguished lineage and some of the class of nouveaux riches—George Washington no longer was the "rebel general" who had led the fight against British "tyranny." Instead, he became the avatar of Anglo-Saxonism, most notably in Albert Welles's 1879 book *The Pedigree and History of the Washington Family, derived from Odin, the Founder of Scandinavia, B.C. 70*. Martha Washington mattered as much as her husband when wealthy Americans sought to imitate the early republic's "court circles." George Washington, they argued, was a man too refined for the raw democracy the United States was beginning to represent. They yearned for the glorious days of Virginia aristocracy and Washingtonian refinement, an American past when, as Karal Ann Marling put it, "a 'Republican Court' still flourished—and everybody else still knew their places."[29]

Rufus Wimore Griswold's *The Republican Court; or, American Society in the Days of Washington* (1854 and reissued in 1868), a book primarily about balls, levees, celebrations, and weddings of notables, Daniel Huntington's *The Republican Court in the Time of Washington*, *or Lady Washington's Reception Day* (1861–1865), a popular painting of one of her Friday levees, a "costume picture" of European-like elegance and a queen-like Martha, as well as Elizabeth F. Ellet's book *The Court Circles of the Republic* (1869) helped inspire the "Martha Washington Tea Parties," where the American elites of the 1870s donned "colonial" garb to raise money for charitable causes, foremost among them the 1876 Centennial Exhibition in Philadelphia.[30] James Russell Lowell had other purposes. In "Under the Old Elm," a memorial poem read at Cambridge, Massachusetts, on July 3, 1875, the hundredth anniversary of Washington's taking command of the Continental Army on that spot, he looked back on the time of Washington: "It was a world of statelier movement then / Than this we fret in, he a denizen / Of that ideal Rome that made a man for men."[31] "Under the Old Elm" has received praise as "the best poem that has yet been written about Washington."[32]

Yet it was the World's Fair, the first in the United States, which launched the "colonial revival" that lingered on roughly until the bicentennial of Washington's birth in 1932. At the Centennial exhibition of 1876, the U.S. Patent Office displayed some of Washington's revolutionary relics, including his general's uniform, which George Washington Parke Custis had lovingly displayed and occasionally worn until just before the Civil War. Also on display were Washington's folding cot and tinware. Such artifacts connected visitors across the generations to the Father of His Country. A different sort of "Washingtoniana" was of entirely new manufacture—handkerchiefs, bookmarks, and other souvenirs embossed or imprinted with Washington's likeness, "Century Vases" adorned by a portrait bust of the Founder in the company of an Indian chief, a buffalo head, and the American eagle, as well as "colonial-style" furniture named for Martha Washington and other figures from the Federalist era.[33]

Such excursions into the make-believe of historical kitsch, the cultural historian Karal Ann Marling wrote, were "gestures toward the special, material intimacy with the past that the centennial generation craved."[34] Intimacy with the past was expressed in other ways as well. In the spring of 1891, a Stan V. Henkels opened two auctions in Philadelphia. Henkels had jumped the bandwagon of foundation-era merchandising in the wake of the centennial of 1876. Now the auctions of "Washingtonian and rare American literary and historical curiosities" offered items such as a catalog of the library of Mount Vernon, Washington's personal world atlas, a book that had belonged to his mother, of lock of his hair, the silver plate from his coffin, numerous signed manuscripts, and—an item altogether novel and unprecedented: "Gen'l Geo. Washington's Manuscript Prayer Book, entitled the 'Daily Sacrifice.'" Henkels claimed he had found the manuscript in a trunk he had received from the Washington family. He was not the first to see the trunk, though. Experts from the Smithsonian, too, had taken a look at the contents and rejected them as worthless. Henkels, however, had a different view: "This gem is all in the handwriting of Geo. Washington, when about twenty years old." Henkels sold it as genuine, for $1,250.[35]

Henkels was wrong. Washington's prayer book, this *"most hallowed of all his writings,"* was a fake.[36] Debunkers slammed it, mainstream academics and journalists didn't even mention it. But the prayer book did not go away. From its reprint in W. Herbert Burk's *Washington's Prayers* (1907), it branched out into evangelical Christian circles, remaining popular even today. It is reproduced on the website of Pat Robertson's Christian Broadcasting Network, CBN.com, was a declared favorite of the evangelical minister and author Tim LaHaye, and a welcome source of reference for televangelist D. James Kennedy. And Washington impersonator James Manship, who appears frequently at public functions and prays with children at scouting events and in schools, campaigns tirelessly to convince people that the prayer book is an authentic document. The Father of His Country, Manship pontificates, was no deist, but a "prayer warrior."[37] Fascination with the Father of His Country blazed around more secular campfires as well. When the Hall of Fame opened in Brooklyn, New York, in 1899, it was Washington who received the most first-place votes (Lincoln came in a close second). In 1902, schoolchildren in at least one Pennsylvania town chose Washington as an exemplar over Lincoln by a substantial margin. A similar pattern emerges from the periodical literature of the time. Between 1870 and 1900, the *New York Times* published ninety-six pieces about Washington (as compared to sixty-two about Lincoln).[38]

Characteristically in these writings, "Washington the lover, the dancer and the courtly aristocrat displaced the rather abstract figure who once stood for national unity, moral rectitude, self denial and a stoic devotion to duty."[39] The same can be said about the products from writers and artists of the time. Paul Leicester Ford's biography of 1896, for instance, challenged writers who were interested solely in their subject's "greatness," introducing instead chapters on Washington's relations with his family, social life, and more.[40] Ford was able to draw on the fourteen-volume edition of *The Writings of George Washington* his brother, Worthington Chauncey Ford, had published in 1889, the year of the Inaugural Centennial, not least for such a savory topic as "Washington's relations with the fair sex." Scenes from Washington's happy domestic life also were staples in the work of artists like John Ward Dunsmore and Henry A. Ogden. Their works found their way into private collections, though they were mostly used as illustrations in commercial publications—from magazines to books, from advertisements to art calendars. A similar set of illustrations, by Howard Pyle, was used for Woodrow Wilson's 1897 biography of George Washington.[41]

Late nineteenth-century depictions of Washington's romantic life almost invariably conveyed the humanity of the Father of His Country. Yet by all accounts, the love of his life was Martha Washington, and, thanks to the efforts of the D.A.R., by the late 1890s their wedding anniversary had become a day to be commemorated. The celebration, Barry Schwartz has shown, reawakened artistic as well as public interest. A number of paintings—by Jean Leon Gerome Ferris or John Ward Dunsmore, for example—depicted the first couple. In 1896, the United States Treasury introduced a new back design for the $1 Silver Certificate, bearing the dignified portraits of Martha Washington and George Washington.[42]

$1, Silver Certificate, 1896, back, with portraits of Martha Washington and George Washington (7.42 × 3.125 in.) (American Numismatic Association Money Museum).

Washingtonian refinement and knowing one's place speak from the bill's design, which thus is yet another example of the way an elite society appropriated the founders. In this instance, society's highest strata crowned the Father of His Country the father of their own good taste, with Martha as a sidekick, a founding mother to go with the founding father. As the *Indiana Democrat* wrote on February 20, 1901: "Persons fortunate enough to possess a one-dollar Silver Certificate have an excellent picture of Martha Washington, the wife of the Father of His Country."[43] Washingtonian refinement turned historical kitsch also speaks from Rudolf Siemering's 44-foot equestrian statue of George Washington. The statue, which is modeled after Christian Rauch's 1852 statue of Frederick the Great, was unveiled in 1897 at Eakins Oval, the entrance to Fairmount Park in Philadelphia, but has since been relocated to the front of the Philadelphia Museum of Art. It shows General Washington sitting majestically on a horse; a field glass suggests that he is leading troops into battle. Below the statue, figures of Native Americans and indigenous animals add a distinctly American flavor, as do female allegories representing "America." To commemorate the new monument, authorities employed Augustus Saint-Gaudens's medal struck in 1889 for the centennial of Washington's first inauguration. The obverse of the official Centennial Anniversary medal showed Houdon's famous bust.[44]

The Centennial Anniversary of 1889 had also brought with it lavish exhibitions of Washingtoniana, from relics (Washington's inkstand, saucers, cushions, and furniture used by Washington in New York's City Hall) to collections of portraits. All these memorabilia presented a distinctive picture of Washington and his era, as did the Centennial celebrations, which set the stage for society's elites to crown the Father of His Country the father of their own refined taste. At the Inaugural ceremony, national unity was reaffirmed, and the audience, which included President Benjamin Harrison, listened to lessons to be learned from the Father of His Country. The following morning brought a parade dedicated to "the miracle of America." The pageantry was truly suggestive. It was organized by unions, working people, tradesmen, firemen, cops, schoolboys, the Tammany Irish, Italian clubs, German marching and singing societies, as well as representatives of lesser-known groups such as the Hebrew Orphans' Asylum Band. Each of these motley groups had its own division in the parade. But the first division consisted of New Americans, represented by ethnic societies, their bands, and a series of floats interpreting American history as successive waves of immigration. On hindsight, we can say that the colorful pageantry only pasted over a profound struggle for the preservation of the social and economic order. Workers especially felt threatened by new arrivals, who by the 1890s mostly came from southern and eastern Europe. And a militant nativism had become too blatant to be overlooked.[45]

What all these Gilded Age appropriations of George Washington show are, first, the anxieties of the "more cultivated" classes; second, an awareness, also on the part of ordinary men and women, of the economic crisis of 1893; and third, an awareness of the moral decay of the Gilded Age, epitomized by Mark Twain and Charles Dudley Warner's novel *The Gilded Age* (1873) and, in a different medium, by John Haberle's trompe l'oeil painting *Changes of Time* (1888). In Haberle's wondrously illusionistic artwork, a range of currency bills appears to be pinned to a wood cabinet door. But the bills, which bear the portraits of various presidents, from Washington to Lincoln to Grant, look frayed and yellowed, suggesting that the nation's public figures—like the values they represent—are susceptible to the changes of time. While their images toy with the idea of graven idols, the painting clearly served a political purpose, inviting viewers to test their perceptual skills to see if they could discern between truth and illusion. Truth, for some people, was that without great men such as George Washington there could be no civilization, only mediocrity and corruption. Madeleine Lee, the main protagonist in Henry Adams's novel *Democracy*, is not the only one to establish the difference between past and present in terms of pure and unclean—"everything Washington touched, he purified ... everything we touch seems unclean."[46]

Throughout the Gilded Age, Washington embodied the ideals that America's elites seemed to betray. The sculptor Lorado Taft, for instance, said about his 1901 bronze statue of Washington that he had intended "a touch of the ideal, to show 'The Father of His Country' rather than the General." For Taft, the memory of Washington was a model for, rather than a model of, a crass and mediocre society. This appears to have been the intention also of William Pelissier, who at the turn of the century had a play *The Father of His Country* copyrighted. In 1901, Robert Louis Weed's play *King Washington* was produced at Wallack's Theatre in New York. And in a poem published in the *Chicago Daily Tribune* in 1910 to commemorate Washington's birthday, Washington is asked: "You, who were Freedom's chosen spear—/ Her organ—/ Would you have traded, had you known, / The occupant of England's throne / For Rockefeller or for Pier-Pont Morgan?"[47] Other commentators, including the fictional Senator Ratcliffe from Henry Adams's *Democracy*, questioned Washington's relevance to this modern era, except as a model of antiquated virtue.

Visitors to the Centennial Exhibition held in Philadelphia in 1876 jokingly referred to a statue that showed the Father of His Country as soaring heavenward on the back of an American eagle as "Washington on a Lark." On its cover commemorating the 1889 centennial of Washington's first inauguration, *Judge* magazine featured Uncle Sam towering over a tiny first couple, dressed in their quaint colonial costume. As Uncle Sam leans over to shake George Washington's hand, a poem titled "A Big Boy's Welcome" notes that "things have changed since you were here," including the expansion of the nation to forty-two states.[48] And Marietta Hawley under the alias of "Samantha at the Centennial" irreverently exclaimed:

> Oh! what feelings I did feel as I see that coat and vest that George had buttoned up so many times over true patriotism, truthfulness and honor. When I see the bed he had slept on, the little round table he had eat on, the wooden bottomed chair he had sat down on, the belluses he had blowed the fire with in cold storms and discouragements. ... Why they all rousted up my mind so..., as much so as if my emotions had been all stirred up with that little hatchet that G. W. couldn't tell a lie with.[49]

Irreverence speaks even more loudly from Ambrose Bierce's "George the Made-Over," a fierce attack on the sanctity that had been heaped on Washington's memory and his image. Americans, Bierce caustically remarked, had made the Father of His Country too virtuous to be human. Portraits of him were too idealized, resembling religious icons, and historians only inflated his intellectual and military abilities. In addition, romancing biographers in the wake of Parson Weems were adorning Washington with all kinds of improbable attributes, leaving nothing of the "natural" man, instead dishing up a "public prig." Hence, Bierce wrote, "You can no more love and revere the memory of the biographical George Washington than you can an isosceles triangle or a cubic foot of interstellar space."[50] As if the damage inflicted on George Washington by the unholy triumvirate of portrait-painters, historians, and biographers were not enough, his memory, Bierce continued, had suffered a "supreme indignity" from "the Sunday-scholiasts, the pietaries, the truly good, the example-to-American-youth folk." These "canting creatures" had sucked Washington completely dry, both to have available an "example" to "the unripe intelligences of their following" and in their very own interest. Bierce was unforgiving: "In order that George Washington may be acceptable to themselves, they have made him a bore to everyone else."[51]

Biercean-style irreverence would not have been tolerated a generation earlier. But at the close of the century, adulatory tributes, Weems's in particular, were scoffed at both by professional historians and by writers bent on disabusing their readers from too much didacticism and, as Karal Ann Marling put it, from "seeing colonial history-in-the-round as a place of refuge from the present."[52] Finally in the 1920s, George Washington himself came to bear the brunt of iconoclastic scrutiny and attack. In his 1926 biography, William E. Woodward (who had invented the word "debunk" in his 1923 novel *Bunk*) represents the Father of His Country as stupid, ignorant, greedy, and selfish, an incorrigible womanizer who combined the vices of a modern businessman, a southern slave driver, and a western Indian killer. Moreover, in Woodward's vitriolic pen, Washington emerges as a poor general who owed his success to mere luck. Also among the debunkers was the English writer Rupert Hughes, who in 1926 started a multivolume biography to strip Washington of whatever good been said about him. Ironically, however, by the end of the third volume, subtitled *The Savior of the States*, Hughes had come to celebrate his subject more enthusiastically than any filiopietist had done before, Weems included. George Washington, Hughes now wrote, was actually "one of the most eager, versatile, human men that ever lived."[53]

Iconoclasts may have attacked George Washington on all kinds of issues, though they unquestioningly left intact the traditional gender hierarchy. That hierarchy typically was keyed to the classification of public and active versus private or domestic and passive. Male protagonists were coded as image carriers of the *vita active*, while females appeared as mere showpieces, passive objects to be looked at. Put differently, insofar as women occupied a positive space in the symbolic constitution of the United States, it was in figurative symbols of liberty and republican virtue, an iconography that underscores their passivity in public forums. Liberty as well as the republican virtue of the "fair daughters of Columbia," as women were often called, evoke a purity of status or innocence of experience under masculine protection, categories that preclude independent female activity.[54] Martha Washington was no exception in this regard. Jared Sparks set a precedent in his *Life of George Washington* when in 1839 he summed up her account in these words: "Affable and courteous, exemplary in her deportment, remarkable for her deeds of charity and piety, unostentatious and without vanity, she adorned by her domestic virtues the sphere of private life, and filled with dignity every situation in which she was placed."[55] Sparks writes both for and from a belief system that accepted real women only as the wives of their better-known husbands and that applied the opprobrium "masculine" to politically or intellectually active women.[56]

Among the revolutionary leaders, only Thomas Paine addressed women's rights in a different fashion. "Man with regard to [women], in all climates, and in all ages," he wrote in 1775, "has been either an insensible husband or an oppressor." Paine's contribution for the *Pennsylvania Magazine* also details the exclusion of women from public life: "[M]an, while he imposes duties upon women, would deprive them of the sweets of public esteem, and in exacting virtues from them, would make it a crime to aspire at honor." Still, women do not seize their rights in Paine's writings. They remain the supplicants of a masculine world of patriarchs. "'Be not our tyrants in all,'" runs Paine's imagined version of this supplicating voice. "'Permit our names to be sometimes pronounced beyond the narrow circles in which we live....'"[57] There is hardly a better example of the "narrow circles" in which women lived than William Blackstone's commentary on marriage: "By marriage, the husband and wife are one person in law: that is, the very being or legal existence of the woman is suspended during the marriage [...] incorporated and consolidated into that of the husband: under whose wing, protection, and *cover*, she performs every thing; and is therefore called in our law-french, a *feme-covert*."[58]

The "incorporation" of woman's existence into that of the husband cannot, of course, be separated from the economic order that based value on property. As Mary Poovey argues, "a woman's sexual infidelity challenged not only the security of the paternal relation and the man's exclusive right to property, but also the illusion that women were 'fixed' as reproductive (not sexually autonomous) beings, as dependent (not socially autonomous) subjects, and as uniformly 'other' to man."[59] Their status as dependent "others" who were excluded from ownership makes women functionally equivalent to commodities (even money) in the exchange between them and men. Women's worth is not intrinsic but derives from their valuation by the male subject, from his "imprint," which becomes the standard of measure (the *étalonnage*, to use Luce Irigaray's term), in relation to a third.[60] That third may well be the nation, as the following episode demonstrates. In 1870, the story of a founding mother came to the fore, to go with the countless stories of the founding father. The "mother's" name was Betsy Ross, a Philadelphia seamstress who, according to her grandson, who promoted the story, in 1776 sewed the first national flag. The story is apocryphal, a fiction, yet it is "a comfortably domestic story: George and Betsy get together to conceive a flag—and a nation." There is a considerable historic irony in the fact that the year before the Betsy Ross story broke, Elizabeth Cady Stanton and Susan B. Anthony had founded the National Woman Suffrage Association. The message that organization was sending out certainly had little in common with the picture presented by Betsy Ross doing a traditional woman's job of sewing at home.[61]

11

Towards the Bicentennial of 1932

The story of Betsy Ross sewing the first national flag faithfully registers the classification of public and active versus private or domestic and passive that framed the traditional gender hierarchy. Male protagonists were coded as image carriers of the *vita active*, while females appeared as mere showpieces, passive objects to be looked at. I have shown elsewhere to what extent the representation of women on the currency too concealed and enshrined their exclusion from the public world of markets and politics. As Virginia Hewitt so aptly put it, the portrayal of women merely constituted "soft images to give hard currency a good name."[1] By the 1920s, the good name of America's currency had declined noticeably, even though the notes were of considerable size—7.42 × 3.125 inches. Notes issued after 1928 are much smaller—6.14 × 2.61 inches. The reduction in size—from "horse blankets" to "pocket change"—was not the only directive issued by Treasury Secretary Andrew W. Mellon. Mellon also acted on a committee recommendation to fundamentally redesign the visual order on existing notes. When the redesign was accomplished, the flood of arbitrarily selected pictures had been curbed: Now there were only a few select examples of "national" architecture, a scene from the nation's history (the signing of the Declaration of Independence), and the portraits of "the Presidents of the United States."[2]

Limiting portraits on the currency to those of "the Presidents of the United States" was the work, again, of Treasury Secretary Mellon's special committee, which decided that such portraits "have a more permanent familiarity in the minds of the public than any others."[3] One understands the sentiment. "No people," President Calvin Coolidge said in an address delivered in Fredericksburg, Virginia, on July 6, 1922, "can look forward who do not look backward."[4] Coolidge was only too happy to follow his own advice, but his description of George Washington as "the first commercial American"[5] sounds odd to modern ears, as if the nation's heritage was a simple matter of dollars and cents. (An entrepreneurial Washington was, at least, different from the treacly myths about him that had reigned supreme for so long). And the President's visit, in the summer of 1924, to Washington's birthplace had drawn attention to the recently constituted Wakefield Memorial Association, founded to buy the thousand-acre property.[6] President Coolidge's actions provided a model for many Americans to seek, as the literary historian Alfred Kazin put it in 1939, "the comfort of their grandfathers."[7] Indeed the portraits of "the Presidents of the United States" on the redesigned currency offered a firm footing in the midst of social and economic chaos, tendering comfort and solace, and confirming the sociologist Michael Schudson's belief that "the past is constantly being retold in order to legitimate present interests" and to elaborate present ideals and realities.[8]

Among the present ideals and realities was the centering of monetary politics on technocrats far removed from the legislative process. Monetary politics, Roy Kreitner summarizes, ceased to be the subject of hypnotizing public interest and seemingly endless debates in Congress. In a long process, begun around 1870, monetary politics was "beaten down, tamed … placed in the context of the kind of expertise that could dampen conflict."[9] Also among the present ideals and realities were new roles for fathers. As Ralph LaRossa has shown in *The Modernization of Fatherhood*, in the 1920s a veritable "culture of daddyhood" arose, intense efforts to sanctify men's relationships with their children.[10] Popular magazines of the time bear out the reinvention of fatherhood. *Outlook* magazine in 1919 even blared out that fatherhood was "the greatest American invention," an experience that all men should embrace. If fatherhood became a serious pursuit, as serious as any pursuit in the business world, that world was itself ready to celebrate fathers, metaphorical ones, that is.

In the 1920s, George Washington was frequently cast as a modern-day Henry Ford, who became a celebrity in the age of Presidents Harding and Coolidge. Already Woodrow Wilson had described Washington as "a man fit either for the frontier or the council-room."[11] But it was the George Washington of the 1920s who became, in Karal Ann Marling's words, "a peculiar mixture of solid, Republican business acumen and petty Rotarian vice," a Babbitt from the colonial past.[12] Construed thus, the Father of His Country was a model for an American people whose business, President Coolidge remarked, was business.[13] The historian Claude Gernade Bowers, who in the 1930s would become Franklin D. Roosevelt's minister to Spain, was less enthusiastic. As a champion of the Democratic cause he had little good to say about the "aristocracy" of the Federalist era, and thus describes the Father of His Country as "a rather hard businessman, a forerunner of the modern captain of industry." Other commentators saw in Washington a man of the people. The *Chicago Daily Tribune* pictured him as working alongside his laborers, while in a 1924 painting by Frank Schoonover the young Washington is imagined as a rugged outdoorsman in buckskins, quill in hand, surveying the mountain landscape. Schoonover's painting is titled *Whatever He Did He Did Well*, a phrase from Lucy Madison's biography of the same year, which Schoonover illustrated.[14]

One of the many apocrypha that have survived from "Parson" Weems's writings is George Washington praying for guidance at Valley Forge on the evening before crossing the Delaware River on Christmas Day, 1776. The story made for a key scene in *America*, the last of D. W. Griffith's silent epics. The film was released in 1924. In 1925, tens of thousands of Klansmen marched down Pennsylvania Avenue and held a rally at the Washington Monument, as proof of their earnest patriotism.[15] In 1926 the *North American Review*, a thoroughly mainstream journal, published an essay by Hiram Evans, the imperial wizard of the Ku Klux Klan, on the subject of "Americanism." Evans claimed to speak for a marginalized white majority, the "Nordic race," which, for all its "faults," had "given the world almost the whole of modern civilization." Now, Evans concluded, the time had come for these "plain people" to form a new "movement."[16] The resurgence of the KKK in the 1920s fits smoothly in a long history of segregating and, on occasion, excluding specific cultural, ethnic, and religious groups. From the 1850s, the Know Nothing Party attacked Catholics and immigrants. In the early twentieth century, proponents of eugenics warned about the "pollution" of the nation's gene pool by former slaves, the feeble-minded, and newcomers of "inferior" races. The societal environment of the 1920s was no different. World War I had momentarily suspended these animosities while American nationalism declared itself in other directions. After the war, the nationalism that came to the forefront in 1920 essentially continued its prewar trends, except on an elevated level and with different targets. Catholics again suffered, and so did Jews, especially after the Russian Revolution and the appearance of the "Protocols of the Elders of Zion," which reached the United States in 1918. Overall, however, segregation and animosity towards specific cultural, ethnic, and religious groups became more poignant from the 1920s. Distrust of entanglements with Europe and commitment to isolation, economic depression, fresh waves of immigrants, and an increased crime level led many Americans to blame minority groups for the post-war environment.[17]

The American press readily fueled the hostility by continually commenting on the rising "crime wave" and speculating on the wave's foreign origins. An arbitrary anti-foreignism thus extended from coast to coast in the 1920s and on a more violent and expansive level than prior to World War I. The burning of the town of West Frankfort, Illinois, in 1920 is but one example of the violence-driven animosity towards foreigners, in this instance, mostly Italians, who were beaten, burned, and left homeless. The town was taken over by a mob of more than 3,000. But the most notorious of the groups mobilizing the emotional ferment of the period was the Ku Klux Klan, which within a few years reached an all-time peak membership in 1924—the year that not only saw the passing of the Johnson-Reed Act, which sharply reduced the number of immigrants and set quotas that privileged people from "Nordic" countries, but also the dedication of various Confederate memorials, including the Robert E. Lee statue in Charlottesville, Virginia, whose planned removal was the pretext for the "Unite the Right" rally there in August 2017.[18]

Another rally took place in the Jamaica neighborhood of Queens in 1927, in the course of which some 1,000 hooded Klansmen fought the police. One of those arrested on the scene was Fred Trump, the father of Donald J. Trump. The charge against Fred Trump—"refusing to disperse"—was later dropped.[19] Still, the Klan of the 1920s was no fringe group, as millions of nonmembers agreed with its politics. Its rebirth and rise to a four-million membership by 1924 was spurred by another film by D. W. Griffith—the 1915 *The Birth of a Nation*, then the most expensive as well as the most widely seen film that had yet been made. The film, which is based on Thomas Dixon's 1905 novel *The Clansman*, shows rampaging mobs of ex-slaves being brought to reason by the KKK. For President Woodrow Wilson, who saw the film in the White House, Griffith's work was "teaching history with lightning"—armed and mounted Klansmen lynching a black villain, saving the honor of southern womanhood, and obviating the ominous prospect of blacks exerting their voting rights.[20]

Five years after the release of *The Birth of a Nation*, members of yet another previously marginalized group were exerting their voting rights. On June 4, 1919, Congress had passed the 19th Amendment to the Constitution. It was finally made law on August 18, 1920, when Tennessee ratified it. On election day 1920, millions of American women exercised their right to vote for the first time. The Amendment, needless to say, had drawn fierce opposition, accompanied by dire warnings that, as the *New York Times* wrote on May 5, 1912, men may not be "firm and wise enough and, it may as well be said, masculine enough to prevent them." Such comments only underline Linda Gordon's finding that the KKK of the 1920s supplied a way for its male members to confirm their manliness: "As more men became white-collar workers, as more small businesses lost out to chains, as the political supremacy of Anglo-Saxons became contested, as more women reached for economic and political rights," the Klan "organized performances of masculinities and male bonding through uniforms, parades, rituals, secrecy, and hierarchical military ranks and titles."[21]

The rebirth and rise of the KKK as well as of other groups on the political far right cannot be separated from the cultural anxieties of men, who were concerned about their loss of authority. That loss is evident also from the dramatic decline of the degree to which boys accepted their fathers as role models. Although immigrants in general were facing much hostility in the 1920s, immigrant fathers experienced their sex-role identity as particularly strained. Immigrant fathers, Robert Griswold found, were "Poles or Italians who lived in America, but their children were Polish-Americans or Italian-Americans who knew more of Washington and Lincoln than of Pilsudski or Garibaldi."[22] If first-generation fathers confronted an inevitable sense of loss, fathers in general, who were concerned about their sons' "masculine development," began to clamor for a "toughening of American manhood."[23]

Was there any refuge from the present, a make-believe alternative to change and the alienation of fathers from their children? Printing and, by extension, encountering the portraits of "the Presidents of the United States" on the new currency constituted a performance of masculinity that provided a sense of permanence, continuity, and stability. But the 1920s also saw larger-than-life acts of solemn remembrance. These were usually done in granite (or limestone, marble, or concrete, for that matter) and on a grand scale, as if their sole purpose was to overwhelm with the majesty of the nation's glorious past. In the following, I will deal with two of these "rallying points of stability," to borrow the words of the British historian David Cannadine, the Princeton Battle Monument and Mount Rushmore.[24]

The Princeton Battle Monument is a 50-foot monument commemorating the Battle of Princeton of January 3, 1777, which marked a decisive victory for the Continental Army under Washington. The massive lime-stone sculpture was dedicated in June 1922, by President Warren G. Harding (who had dedicated the Lincoln Memorial only ten days earlier). The idea for the memorial dates from 1887 but fund-raising and the search for a suitable site bedeviled the project for twenty years. By 1907, enough money had been raised to select a sculptor, Augustus Saint-Gaudens. Saint-Gaudens died in the same year and his follower, Frederick William MacMonnies, who had been Saint-Gaudens's student, in early 1912 came up with the first design ideas. MacMonnies suggested "a stone or granite pylon with a great bas-relief on the face and inscription on the back. The bas-relief represents that moment in the war just before the Battle of Princeton when the armies were much discouraged, but sustained by the unquenchable patriotism of Washington."[25] Seated on his horse, George Washington was the dominant figure in the original design. Next to him was an allegory of Victory, raising the Star-Spangled Banner in triumph.

MacMonnies continued to work on the design. Meanwhile, World War I had begun, and the artist found himself in Paris. In September 1914, British and French forces stopped a German offensive at the first Battle of the Marne. MacMonnies associated the Allied victory in Europe with Washington rallying his troops at Princeton in January 1777 for the first substantial American victory in the Revolutionary War. More than two years before the United States entered the war, MacMonnies thus writes to his wife: War "seems real, and heroism and sacrifice seem natural and unpretentious." The event of the Marne greatly altered the artist's perception of the subject; by 1918 he considered the work's central idea in the following terms: "disaster, defeat, misery, suffering despair—triumphed over and forgotten and cast aside by the unconquerable spirit of love of liberty." Thus, the monument became, "not an anecdotal narration" of a historical event but, as MacMonnies's wife, Alice Jones MacMonnies, made clear, "the presentiment of character in supreme crisis [...] the unfailing vision of Washington, pointing the way [...] to turn the tide at Princeton at the most fateful moment of the Revolution. It is the epic of the lost cause; of defeat turned into victory by the miracle of supreme heroism, sacrifice, vision, and faith, which triumphs over despair. It is dedicated to all lost causes heroically supported; to Thermopylae, Gallipoli, Princeton, and the Marne."

As we will see in the following chapter, the ability to turn defeat into victory, heroism, sacrifice, vision, and faith, which triumphs over despair are the supreme qualities of a great president. Between 1927 and 1941, the monumental heads of four great presidents—Washington, Jefferson, Theodore Roosevelt, and Lincoln—were sculpted out of Mount Rushmore's granite under the guidance of Gutzon Borglum.[26] The four heads—each measuring 60 feet from chin to scalp—symbolize 150 years of the United States, from its founding to expansion to preservation to imperial power. The dominant head is that of America's first president, which clearly shows the influence of Stuart's enduring Athenaeum portrait (though Borglum also cited the influence of Rembrandt Peale and Houdon's masks). It is estimated that the Father of the Country's head, as well as the heads of the other three presidents will still be around 10,000 years from now, which makes Mount Rushmore a monument that literalizes permanence, continuity, and endurance—"patriarchy fixed in stone," in the words of art historian Albert Boime.[27]

When the monument opened in 1941, it was also a triumph to male America. What could be more masculine than dynamite, jackhammers, chisels, and drills—and a cadre of over four hundred workers blasting away some 450,000 tons of granite in the process (and leaving the debris at the memorial's base). For Albert Boime, Mount Rushmore represents "the triumph of modern civilization over [...] geography [...] God-created man now recreates Mother Nature in his own image, realizing through modern technology the old myth of the artist as usurper of the Creator's prerogative."[28] Gutzon Borglum himself had described the monument's scale as truly "soul-stirring," adding that this quality "should be incorporated in all national expression—consciously and deliberately in scale with its importance—in scale with the people whose life it expresses." The rhetoric but thinly conceals Borglum's elitism and right-wing ideology.[29] Yet other public buildings of the time were also built "in scale" with their importance—the Washington Monument, the White House extension, the Union Station, the Lincoln Memorial (built to resemble a Greek temple, dedicated in 1922, and reproduced on the $5 Legal Tender and Federal Reserve notes of the series of 1928), the Arlington Memorial Bridge, the Jefferson Memorial, as well as various government buildings surrounding the United States Capitol. As the contemporary architect Cass Gilbert phrased the agenda, public buildings should inspire "just pride in the state," and be "a symbol of the civilization, culture, and ideals of our country."[30]

The original idea for the Mount Rushmore memorial goes back to 1923, when South Dakota State Historian Doane Robinson proposed to carve images of Western heroes into the Black Hills as a means to attract tourists. Gutzon Borglum, who was hired for the project, rejected both the site and the theme, envisioning instead a national monument of massive scope and significance. More than three million people each year visit the "Shrine of Democracy," a testimony to Mount Rushmore's unbroken popularity. The monument has also been translated into numerous other media, including postcards, decorative plates, jewelry, decanters, postage stamps, commemorative coins, and other items available for purchase on the site, thus enabling visitors to bring a piece of their tourist experience home with them. And the golden jubilee of the Mount Rushmore National Memorial in 1991 provided the occasion for three new commemorative coins, a half dollar, a silver dollar, and a $5 gold piece.[31]

In the creative imagination that produced this "national shrine" (as President Calvin Coolidge called Mount Rushmore in 1927, shortly after its dedication), George Washington reigns as the unequivocal father figure, the strong and wise ruler for the "common man."[32] Yet a likeness in granite does not reveal anything about the inner person. Rather, its bigness silences the nation's fears, its cultural insecurities, its fractured, diverse communities, perhaps even its guilt. The same can be said about its literary equivalents, historical romances such as S. Weir Mitchell's, whose multivolume cycle began in 1904 with *The Youth of Washington*. Each volume constitutes a larger-than-life act of solemn remembrance, of national prowess and pride that, ironically, appeared at roughly the same time as psychoanalysis began its triumphal march across the United States.[33] However, cultural fears remain unspoken not just in genuinely "portentous" products ("portentous" in the sense of pompous, and also in "portending," for instance a national dread), but as well in more modest achievements, such as, for instance, the more than twenty-five paintings of George Washington created by Jean Leon Gerome Ferris. Ferris's paintings, of which *Washington and His Family* is perhaps the best known, were widely reproduced on magazine covers, illustrated calendars, and postcards. Although Ferris claimed that his works were more "realistic" and "human" than others, they are nevertheless just as idealized as Junius Brutus Stearns's paintings of the 1850s or Edward Savage's *The Washington Family* of 1796.

Ferris's homages to the Father of His Country, as well as an additional fifty or so canvases from the Revolutionary era were the perfect fit for a period of colonial revival. While their romanticism had a special appeal to the antimodern streak that underlay Victorian America, they likewise provided uplift during the Great Depression, and were still reproduced from the late 1940s. The entire body of Ferris's works, which came to be known as the "Archive of '76," was first exhibited in the chamber of Independence Hall where Washington was inaugurated in 1793, and later in Congress Hall, before it passed into the public domain and the collection of the Smithsonian's division of history, just in time for the bicentennial of 1932. Also just in time for the bicentennial Ferris finished *Betsy Ross, 1777* and *Washington's Inauguration at Philadelphia*. A number of Ferris's paintings were used as historical illustrations in the 15-volume *Pageant of a Nation* series issued by Yale University Press between 1925 and 1929.[34] *Betsy Ross, 1777* depicts the Philadelphia seamstress showing Major Ross and Robert Morris how she cut the stars for the American flag. George Washington sits in a chair on the left; a young girl is looking at him, thus completing a veritable family tableau for the Founding Father and the Founding Mother.

In *The Painter and the President, 1795* (c. 1916–1920), Ferris imagined the making of the Washington mythology. The scene is Gilbert Stuart's studio. Across a small table to Stuart's left, George Washington poses placidly, legs crossed, while Martha Washington—seated to Stuart's right and immediately beside the canvas—appears to offer the painter some advice. Martha's velvety dress and mobcap, the fashionably dressed young men and women behind her, and the artist's accouterments lying around the room all smack of colonial-revival "realism." Through interaction among appropriately costumed figures, Ferris retells the story behind an episode from the Father of His Country's life: the creation of the Athenaeum portrait, which sits in Stuart's easel in the center of the painting. Nothing could be further from the unpleasant atmosphere Washington recorded in his own version of the sitting. But to cast Stuart in the role of official court painter had been done before. Carl H. Schmolze's 1858 *Washington Sitting for His Portrait to Gilbert Stuart* had captured the celebrity and mythic level attained by the Athenaeum at a time that has gone down as the "commemorative period of the nation's history." Yet whereas Schmolze rendered a well-dressed, almost aristocratic group in a luxurious studio space, Ferris created a much cozier version of the past for an audience entranced by the romance of colonial America. *The Painter and the*

Jean Leon Jerome Ferris, *Betsy Ross, 1777 / L.L.G. Ferris*. Reproduction of oil painting from series *The Pageant of a* Nation. Cleveland, Ohio: The Foundation Press, Inc., July 28, 1932 (photograph retrieved from the Library of Congress, Prints and Photographs Division).

President was little appreciated until the observances of the 1932 bicentennial of Washington's birth landed the picture on giveaway calendars and in the color supplement pages of popular magazines.[35]

The Bicentennial of 1932 also looms large in a 1931 pageant, *The Father of His Country*, by Esther C. and Lawrence A. Averill. Its five episodes begin with Washington returning safely from a campaign in the French and Indian War, go on with Washington taking command at Cambridge, lead the audience through the events of the Revolution, show him as President and at home at Mount Vernon, and ends—in 1932, with a processional in which Washington's name is spelled out, each letter synonymous with some kind of memorial to the Father of His Country. Whereas playwrights like the Averills or artists like Ferris, John Ward Dunsmore, Henry A. Ogden, Percy Morgan, and Howard Pyle made a living from the romantic appeal of colonial America, the post–World War I iconoclasts' purpose was to dismantle the prevailing filiopietism by cataloging George Washington's purported flaws. Later scholars like John C. Fitzpatrick discredited most of these claims, though the work of these "grand dukes of debunkery," as Edward G. Lengel has called them, had its effect. By the late 1920s, as the bicentennial of Washington's birth was approaching, the pedestal began cracking under his feet.

The particular symbolic value invested in the Father of His Country had not grown suddenly ineffectual, however. Already by the early years of the twentieth century, the popularity of the Washington cult was surpassed by Lincoln's. Popular media indexes, for instance, show Lincoln to be written about much more often than Washington, whose dignified restraint and aloofness of his image undermined his popularity. By 1945, national opinion polls also placed Lincoln above Washington, largely because Lincoln was seen as "a greater humanitarian, more down to earth, more of a people's President."[36] The assessment has not changed much until today. Although professional historians complained, Lincoln is usually rated as the nation's greatest president, with Washington ranked second. These historians, Gordon S. Wood among them, could take some consolation from the fact that this general trend showed some sharp fluctuations. Between 1925 and 1932, Lincoln's leading place was lost as the nation planned for, carried out, and reflected upon its year-long celebration of the two-hundredth anniversary of George Washington's birth—the most extensive celebration ever held for a national leader.[37]

The Bicentennial took many years to prepare. President Calvin Coolidge signed the bicentennial bill in December of 1924, with February 22, 1932, designated as the official bicentennial birthday. En route to the Bicentennial, the United States Mint in 1926 issued the Sesquicentennial of American Independence half dollar, which paired Washington's bust with that of the living president, Calvin Coolidge.[38] The Bicentennial itself was marked by some truly outrageous activities. Sol Bloom, the New York congressman whom President Herbert Hoover appointed to the directorship of the Bicentennial Commission, drew on his earlier career as a public relations man and musical entrepreneur to create a patriotic extravaganza, enlisting celebrities right and left. Jimmy Doolittle, an aviator, loaded into his mail plane a middle-aged great-great-great-grandniece of the first president and flew over every part of the nation where Washington had actually traveled, covering 2,600 miles between dawn and dusk on July 25, 1932. Bloom also organized public events, masquerades, radio shows, and patriotic concerts, he had Washington's name and face put on souvenirs and trinkets, and he had streets and buildings named after the Father of His Country. Framed cardboard versions of Stuart's "Athenaeum" portrait were issued by the Commission, finding their way into virtually every schoolroom in America. Millions of pages of print were also published, including hundreds of playlets tailored for production in schools or pageants. Teachers' manuals were crammed with ideas for instilling patriotism in the young through engaging in elaborate rites—disguising as postage stamps, snipping five-pointed stars out of scraps of old bedsheets, crossing let's-pretend rivers muffled in

Jean-Antoine Houdon, Washington bust, 1785 (25 × 18 × 18 in.) (Dallas Museum of Art, gift of Ronald E. Fritz).

tablecloths or, for young girls, playing at Betsy Ross making the Stars and Stripes for George Washington.[39]

Sol Bloom also got on the front page with his efforts, per congressional mandate, to select an unimpeachable likeness of the Father of His Country. The chosen likeness would have "official sanction and be issued in hundreds of thousands of copies as part of the observance of 1932."[40] Whatever the image finally picked, it would appear on stamps, a bicentennial medal, a commemorative quarter, be distributed to the country's schools and, even more important, it would serve as the official logo for the United States George Washington Bicentennial Commission. In order to find a definitive portrait, a special "portrait committee" was established, though the committee, a mutually despising company composed of art critics and historians, could not agree on a single portrait. Finally, Houdon's bust of 1785 gained a majority and was duly photographed by an Austrian named Jaffé.[41]

Secretary of the Treasury Andrew Mellon lost no time in making one of the commission's "authentic" photographs the model for artists competing for the design of a new circulating coin, the Washington Quarter. The coin debuted on August 1, 1832. Although it was trumpeted as the numismatic plum of the decade, only some six million pieces of it were minted and distributed that year, as the nation's economy was in such a slump that additional pieces were not needed in commerce. Since, the Washington Quarter has been circulating in numerous combinations of metals, the loss of its silver, in 1965, included. Though intended as a commemorative, the Washington Quarter has become *the* twenty-five-cent piece used by Americans, one of the most popular coins ever produced by the United States Mint. New quarters are minted each year with the date changed but nothing else.[42] The Washington Quarter may have become Americans' day-to-day coin, but critics never regarded it as providing an artistic "statement." As Cornelius Vermeule wrote, John Flanagan's portrait of Washington was merely "a symptom of the frozen, conservative classic naturalism that affected U.S. governmental sculpture in the generation from 1932 to 1950."[43] The designs and models submitted by Laura Gardin Fraser had been much more vibrant, and they were preferred by nearly everyone except the Treasury Secretary, who had the last word in the decision. It also did not help that, perhaps as compensation, Fraser was the winner of the competition for the Bicentennial medal authorized by Congress.

A notable exception to the bizarre happenings of the Bicentennial was the appointment of John C. Fitzpatrick to the editorship of *The Writings of George Washington*, published in 37 volumes between 1931 and 1944. Fitzpatrick died before all the volumes were published, though his involvement during this prolonged effort set many of the standards for the management of manuscripts in the Library of Congress. As Fitzpatrick and his team were gearing up, the U.S. Postal Service contributed to the bicentennial by introducing a special twelve-stamp set bearing Washington's portrait, with Stuart's "Athenaeum" portrait on the two-cent stamp. Known as "The little red stamp," it not only moved the bulk of the nation's personal mail but also became the subject of a popular poem by Sam Walter Foss.[44] Yet it is Norman Rockwell's painting *The Guiding Influence* which most fully captures the bicentennial's intention of perpetuating the Washington myth. Rockwell showed an earnest and well-groomed young man sitting at his desk. A copy of Houdon's bust is placed before him, while above him we see an image of what the all-American youth is contemplating so deeply—George Washington, in heroic pose, his outstretched left arm raised and pointed ahead. Most likely the fresh-faced calendar boy is working on a composition on the Father of His Country, as did hundreds of thousands of young students during the year of the bicentennial celebration. Writing compositions, learning by heart and reciting poems to and

Norman Rockwell, *The Guiding Influence*, reproduction of painting in *History of the George Washington Bicentennial Celebration*, vol. III (1932), frontispiece.

about Washington, boning up on facts and cramming other bits of useful knowledge—all to preserve an imaginary Washington that would provide young people with a model for and stimulus to moral behavior. Unsurprisingly, Rockwell's work—which Sol Bloom had titled "the guiding inspiration"—served as a government poster and a Sears catalog cover that was sold framed and ready for hanging in a boy's room; it was used as the frontispiece to volume 3 of the *History of the George Washington Bicentennial Celebration* and, later, as the frontispiece in Dixon Wecter's book *The Hero in America*.[45]

V

The Preservation of Our Folklore

The Bicentennial of George Washington's birth coincided with the Great Depression. Uplift was essential then. While Norman Rockwell's *The Guiding Influence* provided just that, the Iowa painter Grant Wood had other purposes. Among his numerous paintings about the mania for all things Revolutionary, two stand out. One is *Daughters of Revolution* (1932), in which three superannuated DAR matrons are celebrating their annual Martha Washington tea in front of a distorted reproduction of Leutze's *Washington Crossing the Delaware*.

The other is *Parson Weems' Fable* (1939), in which Wood playfully captured the moment when the self-declared parson "discovered" the story of young Washington informing his father, "I cannot tell a lie." In the painting's foreground, a smirking Weems raises a curtain with his right hand while gesturing with his left toward the "historic" scene. Young George, in turn, holds the hatchet in his left hand and points to it with his right, while his father clutches the cut-down cherry tree and gestures toward his son.

These as well as numerous other details are Grant Wood's way of calling attention to the ways in which the past is always mediated by representations that elevate stories like Weems's and paintings like Stuart's or Leutze's to the status of national mythology. Yet Wood, once he had come to elaborate a "born-again" narrative of how he had rejected "outlandish" modernism and embraced homegrown sources of inspiration, did not seek to disparage the value of such unifying myths themselves. As he asserted in 1940, "*the preservation of our folklore is more important than generally realized.*"[1]

12

George of Many Perceptions

One man to realize the importance of America's folklore was J. C. Leyendecker, whose famous cover of the *Saturday Evening Post* for February 23, 1935, pictures George Washington on bended knees, praying for guidance at Valley Forge on the evening before his famous crossing of the Delaware River on Christmas Day, 1776.[1] The Valley Forge tale is one of the many apocrypha that have survived from "Parson" Weems's writings. It appeared for the first time in an article Weems wrote for *The Federalist* in 1804. He then included it in the 1809 edition of his *Life of Washington*.[2] Weems's source is unknown, and the later explanation, in the unpublished memoirs of a Presbyterian minister by the name of Nathaniel Randolph Snowden, that it came from a Quaker who had discovered Washington in prayer is dubious, to say the least. Still, the story was eagerly accepted as a fact. It appeared in one of Wilkins Tannehill's *Tales of the Revolution* (1834), in George Lippard's *Washington and His Men* (1849), and in *Blanche of Brandywine* (1856), John Brougham's stage adaptation of Lippard's romance of the same name. In 1852, Benson J. Lossing's *Pictorial Field-Book of the Revolution* retold the legend with new details, such as that Washington had tied his horse to a tree nearby and that his face had been "suffused with tears." The legendary incident is a staple also of A. W. Quinley's novel *Valley Forge* (1906), as well as of some six plays between 1875 and 1935 (most of which are deservedly forgotten, Maxwell Anderson's play of 1934 excepted). *Washington at Valley Forge* (1908) has the distinction of being the first Washington film on record. (Another film with the same title was made in 1914.) Washington at prayer made for a key scene in *Washington Under the American Flag* (1909) and in *America*, the last of D. W. Griffith's silent epics (1924). An 1866 painting by Henry Brueckner, which shows the kneeling General in a snowy scene complete with a few soldiers huddling over a fire in the background, was engraved in the same year by John McRae and served to commemorate the 150th anniversary of the Valley Forge encampment on a 2-cent postage stamp in 1928. Leyendecker's rendering of the prayer was printed on a 13-cent Christmas stamp in 1977. The year before, Arnold Friberg had put on display the best-known modern version of the Valley Forge prayer to commemorate the Bicentennial.[3]

Grant Wood's summons to the "preservation of our folklore" is also played out in a number of films of the Depression era, which told people what kind of situation they were in and how they might or might not cope with it. In *The Phantom President*, for instance, four former presidents—Washington, Jefferson, Lincoln, and Theodore Roosevelt—emerge from large picture frames to do a song-and-dance routine, singing "The Country Needs a Man."[4] *The Phantom President* was released in 1932. With Franklin D. Roosevelt running, there was no need for a stand-in for the actual candidate. But the film prepared the country for what FDR was going to say a year later in his first inaugural address: "[T]he only thing we have to fear is fear itself."[5] As president, Roosevelt actively cultivated the image of a caregiver or male role model, not least with the help of his "fireside chats," in which he invited Americans over the networks to "tell me your troubles." The first of these chats ended with the words, "Together, we cannot fail."[6] By that time, Roosevelt already had instigated an inspirational, political film, with his own message featured in the title song: "The Road to Better Times is Open Again."

To many Americans who actually took to the road, the song must have sounded like a sick joke. In a 1937 photograph taken by Dorothea Lange near Tracy, California, a Missouri family of five who are seven months from the drought area find themselves stranded on U.S. Highway 99. The photograph shows the woman with her young children (one of them sick) and a broken-down vehicle loaded like a Conestoga wagon, with all her worldly possessions. The husband apparently has gone for help and there is no one else in sight. Her fate, and that of her family, hangs in the balance.

Dorothea Lange's photograph sums up the nightmares of the decade, not just for wives and children but also and especially for fathers, who felt that their sense of manhood and personal identity was being destroyed. As Robert Griswold wrote in *Fatherhood in America*: "For the millions of fathers who lost their jobs, farms, and income because of the Depression ... the patriarchal order based on male breadwinning, fatherly responsibilities, and female economic dependence" was severely shaken.[7] One way for fathers to demonstrate their maleness in the 1930s was to establish closer ties with their children. "Tell them a story every night," *American Home* advised fathers in 1935.[8] This is precisely what *The Phantom President* did. In the film, a propaganda piece done by Warner Bros. for the NRA in 1932, the song "The Road to Better Times is Open Again" is created by a musician at his piano, trying to write music, with portraits of Washington, Lincoln, and Woodrow Wilson on the wall. But he naps, and the three presidents appear reading a newspaper about how the NRA has created one million jobs. When the songwriter awakes, Washington tells him he's been watching over the country for more than a hundred years.[9]

Movie audiences went home feeling that the Father of His Country would continue to watch over the country for another hundred years. On occasion, God would provide additional help, as in Irving Berlin's "God Bless America," composed on the eve of World War II. "[W]hile the storm clouds gather far across the sea," music audiences would hear in 1938 America, God was implored to "stand beside her and guide her / Through the night with a light from above...." A light from above in fact shines on George Washington standing on an elevated platform while presiding over the Constitutional Convention. The scene is from Howard Chandler Christy's 20-by-30-foot oil painting, on display in the Capitol's Rotunda since its unveiling in May 1940. Christy's Washington strikes a stately pose. Not only is he physically larger than any other of the thirty-nine delegates depicted in the painting. More importantly, Washington is not facing the Convention. Instead, he gazes into the future. The pose conveys the idea that the Father of His Country is standing above the political arguing, while he is nevertheless able to influence others by his moral example. This notion is underscored by the light, which streams into the chamber highlighting him and simultaneously emanates from him, reflecting on Hamilton, Franklin, and Madison, who sit in front of the stage.[10]

By the time Howard Chandler Christy's gigantic oil painting was unveiled, the surprise attack on Pearl Harbor was just over a year and a half away. The bombing of Pearl Harbor and America's entry into World War II not only got the country out of its economic crisis. It also rescued fatherhood from its shaky status during the Depression. As millions of men enlisted in the armed forces, the sacrifice fathers were making at one and the same time

Dorothea Lange, *"Broke, baby sick, and car trouble!"* February 1937. Gelatin silver print. Farm Security Administration (FSA) (Library of Congress, Prints and Photographs Division).

"restored men's breadwinning abilities" and "reaffirmed fathers' critical role in the health of the republic."[11] In the brave fight for democracy, moral uplift was once again in demand. On the morning of December 7, 1941, Admiral Thomas C. Hart, who then was commander in chief of the U.S. Asiatic Fleet, cited George Washington's integrity and self-sacrifice as an inspiration for all Americans.[12] The Admiral's words, spoken amid the carnage at Pearl Harbor, not only fit the shift in the image of fathers; they also mark a move toward a more conservative set of values, something that came to shape the country's social and political climate for years to come. General Eisenhower, too, claimed Washington as his military exemplar, calling him "the greatest man the English-speaking world ever produced." Eisenhower's troops may have had less use for a bewigged gentleman warrior, but a humorous movie about America's first soldier was popular in army camps in 1943. The movie, *This Is the Army*, starred Ronald Reagan as a GI producer who entertains the troops with a musical review of the American heritage they are defending. Irving Berlin, who in 1938 had composed "God Bless America," plays a skinny doughboy from World War I. Standing before his tent he croaks: "If George Washington were alive today / He'd pick up his sword, / And then he'd say—/ This is our country...."[13]

Washington did pick up his sword in "The Man Who Stole the Sun," one of the first of the Superman comics.[14] More serious is Sidney Kingsley's play *The Patriots*, produced for the first time at the National Theatre in New York in 1943. The play dramatizes the multiple conflicts among the founders under Washington's presidency. Thus, the Father of His Country has to check the quarrels between Madison and Hamilton, or deal with Jefferson threatening to leave the cabinet. A speech by Washington finally turns the tide. "The fabric is crumbling," he says to Jefferson. "Our republic dying. We must bolster it, somehow—someway." Thereafter, all fight to the finish, providing much-needed patriotic fuel to a war-tried audience that could hardly have missed the analogy between the dark days during the early republic and the present.[15] In Howard Fasts's 1942 novel *The Unvanquished* Washington appears not as president but as a military hero. The period treated is the beginning of the War of Independence, from the disastrous New York campaign in the summer of 1776 to the crossing of the Delaware River on Christmas Day of the same year. For the greater part, readers are exposed to an unbroken chain of dismal failures, desertions, disappointments, increasing hopelessness, doubt, uncertainty, and loneliness—until the men get ready to cross the river. Then everyone knew, "with fierce joy, that this was not the end, that for their kind there could never be an end, but only new beginnings." For Washington, the baptism in the river effects a magical transformation. As Fast wrote in his afterword: "But the man who had set out across the Delaware as a Virginia farmer, as a foxhunter, became on the other shore something else, a man of incredible stature, a human being in some ways more godly and wonderful than any other who has walked this earth."[16]

Almost thirty years after *The Unvanquished*, Howard Fast wrote another novel on the crossing of the Delaware. *The Crossing* (1971), became the basis for an historical TV film that went on air in January 2000, a timely lesson in leadership for the era of George W. Bush. In 1942, however, the publication of *The Unvanquished* marked a profound change in portrayals of the Father of His Country, from cataloging Washington's purported flaws, as was the agenda of the debunkers, to humanizing him. Howard Fast's Washington is neither the stately demigod of republican art nor the at once haloed and priggish Father in the Parson Weems tradition. "All the debunking in the world," Fast sounded in the afterword, "cannot change the facts of [Washington's] wonderful simplicity, his complete unselfishness, his humble respect for those who asked him to leave his home and fight a revolution."[17]

As Howard Fast was at work on *The Unvanquished*, increasing numbers of Americans were being asked to leave their homes and fight, not a revolution so much as foreign military powers threatening to conquer the world. It should not surprise anyone that the demand for mythic stories or grand narratives then became more intense and the moral inspiration from even the crudest myth more deeply felt. All kinds of heroes became subjects of tremendous interest for historians as well as for literary scholars.[18] This has important implications for our understanding of the metaphorical father. The metaphorical father does not speak for himself; to be known, accepted, or believed in he must be articulated in vivid images. To simply declare him performatively as the Father of His Country is not enough. The metaphorical Father of His Country cannot be a model without help. The help he needs to be kept alive is commemoration. Commemoration, Émile Durkheim told us, revivifies "these most essential aspects of the collective consciousness [...] the glorious souvenirs which are made to live again, and with which [people] feel that they have a kinship."[19]

Commemoration of the metaphorical father has taken many forms. From the time of his death in 1799 to the present day, every generation of Americans has seen the Father of His Country in the context of its own concerns. The fading concept of greatness, together with a changed understanding of the presidency—from presidential restraint and the domination of Congress to the concentration of power in and the focus of people on the "imperial" President (the term is Robert G. Denton's)—and, not to forget, societal trends that diminished the significance of fathers, metaphorical fathers included, precipitated Washington's descent. A 1937 screwball comedy by the title *Marry the Girl* bears this out.[20] In this film, Washington appears as a mentally unbalanced inmate of a Dr. Hayden Stryker's Fairview Sanitarium. Dressed impeccably in a lounge suit, the Father of His Country strides by without saying a word as two newspaper men look behind a Stuart portrait of Washington for a missing cartoon. While the film's bent depiction lends a special appeal given the notorious rigidity of Washington's public persona, it is also an early indication of a deeper skepticism. Skepticism of George Washington as a heroic father figure worthy of emulation culminated in the overall rejection of paternal authority during the 1960s.

In *Wild in the Streets* (1968), which became a kind of "cult" film for the counterculture, the main character, twenty-four-old Max Frost (played by Christopher Jones), is a pop-rock singer and teen idol who becomes a leader and spokesman for rebellious youth. As a price for handing over his mass following to the Democratic candidate for the presidency, Frost demands a reduction in the voting age—to fourteen, which Congress approves after Frost and his friends send it on an "acid trip" by spiking the D.C. water supply. With his supporters enfranchised and massing the streets, Frost is handed the Republican nomination and wins the presidency in a landslide. In his capacity as POTUS, he embarks on a program of "generational cleansing," ordering everyone over thirty-five rounded up and sent to "groovy" rehabilitation camps. "Some of them are really gonna dig it," Frost promises.[21] George Washington was definitely not among them, as he was frequently shown as disapproving of the counterculture and its life-style. An article by Marshall Fishwick reprinted a poster that depicts the Father of His Country dressed in leather thong jacket, bell bottoms, and platforms. He stares out of his Stuart-like portrait and asks: "What's This Country Coming To?"[22]

The difference between counterculture lifestyle and Washington's dismay reflects a deep-lying tension, described by Jeff Smith as follows: "Countercultures cannot lay claim to mainstream institutions because the mainstream is what they are defined against."[23] At the same time, the tension only underscores Washington's remoteness, which in turn accounts for his diminishing relevance. As early as February 22, 1944, an editorial in the *Boston Herald* proclaimed: "Everybody feels as if he knows Lincoln and merely knows of Washington ... to most of us he still remains austere, unapproachable, a sort of plaster saint, a figure who matured long before his time and never ripened or mellowed."[24] Whereas many people felt that Washington was a remote and cold figure, as though sculpted in marble, Lincoln tended to be talked about in terms of a high-definition, warm presence. Surely this had something to do with character and, not to forget, the assassination, as well as the fact that Lincoln, taken against other elected leaders in world history, was just plain good. But on top of that, it seems that from the post–Civil War era onward America needed a warmer father-figure than the sculpted Washington image could provide.

The mood changed somewhat in the 1950s, as historians tried to make sense of Washington's alleged remoteness. For Marcus Cunliffe, Washington was essentially a figure "of the *eighteenth* century," and his alleged remoteness both cause and effect of historical circumstances.²⁵ Washington's remoteness remained topical for the next generation of historians. "Washington was a thoroughly 18th-century figure," Gordon S. Wood wrote in 1992. "So much so, that he quickly became an anachronism. He belonged to the pre-democratic and pre-egalitarian world of the 18th century, to a world very different from the world that would follow. No wonder then that he seems to us so remote and so distant. He really is. He belonged to a world we have lost and we were losing even as Washington lived."²⁶ Professor Wood's remarks are pertinent. Remoteness and distance are necessary conditions for Washington's status as a moral exemplar. Too much closeness leads to disenchantment, even profanization. Better not to know too much, lest the aura and charisma are destroyed. Thus to imagine the Father of His Country as ordinary or even defective makes it impossible to bow in awe to a greater-than-life being. On the other hand, Wood's remarks can also be read as a warning. While Washington and his time have often served as a place of refuge from the present, a make-believe alternative to change, the opposite alternative, to view the patrician past of George Washington as a benchmark against which the present could be measured, is not always an option in an age that has seen the end of heroism, and that finds it difficult to acknowledge any authority, least of all an authority based on traditional concepts of masculinity. Only orthodox dogmatists seem able to still uphold ideals of perfection.

Skepticism of this kind became a broader phenomenon in the decade preceding the Bicentennial of 1976. *Sweet Funk*, a 1963 oil painting by Phillip Hefferton remodels the Washington from the one-dollar bill, transforming it into a brick wall. It is tempting to see the monumentalization of the national monetary icon as a preemptive reinforcement against the series of seismic shocks the country was soon to undergo. These shocks were brought on chiefly by political assassinations, the protests of African Americans and of the nation's youth, the Vietnam War, and Watergate. To which should be added the women's movement and the gay liberation movement, with their scathing critiques of traditional concepts of masculinity and their demands for inclusion and equality in the public arena. In the realm of culture, familiar symbols and frames were replaced by the mundane signatures of pop art. In the academy, revisionists began to challenge traditional interpretations of the nation's past and contest the conventional "western" perspective. The self-identification on the basis of ethnicity, race, or gender paved the way for the questioning of all fixed or transcendent categories of meaning, including the reverence for "dead white men," especially slaveholders and others directly associated with racial oppression.²⁷

In keeping with its policy of not naming schools for former slave owners, the New Orleans School Board in 1997 changed the name of George Washington Elementary to Dr. Richard Drew Elementary, honoring a pioneering African American surgeon. The school board's action sparked nationwide controversy, including an op-ed piece in the *New York Times*.²⁸ In contrast, when revisionist historiographers expanded traditional heroic tales with chapters on "Washington as a slave-owner" or "Washington as a colonizer at the expense of Native Americans," the public did not take much notice.²⁹ Of course, it was slave labor, along with land speculation, that made Washington one of the richest men in Virginia. Still, he professed pity for "these poor wretches" and detested the idea of offering his slaves in a public sale. In 1794, Washington wrote of his earnest desire "to liberate a certain species of property which I possess, very repugnantly to my feelings." And by 1797, he wished "that the Legislature of this State [of Virginia] could see the policy of a gradual Abolition of Slavery."³⁰

All this goes to show that memory matters. Memory, the historian T. J. Stiles wrote recently, makes meaning. Memory also makes politics, and politics makes memory, especially in the popular imagination. In the context of "postmodernity and multiculturalism," naturally, many icons were subjected to iconoclastic interpretations. America's presidents too were not immune to these changes. As Karal Ann Marling suggested, more than a century of overexposure and mythmaking, the cacophony of Washington's multifarious popular culture presence, and the battles over debunking all contributed to dilute a clear definition of what Washington might be for Americans. Several variations on Emanuel Leutze's iconic painting bear this out—Roy Lichtenstein's lost painting of 1952, Larry Rivers's 1953 painting of an anxious Washington, or Edward Sorel's burlesque version of Leutze's masterpiece, *Nixon Crossing the Delaware* (1973).[31]

In 1975, Robert Colescott's *George Washington Carver Crossing the Delaware* altogether did away with the Father of His Country, replaced by Carver, in the same uniform and pose, while Leutze's oarsmen correspond to familiar racist portrayals of African Americans, from minstrel-show personnel to figures from commercial logos, thus exposing the immensity of stereotyping.[32] Replacement is the strategy of choice also for the artists who in 2018 produced "Trump Crossing the Delaware." The satirical piece, which was put on the cover of Trevor Noah's *The Donald J. Trump Presidential Twitter Library*, depicts America's 45th president together with his most loyal advisors, who are "following his detailed orders as they row across a river of liberal tears. As in life, Trump has surrounded himself with a diverse staff of loyal white people, each believing that he or she is the grownup keeping the boat from sinking."[33]

The theme of shipwreck already loomed large in Peter Saul's pop-art-inspired *Washington Crossing the Delaware*, from 1975, in which a dazed-looking general holds up a comically small flag while his horse, like the soldiers, spills out of the precariously pitching boat. While Saul transformed Leutze's iconic painting into a cartoon-like image of mayhem, Robert Arneson in the year of the Bicentennial sculpted Washington as a wine-bibbler with a glazed-ceramic portrait head titled *Can You Suggest a '76 Pinot Noir*, thus probing a patrician, and to some extent superficial, dimension of his subject in a bold and humorous way. Also in 1976, Arneson created a ceramic sculpture *George and Mona in the Baths of Coloma*, in which the apparently naked Father of His Country casts a lecherous smile upon a fetching Mona Lisa. The two icons are sitting together in a pool of water. Arneson later claimed, ironically, that the low level of water symbolizes the declining value of the dollar. The sculpture certainly has something to say about America's money. To Mark Thistlethwaite, "Washington's green countenance, scored with lines, purposely suggests the form in which Stuart's portrait is seen daily: the 1796 'Athenaeum' image on the dollar bill."[34]

There is hardly a better way to bring to the fore the "sacredness" of an object than to desecrate or vilify it. In 1779, for instance, the provisional government of Pennsylvania commissioned a Washington portrait, both to show the respect due the general and to give an impetus to emulation. A few years later, the portrait was mutilated by unknown perpetrators. The act was duly seen as "a deed of darkness […] for the sons of Lucifer," as if they had desecrated a religious icon.[35] The storm of indignation echoes the understanding, in the Christian tradition, that each human face was at once unique and a reflection of the divinity. In each act of mutilation, disfigurement, defacement, or desecration there is, therefore, at least an implicit acknowledgment, on the part of iconoclasts, of the object's "sacredness." This is also true of less dramatic forms of violations. During the Bicentennial Year, 1976, Washington appeared on the front cover of *MAD* Magazine—crossed with Alfred E. Neumann, the magazine's fictitious mascot and cover boy, and with his teeth recovered, though a front tooth is missing. A short letter to Gilbert Stuart completes the picture: "Dear

Mr. Stuart: I really do not believe this to be a good likeness of me. It would best remain unfinished."[36]

More recent is a birthday card featuring Stuart's Washington bearing a big grin. Below the image was written: "George on Prozac." The card obviously suggests that a smiling Father of His Country is possible only when he is under the influence.[37] The technical term for strategies that playfully turn icons against themselves without destroying recognition of them as icons is *détournement*.[38] *Détournement* also speaks from Phillip Hefferton's paintings. *Sinking George*, a 1962 composition, makes use of the ship-of-state metaphor to ridicule Washington by depicting him as vanishing from view. In *Sweet Funk* (1963), Washington's face from the one-dollar bill is transformed into a brick wall, literally monumentalized.[39] My personal favorite among subversive deflections from "normal" conventions of mainstream or official (state-sanctioned) culture is a cartoon speech balloon coming from George Washington's mouth saying, "I Grew Hemp!"[40]

The "I Grew Hemp" cartoon is an innocuous diversion (another meaning of the word *détournement*) when compared to a 1994 acrylic painting by Alfred J. Quiroz. The artwork, which is titled *George Washington Inspects the Hemp Crop* and is now privately owned, sets a happy Washington between a guffawing gentleman with a clay pipe and a grinning, corn-cob-pipe-puffing slave. It is apparent that the three men have indulged in the consumption of marijuana. The painting not only parodies the numerous representations of Washington as a gentleman farmer; its subversive scorn also targets representations of him as a tedious unsmiling prig. And, as someone under the influence, Washington appears utterly unheroic.[41] Quiroz's painting may even have served as inspiration to Thomas Pynchon, in whose novel *Mason & Dixon* (1997) the title characters visit Washington at Mount Vernon, where they are invited to sample the retired President's newest cash crop—a patch of marijuana he has planted in the back. The Father of His Country gives signs that he has already tried his own crop, as he stares into the shiny buttons of Jeremiah Dixon's coats and, additionally, threatens Charles Mason, the British surveyor, with a ghoulish vision of cannibalism.[42]

Subversive practices, such as tampering with the Fairman vignette or caricaturing the Father of His Country as a consumer of marijuana, foreground the gap between the sacred and the profane, between being and appearance. Subversive practices are also irritating, as they question, reverse, or even negate claims to legitimacy. They challenge traditional concepts and beliefs, much as they spark off new ones. In general terms, discourses circulating in society are meaningful only differentially, in relation to other elements. During the Civil Rights movement, for instance, African American leaders saw George Washington as the epitome of the powerful and the white elitism that had kept them in bondage for so long. Thus in 1970, James Gadsen produced an artwork in which a white ominous George Washington (still shaped in the Stuart portrait) looms large over black Americans of humble origin.[43]

Political caricatures are nothing new. During the American Revolution, caricatures made a fundamental contribution to the political debate, demystifying power and royal prerogative, and encouraging the involvement of ordinary people with political affairs. They performed these tasks by presenting controversial issues (like liberty) in a simple, concrete, and memorable way, and the main actors on the political stage as unheroic and fallible mortals. A 1789 engraved cartoon titled *The Entry* depicted George Washington riding to his inauguration in New York City on a donkey led by David Humphreys; a doggerel beneath read: "The glorious time has come to pass / When David shall conduct an ass."[44] The popularity of satirical images when they were first published suggests that they struck a chord. Caricatures, desecrations, vilifications, or similar acts of debunking articulate specific political attitudes and mentalities, but they do not annihilate the "sacredness" of an object. On the contrary, when the Father of His Country is depicted as an object of parody, he is lampooned for those qualities for which Americans revere him—honesty, piety and virtue, and, especially today, for the omnipresence of his image. For, judging from the sheer number of visual and verbal representations, George Washington is most likely the most widely featured, seen, and known figure in world history.

The anti-heroic and minimalist style that prevails in the arts today at one and the same time articulates and encourages a deep skepticism about heroic views of history and politics. In this context, the Father of His Country is de-heroized, made contemporary, his status of glamor and glory transformed. As Barry Schwartz writes, "the transformation is inevitable. To expect that a nation should turn out, year after year, in heartfelt veneration for a man who died many years ago is to make unrealistic demands on its capacity for emotional attachment."[45] Although the national icon has been bled of much of its significance, some meaning must remain. A Gary Larson cartoon, "Washington Crossing the Street," demonstrates the adaptability of Washington's myth, and its instant recognition. The fact that Americans find humor in the scene asserts the continued strength of Washington's myth.[46]

The paradox of increasing irrelevance but constant reverence and recognition only shows that the Father of His Country is not fading from America's collective memory. On the contrary, the symbol of George Washington still resonates within the American consciousness. The Washington Monument still stands as the pinnacle of the nation's capital and remains an omnipresent icon. Although Far Side comics and abundant advertising may signal a growing cynicism, Americans apparently still need George Washington. "The more modern we become," Karal Ann Marling wrote, "the more desperately we cling to our Washingtons, to our old-fashioned heroes, to an imagined colonial past, to the good old days when patriots stood firm on their pedestals."[47] The "good old days" is, of course, a veiled reference to a time without political assassinations, the protests of African Americans and of the nation's youth, the Vietnam War, Watergate, the women's movement, and the gay liberation movement, all of which challenged traditional concepts of masculinity. What brings these "good old days" back is stories, compelling stories that is, not the collective "infantile phantasy" Americans had turned the Father of His Country into by the 1960s.

James Thomas Flexner, who had raised the charge of "infantile phantasy," set out to recreate George Washington as America's "indispensable man." His four-volume biography, published between 1965 and 1972, became phenomenally successful. It "far outsold anything written about the first president since Mason Locke Weems." The reviews also were almost uniformly superlative. As Thomas Lask trumpeted in the *New York Times*, "Mr. Flexner brought the hero down from Olympus to where we can see him whole and see him plain."[48] Flexner himself described his intention in similar fashion, claiming that he had "replaced the marble image with a warm and appealing human being," making him a more attractive leading man.[49] So attractive was the image Flexner had created that in the early 1980s Hollywood producer David Gerber approached Flexner's lawyer about the possibility of producing a television miniseries based on the biography. The three-part miniseries, which went on air on April 8, 10 and 11, 1984, covers Washington's life in the French and Indian War, in the years leading up to and during the Revolutionary War, and in his triumph over the British and return to Mount Vernon. It may not have been the smashing success Flexner and his producers had hoped for, but it nevertheless brought the Father of His Country back into the "national spotlight."[50]

The miniseries, Flexner ruefully remembered, would have been much more successful if it had enmeshed George Washington in "sex and violence."[51] Possibly so, though mysticism and spookiness also might have added to the series' popularity. For mysticism and spookiness, Americans were ready after 9/11. In 2005, a book titled *An Autobiography of George Washington* began to fill the shelves of bookstores and the virtual spaces of Amazon and other distributors. The book's success shows that, in Edward Lengel's words, the floodgates had been opened, and mythmaking had "taken on new energy."[52] One such myth sprang up around West Ford, George Washington's infamous "slave child," whose story was popularized by Linda Allen Bryant, a West Ford descendant, in the late 1990s in the wake of the Thomas Jefferson-Sally Hemings revelations. Bryant's revelations turned her into a celebrity. She appeared on television on *Today*, *Frontline*, the History Channel, and MSNBC, and was interviewed approvingly by *Newsweek*, the *New York Times*, the *Washington Post*, and other magazines and newspapers. In 2000, PBS produced a documentary, *George and Venus*, highlighting the slave girl with whom Washington allegedly had fathered a son, West Ford. Bryant's campaign peaked when in 2001 she published a book titled *I Cannot Tell a Lie: The Story of George Washington's African American Descendants*. "Washington is one of my grandfathers," Bryant boldly declares in her book, and West Ford "his son."[53]

If Bryant was piggybacking on the Sally Hemings scandal, taking advantage both of contemporary concerns about race and a taste for the savory, other forms of mythmaking took the opposite direction, piety. Quotations about Washington's religiosity were no less spurious than "All the Presidents' Girls,"[54] though they gained renewed popularity in the first decades of the twenty-first century. The so-called Washington Prayer or Prayer Journal, modified in the nineteenth century from Washington's Circular to State Governments of 1783, was discovered as a fake right after it was sold at auction in 1891.[55] Yet this "*most hallowed of all his writings*" is still making its round in order to lend support to the belief that the Father of His Country was a practicing Christian. It even circulates in the corridors of power. Speaking in the House of Representatives on April 21, 2009, Congresswoman Michele Bachmann quoted the spurious prayer, adding that on the day of his inauguration Washington insisted "that unless the citizens of our country imitate the example of Jesus Christ, that we would not be a happy Nation. What a clear contrast between our first President and our current President."[56]

Ironically, after Washington's death clergymen often had difficulties "proving" beyond doubt that Washington actually was a "Christian."[57] In this day and age, the use, by a congressional representative, of a fake George Washington prayer to bash an unloved president, in this instance Barack Obama, shows the extent to which religion has become instrumentalized in American politics. Examining the public messages of United States' political leaders over the past seventy-five years, David Domke and Kevin Coe have shown that politics today is defined by a calculated, deliberate, and partisan use of faith that is unprecedented in modern politics. Beginning with the election of Ronald Reagan in 1980, America has seen a no-holds-barred religious politics that seeks to attract voters, identify and attack enemies, and solidify power.[58] Politicized Christianity also underwrites the various defenses of the national motto, "In God We Trust," ever since it was added to the Pledge of Allegiance and put on the currency in the 1950s. Since then, it has been and presumably always will be the declared intention, on the part both of the Department of the Treasury and of the Department of Justice, to "actively defend against challenges to the use of the national motto," in court and elsewhere.[59]

The phrase "In God We Trust" originated in the years of the American Civil War, though it became the national motto only by an Act of Congress of July 30, 1956. Two years before, the U.S. Capitol's Congressional Prayer Room had been established by a House Concurrent Resolution. The room's inspirational uplift comes from a stained-glass window depicting General Washington praying in the snow at Valley Forge. America's lawmakers must have known that Washington at prayer was merely one of "Parson" Weems's fables, but at the time the religious faith of the Father of His Country and of the nation's representatives were conveniently used as a response to "godless" communism. George Washington "didn't cringe during eight long years of warfare," Wilber M. Brucker, a former secretary of the Army, declared in 1967; the American nation should therefore follow the Father's example, "tighten its belt and resolutely turn again to the grim task of destroying Communist aggression."[60] Destroying Communist aggression was no longer the United States' premier goal at the end of the 1970s, though many Americans then felt that the country was being "kicked around" both at home and abroad. On November 13, 1978, *Time* magazine struck the "To the Rescue" theme, picturing, on the front cover, George Washington as a champion of old-time virtues, an advocate of strength at home, and no entangling alliances abroad. Even with one black eye, he managed a reassuring smile.[61]

George Washington's picture on the front cover of *Time* magazine is ample proof that the Father of His Country still resonated within the American consciousness. Popular culture, too, found useful a rather martial George Washington, featuring him in a series of comics beginning in the 1980s. In *Time Masters* #4, for instance, he is to be assassinated by members of the Illuminati order, though of course he survives the evil scheme.[62] But it was the 250th anniversary of Washington's birthday in 1982, a year into Ronald Reagan's first term as President, that became "an occasion that could not decently be ignored." Mount Vernon was being refurbished, and the Smithsonian's National Museum of American History mounted an exhibition that added depth and luster to the memory of "a larger-than-life figure to whom piety and reverence were naturally due."[63] Titled *George Washington: A Figure Upon the Stage*, the show at the Smithsonian brought together a plethora of Washington uniforms, camp chests, chairs, bric-a-bracs, but also his candlesticks, plates and glassware. Writers and journalists openly expressed their admiration for the features that made Washington interesting again—his character, his dignity, and his charisma.

As George Washington rose to new prominence, America's sitting president celebrated the beginning of his second term with a round of televised balls, galas, parties, and other celebrity-packed functions, including Super Bowl XIX on January 20, 1985. For Mr. Reagan to be able to toss the coin to begin the key football game of the year it had been necessary to postpone his inauguration for a day—a truly "mannerly and polite gesture," as Karal Ann Marling found. At half time—the eventual winners, the San Francisco 49ers, were already leading over the Miami Dolphins—the giant scoreboard lit up in a patriotic tribute to America, the next day's inauguration, and President Reagan. In addition, an electrified George Washington was blinking down at his late twentieth-century children. The shot faded abruptly, to a closeup of a cheerleader's bosom and a battery of commercials. When the cars and beers had been sold and the scoreboard loomed into sight once more, the Father of His Country was gone. But Washington is never gone for long. The 200th anniversary of his death in 1999 again gave rise to numerous events, academic and popular, including a reenactment of his funeral at Mount Vernon on December 18, 1999.[64]

Funerals are always special, not just George Washington's. In the mid–1980s, Californians could be laid to rest in the Court of Liberty at Forest Lawn cemetery beneath a giant mosaic wall depicting Washington praying at Valley Forge. The image persists. In 2008, the conservative Family Research Council claimed on its website: "We have no record of Washington's prayer that Christmas Eve, but we know he prayed."[65] The image of Washington at prayer reflects deep, resilient strains of piety and patriotism in American society. The commitments ensuing from these values have been said to lead to the good social order, especially for men. They restrain men's "anarchic" sexuality, binding them to identities as fathers within the "traditional" family.[66] In order for the good social order to become reality, the FRC's Prayer Team organizes citizens to pray for specific political policies. Other organizations sing from a similar hymn sheet.

On the occasion of Washington's birthday in February 1999, Pat Robertson's Christian Broadcasting Network published the following wisdom on its website: "Washington's stature, you see, is of the biblical kind. When the Old Testament writers judged a leader, it was always in moral, not political, terms. Rulers might conquer a vast empire—but if they neglected their spiritual duties, they were dismissed as men who 'did what was evil in the sight of the Lord.'" As befits a sermon, readers are then encouraged to "make resolution. Next year for Washington's birthday, instead of rushing out to the malls, let's teach our kids that Washington was not just our first president, but a man of moral excellence. Teach them that they should seek after the kind of moral excellence in their lives that Washington personified: the kind that arises, not only from accomplishment, but from character. [...] Otherwise, we may forget why Washington is remembered as the 'Father of our Country'—and that would be a terrible loss."[67]

The Christian Broadcasting Network credits the entire text to a 1999 a radio commentary also titled "Why Washington is 'The Father of our Country.'" The commentary was by Chuck Colson, a former special counsel to President Nixon who spent time in prison after Watergate and subsequently established a Christian prison ministry. In the commentary, Colson repeated the tale of a Quaker finding George Washington at prayer in the snow, and he insisted that the Father of His Country was "a man of profound Christian piety." CBN has the entire transcript of Colson's broadcast online, and also provides a link to the alleged "Prayer Journal" of George Washington.[68] CBN does not, however, provide an editorial comment on Colson's premier source, William J. Bennett's book *Our Sacred Honor*, a collection of stories, songs, letters, poems, and speeches by and about the Founders, which was published in 1997 to provide "words of advice," especially for children.[69]

Gun rights advocates found useful other "words of advice" from the Father of His Country: "Firearms stand next in importance to the Constitution itself. They are the American people's liberty, teeth and keystone under independence. The church, the plow, the prairie wagon and citizens' firearms are indelibly related." Did Washington really say that? If he did, he would have been living at a different time. Prairie wagons definitely were not part of everyday life when the first United States Congress met. The text, known as the "Liberty Teeth" quote, nevertheless could be found on numerous websites. Today it is so well known as a fraud that even the pro-gun Second Amendment Foundation warns that use of it is "counterproductive." Still, many people—including FOX's Sean Hannity in January 2013—keep using it. The spurious quotation is also used as factual in a book by William James, titled *The Constitution and What It Means*. As for websites, a good choice is *Deseret News*, owned by the Church of Jesus Christ of Latter-Day-Saints. Its website claims that it is the first news organization and longest continuously-operating business in the state of Utah. Its mission is "to be a leading news brand for faith and family oriented audiences in Utah and around the world."

On April 25, 1994, *Deseret News* published on its website an article titled "Firearms are Vital for Society."⁷⁰ Whereas the "Liberty Teeth" cannot in good conscience be traced back to George Washington, the Father of His Country did have something to say on the topic of firearms: "A free people ought not only to be armed, but disciplined; to which end a Uniform and well digested plan is requisite: And their safety and interest require that they should promote such manufactories, as tend to render them independent on others, for essential, particularly for military supplies."⁷¹ It is difficult to deduce from this statement the image of George Washington as a gun rights advocate. That image has typically been adopted by periodic conservative "revolutionaries" who seek to return to first principles—Civil War Confederates, members of the "Tea Party" movement, evangelical Christians, and Christian nationalists.

Is it too harsh and one-sided to say that the United States is well on its way to becoming a nation of religious fanatics? A September 16, 2007, poll from Vanderbilt University's First Amendment Center showed that 65 percent of Americans believe the founders intended the United States to be a Christian nation and 55 percent from that poll thought the United States Constitution established the U.S. as a Christian nation.⁷² It's true that many (but not all) of the founders were Christians. And it's also true that the Protestant majority dominated the nation's institutions for much of the country's early history. But the United States Constitution nowhere mentions God or Christianity. The United States is not now and never has been a Christian nation in any official or legal sense of the term. If anything, it is a secular democracy with First Amendment protections, and it is precisely because of these protections that people are more free to say and believe outrageous things than anywhere else on Earth. Thanks to First Amendment protections, for instance, Americans are also free to say and believe that George Washington will reincarnate in one form or the other. In a book titled *Born Again*, one Walter Semkiw, founder of IISIS, the Institute for the Integration of Science, Intuition, and Spirit, identifies (with some help from the Egyptian spirit guide Ahtun Re) former Army General Tommy Ray Franks as the reincarnation of the Father of His Country. Franks apparently remains unaware of his true identity, nor does he suspect that his wife, Cathy, is actually Martha Washington, though Tommy Franks is not a bad choice. He is a distinguished military leader, whom President George W. Bush in 2004 awarded a Medal of Freedom for leading the invasion of Afghanistan and Iraq.⁷³

Towards the end of the twentieth century, Washington's ghost was sighted in Annapolis, Valley Forge, Philadelphia, Williamsburg, and of course Alexandria, where he is still a staple of spirit tours, riding his white horse about historic Woodlawn Plantation. Nor does the spirit have any reservations about new media. In a 2008 episode of *Haunted Travels* on television's Travel Channel, for instance, he saves the entire 20th Maine Regiment from being routed by Confederate troops. The episode on television was meant to bring alive the Civil War Battle of Gettysburg. The story itself goes back to an article published in *Hearst's Magazine* in June 1913, "Through Blood and Fire at Gettysburg."⁷⁴ In this day and age, the ghost's schedule has tightened. In 2008, Washington's ghost appeared in a conservative satirical movie, *An American Carol*, in which John Voight, playing a decidedly Christian Founding ghost, castigates a character named Michael Malone (a thin disguise for filmmaker Michael Moore) for his lack of patriotism by showing him the carnage at the World Trade Center after 9/11. But it was TV rather than the big screen that seemed to attract Washington's ghost the most. He appeared in *The Crossing* (2000), in *Benedict Arnold: A Question of Honor* (2003), in the miniseries *John Adams* (2008), and, in a dubious role as a child-eating cannibal, in an episode of the Showtime series *Masters of Horror* titled "The Washingtonians."⁷⁵

Productions of this kind may have turned Washington's ghost into a media celebrity, yet, Edward Lengel objects, they also routinely distort or ignore historical facts. The phenomenon is not new. George Washington was still alive when artists and storytellers embellished aspects of his life to make him accessible to a wider audience or to remind audiences that there was something in him that they may have overlooked. Take, for instance, Washington the revolutionary hero, the figure captured by Charles Wilson Peale in the 1770s and embraced by nineteenth- and twentieth-century global revolutionaries and their sympathizers. This figure has been all but replaced by the dignified restraint and aloofness of President Washington, beginning with Gilbert Stuart's notoriously unmilitary likenesses.[76] The patrician image of George Washington, originally captured through neoclassical conventions, remained appealing through the present, with few exceptions. In the 1990s, a pair of avant-garde Russian émigré artists found significance in a less patrician image. Noting the impending bicentennial of Washington's death, Vitaly Komar and Alex Melamid called "on everyone who believes that the revolutionary legacy of the Founding Fathers is threatened with extinction to create a work devoted to this patriotic theme." Their own artwork, *Washington Lives II* (1995), blended the composition of Stuart's "Lansdowne" portrait (a standing Washington, dress sword in hand, national iconography of eagle and shield at his feet) with the conventions of Social realism (modern dress, in this instance a business suit; right hand gesturing upward in the style of 1930s Soviet propaganda). In exhorting artists to "join us in celebrating America's greatest revolutionary hero," Komar and Melamid returned to the grounds of Washington's earliest national significance.[77]

Hardly a celebration of America's greatest revolutionary hero is the 1995 film *The American President*. However, the film is noteworthy for its opening sequence, which shows a bust of George Washington in profile, which then cross-dissolves to a closeup of the Stars and Stripes, a heraldic eagle, and various artifacts calling up American history, the nation, the presidency, and, importantly, the mythic and historical associations that attend to the office in past and present. The film was written by Aaron Sorkin, who went on to write *The West Wing*. The fictional president, Andrew Shepard, is played by Michael Douglas, while Martin Sheen, the POTUS of *The West Wing*, appears as A. J. McInerney, the White House Chief of Staff.[78] In 1997, the musical *1776* was revived. The play, by Peter Stone and Sherman Edwards, had premiered on Broadway in 1969, received a Tony Award for Best Musical, and was made it into a film adaptation in 1972. Unlike *The American President*, which is more of a romantic comedy, *1776* really is all about the American Revolution—"a revolution, damn it!" John Adams, the protagonist, exclaims shortly into the second act. George Washington is not part of the cast but is present only through the dispatches he sends to the delegates to the Continental Congress from his headquarters as commander in chief of the Continental Army. The play ends on the eve of July 4, as the delegates sign the Declaration of Independence, the Liberty Bell ringing to a fevered pitch in the background.[79]

After the terrorist attacks of 9/11, Henry Kirke Brown's bronze equestrian statue of George Washington in New York City's Union Square became an impromptu site of mourning. While its original purpose as a symbol of democracy was not altered, the candles, graffiti signs, and stuffed animals left by mourners charged it with another purpose. To the symbols of loss and affection were added a reaffirmation of the heroism and classical ideals that artists from Houdon and Greenough had bestowed on the Father of His Country, exactly the qualities desired by Americans in a post–9/11 quest for America.[80] These desires were also satisfied with the publication in 2005 of David McCullough's book *1776*, which is almost all about the famous battles of that first year of the American revolution. The theme of Washington's military leadership is trumpeted by the book's cover, which bears a reproduction of John Trumbull's *Capture of the Hessians at Trenton*. McCullough's book was spectacularly successful, becoming a *New York Times* bestseller. The publishers, Simon and Schuster, followed it up with an illustrated edition in 2007. Five years later Random House's Quercus came forth with a biography by the British historian Stephen Brumwell. His *Gentleman Warrior* depicts the Father of His Country as a pugnacious fighter, an impetuous man of action. The book brings to mind activities and beliefs that had long been forgotten or neglected as the Father of His Country came to be pictured as formal and seemingly impenetrable. On the book's cover is, appropriately, a detail from another painting by Trumbull, *The Death of General Mercer at the Battle of Princeton, January 3, 1777*.

Washington's daring attack on a Hessian fort also figures prominently in a more recent web document titled "Why is George Washington considered the Father of this nation?" It was published by *ThisNation.com*, a self-described "general American government and politics information site."[81] Readers learn that, as Commander in chief, "Washington's determination, leadership and refusal to give up made the difference between victory and defeat on more than one occasion," including at Trenton. Reverence for Washington is also owed to his "character and reputation," which was so powerful that he became the "indispensable man" at the Constitutional Convention of 1787. Since the piece purports to have been prompted by Presidents' Day, we are also told that Washington was unanimously elected as the United States' first president and that, as chief executive, he wielded the power of the office capably and responsibly, always downplaying his stature as president, seeking "only to serve his country all the days of his adult life." To lend additional weight to the kudos, Washington is allowed to speak for himself: "And certain I am, whensoever I shall be convinced the good of my country requires my reputation to be put in risque, regard for my own fame will not come in competition with an object of so much magnitude."[82]

The text from *ThisNation.com* no doubt portrays Washington as a great president. Unsurprisingly, the question what makes a great president has been asked from the beginning of the presidency. While answers have been sought by a variety of means, the results are usually given in a ranked order. Altogether, polling games seem to have gained in popularity, though presidents tend to be rated in political rather than in moral terms. Sometimes, "personal qualities," "character," or "integrity" are used for evaluation, with answers expected to provide moral stimulus. At an event hosted by the University of Louisville's McConnell Center for Political Leadership on February 20, 2017 (Washington's birthday aka Presidents' Day), University of Virginia presidential scholar Barbara Perry discussed the traits that make a great president. The definition of presidential greatness that Professor Perry used stems from Aaron David Miller: "Preserving the country when facing an existential challenge."[83] Hence the three greatest Presidents: Lincoln (because he saved the Union); Washington (because he solidified the nation's founding); and Franklin D. Roosevelt (because he weathered the Great Depression). Each one of the three great Presidents provided purpose, direction, and motivation.[84] Also for Presidents' Day 2017, C-SPAN conducted a survey among historians. Overall, Lincoln ranked first for the third consecutive time since 2000; Washington again ranked second, followed by Franklin D. Roosevelt, Theodore Roosevelt, and Dwight D. Eisenhower. Ronald Reagan came in ninth, up one place from 2009. C-SPAN asked almost one hundred historians to look at ten different qualities of leadership. Lincoln's top scores were for crisis leadership, administrative skills, vision, setting an agenda, and the pursuit of equal justice for all; Washington was the undisputed leader in moral authority and performance within the context of his time, as well as, surprisingly, economic management.[85] The very first poll in which historians and / or other respondents were asked to rate the presidents of the United States was conducted by Arthur M. Schlesinger in 1948. Schlesinger did not then specify any criteria for the ratings, though the top three were the same as in 2017—Lincoln, Washington, and FDR; also rated great were Wilson, Jefferson, and Jackson.

In 1962, Schlesinger conducted a new poll, with almost identical results. The results also did not change much when different methods were employed, such as a much larger sample, a random sample, or ranking the presidents on a number of different dimensions or categories, instead of or on top of overall rankings as, say, the ten best or worst in history. In 1982, Robert K. Murray and Tim H. Blessing sent out nearly 2,000 questionnaires to historians, then determined *post hoc* the criteria the respondent had utilized. The results were no surprise—the four Greats were Lincoln, FDR, Washington, and Jefferson. Seventeen years later, William J. Ridings, Jr., and Stuart B. McIver published a book titled *Rating the Presidents*, which presented the combined results of two polls they had conducted. The top four? Not much variation: Lincoln, FDR, Washington, and Theodore Roosevelt. Similar results were obtained by the third Schlesinger poll, conducted by Arthur M. Schlesinger, Jr., in 1996, nearly fifty years after his father began the presidential polling game: Lincoln, Washington, and FDR were rated great.[86]

Polls addressing the general public were introduced almost simultaneously with the elder Schlesinger's poll. In 1945, the University of Denver's National Opinion Research Center asked for the two or three of the greatest men (not women) who ever lived in the United States. The question did not specify that presidents were to be named, though seven of the top twelve mentioned were presidents, the top three being Franklin D. Roosevelt, Lincoln, and George Washington. Interestingly, eight of the twelve top men were figures of the twentieth century. Similarly, when ABC News in February 2000 asked for the greatest American presidents, six of the top eight were from the twentieth century—Kennedy, Franklin Roosevelt, Reagan, Clinton, Theodore Roosevelt, and George H. W. Bush.[87] Presentism, critics pointed out later, is unavoidable when the general public is being polled. A drastic example of the presentist fallacy dates from 1956, when a Gallup poll was abandoned when it became obvious that the general public did not know enough about the nation's past to give a meaningful response to the question, "What *three* United States Presidents do you regard as the *greatest*?" The incomplete results had Franklin Roosevelt, Lincoln, and Washington as the top three, but the five most recent presidents—including Herbert Hoover and Calvin Coolidge—also all made the list.[88]

More recent polls are likewise skewed because of presentism. These polls often put Ronald Reagan in first place, a choice that appears rather myopic as far as history goes. A 2011 Gallup poll, for instance, had Reagan in first place, followed by Lincoln, Bill Clinton, and George Washington. In another Gallup poll, done in 2009, the order was Reagan followed by Kennedy, Lincoln, Franklin Roosevelt, and Washington. Unsurprisingly, Reagan was also ranked as "the best president" since World War II (Quinnipiac University, 2017), coming in third place among "the most important presidents of the 20th century" (NBC News / *Wall Street Journal*, 1999).[89] In a 2006 book titled *The American Presidents Ranked by Performance*, Reagan is number 34, much lower than in polls addressing the general public.[90] Presentism is also a cause of misrepresentation. In a Gallup poll done in 1956, only some 47 percent of respondents designated George Washington one of the three greatest presidents, a steep drop from Washington's prestige in the nineteenth century. From 1975 to the present, however, the level hovered around 25 percent. This is still high after 200 years, and if presentism is factored in, we cannot in good conscience follow Barry Schwartz or Scott Casper, who have posited a significant decline in Washington's relevance to Americans. Moreover, results of polls and rankings should be taken with a grain of salt. The assumption that people's choices and preferences are based on reason is not always tenable. More often than not, they result from affect. Because people do not always consciously know what they want, decisions may be "predictably irrational," examples rather of "miswanting."[91]

As informative and useful as polls rating the presidents may be, they are all flawed for failing to specify the criteria to be used in the ratings. Many of these polls do not even ask respondents to rank the presidents in the order of greatness, leaving the task to the researchers, who compute a mean score from the categories in which the respondents placed them. In *The American Presidents Ranked by Performance*, the authors have used their own rating system. Relying on published scholarship, Charles F. Faber and Richard B. Faber focused on accomplishments and performance in some of the most critical aspects of the office: Foreign Relations; Domestic Programs; Administration and Intergovernmental Relations; Leadership and Decision Making; and "Personal" Qualities.[92] Each president is scored in his fulfillment of each aspect of the office, and an analysis is provided for all the scores. So how did George Washington do on individual scores? The Fabers ranked the Father of His Country first in both Administration and Intergovernmental Relations and Leadership and Decision Making (the latter in a tie with Jefferson and Lincoln); he was placed third in Foreign Relations and came in second in "Personal" Qualities.[93]

George Washington's "Personal" Qualities speak directly to his image as the metaphorical father, and thus should be treated in some detail. The Fabers' account begins with Washington's heroic persona, which did not fail to capture the popular imagination: Merely seeing him was enough to convince most men and women that he was the leader of the nation. As the nation's first president, Washington instilled pride in citizens, who united behind the charismatic leader. He distinguished himself by his comportment and dignity, and he increased the stature of the presidency, for instance by envisioning the United States as a mighty nation among other powers. Washington also increased the power of the presidency, not least through decisive actions such as vanquishing the Whiskey Rebellion. He was able to transform his formal power into political authority, though he nevertheless made people think that the president was "on their side." The confidence and support he won—not least by journeying through all thirteen colonies—unified the nation at a critical time in history. Disliking pomp, Washington reached out to people and made himself accessible to the public, who considered him trustworthy and as acting on a firm set of moral values and principles. By all accounts, he was personally honest, exhibiting high standards of personal morality and setting a precedent for future presidents, what James Rees, a former director of Mount Vernon, came to call "leadership lessons."[94]

The six scores cited above (Foreign Relations; Domestic Programs; Administration and Intergovernmental Relations; Leadership and Decision Making; and "Personal" Qualities) provided the basis for the Fabers' overall ranking, in which George Washington comes in second place, narrowly trailing "Honest Abe" Lincoln by just one point.[95] Had Washington done better in Domestic Programs (in 2006, he came in 15th place, with Martin Van Buren; in 2012, he was ranked 17th), the Father of His Country might easily have topped the list as America's greatest president. For the Fabers, appearances and background factors, as well as character traits such as idealism or courage were irrelevant. Still, their book stands out, as most of the ratings done by other individuals more or less closely follow Arthur M. Schlesinger's first poll. That is to say, authors would identify from seven to ten presidents whom they believe to be great and then explain why they were great. Clinton Rossiter in *The American Presidency* gave his highest praise to active presidents, especially to those who led the nation through times of crisis—hence, Washington is followed by Jefferson, Jackson, Lincoln, the two Roosevelts, Wilson, and Truman. Activism is a watchword also in Herman Finer's 1960 book *The Presidency: Crises and Regeneration*, which applauds the usual honorees: Washington, Franklin Roosevelt, and Lincoln. Finer also adds power to his list of criteria, and for good reason. Political power becomes concentrated in the executive, focused on the president, primarily during times of crisis.[96]

A year after the assassination of John F. Kennedy, an Eric Sokolsky published a book titled *Our Seven Greatest Presidents*. His hero, JFK, made the list of seven, together with Franklin Roosevelt, Truman, Jefferson, Jackson, Polk, and Lincoln. The nation's first president did not make the top seven. George Washington, it seems, then was not enough of an activist for the tastes of a liberal journalist.[97] In 1966, Stanford historian Thomas A. Bailey came to a different estimation: "If we must rank presidents, *Washington, in my judgment, deserves the place at the very top*." George Washington, Bailey continues, "made no major mistakes—something that cannot be said of any of his successors who served long enough to make a mistake."[98] Just over a half century later, the Pulitzer Prize–winning historian Gordon S. Wood again warned against diminishing Washington's "unique greatness." To do so would be a mistake because "Washington had challenges and responsibilities that no other president, including Lincoln, has ever faced. Lincoln saved the Union, but Washington created it. Without Washington there might never have been a United States for Lincoln to save."[99]

13

Washington's Unique Greatness

The sheer bulk of recent scholarship seems sufficient proof of Washington's "unique greatness." John C. Fitzpatrick's compilations of Washington's papers, published in 30 volumes between 1931 and 1944 became standard for many years, as will the Papers of George Washington project, edited at the University of Virginia since 1968. Important biographies too underline the Father of His Country's greatness—multivolume works by Douglass Southall Freeman (1948–1957) and James Thomas Flexner (1965–1972); single-volume lives by Marcus Cunliffe (1958), John R. Alden (1984), Robert F. Jones (rev. ed. 1986), John E. Ferling (1988), and, more recently, by Joseph Ellis (2004), Ron Chernow (2010), and John Rhodehamel (2017). To these should be added collections of essays and articles by James Morton Smith (1969) and Don Higginbotham (2001), as well as countless studies of particular aspects of Washington's life and career.[1] A number of these instances of excellent scholarship address Washington's "unique greatness," though none as directly as Richard Brookhiser, who set out to show "how a great man navigated politics and a life as a public figure."[2]

Brookhiser's "moral biography" of 1996 draws, as Plutarch did in his *Lives of the Noble Grecians and Romans* (a book that was popular during Washington's time), on "the power of example."[3] As soon as Brookhiser's book was published, however, studies of single individuals in the making of history—and studies of great white men in particular—went out of fashion, becoming replaced by studies of class, family, gender, race, and ethnicity.[4] At the same time, Washington's "unique greatness" became the domain of the nation's cultural institutions honoring, for instance, the 200th anniversary of his death by performing the premiere of "Behold This Man: George Washington" at the Kennedy Center in Washington, D.C. A total of at least twenty-four conferences, seminars, and exhibits took place around the country in 1999. Some of the exhibits showcased, among other things, Washington's false teeth, bits of his hair, letters, clothing, and other personal relics. Washington's funeral was lavishly enacted at Mount Vernon, an event that on December 18, 1999, drew 5,000 visitors and was covered in a live, three-hour broadcast on C-SPAN.[5]

Public events, especially exhibitions, allow people to come and pay tribute to the man who stands for everything that their country ideally represents. They come to learn more about the man behind the familiar figurehead. They come for vicarious experience of a better time. What they get is beyond what could be had by sitting at home with a book or a tablet or standing before a painting or sculpture. Public events provide a sense of closeness that neither the printed page nor the screen nor the painted canvas nor the sculpted stone can convey. Public events make possible an experience that, as Edmund S. Morgan wrote reviewing a 1999 Washington exhibition at the Huntington Library, can be enjoyed sensually, theatrically, even spiritually, and thus appeals to the affective elements of people's consciousness and relationships, elements that organize into "structures of feeling," in Raymond Williams's words.[6]

The creation of such an experience constitutes the Father of His Country as a social or institutional object, a fact only by human agreement. Phrased differently, George Washington becomes the Father of His Country because people believe and accept him to be that. To simply declare him as the Father of His Country is not enough, no matter how sophisticated or worthy the criteria for greatness are. The metaphorical father acquires meaning also when he is used to "frame" present-day events, or to "key" such events to moments in the past associated with him. Keying present-day events to the past is, Barry Schwartz explains, "an act of recognition, a pairing in which an object (or an event, an act, an emotion) is identified by placing it against the background of an appropriate symbol." George Washington has been an "appropriate symbol," a frame for American values, aspirations, and experience, for more than two hundred years. By the same token, the Father of His Country "frames" present events when they are convincingly "keyed" to his life.[7]

"Keying" present events to George Washington's life and, in doing so, using the Father of His Country as a "frame," is evident from any number of inaugural addresses. Presidential inaugurations are central elements in America's secular or civil religion, its "creed," as Thomas Jefferson called it. The sheer emotional weight and ceremonial pomp of an inauguration justifies its description as a "religious happening," the "sacrament of [American] democracy."[8] The religious context defines the president's role as "the custodian of national values," America's "national priest," and "the representative of the nation before God and praying for the nation."[9] In this capacity, the president delivers his inaugural address, said to be "the most liturgically meaningful, carefully crafted, and listened to pronouncement in American public life."[10] Not all these properties may apply to individual addresses, though many of them have invoked the Father of His Country, be it in the rhetorical context, the argument, or for effect. Some addresses, especially in the early years of the republic, did so only indirectly, as when James Madison in March 1809 pledges himself to follow the "examples of the most revered authority."[11]

When Martin Van Buren took the oath of office in 1837, he felt compelled to invoke the "forbearance" with which the "forefathers" had approached slavery, a subject of great "delicacy" already at the foundation. And, like "the venerated fathers of the Republic," Van Buren vows to oppose any attempt on the part of Congress to abolish slavery "against the wishes of the slaveholding States."[12] The preservation of the union acquired much greater urgency in James Polk's inaugural address. As regards slavery, Polk pledged himself to "sacredly and religiously observe" the "compromises which alone enabled our fathers to form a common constitution for the government and protection of so many States and distinct communities, of such diversified habits, interests, and domestic institutions."[13] Zachary Taylor, too, vowed to follow the Constitution as his guide, adding that for its interpretation, he would always follow "with reverence" the "example who was by so many titled '*the Father of his Country*.'"[14] Zachary Taylor was the first president to explicitly refer to "our own beloved Washington" in an inaugural address. This is somewhat surprising as all of Washington's successors saw themselves or were seen as "new" or "second" Washingtons. Taylor too had good reason for his reverence, as he was described as "the very one / God chose to train a Washington."[15]

Taylor's successor, Franklin Pierce, likewise invoked "the Father of His Country."

Washington, as well as the founders at large, receive praise not only for their "broad and intelligent comprehension of rights and an all-pervading purpose to maintain them and for good reason" but also for not wasting "their energies upon idle and delusive speculations." These words were a code for abolition, which Pierce regarded as a threat to the Union. Pierce avoids the word slavery, however, offering instead an oblique reference to an "important subject" he wanted to put to rest. During his presidency, Pierce championed and signed the Kansas-Nebraska Act, which nullified the Missouri Compromise of 1820. The action alienated many Northerners, while many whites in the South applauded. It did nothing to stem regional conflict.[16] The sectional crisis only was made worse by Pierce's successor, James Buchanan who, in attempting to gain the admission of Kansas into the Union as a slave state, alienated both Republican abolitionists and Northern Democrats. Unable to address the nation with a unifying principle, Buchanan failed to deal with secession. In his final message to Congress, on December 3, 1860, he denied that the states had a legal right to secede while he also held that the federal government legally could not prevent them. Whereas the latter statement was anathema to the North, the former outraged the South. South Carolina seceded on December 20, 1860. In his inaugural address of 1857, Buchanan had deplored the growing divisions over slavery and its status in the territories. The solution he offered called for popular sovereignty and a federal slave code protecting the rights of slave-owners in any federal territory. Buchanan did so in the hope "that the long agitation on this subject is approaching its end, and that the geographical parties to which it has given birth, so much dreaded by the Father of his Country, will speedily become extinct."[17]

The legacy that Buchanan bequeathed to his successor was terrible. Abraham Lincoln had frequently referred to Washington when rebutting secessionists in debate. A year into his presidency, he recommended that the "immortal Farewell Address" be read out on Washington's birthday; and he had Washington's first general orders read out to the Army and Navy.[18] In all these instances, Lincoln's words reveal nostalgia for an idealized Old Republic in the days of the Founders. Their world seemed simpler, purer, better somehow. Yet it was vanishing, and so Lincoln had no use for George Washington in his inaugural addresses. Andrew Johnson, who succeeded the martyred president, had no inauguration. In Ulysses S. Grant's inaugural address, the Father of His Country again draws a blank. Hence we have to wait for Rutherford B. Hayes, who a year after the centennial of the Declaration of Independence opens his speech with a gesture of deference to Washington as the one who began the "public ceremonial" that by 1877 had become "a time-honored custom."[19] Four years later, James Garfield pays his respect to the "fathers," whose "fervent love of liberty ... intelligent courage [and] common sense" established a "National Union" under the Constitution—with twenty-five states added to the Union since.[20] The Constitution also was tone-setting in Grover Cleveland's first inaugural address. On March 4, 1885, he summoned his audience to "renew the pledge of our devotion" to that sacred document. Cleveland also did not forget to defer to "the Father of His Country" who had "commended the Constitution for adoption," seeing it as "'the result of a spirit of amity and mutual concession.'"[21] Benjamin Harrison's inauguration, in 1889, was accompanied by all the pomp of the colonial revival and the invention of the "republican court." With the centennials of the Declaration of Independence, the battle of Yorktown, and the adoption of the Constitution behind, the grandson of the ninth president, William Henry Harrison, proudly proclaimed that the nation will soon "have fully entered its second century." The happy prospect was reason enough for Benjamin Harrison "to find inspiration and guidance in the teachings and example of Washington and his great associates."[22]

In Grover Cleveland's inaugural address of March 4, 1893, the tone is much more somber. Cleveland deplores the widespread habit of securing "bounties and subsidies" from the government, a form of "paternalism" that is "the bane of republican institutions," a national disgrace which in his view "degrades to the purposes of wily craft the plan of rule of our fathers [...] perverts the patriotic sentiments of our countrymen [...] undermines the self-reliance of our people [and] stifles the spirit of true Americanism and stupefies every ennobling trait of American citizenship." This is the voice of the strict father, in whose view the functions of government "do not include the support of the people."[23] Cleveland's successor, William McKinley, had other worries. Faced with mass immigration and a rising illiteracy, he urges "the spread of knowledge and free education" as the royal road to "a safer, a better, and a higher citizenship." The promotion of this, he says, must be undertaken "with the zeal of our forefathers."[24] In his second inauguration, McKinley again invokes "the faith of the fathers," albeit for different reasons. McKinley had led the nation into the Spanish-American War, winning Puerto Rico, Guam, and the Philippines for the United States. (He also promised independence to Cuba, though at the time it remained under the control of the U.S. Army.) At the height of imperialism, the interventionist agenda is unmistakable: "Our institutions will not deteriorate by extension, and our sense of justice will not abate under tropic suns in distant seas."[25] This was on March 4, 1901. Six months later, McKinley was dead, shot by a second-generation Polish-American anarchist in Buffalo, New York, and succeeded by his Vice President, Theodore Roosevelt. In 1904, Theodore Roosevelt was elected as the 26th president. He had been the driving force already for the Progressive Era in the United States, advocating measures that required a larger regulatory role for the government. Many of the reforms he proposed during his second term failed to pass Congress, though his ambitions are reflected in his first inaugural address, in which he concluded that the tasks lying ahead were different from the ones "our fathers" faced, though they must be undertaken and faced in their "spirit."[26]

Neither Theodore Roosevelt's immediate successor, William Howard Taft (whose conservatism frustrated Roosevelt), nor Woodrow Wilson (whom Roosevelt criticized for keeping the country out of the war with Germany) made any references to Washington in their inaugural addresses. In 1921, renewed "belief in the divine inspiration of the founding fathers" came with Warren G. Harding, who is perhaps better known for sounding the theme of "return to normalcy." By this, Harding meant a return to the way of life before World War I: "America's present need is not heroics, but healing; not nostrums, but normalcy; not revolution, but restoration; not agitation, but adjustment; not surgery, but serenity; not the dramatic, but the dispassionate; not experiment, but equipoise; not submergence in internationalism, but sustainment in triumphant nationality." Harding defined the latter in the following terms: "[T]he America builded [sic] on the foundation laid by the inspired fathers, can be a party to no permanent military alliance. It can enter into no political commitments, nor assume any economic obligations which will subject our decisions to any other than our own authority."[27]

President Harding proved true to his word. Under his administration, the United States would not join even a scaled-down version of the League of Nation.[28] His successor, Calvin Coolidge, had no place for Washington in his inaugural, not so much because he reputedly was a man who said very little (his inaugural speech is one of the longest on record) than for his political convictions: As an advocate of small government and laissez-faire politics, Coolidge had little in common with the Father of His Country. As Coolidge remarked in an address to the American Society of Newspaper Editors in 1925, "the chief business of the American people is business."²⁹ Business or, rather, the economy also was important for President Herbert Hoover, as was the bicentennial of Washington's birth, the celebrations of which he oversaw. Yet the Wall Street crash, which struck less than eight months after Hoover took office, sent the economy on a downward spiral. This set the stage for his overwhelming defeat in 1932 by Franklin Delano Roosevelt, who promised a New Deal.

The nation's "distress," Franklin Delano Roosevelt said in his first inaugural address, "comes from no failure of substance," but was the doing of "unscrupulous money changers." Still, the situation was not nearly as serious as "the perils which our forefathers conquered because they believed and were not afraid."³⁰ Four years later, the nation remembered the 150th anniversary of the Constitutional Convention and FDR again invokes the "forefathers," appropriately for having "created a strong government with powers of united action sufficient then and now to solve problems utterly beyond individual or local solution." In the spirit of the forefathers, the President emphasized the role of the federal government in promoting "the general welfare" and securing "the blessings of liberty."³¹ At the beginning of Franklin Roosevelt's third term in office, the nation was being drawn into World War II. In his inaugural address is, therefore, an urgent reference to those presidents who had faced similar challenges: "In Washington's day the task of the people was to create and weld together a Nation. In Lincoln's day the task of the people was to preserve that Nation from disruption from within. In this day the task of the people is to save that Nation and its institutions from disruption from without." This, the President said in conclusion, is "the destiny which Washington strove so valiantly and so triumphantly to establish." Four years later, Roosevelt felt contented that the "sacrifice that we may make in the cause of national defense" had been justified, for "the preservation of the spirit and faith of the Nation."³² Invoking the Father of His Country in the fourth inaugural would have been gratuitous.

Post-World War II America generally had little use for the Father of His Country. By the time of Kennedy's presidency, Washington no longer seemed to serve any purpose except as an image on the one-dollar bill. Between 1961–1981, there are no direct references to George Washington in any of the inaugural addresses. At best, there are meek echoes of the "bold and brilliant dream" of the "founders of this Nation." Their "long quest for freedom," Jimmy Carter said on January 20, 1977, was a quest that was still awaiting its "consummation." Thus, Carter, who became the first president to take his presidential oath on the bible George Washington had used in 1789 (George H. W. Bush was next), urges "a fresh faith in the old dream."³³ No such note had been struck by Harry S. Truman in 1949, or in Dwight Eisenhower's two inaugurals. However, Eisenhower in 1953 deemed it necessary both to "beseech God's guidance" and to invoke "the abiding creed of our fathers. It is our faith in the deathless dignity of man, governed by eternal moral and natural laws."³⁴ Had fathers become dispensable? Many people in the 1950s did not like fathers, including the youthful protagonist in J. D. Salinger's *The Catcher in the Rye*, for whom fathers—as well as adults in general—are simply "phony." In Tennessee Williams's *Cat on a Hot Tin Roof* (1955), Big Daddy is bullying and damaging his children.³⁵

What about metaphorical fathers, then? Eisenhower, for his part, "idolized" George Washington. Other than that, the nation appears to have had other concerns then, summed up by William Faulkner in his Nobel Prize acceptance speech on December 10, 1950: "There is only one question: When will I be blown up?"³⁶ Such words are not, of course, appropriate for an inaugural address. As Eisenhower saw it in 1953, the United States were part of a world going through "a century of continuing challenge [...] a time of recurring trial." These were cautious words; four years later, Eisenhower's language was much more explicit, pointing to the danger posed by the "divisive force [of] International Communism." The premier goal therefore was "the brotherhood of all."[37] In 1959, as Eisenhower was about to finish his second term in office, John Farrow created a film, *John Paul Jones*, which features a tough George Washington, who in a key scene lectures the title character like a naughty schoolboy, asking him, "What are you fighting for, the principle of liberty or promotion?"[38] The subtext seems clear: With Eisenhower to be gone soon, the nation was in dire need of a strong, experienced leader to deal with racial tensions at home and an international Cold War, the threat of atomic warfare included. These were the topics also in John F. Kennedy's inaugural address of 1961, which summoned citizens "to bear the burden of a long twilight struggle, year in and year out, 'rejoicing in hope, patient in tribulation'—a struggle against the common enemies of man: tyranny, poverty, disease and war itself."[39] Domestic issues were foremost in Lyndon B. Johnson's inaugural address of 1965. With the "Great Society" at the top of his agenda, LBJ reminded his audience of the "American covenant […] Conceived in justice, written in liberty, bound in union, it was meant one day to inspire the hopes of all mankind. And it binds us still."[40]

Richard M. Nixon in 1969 hailed the moon landing, and he also tuned the nation up to the bicentennial of the American Revolution, defining the meaning of this portentous event for the present in this way: "we helped make the world safe for mankind." At home, however, the prospect was bleak: "We are torn by division, wanting unity." To overcome America's spiritual crisis, the President deemed it necessary to listen, not to George Washington or the other founders, but to "the better angels of our nature."[41] In 1973, Nixon saw the nation standing "on the threshold of a new era of peace in the world." This prospect would open an opportunity "to do more than ever before in our history to make life better in America." Yet the opportunity must be realized, not by the government but by individuals accepting "responsibility." Nixon therefore would "offer no promise of a purely governmental solution for every problem. We have lived too long with that false promise." Now, he declared, "the time has come for us to renew our faith in ourselves and in America." That faith, Nixon said, "has been challenged. Our children have been taught to be ashamed of their country, ashamed of their parents, ashamed of America's record at home and its role in the world." This is followed up by a summons to "be proud."[42]

Pride in, not shame of, country, parents, and America's record and its role in the world was transformed into a full-blown creed with the advent of Ronald Reagan. It does not come as a surprise that beginning with the Reagan presidency, George Washington has been directly referred to or invoked in five out of the nine inaugural addresses given to date, and almost always as the Father of His Country. In 1981, Ronald Reagan also became the first president to address his audience from the west front of the Capitol. Reagan opened his speech with the image of President-elect Washington resting his right hand on the Bible for the first solemn oath of office; he then pointed, in a most telegenic gesture, to "the monument to a monumental man: George Washington, Father of our country." Washington may not have liked the spectacle, as he took the oath of office in public but then went inside to read out his inaugural address. As if in awareness of this, Reagan described George Washington as a "man of humility who came to greatness reluctantly."[43] President Reagan's praise for George Washington may have been the work of a script-writer, but Reagan also had been a self-professed admirer of Washington since his days as a movie actor. His televised state visits to Colonial Williamsburg buoyed up a renewed interest in George Washington, much as his call for a return to traditional American values became a fitting backdrop to the 250th anniversary of Washington's birth in 1982. Additionally, President Reagan frequently evoked Washington in his speeches—and often in a religious context. Speaking on May 6, 1982, for instance, Reagan declared that "the most sublime picture in American history is of George Washington on his knees in the snow at Valley Forge."[44]

The story of General Washington kneeling in the snow and praying to God for deliverance is the foremost one of "Parson" Weems's fables. President Reagan's genius was to transform storytelling into political leadership. Accordingly, for his second inaugural address in 1985, he once more opened the patriotic lexicon on that same page: "This is … the 50th time that we the people have celebrated this historic occasion." Using a hackneyed conceit, Reagan then described history as a "ribbon, slowly unfurling … a journey." The times, Reagan said, have changed: "When the first President, George Washington, placed his hand upon the Bible, he stood less than a single day's journey by horseback from raw, untamed wilderness. There were 4 million Americans in a union of 13 States. Today we are 60 times as many in a union of 50 states." January 21, 1985, was a bitterly cold day. The ceremony took place inside the Capitol, where the President summoned his audience to "hear again the echoes of our past: a general falls to his knees in the hard snow of Valley Forge."[45]

Ronald Reagan's successor, George H. W. Bush, was inaugurated on January 20, 1989. He, too, began his speech by invoking the memory of Washington: "I've just repeated word for word the oath taken by George Washington 200 years ago, and the Bible on which I placed my hand is the Bible on which he placed his. It is right that the memory of Washington be with us today not only because this is our bicentennial inauguration but because Washington remains the *Father of our Country*."[46] Four years later, Bill Clinton collapsed the rhetoric of Reagan and Bush senior: "When George Washington first took the oath I have just sworn to uphold, news traveled slowly across the land by horseback and across the ocean by boat. Now the sights and sounds of this ceremony are broadcast instantaneously to billions around the world." A world, Clinton continued, in which "ambition for a better life is now universal."[47] In 1997, Bill Clinton again refers to the Founders, who, he said, "taught us that the preservation of our liberty and our Union depends upon responsible citizenship."[48] Clinton's successor, George W. Bush, did not evoke Washington in his inaugural address, though after 9/11 he expressed his passion around other campfires.

In 2009, Barack Obama readopted Ronald Reagan's quotation from the Valley Forge fable, expanding on it in his conclusion: "In the years of America's birth, in the coldest of months, a small band of patriots huddled by dying campfires on the shores of an icy river." Never mind that the winter of 1776–1777 was one of the mildest. What matters is the image and the patriotic sentiment that can be pulled from the Valley Forge story. At that crucial moment in the Revolutionary War, Obama reminded his listeners, "the father of our nation ordered these words to be read to the people: 'Let it be told to the future world … that in the depth of winter, when nothing but hope and virtue could survive … that the city and the country, alarmed at one common danger, came forth to meet it.'" Barack Obama invoked the nation's founding moment—the American Revolution—no fewer than four separate times in his attempt to chart a proposed path through the difficult years to come. Significantly, the address has been dubbed a "dad speech," with George Washington figuring as the transcendental Über-Vater. Yet when Obama invokes "a new era of responsibility," and calls upon citizens to "set aside childish things," he sets himself up as a metaphorical Father, just as his predecessors from Ronald Reagan on had wanted to be seen as reincarnations of the Father of His Country.[49] Obama only took the evocation of George Washington one step further when he used the phrase "so help me God" as he took the presidential oath of office.

In doing so, he tapped into the story that Washington had added the phrase to his own oath of office on April 30, 1789.

The story of the oath has stood for generations, and the phrase—not mandated by the Constitution—has been used at least since 1881, when Chester A. Arthur took the oath of office. A tradition dating from George Washington may be fake news, but it carries a lot more weight than one dating from the lowly Chester A. Arthur, and advocates of the phrase have gone out of their way to "prove" that Washington used it in 1789. There is, however, no evidence that the Father of His Country said, "so help me God." The first report that George Washington used the phrase did not appear until 1854, in Rufus Wilmot Griswold's *The Republican Court*, which draws on the word of seventy-one-year-old Washington Irving who had attended the ceremony as a six-year-old boy.[50] Old habits die slowly, though. In April 2014, for instance, a blogger left a message on the website of the Family Research Council complaining that there still are "some people confused enough or mendacious enough publicly to express doubt that George Washington actually added those words to the constitutionally prescribed presidential oath."[51]

Donald Trump, too, had "so help me God" follow his oath of office, though it came with a lesser degree of drama, and without reference to the Father of His Country. No one really knows what Trump thinks about George Washington, whether he thinks about him at all, or whether the notion of "Father of His Country" makes him think about his own father. Fred Trump, for what we know, was an overbearing if not abusive father. The same can be said about the fathers of Kennedy, Nixon, and George W. Bush. Ronald Reagan's father was an alcoholic. Bill Clinton and Barack Obama lacked fathers altogether, which puts them in a boat with George Washington. Washington's father, Augustine Washington, died in 1743, when son George was only eleven years old. From what little we know, the relationship, though tragically short, was typical for that time in history. Yet Washington rarely mentioned his father, nor did he often speak of him. The most significant record is from 1784, when he said, somewhat introspectively, that he had "early been deprived of a father." It is probably not too far-fetched to say, as William H. Wilbur noted in 1970, that the father must have had quite a significant impact on the son.[52]

One can only speculate what that impact was like, though in light of more than two hundred years of presidential history one is inclined to believe that the presidency seems to be at least partly an obsession with proving oneself to a disapproving or absent father. And mindful of the unflagging interest in a "Father of His Country" it is also tempting to think of some kind of reinforcing cycle there between Americans' need for a father and the aspirants' to the office similar need. But these are mere speculations, and one is on safer ground to point to two key functions of an inaugural address, to unify the audience, with appeals to George Washington appealing to the audience's emotions and desires, and, secondly, to rehearse "communal values drawn from the past."[53] Thus, whether viewed positively as embodying American ideals of leadership and character, or negatively as embodying the nation's deepest contradictions and historical flaws, Americans have always re-created Washington to suit their own agendas and have found in his life and career characteristics and episodes applicable to their own lives and times. They have constructed their versions of him from actual events of his lifetimes. Or they have built their images upon previous ones—as witness the myriad variations on Gilbert Stuart's patriarchal "Athenaeum" portrait.

Today, the face of the nation seems hopelessly commercialized, especially every year around "Presidents' Day," which used to be George Washington's birthday, always observed on February 22, but now moved by the Federal government to the third Monday in February, whatever date that may be. Only nine states currently identify "Washington's Birthday" as the sole commemorative event. Twenty-four states observe a "Presidents' Day" as a holiday. In total, forty-one states observe some form of holiday commemorating either the birth of George Washington or "Presidents' Day." Some states observe Washington's birthday or a Presidents' Day in conjunction with celebrations also honoring Lincoln and Jefferson. Arkansas honors both Washington and civil rights activist Daisy Gaston Bates. The states of Georgia and Indiana commemorate Washington's birthday on December 24. New Mexico's "Presidents' Day" falls on November 4. Nine states have no legal holiday at all commemorating any president.[54]

To honor and commemorate fathers and forefathers, as well as to celebrate fatherhood and male parenting, is the purpose of Father's Day. By the end of the first decade of the twenty-first century, Father's Day again was in great demand, as the political climate then was dominated by the discourse of "family values." In 2009, for instance, BellaOnline℠ put on its "Christian Literature" website an article titled "A Father's Importance." Its author, Diana Pederson, pleaded with Americans not to forget "about the importance of a father in the lives of their children. Thanks to today's divorce rates, too many children spend only a few days a year with their fathers." And mindful of the upcoming Father's Day, Ms. Pederson also had a recommendation to make, "a special book that could be used to show your appreciation for your Father." The book that "best serves this purpose" in her opinion is *The Embrace of a Father*, by Wayne Holmes.[55]

Although the first modern Father's Day church-service celebration was held in Fairmont, West Virginia, as early as 1908, Father's Day was not officially recognized as a holiday until 1972, during the presidency of Richard Nixon.[56] Seven years later, President Jimmy Carter decided to declare Father's Day officially. Fathers were expected to play a bigger role in raising children, the President noted, calling upon dads to take on greater responsibilities in family life. With his speech, Carter publicly acknowledged the importance and value of fatherhood in America, a sentiment that only increased in the decades to follow, reinforced for instance by the *Cosby Show*, which aired for eight seasons on NBC between September 1984 and April 1992. The *Cosby Show* provided the very model of proper parenting, earning its protagonist, Cliff Huxtable, the honorary title of "Greatest Television Dad."[57] A year into the new millennium, George W. Bush also issued a "Father's Day" proclamation. After reflecting on the importance of fathers and honoring their vital role in the lives of children, and after also going through the history of the holiday, Bush encouraged "all Americans to express love and respect for their fathers, as well as appreciation for the vital contributions of fathers to families and to society." In his capacity as president, Bush went on to direct "the appropriate officials of the Government to display the flag of the United States on all Government buildings on this day. I also call upon State and local governments and citizens to observe this day with appropriate programs, ceremonies, and activities."[58]

Take notice: Bush's proclamation reads "Father's Day." This is at odds with normal English punctuation guidelines, which indicate that the holiday should be spelled "Fathers' Day" (as it is a plural possessive). Common usage, however, dictates that the ostensibly singular possessive "Father's Day" is the preferred spelling. "Father's Day" also extends to metaphorical fathers. In 2008, for instance, President Bush presented his economic recovery plan seated in front of Gilbert Stuart's patriarchal portrait of George Washington, that is, in front of the face of the nation and, figuratively speaking, under the gaze of the Father of His Country, who is peering over his successor's shoulder.

Father's Day, Washington's birthday, Presidents' Day—observing them constitutes rituals that many Americans find meaningful. From the early 2000s, public discourse in America has resonated with "family values," and responsible fatherhood has been seen, especially among the middle classes, as not only helping the children but also as greatly enhancing men's lives. In late 2009, Phillip Longman, a journalist, even predicted the return of patriarchy. By patriarchy, Longman explicitly does not simply mean "that men rule." He conceives of it as a value system that requires men to marry and have children, thus keeping birthrates high. Declining birth rates, Longman argues, has been the legacy of the baby boomers (whom he also sees responsible for values like gender equality). Longman's conclusion is quite disturbing. No advanced civilization, he writes, has been able to ensure its continued existence while foregoing a patriarchal order. The re-election in 2004 of George W. Bush to the presidency thus is proof that the new trend had already set in. As Longman points out, in states that voted for Bush, fertility rates were 12 percent higher than in states that voted for Senator John Kerry. Bush's re-election therefore marks the return to a more traditional family order, together with "a strong identification with one's folk or nation."[59]

George W. Bush in front of Gilbert Stuart's portrait of George Washington (REUTERS/Kevin Lamarque).

For the generation before, notions like nation, folk, or fatherhood had been of much less relevance. As the sociologist Leonard Benson put it in a 1968 book, "Father is not a very impressive figure in American life." Another sociologist pronounced that a "father's absence from the home is not a major factor in behavioral problems or low achievement test scores in young children."[60] One wonders what kind of father these scholars imagined. If it was one whose essential purpose was to ensure a stable family system, breadwinner, not caregiver would have been the marker of his identity. The two terms—breadwinner as opposed to caregiver—only indicate the deep ideological divide over the role of men in the family. "American society is fundamentally divided and ambivalent about the fatherhood idea," David Blankenhorn wrote. "Some people do not even remember it. Others are offended by it. Others, including more than a few family scholars, neglect it or disdain it."[61] The fatherhood idea seems once and for all and forever grounded in a larger debate over gender roles. "Trump's slogan 'make America great again,'" Rebecca Solnit wrote in *The London Review of Books* in January 2017, "seemed to invoke a return to a never-never land of white male supremacy where coal was an awesome fuel, blue-collar manufacturing jobs were what they had been in 1956, women belonged in the home, and the needs of white men were paramount."[62]

Solnit may have exaggerated in her critique of patriarchy and problematic images of maleness, yet there undeniably exists a distinctive concept of manhood, one that stresses the man's place as the undisputed head of the family, leads men to think of child care as women's work, and emphasizes an emotional distance that makes warm, nurturant relations with children difficult to achieve. Toxic masculinity inspires anger, and the man becomes a threat. His job is to go out, earn the money, and punish the kids when he gets home. This image of masculinity and fatherhood may strike one as a caricature, though it is one that a majority of Republicans subscribes to. In contrast, about the same percentage of Democrats, roughly two thirds, say that American culture has generally changed for the better since the 1950s.[63] Is it that for them, the blurring of gender roles has led to the separation of masculinity and responsible paternity, which thus became dissimilar cultural categories?

Although fatherhood as such transcends politics, the diminished significance of fathers in the 1960s and 1970s cannot be separated from the descent of George Washington's reputation and importance. His birthday often was rather the pretext for a long weekend. This may not be such a bad thing in itself, if one is prepared to see the virtue of securing time away from economic activities and dedicating more of one's time to family and community. But in the 1960s and 1970s, towns and cities abandoned or canceled their traditional celebrations because of a lack of public interest. Even the United States House and Senate no longer assembled for the annual reading of the Farewell Address.[64] The erosion of traditional rituals should not be taken to mean that Washington's image was fading completely from the collective memory. Washington's birthday is simply not the chief method of his commemoration. Emotional attachment to the Father of His Country can assume other, less grandiose forms than annual parades, feasts, and balls. When presidents of the United States habitually cite George Washington's example in their inaugural addresses or else pose in front of Stuart's "Athenaeum" portrait, they at one and the same time identify with the nation's past and evoke Washington's memory. Other iconic reminders of the Father of His Country can be found on city landscapes, especially in the nation's capital, where they overwhelm every other figure in America's history.[65] The memory of the Father of His Country also lives on in the places named for him: Rivers and streams, mountains and lakes, colleges and universities, counties, cities and towns, the capital city, one state—not to mention the thousands of streets and businesses, and the hundreds of thousands of people that still carry his name. On a more modest scale, iconic reminders also appear on postage stamps (two of which show George Washington at prayer).

For modern Americans, George Washington is indelibly connected to the one-dollar bill. His iconic portrait endures not just on the currency, though. It also became the schoolroom Washington, gazing down on students throughout the day, as well as the TV Washington, serving as the patron saint for Peter Jennings's economic coverage on the ABC evening news. Popular print imagery too has appropriated the iconic representation of Washington, including on book covers.[66] Businesses too love George Washington, who sells everything from coffee to soap to baking powder to soft drinks. You can even sell cigars in his name. Or travels to the most unlikely places. The face on the dollar bill also advertises big February sales in department stores and used-car lots. Or else, you can acquire bottles, belt buckles, hats, hatchet-shaped cookie cutters, ice cream molds, fans, medallions, chairs, chocolate wraps, paper tissues, T-shirts (worn, for instance, by students at George Washington University), and other objects bearing Washington's likeness. Such "outpourings of junk," in Karal Ann Marling's memorable words, may well constitute a relapse into infantilism.[67] But that junk, or kitsch, not merely sells the past to the future, thus contributing to the manufacturing of consent. Junk or kitsch is the expression of the soul. It reveals an inner need to internalize the Father of His Country as an object of emotional attachment.[68]

The art historian Mark Thistlethwaite has a different view. Analyzing the form, content, and context of several diverse images from recent years (editorial cartoons, advertisements, magazine covers, etc.), he concludes that Washington's dollar bill visage functions "as the nation's personification of late capitalism," a potent visual synecdoche for the nation, its economy, and its consumerist culture. Thistlethwaite also claims, justly I think, that such familiar usage of a national foundational leader and hero is "uniquely American," even though Washington's dollar bill image has also made it onto luxury women's boots by the Italian label Balanciaga.[69] Altogether, the "trivialization" of the Father of His Country should be seen as a way of upholding the iconic properties of his image, albeit around rather inconspicuous campfires. Max Weber would have said that America's national icon has undergone routinization ("*Veralltäglichung*").[70]

Americans are also fond of remembering the Father of His Country with the help of new media. "The Captioned Adventures of George Washington," on Tumblr's LadyHistory, has become a hugely popular series. It pairs classic pictures of George Washington with contemporary (and sometimes quite irreverent) captions. Leutze's *Crossing of the Delaware*, for instance, is captioned "let's yankee doodle this shit." A few years ago, Savage's *Washington Family* was captioned to make the liveried servant say "Hey George, Mount Vernon just hit 100,000 fans on Facebook." To which Washington answers, "Well, huzzah, Are they all coming to visit?" Martha Washington has the final word: "I better make another ham." Yet another example depicts George Washington on his death bed, captioned "delete my browser history."[71] A new website on George Washington that opened on February 22, 2011, pursued more serious goals. The site included a blog, background information, and a message board for the community. The site's founder, Richard Lim, who also contributed the "Father of His Country" article to Mount Vernon's *George Washington Digital Encyclopedia*, intended the site to become "one of the premier George Washington centers on the internet and a meeting point for Washington scholars and enthusiasts alike." It was not to be, though. The domain, http://www.firstinpeace.com, was on sale in early 2018, though Lim's George Washington site on Facebook, reputedly with over 20,000 followers, is still active.[72]

Another popular culture representation of Washington is the video game *BioShock Infinite*. Released in 2013, it is the third game in the BioShock series. The Father of His Country looms large in it, first as a statue in the Garden of New Eden, which serves as a peaceful place of prayer and contemplation in the city of Columbia. Visitors are led to three statues, Benjamin Franklin holding a key, Thomas Jefferson holding a scroll, and George Washington holding a sword. Most visitors will pray to the statue of Father Washington. There are, of course, also the bad guys. One of the many foes players will encounter is a creepy automated Washington. A Frankenstein look-alike, "George Washington" is utterly fearless, a clockwork terminator who, like other "Motorized Patriots" keeps coming back forever, relentlessly.[73] June 30, 2014, saw the release of "George Washington vs. William Wallace," an episode in Season 3 of Nice Peter & EpicLloyd's *Epic Rap Battles of History*. The episode begins with Washington insisting on the "difference between you and me, Willy / I fought 'till I was actually free, Willy / I got my face on a quarter / you got drawn and quartered / Tortured on the orders of a king, really?" Wallace responds by calling Washington "Founding Father, but no children / Crossed the Delaware, but your soldiers couldn't swim," and he concludes, "You're the Father of Your Country, but I'm your daddy...."[74]

Two years later, Audible Originals began a series, *Presidents Are People Too!* In the George Washington episode, which went on air on April 3, 2017, hosts Elliott Kalan (a former Daily Show head writer) and Alexis Coe (a historian and author, currently at work on a biography of George Washington, under the working title *You Never Forget Your First*), attempt to recast George Washington as a real-life person, exploring topics like the Washington myth, his role as a major whiskey distiller, or his life as a slave-holding planter.[75] In

February 2018, an interactive online experience titled "Be Washington" opened in Mount Vernon's Donald W. Reynolds Museum & Education Center. The experience allows participants to "step into the shoes of the first president and commander in chief and make the very same decisions he had to." In doing so, participants can discover key moments in George Washington's life (the 1777 Battle of Trenton, the 1783 Newburgh Conspiracy, the Genet Affair of 1793, and the Whiskey Rebellion of 1794) and hear from most of his important advisors (Jefferson, Hamilton, and Madison). Each of the four scenarios takes an estimated 18 minutes to complete. Players can visit the Interactive Theater, go through the experience at home or in the classroom, or sign up for a private session by appointment.[76]

The "Be Washington" experience no doubt will increase visits to Mount Vernon, which already attracts an average of one million guests each year. Mount Vernon is the most popular shrine to the Father of His Country by far, visited by a total of 85 million since 1860, when the estate officially opened to the public. Other historic monuments to attract massive visits, such as the Washington Monument and Washington's birthplace in Wakefield, as well as the many places between Boston and Savannah that the Father of His Country visited and that can now proudly announce that "George Washington slept here."[77] George Washington never became a parent himself, though he had any number of substitute children, in his military family as much as at Mount Vernon. But "the most important category of substitute descendants," Richard Brookhiser contends, was "the future generation of Americans."[78]

Washington chose the role of father of future generations consciously. In the spring of 1783, as peace was approaching and the Continental Army was winding up its affairs, he twice used a striking phrase. In a letter to a staff officer, he gave expression to his hope that the "Peace & Independency for which we have fought" would be "a blessing to Millions yet unborn." And in the "Circular to State Governments" he warned that "our fate" was bound up with "the destiny of unborn Millions."[79] When Washington talks about posterity, he must have known that he would never see most of them. They would be strangers to his blood, as well as strangers to him in time. But as Brookhiser aptly puts it, "Mentioning them was an act of adoption."[80] Who, then, are George Washington's "adopted political heirs," those who still believe that the Father of His Country "was and would continue to be there for them"?[81] An inconclusive list would contain people who choose to name a plaza outside a new federal building after George Washington; people who leave "Happy Birthday" posts on the George Washington Facebook site; people who bake George Washington meatloaves, creating an edible icon; people who get excited about news of strands of Washington's hair recently found in an almanac from 1793; or people who around Father's Day 2018 disseminated on social media a Lansdownesque image of George Washington inscribed with "America, I am your father." The post drew any number of likes and comments, such as "Happy almost Father's Day to the Father of our Country," "I wish he could come back," "if you could only see your country today," or "we NEED him instead of this guy we got now."[82]

Likewise among Washington's "adopted political heirs" would be people who scatter the ashes of loved ones on the grounds of Mount Vernon; the visitors who leave the premises loaded with Mount Vernon Folk Art Christmas Tidings and other souvenirs; descendants of Revolutionary War officers in the Society of the Cincinnati who some years ago donated to the Mount Vernon Ladies' Association a bronze copy of Houdon's marble statue in the Virginia State Capitol; the 150 or so uniformed "soldiers" (actually schoolchildren) who still meet every Christmas Day afternoon on the banks of the Delaware River, in Pennsylvania's Washington Crossing Historic Park, to recreate that fateful day in 1776 by rowing across the river in "authentic reproductions" of the boats used in Washington's surprise attack on Trenton (high winds scuttled the re-enactment in 2017).[83] Also on the list would be that faithful representative braving scorn and derision to deliver the Farewell Address to an empty House or Chamber. Mark S. Wilson also would make the list, for carving an Americana Totem Pole in red pine, for display at the Yankee Doodle Country Store in Canastota, New York. The mixed-media column features familiar symbols of American democracy including a bald eagle, the Liberty Bell, and the Constitution. Below the scroll, Washington sits atop an original flag of the U.S.A. and a white pillar of justice. And, last but not least, an "adopted political heir" no doubt is an ambitious young man by the name of Dennis Rudenko, who is planning to build an innovative seven-story building in the San Francisco area, whose front will resemble the quarter dollar. As the Ukrainian entrepreneur said, the quarter dollar is "the longest-serving, unchanged coin design that every American has in his or her pocket," and it depicts "America's first president."[84]

All these people, in one way or the other, have taken the Father of His Country into their minds—internalized him as an object, as psychoanalysts put it. Internalizing, Richard Brookhiser wrote, is something everyone must do to grow up. Living as a man or a woman depends on images we carry with us. Most people internalize their parents as objects, for good or for ill, supplementing them with aspects of important mentors. These images are not fantasy figures but rather models, based on the actual behavior of others and shaping the actual behavior of ourselves. A political father can serve as a model for a nation as a whole—for its citizens individually or for all of them acting together. By their common exposure to icons, shrines, place names, observances, rituals, currency notes, etc., millions of people are drawn into a moral communion, called a *participation mystique* by anthropologists, and through this relationship the continuity of their political tradition is reinforced at the same time as their felt fatherlessness is assuaged. Fatherhood does not come naturally, though; if fathers are to set an example to their children, both training and an act of will are required. George Washington had both. He was "a man who follows through. This is why it was particularly appropriate that George Washington came to be known as the father of his country, for he was the founder, above all others, who followed through."[85]

Epilogue:
If George Washington Had Not Been the Father of His Country

I began this book by advancing the importance of fathers, both biological and metaphorical ones, each appearing in two different guises, the "strict father" as opposed to the "nurturant parent." After showing how, by an act a symbolic regicide and patricide, the exalted title of "Father of His Country" was transferred from George III to George Washington, I spent some time unfolding the title's genealogy. The *pater patriae* of Roman antiquity reemerged as "patriot king" in the English Enlightenment, when it was also rendered, in a literal translation, as "Father of His Country" or, in French, as *père de la patrie*. German-speaking Protestants were familiar with *des Landes Vater* from Martin Luther's Bible translations. I then discussed the cultural transformations of the national icon. Representations of America's first president as the Father of His Country, I found, articulate individual and collective needs, providing scenarios that elevate, humanize, and deflate him. I ended with attempts to "prove" Washington's "unique greatness" and a discussion of Washington's "adopted political heirs." In this final chapter I reconsider America's relationship with its first president. While commemoration of the Father of His Country has taken many forms over the years, as an icon he became a stylized image of Americans' faith in themselves and in their country. That image originated in the creative imaginations of various cultural elites; it has been manipulated for ideological (patriotic) purposes, at the same time as it has been subject to contested readings.

George Washington was the Father of His Country already during his lifetime. After his death and through the nineteenth century, reverence for him increased. His prominence reached a peak at the time of the bicentennial of his birth in 1932, then, over the next half century, his prestige seemed to be diminishing. Increasingly, the Father of His Country was seen as remote and distant, one of those "dead white men" who are largely irrelevant for a world that was getting ready for Civil Rights Acts or the Equal Rights Amendment. The fading concept of greatness, a changed understanding of the presidency—from presidential restraint to the "imperial presidency" (the term is Robert G. Denton's)—and, not to forget, the diminished significance of fathers, metaphorical fathers included, no doubt precipitated Washington's descent, which was halted only with the election to the presidency of Ronald Reagan. During his presidency and in the years to follow, George Washington was returned to his former glory and greatness, achieving a new significance, for the American people as much as for the nation's political leaders.

Let's begin with Washington's apotheosis, the primary condition of which was the unique fit between his personal traits and public deeds and the young republic's nation-building. Identification of Washington with the new nation was universal, articulated in the print culture, in public speechifying, in private or not-so-private letters, though nowhere more potently than in the arts. Portrait artists, sculptors, printmakers, copper and steel engravers, and silhouette cutters engaged in producing likenesses of the venerable Father of His Country. Their works cannot be fully understood solely in terms of contemporary aesthetic norms and standards; moral and political concerns were at least as important. Especially portraiture had to serve the nation's moral and ethical standards. For modern Americans, George Washington is indelibly connected to the one-dollar bill. It is the form in which Gilbert Stuart's "Athenaeum" portrait of 1796 is seen daily. The notion that in portraiture, the highest possible closeness to an original is more than an aesthetic axiom can be found already in Shakespeare. In the third act of *The Merchant of Venice*, Bassanio enters Portia's room, opens a leaden casket, and finds—a portrait of his beloved Portia, or rather, "Fair Portia's counterfeit!" Thus Bassanio marvels about the portrait's provenance:

> What demi-god
> Hath come so near creation? Move these eyes?
> Or whether, riding on the balls of mine,
> Seem they in motion? Here are sever'd lips,
> Parted with sugar breath: so sweet a bar
> Should sunder such sweet friends. Here in her hairs
> The painter plays the spider and hath woven
> A golden mesh to entrap the hearts of men,
> Faster than gnats in cobwebs; but her eyes,—
> How could he see to do them? Having made one,
> Methinks it should have power to steal both his
> And leave itself unfurnish'd: yet look, how far
> The substance of my praise doth wrong this shadow
> In underprizing it, so far this shadow
> Doth limp behind the substance.[1]

Bassanio's astonishment stems from his understanding that Portia's portrait is so close to the original, is true and reliable, possessing qualities that portrait painting acquired only in the Renaissance.[2] Yet the perceived likeness exists only ex post. The affective rapture that overwhelms Bassanio is retroactive, directed to a simulation. Hence his "praise" can only do it "wrong." But why "Fair Portia's *counterfeit*"? Modern usage suggests something illicit, like a counterfeit bill, or coin. There is something to this. Until the fifteenth century, the Italian word *contraffare* (like the French *contrefaire*) described the process of artful simulation. This is captured in Shakespeare's "shadow" that "doth limp behind the substance." By the sixteenth century, however, the word *contraffare* had acquired more positive connotations. It now described a technique of representation that produces, not a counterfeit, but something genuine or authentic.[3]

Authenticity should not be taken to mean that there was an assumed identity between an original and its likeness. Portraiture in fact required that the original be transformed, heightened, presented in a dramatic or suggestive pose. In the scene in Shakespeare's play the focus is on the face. For people in the Renaissance, the face was seen as an expression of the soul. A fifteenth-century tract by the humanist Lorenzo Valla expressly distinguishes between the physical face, the *facie* (which Valla relates to *superficie*, surface), and the invisible face (*vultus*) that the canvas reveals in the physical face. The term commonly used for the artistic practice of depicting faces was *rittrare al naturale*, drawing out from nature.

Its past participle survives in the various designations for depictions of faces, as in *ritratto* or, via a related Italian verb, *protrarre*, "portrait."[4] Did Shakespeare sense that in portraiture, an invisible face (*vultus*) had to be made visible in the physical face? And that a successful portrait reveals much more about its subject than immediate perception? A gifted portrait painter, by closely studying his subject's face, sees more in it than a casual observer. Moreover, the painter's artistry necessarily conveys more about a subject than a mere first impression—conveys, that is, "the very innermost essence of a man," including feelings, mental and intellectual abilities, and moral character.[5] In America, these notions became popular thanks to translations into English of writings by the Swiss poet, philosopher, theologian, and physiognomist Johann Caspar Lavater. Especially Lavater's idea that everyone had a unique essence that was externally visible in the physiognomy, became profoundly influential on American portrait painting. Yet an individual's essence was not to be detected by studying faces directly; nor could it be conveyed in words. Instead, Lavater argued in *Essays on Physiognomy*, one should look for signs of these traits in artistic renderings, most notably in portraits. Not all portraits were alike, though. While artistic renderings were capable of drawing out an original's innermost essence, mechanical, superficial likenesses fell short.[6]

A circular from the American Academy of Fine Arts is a good example of the topicality, in early nineteenth-century America, of the distinction between genuine artistry and mechanical, superficial likenesses. The circular bemoans the glut of poor representations of George Washington, "the common, miserable representations of our Great Hero," which are dismissed as a "curse." Only Gilbert Stuart's portraits, the circular asserts, actually resembled the original. This is odd, as Martha Washington had not seen in them any "true resemblance" to the original.[7] Apparently, her predisposition, perhaps the result of her memories of a healthier and happier husband, was no longer topical a generation later. By 1824, the date of the Academy's circular, the confirmed resemblance validated George Washington as a plain citizen. There is no hint of a heroic dimension, only the commonality of a man among the people. The agenda behind this strategy is obvious—to instrumentalize Washington as a moral exemplar in the manufacturing of consent in what increasingly was a middle-class society. At the beginning of the republic, portraits and other representations of Washington were employed not only in efforts to reform morals and propriety but also to increase patriotic feelings. When Washington sat for Stuart in 1796, the nation's future was still in doubt. Washington was the one man around whom all could rally, and what, Chief Justice Marshall pontificated, would more effectively spark the noble emotions of emulation and patriotism than a portrait of the first president? Stuart's serene Washington provided just the right icon. His Washington, the writer and art critic John Neal wrote in an 1823 novel, "was less what Washington was, than what he ought to have been." Neal's sentiment became a commonly accepted position throughout the century. As late as 1880, the *Magazine of American History* printed a passionate plea to establish a "national standard" for Washington's likeness, on the grounds that "the authentication and erection of a standard image to represent the Nation's Father, is an act of sacred dedication to the claims of eternal posterity."[8]

Deification of illustrious personalities usually occurs only *after* their passing away. Not so in the case of "the matchless Washington," whose place "next unto the Trinity" was a matter of fact already during his lifetime. As Marcus Cunlife notes, to his admirers Washington was "god-like Washington," while his detractors complained to one another that he was looked upon as a "demi-god" whom it was treasonable to criticize.[9] Many of the religious or quasi-religious sentiments that gave rise to wave after wave of adulation lived on in the public memory. When Gustave de Beaumont traveled through the United States in the company of Alexis de Tocqueville in the 1830s, he had a first-hand experience of a myriad of statues, busts, columns, and inscriptions dedicated to Washington. De Beaumont's summary is telling: "In America do not look [...] for monuments raised to the memory of illustrious men. I know that this people has its heroes; but no where have I seen their statues. To Washington alone are there busts, inscriptions, columns; this is because Washington, in America, *is not a man but a God*."[10] De Beaumont might also have mentioned the countless treatises on Washington in which the personal pronoun was capitalized ("HE"), which compared Washington to Jesus Christ, referring to him as "savior" or "redeemer," pointing out that Washington's mother, too, was named Mary. Such deification was difficult to swallow for a republican-minded man like John Adams, who in 1812 indignantly noted that Washington worship was a national impiety: "Among the national sins of our country [is] the idolatrous worship paid to the name of Washington by all classes and nearly all parties of our citizens, manifested in the impious application of names and epithets to him which are ascribed in Scripture only to God and to Jesus Christ."[11]

Perhaps the most vociferous rejection of Washington worship stems from John Adams's son, John Quincy Adams. In response to debates about a monument to be erected for Washington's one-hundredth birthday, the nation's sixth president noted in his diary: "Democracy has no monuments. It strikes no medals. It bears the head of no man on a coin. Its very essence is iconoclastic."[12] The target of Adams's wrath is America's "dysfunctional relationship" with its presidents, to borrow from Thomas S. Langston's survey of presidential history. Each president, Langston argues, becomes an icon, a stylized image of Americans' faith in themselves and in their country. But the game of presidential symbol-making only encourages unrealistic expectations, false hopes, and willful misunderstandings. And, Langston adds, the game invites even the best presidents to deceive the public.[13] Langston's survey dates from 1995. But already John Quincy Adams's objection was like the voice of someone crying out in the desert. Washington's "holiness" continued to set the tone for pictorial representations, whose aura of sacredness was beyond dispute. Ralph Waldo Emerson, we have seen, had a Washington portrait hung in his dining room, of which, as he admitted, he simply could not keep his eyes off.[14] Walt Whitman remarked that Washington's portrait was "canonized in the affections of our people."[15] And for William J. Hubard, the "authentication and erection" of a Washington portrait was "an act of sacred dedication."[16] For all these people, a Washington portrait was truly a sacred image deserving of veneration.

When Gilbert Stuart was at work on his portraits of America's first president, it was commonly believed that it was possible to deduce a person's character from his or her face. Focusing on the face thus was a prerequisite for a claim to moral exemplariness. Religious icons are said to have identical claims. Such icons are hung, not only in churches but also, and often primarily, in homes. So, we have seen, were "likenesses" of George Washington.[17] The functional parallels between religious icons and Washington's portrait are not lost even today. In 1963, the year the popular TV series *Father Knows Best* was discontinued, the artist Tom Wesselmann produced a pop-art-style collage titled *Still Life*; the work places a Stuart-like portrait of George Washington next to a TV set, suggesting a religious icon being placed next to the modern equivalent of the domestic fireplace.[18] A year into Ronald Reagan's first term as president, Washington came back solo-ing in John Huston's film *Annie*, by way of Stuart's portrait. In a scene set in the White House, the title character—who afterwards becomes "The Fourth of July kid"—sings "Tomorrow," to the delight of Franklin and Eleanor Roosevelt, who readily join in while the Stuart portrait observes the songfest.[19]

Annie premiered in 1982, the year of the 250th anniversary of Washington's birth. A few years later, a poem titled "The Father of My Country" appeared in one of Diane Wakoski's collections, *Emerald Ice*:

> If George Washington
> had not
> been the Father
> of my Country
> it is doubtful that I would ever have
> found
> a father.[20]

Emerald Ice was published in 1988. By that time, Wakoski had become critical of American poetry's return to a new formalism. "The Father of My Country," which is dated 1964 and was originally published in *The George Washington Poems* in 1967, dedicated to her father and her husband, clearly belongs to the tradition of Allen Ginsberg and other confessionalists. Yet when *Emerald Ice* was published, the poem was criticized as too conservative, snugly fitting the mood of the Reagan era, not least its hostility towards the new women's movement, which had reached an early peak in the failure to getting the Equal Rights Amendment ratified and the withdrawal of its support by the Republican Party in 1980.[21] The ERA was introduced in Congress in 1971 or, rather, it was reintroduced. It was originally written for the National Woman's Party by Alice Paul and Crystal Eastman and introduced in Congress for the first time in 1921. Then and later the Equal Rights Amendment sought to end the legal distinctions between men and women in terms of property, employment, divorce, and other matters. Diane Wakoski, it seems, would have none of all this. Not only is her poem more personal and conversational, more in the mode of William Carlos Williams (*Emerald Ice* won the William Carlos Williams Award in 1989). It also openly flaunts her emotional attachment to George Washington, who appears throughout the poem as a symbolic father figure, a surrogate the speaker can use to talk about her own father. Curiously, that theme was overlooked by critics, as was the fact that Williams in 1925 had referred to Washington as "The Pap of Our Country."[22]

The fact that for Wakoski, the Father of Her Country is simply good for feeling raises a number of questions. Is this a simple case of men making the gods and women worshipping them, to borrow from Frazer (the anthropologist)? Simone de Beauvoir is not the only feminist to claim that women like to have Order and Right—a "magic male essence"—embodied in a male leader. This would make Wakoski's George Washington as it were "the heavenly father demanded by all serious right-thinkers, the absolute guarantor of all values," accepted "not through second judgment but by an act of faith." But can we really say that Wakoski's attachment to Washington is "blind, impassioned, obstinate, stupid; what it declares, it declares unconditionally, against reason, against history, against all denial"?[23] Wakoski's claim on George Washington as a father—"I need your / love" she says in the last stanza—might just as well be taken as an index that from the 1960s, a time when the so-called generation gap between fathers and their children was very real, as real as rising divorce rates and father absences, many American men and women were in search of at least a vague sense of fatherly warmth. For them, what Robert Bly once called "father hunger" was a given, and fathers in general were anything but "not that important." On the contrary, fathers—whether real or metaphorical—provided at least an imagined sense of security at a time when beliefs, convictions, or moral values were no longer commonly held or broadly shared, and what advice one could get tended to be bleak. As Bob Dylan sang in "The Times They Are A-Changin," "you better start swimmin' or you'll sink like a stone."

It comes as no surprise that the demand for mythic stories or grand narratives is most intense and the moral inspiration from even the crudest myth most deeply felt during times of crisis. Yet narratives do not just spring up spontaneously or "naturally." They are always constructed, disseminated, and passed on with a view to the maintenance of power. As George Gerbner noted, "Those who tell stories hold the power in society."[24] This power consists in manufacturing consent, that is, in conveying beliefs, convictions, or moral values that will be broadly shared. By manufacturing consent, by establishing hegemonic rule, the state can imagine the people under its dominance, the geographic territory under control, and the nature of historical legitimacy. One of the hegemonic stories told and retold in the United States is the father narrative, the "dad story," as it were. Allen Ginsberg is not the only one to evoke that narrative, even though he does so in a rather melancholy way, "O Washington—O Father." Ginsberg was a child of the 1950s, a time when an estimated 20–25 percent of American families experienced war-related father absence during any one year. Forty years later, roughly the same percentage of the nation's families with children were without fathers.[25] And today? By 2013, some 17 million children were fatherless in the United States. In view of these "brute facts," Stephen Marche concludes that there simply "is no cure for fatherlessness."[26] This is no problem merely of demographics. Fatherlessness always occurs within wider cultural attitudes, including a lurking hostility toward paternal authority. The American nation itself, David Blankenhorn reminds us, originated in revolt against the paternal authority of the king. "We are the inheritors of regicide, the jealous guardians of power stolen from a societal Old Father. [...] The Old Father says: Stay at home. Obey me. Learn my trade. Marry one of our kind. Do not forget your faith. Cut your hair. Much of the American answer is: I will go West."[27]

Mark Twain's Huckleberry Finn will go West, and Jack Schaefer's Shane already has gone. Set in the Wyoming Territory in the 1890s, Schaefer's novel of 1949 revolves around the mythic conflict between cattle ranchers and homesteaders. Thanks to the intervention of Shane, the conflict is resolved in favor of the homesteaders. Shane, the title hero of this most famous Western of all, is a mysterious stranger, portrayed as an almost divine or supernatural hero, "in that dark and worn magnificence from the black hat with its wide curling brim to the soft black boots. But what caught your eye was the single flash of white, the outer ivory plate on the grip of the gun, showing sharp and distinct against the dark material of the trousers."[28] Yet Shane is not a stereotypical gunslinger. The mystery that surrounds him results from a deep wound left by the absence (or loss) of a father. As Shane is about to ride on, he takes aside Bob Starrett, the eleven-year-old narrator and chief witness of the events unfolding in the Wyoming Territory, telling him, "I reckon it was in the cards from the moment I saw a freckled kid on a rail up the road there and a real man behind him, the kind that could back him for the chance another kid never had."[29]

Shane was initially published in 1946 in three parts in *Argosy* magazine, and then titled *Rider from Nowhere*. The novel was made into a film by Paramount in 1953, directed by George Stevens. Clearly the 1940s and 1950s were a time when the connection between masculinity and responsible paternity was unraveling. Yet writers, ordinary citizens, and political leaders, whatever their other flaws, had not yet lost the idea of fatherhood. They acted on the principle that every child needs a father, however dubious. Fatherhood in those years occurred within broader cultural norms, described by Wini Brines as a "moralistic national family ideology."[30] Within that family model, the President of the United States must have corresponded to the "strict father" model described by George Lakoff. What kind of metaphorical "father" was, then, Dwight D. Eisenhower? Before he became president in 1952, Eisenhower had been a soldier, commanding Allied troops in Europe. The British Field Marshall Bernard "Monty" Montgomery did not think much of Eisenhower as a soldier, but, as he writes in his memoirs, appreciated other attributes: "[Eisenhower's] real strength lies in his human qualities. He has the power of drawing the hearts of men toward him as a magnet attracts the bit of metal. He merely has to smile at you, and you trust him at once."[31]

Eisenhower had lovingly been called "Ike" since World War II. His trustworthiness, together with his conservative and paternalistic attitude must have felt comforting to Americans frightened by the possibility of a nuclear Armageddon. Like his predecessor in office, Harry Truman, Eisenhower indeed projected an image of quiet and serene authority and paternal confidence, enough for John F. Kennedy to call him for advice during the Cuban missile crisis. Yet if Eisenhower was considered as the undisputed "father" of a nation imagined as a family, the cracks in the family fabric were already becoming obvious. It is well to remember, then, that whatever his human qualities, the Eisenhower *image* stemmed from sophisticated media work. It was the image, not content, that decided the elections, first in 1952 and then again in 1956. Eisenhower's opponent in both elections was Adlai Stevenson, a Democrat. Stevenson could never project the image of the nation's "father." Rather, he was seen as too serious and cerebral, if not as patronizing and condescending. John Alsop, a journalist, famously described him as an "egghead," adding that all the eggheads were for Stevenson but there were simply not enough of them.[32]

About a half year into Eisenhower's second term, Americans got to know a different President, one that no longer operated behind the scenes while presenting a public persona of a kindly father. In September 1957, the President sent some 11,000 National Guards to the little town of Little Rock, Arkansas. Their job was to escort nine African American school children through the gauntlet of angry white faces. State police had denied the school children entry into a "white" high school—at the behest of the state governor, who simply ignored the Supreme Court's ruling that racial segregation was unconstitutional.[33] In the long run, however, not even Eisenhower could bring back the traditional roles of fatherhood that had been lost since the time of the Founders—of irreplaceable caregiver, moral educator, head of family, and family breadwinner. It is no coincidence that during these eventful years, Eisenhower left the role of the nation's father to God. In July 1955, he signed a law that made it mandatory for the motto "In God We Trust" to be printed on the currency. The motto became the national motto in July 1956, and on October 1, 1957, the first dollar bills with the motto were released. It is hardly coincidental that the motto "In God We Trust" was ordered to be inscribed on the currency. For a currency that had lost its convertibility, the ringing endorsement of the one God could symbolically compensate for the "financial atheism" of the dollar, restoring faith in a sign that not only lacked the transcendental signified of the gold standard but also was devoid of any reference to a deposit in the government's vaults.[34] A generation later, the dollar's role as a world currency reserve was in jeopardy, its share in the foreign-exchange market in decline, and its purchasing power dwindling. Yet interest in the visual properties of the national monetary icon, its "esoteric political theology," was rising.[35]

Interest in the presidents was rising too. A number of films from the 1970s to the 1990s indulged in what has appropriately been called "live-action presidential heroics." In both John Huston's *Independence Day* (1976) and Wolfgang Petersen's *Air Force One* (1997), the fictional presidents are shown as agents who "at moments of ultimate peril [...] step in and duke it out with the bad guys themselves."[36] Yet the action hero presidents of these films are also fathers or, more inclusively, family men. Even while organizing *Independence Day*'s planet-wide counterattack, President Whitmore has to watch out for his daughter and deal with the death of his wife—a sequence whose sentimentality rivals the death scenes in Victorian romances. President Marshall, likewise, has to worry not just that the terrorist hijackers of *Air Force One* will succeed at destabilizing the former Soviet Union; even more urgently he, too, must protect his wife and younger daughter, who happen to be along on the flight. If anything, Jeff Smith argues in *The Presidents We Imagine*, "action hero presidents are the *ultimate* family men, reacting to dangers that threaten kin and country alike."[37] It does not come as a surprise that both *Independence Day* and *Air Force One* conceive of the nation as a family, running along smoothly, without irksome factions and parties. Politics in each of the two films is either conveniently ignored or reduced to a primordial hand-to-hand combat. Family issues and action heroics are easily linked because they are both formulas for suppressing, adjourning, or at least ignoring politics in the name of an assumed consensus—two different but related consequences of keeping stories focused on the president's person, who is depicted as a leader above party, representing all the people because all the people are family.[38]

Stories about George Washington, too, make use of the nation-as-family idea, thus steering clear of anything overtly political. In 1999, C-SPAN created a series of life portraits of American Presidents. In the first series, *Life Portrait of George Washington*, historian Richard Norton Smith, the author *Patriarch: George Washington and the New American Nation*, and James C. Rees, executive director of George Washington's Mount Vernon, answered questions from across the nation. Many of the callers—including a thirteen-year-old student from the George Washington Middle School in Alexandria, Virginia—wanted to know more about the real Washington: Did he have a sense of humor? Did he have sexual relations with his slaves? Did he really chop down the fabled cherry tree? Did he grow hemp?[39] The answers had little to do with the saccharine myths about Washington that used to be disseminated so widely. But the answers, together with the questions asked, indicate that people have always re-created George Washington to suit their own agendas, and have found in his life and career characteristics and episodes applicable to their own lives and times. People construct their versions of him from actual events of his lifetimes. Or they build their images upon previous ones—from the myriad variations on Stuart's "Athenaeum" portrait to the recycling, on "Whatsoproudlywehail.org," of Oliver Wendell Holmes's belief that Washington's birthday is "Dearer still as ages flow." While it is self-evident that the America for which these people are nostalgic never existed, the values embedded in such symbolic acts of nostalgia are not without their force. They foster a sense of community. They offer a firm footing in the midst of social and economic chaos, even dictating a suspension of business activities. They tender comfort and solace, and they consecrate the stories that keep a big country and a diverse people united.[40]

As long as the values, customs, beliefs, practices, and stories that constitute the way of life of a people are alive and respected, people will continue to think in terms of "We Americans." They will see themselves as part of a larger whole, proud to be American rather than proud to be "different." And they will see themselves as united not by any specific ideology so much as by a compound of old-fashioned values and traditions, last seen perhaps in the patriotic politics of Franklin D. Roosevelt, and of a desire for commonness and "unity of purpose" rather than societal disintegration.[41] The commitment to shared beliefs, values, and traditions also reinforces respect for a man at the nation's founding whose like they do not expect to see again, and a profound distrust of many of the current policies that have no place either for solidarity or civics. As George Washington himself observed at the outset of his presidency in 1789, the president must not "demean himself in his public character" but must act "in such a manner as to maintain the dignity of office."[42] To uphold the memory of the Father of His Country thus at one and the same time articulates an ethical imperative and documents a political ethics.

It is no exaggeration to say that the values Washington stood for more than two hundred years ago remain central to the political culture of the twenty-first century. Not that contemporary presidents actually live up to these values. As Sean Wilentz wrote on the anniversary of Donald Trump's inauguration, it is rather their shortcomings that give the moral example of the Father of His Country its significance.[43] In more general terms, Arthur M. Schlesinger, Jr., wrote in his editor's note to the George Washington volume in the American Presidents Series, "Presidents serve us as inspirations, and they also serve us as warnings. They provide bad examples as well as good. The nation, the Supreme Court has said, has 'no right to expect that it will always have wise and humane rulers, sincerely attached to the principles of the Constitution. Wicked men, ambitious of power, with hatred of liberty and contempt of law, may fill the place once occupied by Washington and Lincoln.'"[44] Nor, I would add, does the nation have any right to expect that a woman may fill that place. Article II, Section 1 of the Constitution lists only three qualifications: that the president be a "natural born citizen," at least thirty-five years old, and a resident "within the United States" for fourteen years.

While these are the Constitution's minimal qualifications, there are and always have been cultural understandings that were never stated explicitly—that the president had to be white, or that the president had to be a man. The first understanding received a serious challenge when Barack Obama was elected president in 2008; the second when Hillary Clinton in 2016 became the first woman to seriously run for the presidency. But as she writes in her memoir of her unsuccessful campaign, "it's not customary to have women lead or even to engage in the rough-and-tumble of politics. It's not normal—not yet. So when it happens, it often doesn't feel quite right. That may sound vague, but it's potent. People cast their votes based on feelings like that all the time."[45] The statement shows that Hillary Clinton was well aware of a basic problem, one that Uri Friedman formulated in *The Atlantic* right after election day—that "to win in a presidential system, women must contend more directly, and on a larger scale, with sexism and stereotypes."[46] The comparison is between presidential systems and parliamentary ones. In the latter, leaders are chosen by their colleagues, and thus are able to bypass a potentially biased general electorate. Following Clinton's defeat, many commentators suggested that she was simply the "wrong" woman. This is far too easy. As Annette Gordon-Reed wrote in her review of Clinton's memoir, "any woman who had been the first to run for president with the backing of a major party would have encountered some of the gender-based scrutiny Clinton faced."[47] They would have encountered that scrutiny for at least two reasons. One is that many Americans, especially white men, felt that women had upended their world and that they now had a chance to vent their anger and frustration. The other reason is that Americans' expectations for their political leaders have been set by generations of male politicians and shaped by generations of male pundits.

Hillary Clinton thus is absolutely right when she states that, historically, "women haven't been the ones writing the laws or leading the armies and navies. […] It's the men who lead. It's the men who speak. […] That's been the case for so long it has infiltrated our deepest thoughts."[48] If Hillary Clinton had in mind the nation's founders, she's of course on the right track, though we can go back much further, to Homer's *Odyssey*. That venerable epic, the classical scholar Mary Beard angrily wrote, stands at the beginning of western culture's practice of reducing women to silence. Indeed, when Telemachus confronts his mother Penelope for having rebuked him and his rowdy buddies, he tells her to get lost: "Nay, go to thy chamber, and busy thyself with thine own tasks, the loom and the distaff, and bid thy handmaids ply their tasks; but *speech shall be for men*, for all, but most of all for me; since mine is the authority in the house."[49] Some two thousand years later, Treasury Secretary Albert Gallatin worried about a shortage of individuals qualified to hold office during the second Jefferson administration. When he suggested that the president consider hiring women, Jefferson replied by spilling out all the cultural understandings that have kept women from the public sphere to this very day: "The appointment of a woman to office is an innovation for which the public is not prepared, nor am I."[50]

And George Washington? It's a moot point to say that he also would not have been prepared to appoint a woman to office. There is no record that he ever was in a situation similar to President Jefferson's. What we can safely say is that the exalted title of Father of His Country at one and the same time immunized Washington against criticism and subverted ideological impetuses for further change, locking them into a "worthier" past. In that past, patriarchal language served to legitimize political authority. Americans or, rather, American males were accustomed to paternal authority. They honored their own fathers and expected their sons to honor them. Accordingly, political leaders who successfully donned the mantle of fatherhood not only elicited considerable citizen respect and deference; they could also rest assured that for most people dissent was too daunting. As Reid Mitchell put it, "The parental metaphor made rebellion a primal sin."[51]

Another consequence of the parental metaphor has been more far-reaching. Since patriarchal leadership was associated with "benign authority," a man could obey a biological or political father without feeling that he forfeited his manly independence or citizenship. This seems true even today. For, the hopes and anxieties associated with Washington's successors demonstrate a desire for a paternal leader, one who, as Robin Lakoff said in her political memorandum on the 1992 campaign, is at one and the same time "a daddy, a king, a god, a hero [...] a champion who will carry that lance and that sword into the field and fight for us."[52] It's the rhetoric of political *fatherhood*, not motherhood, that ameliorates, if not elides, all kinds of fears, of change, of the future, of social decline, of other people. The story of the Father of His Country is a gendered narrative as well as a narrative of gender. As sobering as it may sound, therefore, all the evidence suggests that "a woman leading the United States is not, as many young voters predicted this election cycle, simply a matter of time."[53]

Notes

Prologue

1. Walt Whitman, "To Foreign Lands," from the "Inscriptions" section to *Leaves of Grass*, ed. Sculley Bradley and Harold W. Blodgett (New York: W. W. Norton, 1973), 3.
2. Blankenhorn, *Fatherless America*, 1.
3. *Ibid.*, 61.
4. Stephen Marche, "Manifesto of the New Fatherhood," *Esquire* (June 13, 2014), http://www.esquire.com/lifestyle/news/a28987/manifesto-of-the-new-fatherhood-0614/, retrieved November 28, 2017.
5. "Americans for George," https://www.facebook.com/amerforgeorge and, for information about the group, Kglobal, "Americans for George," http://kglobal.com/results/americans-for-george, both retrieved August 28, 2017. The COINS Act (H.R. 2977) was proposed by Arizona House Republican David Schweikert and two other House Republicans. See United States Congress, https://www.congress.gov/bill/112th-congress/house-bill/2977/text, last accessed November 13, 2017. In March 2011, the Government Accountability Office (GAO, formerly General Accounting Office) also likewise that the $1 note be replaced with a $1 coin. Since, the financial benefit of such a replacement has decreased and the GAO is no longer tracking this action; instead, the GAO recommends that the Treasury be allowed to alter the metal composition of all coins. See United States Government Accountability Office, "Annual Report on Duplication and Cost Savings," May 21, 2019, https://www.gao.gov/duplication/overview, retrieved May 25, 2019.
6. Clinton Rossiter, *The American Presidency* (New York: New American Library, 1960), 11.
7. Miller and Schwartz, "The Icon of the American Republic," 521–23; for "innermost essence," see Pavil Svinin, commenting on Rembrandt Peale's *Patriae Pater*, qtd. *ibid.*, 528; for "the icon acts," see Marie-José Mondzain, *Image, Icon, Economy: The Byzantine Origins of the Contemporary Imaginary*, trans. Rico Franses (Stanford: Stanford UP, 2005), 106.
8. The concept of the *"participation mystique"* originates from Lucien Lévy-Bruhl's book *La mentalité primitive* (Paris: Félix Alcan, 1922).
9. For the "nation-as-family" concept, see Lakoff, *Moral Politics*, esp. 153–61.
10. Cunliffe, *George Washington*, 14.
11. For Cunliffe, Washington was essentially a figure "of the *eighteenth* century." Thus, he dismisses all attempts toward emphasizing the "human" side of Washington as mere "Hollywood-and-historical novel conception[s] of an American hero." *George Washington*, 160 and, for further description and analysis, 161–67. For more recent attempts to "rediscover" or at least to "reconsider" George Washington, see Brookhiser, *Founding Father: Rediscovering George Washington*, and Higginbotham, ed., *Washington Reconsidered*.
12. Stuart Hall, "Cultural Studies: Two Paradigms," *A Cultural Studies Reader: History, Theory, Practice*, ed. Jessica Munns and Gita Rajan (London-New York: Longman, 1995), 199.
13. Washington, Cunliffe argues (*George Washington*, 16), occurs "in any or all of the four following guises: a) *the Copybook Hero*; b) *the Father of His People*; c) *the Disinterested Patriot*; d) *the Revolutionary Leader*."
14. Qtd. in Geraghty, "Donald Trump Is Not Your Father," *The National Review*, April 26, 2016, http://www.nationalreview.com/article/434570/donald-trump-not-your-father, retrieved May 17, 2017.
15. For "living 'tribal' totem," see Albanese, *Sons of the Father*, 144; for "political Father and head of a Great People," see Levi Allen to George Washington, 27 January 1776, *Founders Online*, National Archives, http://founders.archives.gov/documents/Washington/03-03-02-0141, retrieved January 26, 2017.
16. James Wilson, qtd. in Bernard Bailyn, ed., *The Debate on the Constitution*, 1:825.
17. St. George Tucker, qtd. in Bryan, *Washington in American Literature*, 152.
18. Joseph Addison, *Cato*, 1.1.
19. David Humphreys, "A Poem on the Happiness of America," qtd. in Bryan, *Washington in American Literature*, 129.
20. Irving, *Life of Washington*, 5:320, emphases added.
21. Willard, *History of the United States*, 300.
22. Peale, *Portrait of Washington*, 3.
23. Tocqueville, *Democracy in America*, 464.
24. Rev. John S. C. Abbott, qtd. in Blankenhorn, *Fatherless America*, 14.
25. Holmes, "Ode for Washington's Birthday," *The Poetical Works of Oliver Wendell Holmes*, rev. and

with a new introd. by Eleanor M. Tilton (Boston: Houghton Mifflin, 1975), 98.
26. Calhoun, qtd. in Bryan, *Washington in American Literature*, 75.
27. "Ode on the Death of President Lincoln" (1865), qtd. in Butter, *Der "Washington-Code,"* 96.
28. Eric Hobsbawm, "Mass-Producing Traditions: Europe, 1870–1914," *The Invention of Tradition*, ed. the same and Terence Ranger (Cambridge: Cambridge UP, 1983), 263–307, quot.'s 280, 279.
29. Ann Pamela Cunningham, qtd. in Casper, "The Washington Image," 601–602.
30. *Indiana Democrat*, qtd. in "Martha on $1," *George Washington's Mount Vernon*, n.d., http://www.mountvernon.org/george-washington/martha-washington/martha-on-1/, retrieved September 20, 2017.
31. Griswold, *Fatherhood in America*, 115.
32. Boime, *The Unveiling of the National Icons*, 153.
33. Grant Wood, qtd. in Thistlethwaite, "Hero, Celebrity, and Cliché," 143, emphasis added.
34. Marling, *Washington Slept Here*, viii.
35. John Quincy Adams, December 11, 1831, qtd. in Kammen, *Mystic Chords of Memory*, 19.
36. Langston, *With Reverence and Contempt*, 5, 9.
37. Thistlethwaite, *The Image of George Washington*, 3.
38. Marling, *Washington Slept Here*, 20–24.
39. Morgan, *Inventing the People*, 13, 14.
40. Jeff Smith, *The Presidents We Imagine*, 7.
41. "These were the times when the demand for Washington's image was most intense [...] and the moral inspiration from even the crudest likeness most deeply felt." Miller and Schwartz, "The Icon of the American Republic," 537.
42. Thomas Jefferson to George Washington, May 23, 1792, *Founders Online*, National Archives, http://founders.archives.gov/documents/Washington/05-10-02-0267, retrieved January 26, 2018.
43. Robin Lakoff, qtd. in Maureen Dowd, "The 1992 Campaign," *The New York Times* (October 10, 1992), http://www.nytimes.com/1992/10/10/us/1992-campaign-political-memo-knights-presidents-race-mythic-proportions.html?pagewanted=all&pagewanted=print, retrieved February 9, 2018.

Part I

1. "President-elect Barack Obama Named 2009 Father of the Year," *American Chronicle* January 4, 2009, http://www.americanchronicle.com/articles/view/86742, February 8, 2009. Other references in this paragraph are to Elizabeth Kelleher, "Economy Remains Central Issue in Presidential Race" *America.gov*, September 29, 2008, http://www.america.gov/st/elections08-english/2008/September/20080929182957berehellek0.4966089.html, March 16, 2009, and Manuel Swoboda, "Amerikaner wählen stets einen Daddy ['Americans always vote for a Daddy']," Interview with Donna Leon]," *Kleine Zeitung* (Klagenfurt-Graz), October 19, 2008, 112–13, here 112, my translation.

2. Blankenhorn, *Fatherless America*, 84–85; Griswold, *Fatherhood in America*, 219–28. On America's highest office as particularly unenviable, the result of an inevitable mismatch between presidential promises and the structural limitations of the office, see Jeremi Suri, *The Impossible Presidency: The Rise and Fall of America's Highest Office* (New York: Basic Books, 2017).
3. Barack Obama, "Inaugural Address," January 20, 2009, http://www.whitehouse.gov/blog/inaugural-address/. Following is the complete passage from Corinthians: "When I was a child, I spake as a child, I understood as a child, I thought as a child: but when I became a man, I put away childish things" (1 Cor 13: 11). Robert G. Kaiser, "Analysis: President Obama's Swearing-in Ceremony," *The Washington Post*. January 20, 2009, 1pm, http://www.washingtonpost.com/wp-dyn/content/discussion/2009/01/16/DI2009011603008.html; for "Dad speech," see Joel Achenbach, "Achenblog," January 20, 2009, http://voices.washingtonpost.com/achenblog/2009/01/obamas_inaugural_address.html; for the line from *The Sun*, see the CNN press review "World hails 'United States of Obama,'" January 21, 2009, http://edition.cnn.com/2009/POLITICS/01/21/obama.international.press.reaction/index.html, all retrieved January 29, 2009.
4. Barack Obama, "Acceptance Speech," Denver, CO, August 28, 2008, http://my.barackobama.com/barackspeech, January 21, 2009.
5. See Barack Obama, "Being the Father I Never Had," *People*, June 8, 2011, http://people.com/celebrity/barack-obama-fathers-day-essay/, retrieved November 28, 2017. For the NRFC, go to Fatherhood.gov, at https://www.fatherhood.gov/home.
6. See Julia T. Marsh, "Fatherhood, Not Marriage, Is Focus of Obama Family Policies," *Christian Science Monitor*, August 10, 2010, 7. President Obama's belief that the national fatherhood crisis is especially severe within the African American community only goes to show that the debate set off by the Moynihan Report on *The Negro Family* of 1965 is far from over.
7. Obama, *The Audacity of Hope*, 409–10; the book's title originates from an eponymous sermon by Reverend Wright, about Hannah's story, from the Book of Samuel (ibid., 292).
8. Obama, *Dreams from My Father*, 327. The memoir was first published as Obama, at age 33, was preparing to launch his political career in a campaign for the Illinois Senate. It was republished in 2004, following his United States Senate Democratic primary victory in Illinois.

Chapter 1

1. Blankenhorn, *Fatherless America*, 25; for "necessary and not a contingent figure" see Martin Baily, "Concluding Comments," *The Importance of Fathers* (London: Psychology Press / Routledge, 2001), 243–44, quot. 244. For further discussion and analysis of fathers' unique contribution to child development, see *The Role of the Father in Child Development*, ed.

Michael E. Lamb (5th edn. Hoboken, NJ: Wiley, 2010).

2. Donald Barthelme, *The Dead Father* (New York: Farrar, Straus and Giroux, 1975), 129.

3. Brookhiser, *Founding Father*, 193.

4. 1 Chronicles 22:9, 10; cf. a. 28:6: "I have chosen [Solomon] to be my son, and I will be his father." All quotations from Scripture are from the *KJV*, the King James Version.

5. Proverbs 1:7; Matt 6:9; St. John 14:8.

6. The goddess is generally unnamed in the English Bible. In the modern German Bible, in contrast, she is customarily mentioned by name, "Aschera" (English "Asherah"). The reason for this discrepancy is that "Asherah" is translated in Greek as *alsos*, grove, or *alse*, groves. Since the *KJV* used the Greek translation, Asherah's name was lost to English language readers for some 400 years, as was knowledge of her existence. Still, attentive readers might have noticed references to a "queen of heaven" in Jeremiah (7:18; 44:17, 25), another hint that Jahwe may have had a female consort. The female aspect of the divine is known as *Shekhinah* in Kabbalah, treated as a central element of Jewish mysticism by Gershom Scholem in *Major Trends in Jewish Mysticism* (Jerusalem: Schocken, 1941), especially 213–17 and 229–35.

7. See BBC Two, "The Bible's Buried Secrets. Did God Have a Wife?" December 21, 2011, http://www.bbc.co.uk/programmes/b00zw3fl, February 2, 2015, and, for further discussion and analysis, Judith M. Hadley, *The Cult of Asherah in Ancient Israel and Judah: Evidence for a Hebrew Goddess* (Cambridge: Cambridge UP, 2000).

8. Gordon J. Schochet, *Patriarchalism in Political Thought: The Authoritarian Family and Political Speculation and Attitudes Especially in Seventeenth-Century England* (1975; New Brunswick, NJ–London: Transaction Books, 1988), 233. References to Hobbes are to *Hobbes's Leviathan*, reprinted from the Edition of 1651, with an Essay by the late W. G. Pogson Smith (Oxford: Clarendon P, 1909; 1929), 97 (pt.I, ch.13) and 154 (pt.II, ch.20). Also in this connection, see Peter B. Gray and Kermyt G. Anderson, *Fatherhood: Evolution and Human Paternal Behavior* (Cambridge: Harvard UP, 2012).

9. Locke, *Two Treatises on Government*, I, §100.

10. *Ibid.*, I, §100; II, §105, §77–79.

11. See Michael Walzer, "Regicide and Revolution," in *Regicide and Revolution: Speeches at the Trial of Louis XVI*, Ed. with an Introduction by Michael Walzer, trans. Marian Rothstein (New York: Columbia UP, 1992), 1–92, here 25, 15. On the political debates in seventeenth-century England, see Schochet, *Patriarchalism in Political Thought*.

12. Liddle, "'A Patriot King, or None,'" 952–53.

13. Shaftesbury, *Characteristics*, 2:40 and, for "fatherless world," 1:25.

14. "…to resolve on a humble, dutiful and loyal Petition to the King, the common head and Father of *all* his people." *Journals of the House of Representatives of Massachusetts* (Boston: Massachusetts Historical Society, 1976), 45:100; Samuel Davies, "On the Death of His Late Majesty King George II," *Spreading the Gospel in Colonial Virginia*, ed. Edward L. Bond (Lanham, MD et al.: Lexington Books, 2004), 398–413, here 400; for Governor Belcher's speech, see *The Political State of Great-Britain*, vol. 43 (London: T. Warner and A. Rocayrol, 1732), 335–38, here 335.

15. Nathaniel Niles, in Hyneman and Lutz, *American Political Writing*, 1:273.

16. For Jill Lepore, however, "What would the founders do?" is an "ill-considered" and "pointless" question, an instance of "historical fundamentalism." *The Whites of Their Eyes: The Tea Party's Revolution and the Battle Over American History* (Princeton: Princeton UP, 2011), 14, 19. As regards veneration of the "founders," following the bicentennial of Washington's death in 1799, the Delaware History Museum staged an expansive exhibition, *Fathers of Our Country*. The exhibition, which opened on Presidents' Day and was on display through election day, November 7, 2000, featured memorabilia, photographs, and documents from each of the Presidents through George H. W. Bush. For reference, go to Historical Society of Delaware, http://www.hsd.org/Fathers.htm, no longer available as of 2017.

17. Lakoff first developed the idea that we understand the nation metaphorically in family terms in his book *Moral Politics*, chap. 8, esp. 153–61.

18. Martha Nussbaum, *The Monarchy of Fear: A Philosopher Looks at Our Political Crisis* (New York: Simon & Schuster, 2018), 7.

19. Qtd. in Jim Geraghty, "Donald Trump Is Not Your Father," *National Review*, April 26, 2016, http://www.nationalreview.com/article/434570/donald-trump-not-your-father, retrieved May 17, 2017.

20. Zoltán Kövecses, *Metaphor: A Practical Introduction* (Oxford: Oxford UP, 2010), 7. Epistemologically, the "nation-as-family" is an idealized cognitive model ("ICM"), that is, a simplified (even oversimplified) representation of a situation, an event, or a fact. On this, see George Lakoff, *Women, Fire, and Dangerous Things: What Categories Reveal about the Mind* (Chicago: U of Chicago P, 1987), 68.

21. Samuel P. Huntington, *American Politics: The Promise of Disharmony* (Cambridge: Belknap Press of Harvard UP, 1981), especially chapters 5 and 6. Huntington identifies four periods of "creedal passion" in American history—the Revolutionary War, the Jacksonian Age, the Progressive era, and the 1960s—, but as Carlos Lozada has argued, Huntington's book of 1981 was truly prophetic, pointing as it does to the Trump era. "Samuel Huntington, a prophet for the Trump era," *The Washington Post*, July 18, 2017, https://www.washingtonpost.com/news/book-party/wp/2017/07/18/samuel-huntington-a-prophet-for-the-trump-era/?utm_term=.9375e04bcc24, retrieved November 7, 2017. On Trump winning the 2016 election by exploiting the deep divisions in American society, see Abramowitz, *The Great Alignment*.

22. Lakoff, *Moral Politics*, chaps. 5 and 6. For a general discussion of conceptual metaphors, see Raymond W. Gibbs, Jr., *Metaphor Wars: Conceptual Metaphors in Human Life* (Cambridge: Cambridge UP, 2017), especially Chap. 2, 17–56.

23. John Robinson, qtd. in Griswold, *Fatherhood in America*, 10.

24. Donald J. Trump, "Inaugural Address," The White House, January 20, 2017, https://www.whitehouse.gov/inaugural-address, retrieved January 23, 2017. And see George Lakoff's March 2016 blog, "Why Trump?" *The Huffington Post*, March 3, 2016, http://www.huffingtonpost.com/george-lakoff/why-trump_1_b_9372450.html, retrieved December 1, 2016. On the emotional appeal of Trump's politics, see Arlie Russell Hochschild's essay "The Ecstatic Edge of Politics: Sociology and Donald Trump," *Contemporary Sociology* 45:6 (June 2016), 683–89.

25. Lincoln Steffens, "Becoming a Father at 60," *American Magazine* (August 1928), qtd. in Griswold, *Fatherhood in America*, 10.

26. Blankenhorn, *Fatherless America*, 96 and, for further description and discussion of the "New Father," 97–123.

27. See Lakoff, *Moral Politics*, 245–62. Ernst Bloch has used the shifting conceptions of god—from authoritarian transcendence to the embrace of the lowly—as the basis of his utopianism, which he elaborated on in *The Principle of Hope* (Cambridge: MIT P, 1986); see especially chapters 36 and 53).

28. Blankenhorn, *Fatherless America*, 4–5.

29. Bourdieu, "Thinking About Limits," *Theory, Culture, and Society* 9:1 (February 1992), 37–49, here 39.

30. Lakoff, preface to the 2nd edn. of *Moral Politics*, x. See a. Matthew Feinberg and Elisabeth Wehling, "A moral house divided: How idealized family models impact political cognition," *PloS one*, vol. 13,4 e0193347, 11 Apr. 2018, <doi:10.1371/journal.pone.0193347>, March 3, 2019.

31. Donald J. Trump, respectively Republican National Convention acceptance speech, July 21, 2016, full transcript by Brad Plumer, http://www.vox.com/2016/7/21/12253426/donald-trump-acceptance-speech-transcript-republican-nomination-transcript, July 25, 2016, and press conference, January 11, 2017, *The New York Times*, January 11, 2017, http://www.nytimes.com/interactive/2017/01/11/us/politics/live-video-analysis-donald-trumps-press-conference.html, retrieved January 13, 2017.

32. Qtd. in Jim Geraghty, "Donald Trump Is Not Your Father," web document. For Trump's pre-election record, see Michael Kranish and Marc Fisher, *Trump Revealed: An American Journey of Ambition, Ego, Money, and Power* (New York: Scribner, 2016).

33. John R. Talbott, *Obamanomics: How Bottom-Up Economic Prosperity Will Replace Trickle-Down Economics* (New York: Seven Stories P, 2008), 17; for the full results of poll, see 206n17. For the national survey, see NBC Mews / Wall Street Journal Poll, see Study # 6078, Question 17b, December 19, 2007, https://www.wsj.com/public/resources/documents/wsjnbcpoll20071219.pdf, retrieved December 8, 2008. For Eli Zaretsky, see the interview in *Die ZEIT* (Hamburg, Germany), November 17, 2016, 46: "Es gibt keinen Weg zurück" ("There's no way back"). At the time of Obama's election to the presidency, many liberals hoped that he would become the strong Democratic president the United States had not had in over forty years. Ironically, Jon Meacham in 2008 celebrated a strong presidency in a book on Andrew Jackson.

34. Obama supporter, qtd. in Geraghty, "Donald Trump Is Not Your Father," web document.

35. Barack Obama, "Inaugural Address," January 20, 2009.

36. Barack Obama, qtd. in Colvin, "Obama Gives Memorable Acceptance Speech," *ABC Net*, November 7, 2012, http://www.abc.net.au/pm/content/2012/s3627984.htm, retrieved January 19, 2013.

37. Barack Obama, Farewell Address of January 10, 2017, *The New York Times*, https://www.nytimes.com/2017/01/10/us/politics/obama-farewell-address-speech.html?_r=0, retrieved January 11, 2017.

38. Washington, "Farewell Address," *The Writings of George Washington*, ed. Rhodehamel (subsequently abbreviated as *WWR*), 964, 965: "The name of AMERICAN, which belongs to you, in your national capacity, must always exalt the just pride in patriotism, more than any other appellation derived from local discriminations."

39. "Farewell Address," *WWR*, 964. The Federalists in 1793 had had the French ambassador deported for alleged Jacobin insurgence. Incidentally, James Madison (in *The Federalist* #10) explained the difference between a "Democracy and a Republic" in terms of a) "the delegation of the Government, in the latter, to a small number of citizens elected by the rest," and b) "the greater number of citizens, and greater sphere of country, over which the latter may be extended." It is obvious that Madison directed his warning against Jefferson, whose idea of "democracy" was derived from the Greek model of the *polis*. Madison, "The Union as a Safeguard Against Domestic Faction and Insurrection," *The Federalist Papers*, No. 10, November 23, 1787, The Avalon Project at Yale Law School, 2008, http://avalon.law.yale.edu/18th_century/fed10.asp, November 20, 2017.

40. "Farewell Address," *WWR*, 968.

41. References are to President Obama's Farewell Address of January 10, 2017, web document. On Obama's role as "father of his country" and the need for liberals to reframe some of the issues at stake, see Lakoff, *Moral Politics*, 418–26.

42. Brookhiser, *Founding Father*, 185–90.

43. "Farewell Address," *WWR*, 972–76. For a reading of the Farewell Address in its historical context, see Joseph J. Ellis, "The Farewell," in *George Washington Reconsidered*, ed. Don Higginbotham (Charlottesville: UP of Virginia, 2001), 212–49, esp. 220–44, and John Avlon, *Washington's Farewell: The Founding Father's Warning to Future Generations* (New York: Simon & Schuster, 2017).

44. George Washington paid for his portraits out of his own pocket. As for his successors as well as for any number of elected officials since, their portraits mostly were paid for by the U.S. taxpayers—until March 27, 2018, when President Donald J. Trump signed into law the Eliminating Government-funded Oil-painting Act, also known as the EGO Act. See Colin Dwyer, "Congress Takes a Brush to the Budget,

Barring Federal Funds for Portraits," *The Two-Way, National Public Radio*, March 28, 2018, https://www.npr.org/sections/thetwo-way/2018/03/28/597593218/congress-takes-a-brush-to-the-budget-barring-federal-funds-for-portraits, retrieved March 29, 2018.

45. Barbara Perry and George W. Bush, qtd. in Samantha Raphelson, "Fathers of Our Country: How U.S. Presidents Exercised Moral Leadership in Crisis," *NPR*, August 18, 2017, http://www.npr.org/2017/08/18/544523278/fathers-of-our-country-how-u-s-presidents-exercised-moral-leadership-in-crisis, retrieved August 24, 2017.

46. Donald J. Trump, qtd. *ibid.*

47. Maggie Haberman, "A Homebody Finds the Ultimate Home Office," *The New York Times*, January 25, 2017, https://www.nytimes.com/2017/01/25/us/politics/president-trump-white-house.html?_r=1, retrieved January 26, 2017.

48. "President Donald Trump's Remarks at Andrew Jackson's Hermitage," March 15, 2017, *YouTube*, https://www.youtube.com/watch?v=thx5_2jfpiU, accessed June 27, 2017.

49. For one thing, Jackson was *not* a political newcomer when he took office. He may have been that in 1824, but not in 1828, when his election was no surprise to anyone. Nor does he fit the caricature of the hot-tempered gunslinger, the "two-gun Andy" that flitted about in his first biographer, James Parton, as well as in Charlton Heston's movies. And Jackson did *not* impose protective tariffs, he opposed them, just as he opposed the business community. What he did not oppose was general welfare and, for that matter, the powers of the national government. Daniel Feller, "Andrew Jackson and Donald Trump: Outsiders Alike?" OAH Distinguished Lecture, Central Michigan University, Mount Pleasant, MI, June 22, 2017, https://youtu.be/lKsp32G6isI, accessed June 27, 2017. For the "real" Jackson, see Jon Meacham's *American Lion: Andrew Jackson in the White House* (New York: Random House, 2008).

50. Donald J. Trump to CBS moderator John Dickerson, *CBS This Morning*, May 1, 2017, https://www.youtube.com/watch?v=CF8lzCL5ncE, retrieved June 30, 2017.

51. Isaac Kaplan, "What Does Donald Trump See in His Portrait of Andrew Jackson?" *Artsy Net*, January 26, 2017, https://www.artsy.net/article/artsy-editorial-donald-trump-portrait-andrew-jackson, retrieved May 18, 2017. Also useful is William Kloss et al., *Art in the White House: A Nation's Pride* (Washington, DC: The National Geographic Society in cooperation with The White House Historical Association, 1992).

52. Donald J. Trump on *The 11th Hour*, MSNBC, May 2, 2017, https://www.youtube.com/watch?v=i6rq0ZjRp_w&feature=youtu.be, retrieved May 18, 2017. It is not without irony that even a liberal like Jon Meacham celebrated Jackson as a model of a strong president, in the 2008 book *American Lion*.

53. Washington, "Farewell Address," *WWR*, 964; for "*obey* the established Government," see *ibid.*, 968, emphasis added.

54. It was a fictional George Washington who did something like that—in a 1932 film about the good work of Franklin D. Roosevelt's NRA.

55. Washington, "Farewell Address," *WWR*, 969–70.

56. Thomas S. Langston, "Symbolic Presidency," *Encyclopedia of the American Presidency*, ed. Michael Genovese (New York: Facts on File, 2004), 424–25, here 424 and, for further discussion, Greenstein, "What the President Means to Americans," *Choosing the President*, ed. James D. Barber (Englewood Cliffs, NJ: Prentice-Hall, 1974), 121–147.

57. Trump, "Inaugural Address," web document.

58. Marx, *The Eighteenth Brumaire of Louis Bonaparte*, 9.

59. William Penn Adair "Will" Rogers (1879–1935), was an actor and vaudeville performer, humorist, newspaper columnist, and social commentator. His saying, "I bet after seeing us, [George Washington] would sue us for calling him 'father,'" is dated February 22, 1931, and is qtd. in Sterling and Sterling, *Will Rogers' World*, 129.

60. On Donald Trump as a threat to republicanism, see *Can It Happen Here? Authoritarianism in America*, ed. by Cass R. Sunstein (New York: Harper, 2018).

61. Richard Nixon, "Inaugural Address," January 20, 1973, online by Gerhard Peters and John T. Woolley, *The American Presidency Project*, http://www.presidency.ucsb.edu/ws/index.php?pid=4141, retrieved May 18, 2017. For the thesis that Trump's presidency is, in certain ways, the most Nixonian since Nixon's own, see Carl Freedman, "From Nixon to Trump: Metastases of Cultural Power," *Los Angeles Review of Books*, June 4, 2018, https://lareviewofbooks.org/article/from-nixon-to-trump-metastases-of-cultural-power/#, retrieved June 5, 2018.

62. Trump, "Inaugural Address," web document.

63. Jon Baskin, "The Academic Home of Trumpism," *Chronicle of Higher Education*. March 17, 2017, https://www.chronicle.com/article/The-Academic-Home-of-Trumpism/239495, retrieved January 7, 2018. For "permissive egalitarianism," see Leo Strauss, "The Crisis of Our Time," *The Predicament of Modern Politics*, ed. Harold J. Spaeth (Detroit, MI: U of Detroit P, 1964), 41–54, here 47–48.

64. Lakoff, *Moral Politics*, 271–73, quotation 273. Lakoff does not mention him, but when Karl Marx in 1852 described the American republic as "a conservative form of existence," he meant precisely this: That Americans see "the state" as a necessary evil, useful at the beginning of the nation but ideally to be replaced by a "libertarian" society without governmental authority and mediation. Marx, *The Eighteenth Brumaire of Louis Bonaparte*, 21.

65. Obama, "Changing the Odds for Urban America," July 18, 2007, http://barackobama.com/2007/07/18/remarks_of_senator_barack_obama_19.php, retrieved January 21, 2009.

66. Obama, *The Audacity of Hope*, 410.

67. Vice President Al Gore, qtd. in Samuel, *American Fatherhood*, 85.

68. See Peter Rubin, "Family Man," *The New Republic* (April 27, 1998), 12–13.

69. Blankenhorn, *Fatherless America*, 1.

70. Marche, "Manifesto of the New Fatherhood," *Esquire* (June 13, 2014), http://www.esquire.com/lifestyle/news/a28987/manifesto-of-the-new-fatherhood-0614/, retrieved November 28, 2017.

71. William H. Young, *The 1950s* (Westport, CT: Greenwood P, 2004), 222; Haralovich, "Sit-coms and Suburbs: Positioning the 1950s Homemaker," *Looking for America: The Visual Production of Nation and People*, ed. Ardis Cameron (Malden, MA: Blackwell, 2005), 238–63, here 238–43.

72. "Father comes marching home," *Parents* magazine riffed in 1945; qtd. in Samuel, *American Fatherhood*, 14.

73. Salinger, *The Catcher in the Rye*, 7, 12. On fatherlessness in 1950s America and war-induced fatherlessness in particular, see Blankenhorn, *Fatherless America*, 50–60. For "mass deprivation," see *ibid.*, 53. Also useful is Griswold, *Fatherhood in America*, 161–76 and, for *Rebel without a Cause*, ibid., 185–86.

74. Blankenhorn, *Fatherless America*, 105.

75. *Ibid.*, 106. As Elaine Tyler May wrote in 1988, putting fatherhood at "the center of a man's identity" expanded men's role beyond the mere breadwinner, imbuing them with a more nurturing sensibility. May, *Homeward Bound*, qtd. in Samuel, *American Fatherhood*, 15.

76. Saul K. Padover, "George Washington—Portrait of a True Conservative," *Social Research* 22:2 (Summer 1955), 199–222, quot. 218; Howard Swiggett, *The Great Man: George Washington as a Human Being* (Garden City, NY: Doubleday, 1953), 58.

77. As the series clearly embraces the "nurturant parent" model, Staci Beavers praises *The West Wing* as a healthy corrective, not just of family life, but also of public life. "*The West Wing* as a Pedagogical Tool," *The West Wing: The American Presidency as Television Drama*, ed. Peter C. Rollins and John E. O'Connor (Syracuse: Syracuse UP 2003), 175–86.

78. See Frame, *The American President in Film and Television*, chap. 4, "*The West Wing*," 111–73, passim. The pilot script to the series describes Bartlet as "President Josiah (Jed) Bartlet, Democrat of New Hampshire, and a direct descendant of one of the signers of the Declaration." Aron Sorkin, *The West Wing: Pilot Script* (Burbank, CA: Warner Bros. Entertainment Corporation, 2006), 55.

79. Gabriel Spitzer, "Rich are different. They Watch *West Wing*," *Media Life*, May 14, 2001, http://www.medialifemagazine.com:8080/news2001/may01/may14/1_mon/news2monday.html, retrieved January 15, 2017.

80. Chris Lehmann, "The Feel-Good Presidency: The Pseudo-Politics of *The West Wing*," *The West Wing*, 213–21.

81. Naomi Pfefferman, "The Left 'Wing,'" *Jewish Journal*, October 11, 2001, http://www.jewishjournal.com/up_front/article/the_left_wing_20011012, retrieved January 15, 2017, and Stephen Armstrong, "The War on Culture," *The New Statesman*, May 21, 2007, http://www.newstatesman.com/arts-and-culture/2007/05/west-wing-sorkin-television, retrieved January 15, 2017.

82. Robert P. Jones, "The Rage of White, Christian America," *The New York Times*, November 10, 2016, http://www.nytimes.com/2016/11/11/opinion/campaign-stops/the-rage-of-white-christian-america.html?_r=0, retrieved December 23, 2016.

83. Daniel Yankelovich, "How Changes in the Economy Are Reshaping American Values," *Values and Public Policy*, ed. Henry J. Aaron, Thomas E. Mann, and Timothy Taylor (Washington, DC: Brookings Institution, 1994), 16–53, qut. 34.

84. Martin N. Baily, Robert Z. Lawrence, and Kathryn L. Shaw, "The Importance of Fathers," *Economic Report of the President* (Washington, DC: United States Government Printing Office, 2000), 165–98.

Chapter 2

1. Nathaniel Niles, in Hyneman and Lutz, *American Political Writing*, 1:273. Samuel Davies, "On the Death of His Late Majesty King George II," 398.

2. Weems, *The Life of George Washington*, 80. "[H]orrors of civil discord," George Washington, letter to Robert McKenzie, October 9, 1774, in *WWR*, 160.

3. Thomas Jefferson, "The Declaration of Independence as Adopted by Congress," *Concise Anthology of American Literature*, Fourth Edition, ed. George McMichael (Upper Saddle River, NJ: Prentice Hall, 1998), 375–78, quot. 377.

4. On the stormy protests articulated in all forms of media, see Stephen D. Solomon, *Revolutionary Dissent: How the Founding Generation Created the Freedom of Speech* (New York: St. Martin's P, 2016).

5. Jefferson, "Summary View," *Writings*, 120, 107, 110.

6. Paine, "Royal Brute," "law is king," and "King of America," *Common Sense*, 99; "continental form of government," *ibid.*, 95, all in the section, "Thoughts on the Present State of American Affairs." For "first catalyst of change," see Ferguson, *The American Enlightenment*, 110.

7. Ferguson, *The American Enlightenment*, 113. For "still captures the imagination of the American reader" see *ibid.*, 110. On the American Revolution as first and foremost a "literary pursuit," see *ibid.*, 1–21. For a perceptive analysis of the emotional intensity and rhetorical power of *Common Sense*, see Bernard Bailyn, *Fundamental Testaments of the American Revolution* (Washington, DC: Library of Congress, 1973), 11–22.

8. The denomination on the note shown here—"One Dollar and Two Thirds of a Dollar"—is a result of the confusion in the British currency system. One pound was worth 20 shillings; a guinea, a larger gold coin, was worth one pound and one shilling; one shilling was equal to twelve pence; and each penny was divided into four farthings. It was not until 1971 that Britain's currency went metric. Jack Weatherford, *The History of Money: From Sandstone to Cyberspace* (New York: Crown Publishers, 1997), 181.

9. For descriptions of the Maryland notes, see

Doty, *America's Money*, 46–47, and the website of University of Notre Dame, Special Collections, "Colonial Currency," n.d., http://www.coins.nd.edu/ColCurrency/CurrencyText/MD-07-26-75.html, July 7, 2014.

10. Eric P. Newman, *The Early Paper Money of America* (Fourth edition. Iola, WI: Krause Publications, 1997), 445. The phrase was recommended by George Mason to the Virginia Assembly in 1776, as part of the commonwealth's seal. The seal was planned by Mason and designed by George Wythe, who also signed the Declaration of Independence. "Thus always to tyrants" is a shortened version of the phrase "Sic semper evello mortem tyrannis" ("Thus always I bring death to tyrants"). The phrase is sometimes said to have originated with Marcus Junius Brutus during the assassination of Julius Caesar on March 15, 44 BC, though according to Plutarch, Brutus either did not have a chance to say anything, or if he did, no one heard what was said. See *Plutarch's Lives*, the translation called Dryden's, corr. and rev. by A. H. Clough (New York: Colonial Company, 1905), 5: 320–28.

11. Jefferson to Henry Lee, May 8, 1825, *Writings*, 1500–1501; for "extract consensus at all costs," see Ferguson, *The American Enlightenment*, 6.

12. Michel Foucault, "Politics and the Study of Discourse," *The Foucault Effect: Studies in Governmentality*, ed. G. Burchell, C. Gordon and P. Miller (Chicago: U of Chicago Press / London: Harvester Wheatsheaf, 1991), 53–72, quot. 59.

13. Ferguson, *The American Enlightenment*, 188–189; for "Only children can be orphans," see *ibid.*, 37. On the orphan figure in the literature of the time, see Diana Loercher Pazicky, *Cultural Orphans in America* (Jackson: UP of Mississippi, 1998), esp. 51–85.

14. For the extent to which American propagandists depicted Washington as a virtuous replacement for the "tyrant" George III, see Peter Shaw, *American Patriots and the Rituals of Revolution* (Cambridge: Harvard UP, 1981), 15, and Longmore, *The Invention of George Washington*, 202–11. On the colonial renunciation of George III as a deeply traumatic experience, see Winthrop D. Jordan, "Familial Politics: Thomas Paine and the Killing of the King, 1776," *Journal of American History* 90 (September 1973), 294–308.

15. The "god of the clan," Durkheim wrote, can be "nothing else than the clan itself, personified and represented to the imagination under the visible form of the animal or vegetable which serves as totem." *The Elementary Forms of the Religious Life*, 236.

16. Albanese, *Sons of the Father*, 144.

17. Benjamin Rush, qtd. in Bryan, *Washington in American Literature*, 25.

18. Levi Allen to George Washington, 27 January 1776, *Founders Online*, National Archives, http://founders.archives.gov/documents/Washington/03-03-02-0141, retrieved January 26, 2017.

19. Henry Knox to George Washington, 26 November 1777, *Founders Online*, National Archives, http://founders.archives.gov/documents/Washington/03-12-02-0407, retrieved January 26, 2017.

20. Kahler, *The Long Farewell*, 110. The almanac, for which David Rittenhouse furnished the material, was published by Francis Bailey as *Der Neue Gantz Verbesserte Nord-Americanische Calender*. William S. Baker lists it in *Bibliotheca Washingtoniana* (Philadelphia: Robert M. Lindsay, 1889), 6; for a detailed commentary, see York-Gothart Mix, ed., *Deutsch-Amerikanische Kalender des 18. und 19. Jahrhunderts / German-American Almanacs of the 18th and 19th Centuries. Bibliographie und Kommentar / Bibliography and Commentary*, Bd. 1 / Vol. 1 (Berlin-Boston: Walter de Gruyter, 2012), 733–34.

21. Brumwell, *Gentleman Warrior*, 178–79. Washington's retirement from the Virginia regiment may well have resulted from his deep resentment at failing to procure a royal commission in the British Army. Washington likely did not just feel "slighted" or discriminated against. In Paul Longmore's view, therefore, the decision reveals a "significant development" in Washington's "political identity and thinking," so that the year 1757 marked "a step toward republicanism and nationalism." Longmore, *The Invention of George Washington*, 43–44.

22. "A Son Exelence, Monseigneur le General Washington," qtd. in Frank E. Grizzard, Jr., "Father of His Country," *George Washington: A Biographical Companion* (Santa Barbara, CA: ABC-CLIO, 2002), 105–107, here 106. The translation of the poem reads: "May your Statue established by Council, be honoured by Congress, with these honourable words— Lo! Washington! The Father of his Country, the Protector of Liberty!"

23. Henry Knox, letter to George Washington, 19 March 1787, *Founders Online*, National Archives, http://founders.archives.gov/documents/Washington/04-05-02-0095, retrieved October 26, 2016.

24. Gouverneur Morris to George Washington, December 6, 1788, *Founders Online*, National Archives, last modified June 13, 2018, http://founders.archives.gov/documents/Washington/05-01-02-0123.

25. *Pennsylvania Packet*, April 21, 1789, qtd. in Chernow, *Washington*, 561.

26. All qtd. in Grizzard, "Father of His Country," 106.

27. For the full text of "Inscribed" go to "Poems on American Presidents, 1789-1865," Universität Freiburg, Germany, n.d. https://presidents.ub.uni-freiburg.de/index.php, last accessed July 14, 2017. For a close reading of this and similar poems of the era, see Butter, *Der "Washington-Code*," 28–37.

28. Cavitch, "Remembering George Washington," 253. On the formal characteristics of this kind of poetry, see Gordon Bigelow, *Rhetoric and American Poetry of the Early National Period* (Gainesville: U of Florida P, 1960). On the poetry of the time as an art form so thoroughly in the service of "morality and politics" that, except for being in meter and rhyme, it was practically indistinguishable from other forms of discourse, see Michael T. Gilmore, "The Literature of the Revolutionary and Early National Periods," *The Cambridge History of American Literature*, Vol. I, *1590–1820* (New York: Cambridge UP, 1994), 591–93, quotation 593.

29. Munford, "An Oration on the Subject of American Independence...," qtd. in Bryan, *Washington in American Literature*, 54.

30. Bell's letter is repr. in William S. Baker, ed., *Early Sketches of George Washington* (Philadelphia: Lippincott, 1894), 65–80, quotation 77. The letter accompanied Bell's "Sketch of Mr. Washington's Life and Character," which had been published in Annapolis in 1779 and was to be reprinted in *The Westminster Magazine* the following year. Bell's sketch is considered the first Washington biography to have been published in America, though an account titled "Particulars from the Life and Character of General Washington" was published in London in 1778. Mitnick, "Parallel Visions," 58 and 68n4.

31. James Hardie, *The New Universal Biographical Dictionary*, Vol.4 (New York: Thomas Kirk, 1805), 408–33, quot. 426. For "the father of his country and the friend of mankind" as well as for the Philadelphia magazine, see *American Remembrancer*, 37. For the Supreme Executive Council of Pennsylvania, see Mitnick, "Parallel Visions," 57–58.

32. Weems once told Matthew Carey, his Philadelphia publisher: "You have a great deal of money in the bones of old George if you will but exert yourself to extract it." Qtd. in Cunningham, *Popular Images of the Presidency*, 16. Hence Edward G. Lengel quipped, not quite correctly when we consider the notes from the Washington Bank of Westerly, Rhode Island, which were the first notes to carry Washington's portrait, Weems "saw the dollar bill in Washington long before Washington appeared on the dollar bill." *Inventing George Washington* 33.

33. "The dearest and best of all appellations," Weems, *The Life of Washington*, 190. For Washington's "stirred all the father within him," "with a father's joy," "a shepherd father," "private virtues" and "humble imitation," see respectively 122, 123, 166, 297.

34. Erskine's recommendation to the American public was issued in response to news received in January 1800, of Washington's death. *Maxims of Washington*, ed. Frederick Schroeder (New York: Appleton & Co., 1909), vii.

35. De Chastellux, "this great American," and French journalist, qtd. in Weems, *Life of Washington*, 190.

36. Jean-Jacques Rousseau, *The First and Second Discourses* (New York: St. Martin's P, 1964), 146–47. The *First Discourse* was originally published in 1750 as *Discours sur les sciences et les arts*. Its main argument is that the arts and sciences corrupt human morality. In contrast, the "habit" of fathers and children husbands living together "in a common habitation" gave rise to the "sweet sentiment [of] paternal love."

37. Fliegelman, *Prodigals and Pilgrims*, 197–226.

38. Tocqueville, *Democracy in America*, 480. For criticism of Fliegelman, see Schwartz, *American Symbol*, 227n25.

39. For an excellent overview of the transformations of family life, see Steven Mintz and Susan Kellogg, *Domestic Revolutions: A Social History of American Family Life* (New York: Free P, 1988).

40. Max Weber, *The Theory of Social and Economic Organizations* (New York: Oxford UP, 1947), 358. See a. Chernow, *Washington*, 814 and, on the parallels between the adulatory biographies of Washington and contemporary biographies of Jesus Christ, Buddha, Socrates, or Columbus, Albanese, *Sons of the Fathers*, 174. For a history and evaluation of Weems's narrative, see Bryan, *Washington in American Literature*, 92–96.

41. Tuckerman, *The Character and Portraits of Washington*, 33–34.

42. Mitnick, "Parallel Vision," 59 and Fig. 20. *Sacred to Patriotism* is on view at the Fraunces Tavern Museum, New York.

43. Massachusetts paper, in Kaminski and McCaughan, eds., *A Great and Good Man*, 97; John Adams to Thomas Jefferson, September 3, 1816, *Founders Online*, National Archives, last modified June 13, 2018, http://founders.archives.gov/documents/Adams/99-02-02-6627.

44. Gouverneur Morris, qtd. in François Furstenberg, *In the Name of the Father: Washington's Legacy, Slavery, and the Making of a Nation* (New York: Penguin, 2007), 75.

45. George Rippey Stewart, *Names on the Land* (Boston: Houghton Mifflin, 1967) and, for Washington, Kentucky, Q. David Bowers, *Whitman Encyclopedia of Obsolete Paper Money*, vol. 7 (Atlanta, GA: Whitman Publishing, 2016), 221. By 1932, the bicentennial year of Washington's birth, the American map contained a Federal capital, a state, 33 counties, 121 cities and towns, 257 townships, 1140 streets, roads, and avenues, one mountain, three colleges and universities, and uncounted schools and lakes—all named for Washington.

46. Wick, *American Icon*, 150–51, ill. 81; for further description and discussion, see Kahler, *The Long Farewell*.

47. Weems, *Life of Washington*, 168–70.

48. Thistlethwaite, *The Image of George Washington*, 188 and 306, figs.154 and 155. A rare example is a mourning picture done in needlework and watercolor on silk. Cummingham, *Popular Images of the Presidency*, 10–11.

49. Reproductions of David Edwin's engraving, after Rembrandt Peale, are in Thistlethwaite, *The Image of George Washington*, 190 and 265 (fig.88); today, *Apotheosis of Washington* is in the possession of the National Portrait Gallery, Smithsonian Institution. At mid-century, three more apotheoses of the nation's founder appeared, James Burns's *Washington Crowned* (1849), Rembrandt Lockwood's *The Last Judgment* (1854), and Constantino Brumidi's majestic fresco in the Rotunda of the Capitol, *The Apotheosis of George Washington* (1865). See Thistlethwaite, *The Image of George Washington*, 190–92 and 310–12 (figs. 161–164) and, for Brumidi, below, chap.9.

50. Weishaupt's lithograph is dated ca. 1830. For an illustration see Schwartz, *American Symbol*, Fig. 24, from the Huntington Library, San Marino, California.

51. Illustration in Schwartz, *American Symbol*, Fig. 23.

52. Mitnick, "Parallel Visions," 61–62; on the importance of public virtue, see Andrew S. Trees, *The Founding Fathers and the Politics of Character* (Princeton: Princeton UP, 2004), 107–33. For the Chinese glass paintings, see Maggie Cao, "Washington in China: A Media History of Reverse Painting on Glass," *Common-Place: The Journal of Early American Life* 15:4 (Summer 2015), http://common-place.org/book/washington-in-china-a-media-history-of-re verse-painting-on-glass/, retrieved April 13, 2017; for Trumbull's resignation painting, see below, chap.5.

53. Pavil Svinin, *Picturesque United States of America*, and, for "No cottage should be without his likeness...," *American Magazine of Useful and Entertaining Knowledge*, both qtd. in Thistlethwaite, "The Face of the Nation," 38. On the commemorative medal, see Bowers, *Garrett Collection*, 169; on the manifold forms of Washington worship, see Ayres, "At Home with George," Meschutt, "Life Portraits of George Washington," and Robinson, "The Marketing of an Icon," all in Mitnick, ed., *George Washington: American Symbol*; and Schwartz, *George Washington*.

54. Thistlethwaite, "The Face of the Nation," 35–38.

55. Lawrence J. Friedman, "The Flawless American," in *Inventors of the Promised Land* (New York: Knopf, 1975), 44–78.

56. "The Genius of America," qtd. in Schwartz, *American Symbol*, xiii.

57. Edmund S. Morgan, *Inventing the People*, 14.

58. Volker Depkat, "Die Erfindung der republikanischen Präsidentschaft im Zeichen des Geschichtsbruchs," *Zeitschrift für Geschichtswissenschaft* 56:9 (September 2008), 728–42, and "The Grammar of Postrevolutionary Visual Politics," in *Pictorial Cultures and Political Iconographies*, ed. Udo J. Hebel and Christoph Wagner (Berlin-New York: de Gruyter, 2011), 176–97, esp. 179–81, 183–87. On the concept of "hegemony," see the eponymous entry in *The New Fontana Dictionary of Modern Thought*, ed. Alan Bullock and Stephen Trombley, Third Edition (London: HarperCollins, 1999), 387–88387–88, and Perry Anderson, *The H-Word: The Peripateia of Hegemony* (London: Verso P, 2017).

59. Albanese, *Sons of the Fathers*, chap. 5, "Our Father, Our Washington," 143–81, quotation 143. James Madison to William Cogswell, March 10, 1834, *Founders Online*, National Archives, last modified June 13, 2018, http://founders.archives.gov/documents/Madison/99-02-02-2952.

60. Kevin Cope, preface to *George Washington in and as Culture*, ed. the same et al., AMS Studies in the Eighteenth Century 38 (New York: AMS P, 2001), xix.

61. Schwartz, *American Symbol*, 20. On the creation of a sense of unity as Washington's greatest contribution to American life see also Don Higginbotham, *George Washington: Uniting a Nation* (Lanham, MD: Rowman & Littlefield, 2002).

62. Klaus Lubbers, "The Construction of Collective Identity in Early Republican Folk Art," *The Construction and Contestation of American Cultures and Identities in the Early National Period*, ed. Udo J. Hebel (Heidelberg: Winter, 1999), 273–301, here 278 and 280, Fig.8. Robert Hay even claimed that overall in Washington eulogies, religious themes far outnumbered classical ones. "George Washington: American Moses," *American Quarterly* 21:4 (1926), 781–87, especially 782n14.

63. Qtd. in Silverman, *Cultural History of the American Revolution*, 601.

64. Paine, *Common Sense*, 84. *American Crisis*, qtd. in Ferguson, *The American Enlightenment*, 154.

65. Schwartz, *American Symbol*, 45, 85.

66. Washington quotations from Brookhiser, *Founding Father*, 146 and, on Washington's religious beliefs, 145–49.

67. Aspasio (pseud.), "Anniversary Ode," in *Key Concepts in American Cultural History: From the Colonial Period to the End of the 19th Century*, 2nd edn., ed. Bernd Engler and Oliver Scheiding (Trier, Germany: Wissenschaftlicher Verlag Trier, 2007), 315.

68. Literally, "annuit coeptis" translates as "He/she/it nods/has nodded to the undertaken," from L. *annuo, annuere, annui, annutum*, to nod. *Annuit* is either the 3sg. pres. ind. act. or 3sg. perf. ind. act. *Coeptis* comes from *coepio, coepere, coepi, coeptum*, to begin, and is a departicipial noun; hence it can also mean beginning or undertaking. "Annuit coeptis" therefore may well be translated as "He approved of our undertakings." I am grateful to my colleague Johann Köberl (†) for providing this information. On the Roman origin of *annuit coeptis* and, as well, of *E pluribus unum*, see also Gordon S. Wood, "Rambunctious American Democracy," *The New York Review of Books* XLIX (May 9, 2002), 20–23, here 21. The two phrases are only marginally related to the Judeo-Christian tradition, as Michael and Jana Novak want us to believe.

69. Carl L. Becker, *The Heavenly City of the Eighteenth-Century Philosophers* (New Haven: Yale UP, 1932), 31.

70. All qtd. in Schwartz, *American Symbol*, 173.

71. Willard, *History of the United States*, 293.

72. *Boston Magazine*, April 1784, qtd. in Silverman, *Cultural History of the American Revolution*, 517. Supreme Executive Council of Pennsylvania qtd. in Wick, *American Icon*, xiii. For "good for thinking" and "good for feeling," see Albanese, *Sons of the Fathers*, 144. On the adoption of George Washington at once as "an object of emotional attachment and an exemplification of moral values," see Schwartz, *American Symbol*, 6.

73. Williams, *Marxism and Literature*, 132.

74. "[T]he highest existent patriotism," Tuckerman, *Character and Portraits*, 20–21; "as a hero," Meschutt, "Life Portraits," 35.

75. West, qtd. in Silverman, *Cultural History of the American Revolution*, 428.

76. Barratt and Miles, *Gilbert Stuart*, 166–83; Dorinda Evans, *The Genius of Gilbert Stuart* (Princeton: Princeton UP, 1999), 60–73; for Lord Lansdowne's response, see Howard, *The Painter's Chair*, 200–203. I have also drawn in this paragraph on Decker, "Paintings and Sculptures," 23. The more than 1,000 paintings by Stuart include images of

the country's first six presidents—Washington, John Adams, Thomas Jefferson, James Madison, James Monroe, and John Qincy Adams. For the Smithsonian's exhibition, go to https://americaspresidents.si.edu.

77. On artistic strategies of showing individuals as incarnations of ideas or values, see Peter Burke, *Eyewitnessing: The Uses of Images as Historical Evidence* (Ithaca: Cornell UP, 2001), 65–77. The belief that portraits have the power to bring the dead back to life, to make the absent present, and to preserve the portrayed's features for posterity, goes back to Leon Battista Alberti's 1435 treatise *Della pittura* (*On Painting*, trans. and ed. John R. Spencer, New Haven: Yale University Press, 1956, 63).

78. Roy C. Strong, *Portraits of Queen Elizabeth* (Oxford: Clarendon P, 1963), 36. On the affinities of the "Lansdowne" with European state portraiture, see a. Cunningham, *Popular Images of the Presidency*, 130–39.

79. Depkat, "The Grammar of Postrevolutionary Visual Politics," 183–85.

80. Schwartz, *American Symbol*, 34–35 and Figs. 5–8. For Le Mire's engraving, see a. Mount Vernon Collections, http://www.mountvernon.org/preservation/collections-holdings/browse-the-museum-collections/object/sc-5/, last accessed August 3, 2017. For Norman's work, see the New York Public Library's C. W. McAlpin Collection, Section IV, "Fictitious Portraits of Washington," http://web-static.nypl.org/exhibitions/revolution/selection4.html, last accessed August 3, 2017. Both works are treated and reproduced in Wick, *American Icon*, respectively 29–31, and 17, 90–91. For a study of "monarchical" tendencies in the early republic, see Louise Dunbar's eponymous essay.

Part II

1. Gordon S. Wood, *The Radicalism of the American Revolution* (New York: Knopf, 1992), 149–50. For "revered parent" and "dutiful child," see Mercy Otis Warren, *History of the Rise, Progress, and Termination of the American Revolution*, 3 vols. (Boston: Larkin, 1805. Repr. in 2 vols., Foreword by Lester H. Cohen (Indianapolis: Liberty Fund, 1994), http://oll.libertyfund.org/titles/815, 1:302.

2. "The Preceptor," *The Massachusetts Spy*, May 21, 1772, in Hyneman and Lutz, *American Political Writing*, 1:180; for "common tie of nature," see Simeon Howard, "A Sermon Preached to the Ancient and Honorable Artillery Company in Boston [1773]," *ibid.*, 1:202. On the persistence of patriarchy and, especially, of patriarchal language, see Kann, *The Gendering of American Politics*, 4–7.

3. Cooper, "A Sermon on the Day of the Commencement of the Constitution," in Sandoz, *Political Sermons*, 1:643, 653; Hitchcock, "An Election Sermon," in Hyneman and Lutz, *American Political Writing*, 1:299; and Payson, "A Sermon," *ibid.*, 1:537.

4. James Wilson, qtd. in Bailyn, ed., *The Debate on the Constitution*, 1:825; Langdon, "The Republic of the Israelites as Example to the American States [1788]" in Sandoz, *Political Sermons*, 1:959, 965.

5. "The Trenton Ladies' Sonata," in Kaminski and McCaughan, eds., *A Great and Good Man*, 121 (for Nathaniel Currier's lithograph of the reception, see Cunningham, *Popular Images of the Presidency*, 208); Murray, "Sketches of the Present Situation of America," *Selected Writings*, 66, qtd. in Mark E. Kann, "Manhood, Immortality, and Politics During the American Founding," *Journal of Men's Studies* 5:2 (November 1996), 79–103, here 89; Moore, "An Oration on the Anniversary of the Independence of the United States of America," and Addison, "Analysis of the Report of the Committee of the Virginia Assembly," both qtd. in Hyneman and Lutz, *American Political Writing*, respectively 2:1214 and 2:1063.

6. Stone, "An Election Sermon [1792]," in Hyneman and Lutz, *American Political Writing*, 2:846, 854; Evans, "A Sermon Delivered at the Annual Election," in Sandoz, *Political Sermons*, 2:1070; and McClintock, "A Sermon on Occasion of the Commencement of the New Hampshire Constitution [1784]," *ibid.*, 1:802, 806–807.

7. See, on these mutual influences, Lorri Glover, *Founders as Fathers: The Private Lives and Politics of the American Revolutionaries* (New Haven: Yale UP, 2014), and Kann, "Manhood, Immortality, and Politics," 89–90. On America's "national subjectivity" as the dominion of white males, see Dana D. Nelson, *National Manhood: Capitalist Citizenship and the Imagined Fraternity of White Men* (Durham: Duke UP, 1998), and Valerie Melissa Babb, *Whiteness Visible: The Meaning of Whiteness in American Literature and Culture* (New York: New York UP, 1998).

8. Blankenhorn, *Fatherless America*, 12–13; see also Rotundo, "American Fatherhood: A Historical Perspective," *American Behavioral Scientist* 29:9 (September/October 1985), 7–25, for further description and discussion of fatherhood in eighteenth- and nineteenth-century America.

Chapter 3

1. Jefferson, qtd. in Chernow, *Washington*, 600. Jefferson had started out by venerating Washington, had even identified him as a genius; but fifteen years after Washington's death, despite Jefferson's opposition to his presidential politics, Jefferson wrote again to a friend that Washington was a "in every sense of the words, a wise, a good, and a great man," one "whose memory will be adored while liberty shall have votaries, whose name shall triumph over time." Letter to Dr. Walter Jones, January 2, 1814, *Founders Online*, National Archives, last modified June 13, 2018, http://founders.archives.gov/documents/Jefferson/03-07-02-0052.

2. See the collection ed. by Robert M. S. McDonald, *Sons of the Father: George Washington and His Protégés*.

3. François Barbé-Marbois, secretary to the French minister, qtd. in Chernow, *Washington*, 364.

4. Marquis de Lafayette, February 5, 1783, *Founders*

Online, National Archives, http://founders.archives.gov/documents/Washington/99-01-02-10575, retrieved October 26, 2016, emphasis added. For a discussion of Washington's military "family," see Arthur S. Lefkowitz, *George Washington's Indispensable Men: The 32 Aides-de-Camp Who Helped Win American Independence* (Mechanicsburg, PA: Stackpole Books), 2003. The Washington-Lafayette relationship is also a key theme in a big-budget French film about the Revolutionary War. In the film, titled *La Fayette* and released in 1962, Washington (played by Howard St. John) affectionately calls Lafayette "that damn brat." Bolam and Bolam, *The Presidents on Film*, 34–35.

5. Washington, qtd. in Freeman, *George Washington*, 5:435.

6. Chernow, *Washington*, 326, emphasis added.

7. *Ibid.*, 196. For a nuanced discussion of Washington's socialization in the British military system, see Higginbotham, "Washington and the Colonial Military Tradition," in *George Washington Reconsidered*, ed. the same (Charlottesville: UP of Virginia, 2001), 38–66.

8. Chernow, *Washington*, 196; for "a just pretension...," see Washington's letter to Governor Patrick Henry, October 5, 1776, *Founders Online*, National Archives, http://founders.archives.gov/documents/Washington/03-06-02-0367, retrieved October 26, 2016. As a colonial officer in the Virginia Regiment, Washington also brought into play his status as a slave owner, who found "mulattos and negroes" utterly unacceptable as recruits, consequently barring them from carrying arms. Freshly appointed to commander in chief, he characterized New Englanders, in rather unflattering terms, as "an exceeding dirty & nasty people." Even officers for the most part shared the "unaccountable kind of stupidity" shown by the ordinary soldiers. George Washington to Richard Henry Lee, August 29, 1775, *Founders Online*, National Archives, http://founders.archives.gov/documents/Washington/03-01-02-0270, and George Washington to Lund Washington, August 20, 1775, *Founders Online*, National Archives, http://founders.archives.gov/documents/Washington/03-01-02-0234, retrieved October 26, 2016.

9. Burns and Dunn, *George Washington*, 18.

10. Thomas Jefferson, letter to Dr. Walter Jones, January 2, 1814, *Founders Online*, National Archives, last modified June 13, 2018, http://founders.archives.gov/documents/Jefferson/03-07-02-0052.

11. Sewall, "War and Washington," *Poems on American Presidents, 1789–1865.*" Freneau, "American Liberty," *The Poems of Philip Freneau*, ed. Fred Lewis Pattee (Princeton: Princeton University Library, 1902), 1:142–57, quot. 149.

12. Joel Barlow, *The Vision of Columbus; a Poem in Nine Books* (Hartford, CT: Hudson and Goodwin, 1787), 160; Humphreys, "A Letter to a Young Lady in Boston," *The Miscellaneous Works of David Humphreys* (New York: T. and J. Swords, 1804), 196–201, quot. 201; Snowden, *The Columbiad*, qtd. in Bryan, *Washington in American Literature*, 140. For additional examples, see *ibid.*, 120–140.

13. Irving, *Life of Washington*, chap. XXVI, 1:309–24, quotation 311.

14. Irving, *Life of Washington*, 4:517.

15. Hicks directly linked the two subjects in 1836, when he painted versions of *Washington at the Delaware* and *The Declaration of Independence* on opposite sides of a wooden tavern sign. Chrysler Museum of Art, Learning Resource, "Colonial and Revolutionary America, 1610–1776," October 2010, http://www.chrysler.org/files/resources/colonial-america-teacher-resource_07-2010.pdf, accessed November 29, 2017.

16. Chernow, *Washington*, 278. "Nothing is more agreeable ... than good music," "General Orders, June 4, 1777," *Founders Online*, National Archives, last modified April 12, 2018, http://founders.archives.gov/documents/Washington/03-09-02-0600.

17. Henry Knox to George Washington, November 26, 1777, *Founders Online*, National Archives, http://founders.archives.gov/documents/Washington/03-12-02-0407, retrieved January 26, 2017.

18. Chernow, *Washington*, 439.

19. *Ibid.*, 452. For renderings of Washington's leave-taking at Fraunces Tavern, see Thistlethwaite, *The Image of George Washington*, 102–104.

20. Washington, "Circular to State Governments," *WWR*, 516–17.

21. *Ibid.*, 517.

22. Brookhiser, *Founding Father*, 189.

23. Washington, "Circular to State Governments," *WWR*, 518.

24. *Ibid.*

25. Washington, "First Inaugural Address (30 April 1789)," *WWR*, 733.

26. Washington, "Circular to State Governments," *WWR*, 516.

27. Washington, *Rules of Civility*, *WWR*, 6.

28. Washington, "Circular to State Governments," *WWR*, 526.

29. Letter from Nathanael Greene, August 29, 1784, *Founders Online*, National Archives, http://founders.archives.gov/documents/Washington/04-02-02-0056, retrieved October 26, 2016.

30. Letter to James McHenry, delegate to Congress from Maryland, August 22, 1785, *WWR*, 588. For a general account of the anxieties over disunion in the years following Independence see Benjamin E. Park, *American Nationalisms: Imagining Union in the Age of Revolutions, 1783–1833* (Cambridge: Cambridge UP, 2018), 39–47.

31. Letter to James McHenry, August 22, 1785, *WWR*, 588.

32. What also helped was patient prodding especially by James Madison, and Henry Knox's double-barreled appeal to Washington's vanity and patriotism: Should the convention establish a strong new federal government, Knox wrote in 1787, "it would be a circumstance highly honourable to your fame ... and doubly entitle you to the glorious republican epithet—The Father of Your Country." Henry Knox, letter to George Washington, 19 March 1787, *Founders Online*, National Archives, http://founders.archives.gov/documents/Washing

ton/04-05-02-0095, retrieved October 26, 2016. For further discussion and analysis, see Larson, *The Return of George Washington*.

33. *Pennsylvania Gazette*, August 22, 1787, in Kaminski and McCaughan, eds., *A Great and Good Man*, 87.

34. Chernow, *Washington*, 596. On Washington's leadership qualities, see Rees, with Spignesi, *Washington's Leadership Lessons*.

35. Wills, *Cincinnatus*, 170. For Washington's "relational" style of leadership, see Larson, *The Return of George Washington*, 112, and Fred I. Greenstein, *Inventing the Job of President: Leadership Style from George Washington to Andrew Jackson* (Princeton: Princeton UP, 2009), 16–17.

36. Breen, *George Washington's Journey*, 1–3 and chap.3, "The Script: Washington's Defense of the Union," 83–109. For a generous collection of records from the tour, see Kaminski and McCaughan, eds., *A Great and Good Man*, 152–96.

37. Breen, *George Washington's Journey*, 146.

38. *Ibid.*, 192 and Fig. 11, between 114 and 115. "TO COLUMBIA'S FAVORITE SON" was also written as an ode and performed by a choir of singers. Kaminski and McCaughan, eds., *A Great and Good Man*, 154–56.

39. Breen, *George Washington's Journey*, 168, as sung at Newburyport, Massachusetts. In a similar poem from Boston, the recitative has "He comes" followed by the command "bow the knee!" (*ibid.*, 159). The phrase is from a passage in Genesis in which Joseph receives distinction from the Egyptian pharaoh (41:43); "bow the knee!" is the KJV's rendering of the original Hebrew word *"abrech."* In Martin Luther's translation, *"abrech"* appears as "father of the country" (*"Der ist des Landes Vater"*).

40. Breen, *George Washington's Journey*, respectively 120, 191, and 123. For "godlike WASHINGTON," see Kaminski and McCaughan, eds., *A Great and Good Man*, 160.

41. Olney, *History of the United States*, 184; on the poems, see Bryan, *Washington in American Literature*, 149–50; for the Charleston concert, see Brookhiser, *Founding Father*, 80.

42. See Cicero, *Phillipicae*, XIII: 19, 40f.; other possible sources are Ovid (*Fasti*, 2: 127–44) and Horace (*Carmen Saeculare*, III: 5, 2ff.). Andreas Alföldi has traced the genealogy of *"patriae pater"* in Roman antiquity in *Der Vater des Vaterlandes im römischen Denken* (Darmstadt, Germany: Wissenschaftliche Buchgesellschaft, 1971), especially 80–101. *Pater patriae*, Alföldi has shown, originated in the time of Romulus; the honorary title was in common usage during the republican era, reaching a new peak under Caesar (following the end of the civil war) and Augustus, when it became both an honorary title and a political concept. Among Augustus's followers, numerous coins were struck bearing the inscription *Patri patriae* (*ibid.*, 95).

43. To George Washington from James Hardie, January 23, 1792, *Founders Online*, National Archives, last modified June 29, 2017, http://founders.archives.gov/documents/Washington/05-09-02-0292, retrieved September 11, 2017.

44. Samuel Davies, "On the Death of His Late Majesty King George II," *Spreading the Gospel in Colonial Virginia*, ed. Edward L. Bond (Lanham, MD et al.: Lexington Books, 2004), 398–413, here 398.

45. On the importance of Addison's *Cato* for the American colonists and, in particular for Washington, see below, chap. 5. On the trajectory of Roman-style republicanism, from its rediscovery by humanists in Renaissance Italy to seventeenth- and eighteenth-century Britain and, via Algernon Sidney's *Discourses Concerning Government*, to revolutionary America, see John G. A. Pocock, *The Machiavellian Moment: Florentine Political Thought and the Atlantic Republican Tradition* (Princeton: Princeton UP), 1975.

46. See Isaac Kramnick, *Bolingbroke and His Circle: The Politics of Nostalgia in the Age of Walpole* (Cambridge: Harvard UP, 1968), and Jeff Smith, *The Presidents We Imagine*, 16–18.

47. Liddle, "'A Patriot King, or None,'" 953–57, and Bernard Bailyn, *The Ideological Origins of the American Revolution* (Cambridge: Harvard UP, 1967). On Parke's library, see Kevin J. Hayes, *George Washington: A Life in Books* (New York: Oxford UP, 2017), 96, 110–32.

48. Henry St John, 1st Viscount Bolingbroke, *The Idea of a Patriot King*, 1738, ed. Sydney Wayne Jackman (Indianapolis: Bobbs-Merrill, 1965), 41, 45, 47, 52; quotation from *The Craftsman*, 6:251–52. On the fantasy of politics without factions and parties, see Ketcham, *Presidents Above Party*, and Rosemarie Zagarri, "George Washington and the Emergence of Party Politics in the New Nation," *A Companion to George Washington*, ed. Edward G. Lengel (Malden, MA: Wiley-Blackwell, 2012), 490–505.

49. Bolingbroke, *The Idea of a Patriot King*, 46. A good example of Bolingbroke's reception is Thomas Jefferson's insisting, in *A Summary View*, that "kings are the servants, not the proprietors of the people." Jefferson, *Writings*, ed. Merrill D. Peterson (New York: Library of America, 1984), 121.

50. Liddle, "'A Patriot King, or None,'" 960. On the mythologies surrounding George III's reign, see Cunliffe, "The Two Georges," 67, and, for a careful analysis of the king's conduct, Bernard Donoughue, *British Politics and the American Revolution, 1773–1775* (London: Macmillan, 1964).

51. Qtd. in Silverman, *Cultural History of the American Revolution*, 323. Two more odes to the same tune were performed and published during Washington's "Eastern tour" in the summer of 1789. Kaminski and McCaughan, eds., *A Great and Good Man*, 134–36.

52. John Dickinson, *Letters from a Farmer in Pennsylvania to the Inhabitants of the British Colonies* (Philadelphia: Hall and Sellers, 1768), 38; for "dutiful children," see *ibid.*, 17. See, for further discussion, Pierre Marambaud, "Dickinson's 'Letters from a Farmer in Pennsylvania' as Political Discourse: Ideology, Imagery, and Rhetoric," *Early American Literature* 12:1 (Spring 1977), 63–72.

53. On the presidency, with George Washington, as the institutionalization of the neoclassicist ideal of

the patriot king, see Ketcham, *Presidents Above Party*, 29. The idea of a republicanized version of Bolingbroke's patriot king was often misunderstood. When John Adams during his vice-presidency advocated a strong executive presence in the new American government, he imprudently called this the "monarchical principle." This was understood as Adams's desire to declare himself king for life, though it was clearly an echo of the "patriot king." Joseph J. Ellis, *Founding Brothers: The Revolutionary Generation* (New York: Knopf, 2000), 168–69.

54. The Federal Farmer (pseud.), qtd. in Jeff Smith, *The Presidents We Imagine*, 22, and *ibid.* for Franklin and the antifederalists.

55. Kaminski and McCaughan, eds., *A Great and Good Man*, 113.

56. Thomas Jefferson to Edward Carrington, May 27, 1788, *Founders Online*, National Archives, last modified June 13, 2018, http://founders.archives.gov/documents/Jefferson/01-13-02-0120, retrieved July 7, 2018.

57. Hamilton, "The Executive Department," *The Federalist Papers*, No.67, March 11, 1788, The Avalon Project at Yale Law School, 2008, http://avalon.law.yale.edu/18th_century/fed67.asp, for "extravagant tales ... tremble ... blush," and "The Mode of Electing the President," *The Federalist Papers*, No.68, March 14, 1788, http://avalon.law.yale.edu/18th_century/fed68.asp, for "constant probability...," both retrieved Dec. 7, 2017.

58. It is not entirely clear what *"abrech"* means. As a command, the word may be translated respectively as "bow the knee" (as in the King James Version), "on your knees" (as in the 2017 revised version of Luther's Bible), or "prostrate yourself." As an honorary title, it may be translated as "chief steward" or, as in Luther's original version, "father of the country." In the Geneva Bible of 1599, the Bible of the Pilgrims and the Reformation, the word was left standing: "and they cried before [Joseph], Abrech, and placed him over all the land of Egypt." On the different views of *"abrech"* (or Abrek; Heb. אברך, *avrekh*), see "Abrech," *Encyclopedia Judaica*, 2007, http://www.encyclopedia.com/religion/encyclopedias-almanacs-transcripts-and-maps/abrech, retrieved July 6, 2017.

59. "Was Abrech heisse / lassen wir die Zencker suchen bis an den Jüngstentage / wollens die weil verstehen / wie es gedeudscht ist." ("What abrech means / the wranglers may be searching for till doomsday comes / meanwhile we'll understand it the way the German language renders it," my translation.) Deutsches Textarchiv (DTA) by the Berlin-Brandenburgische Akademie der Wissenschaften, http://www.deutschestextarchiv.de, retrieved May 31, 2016.

60. Luther, *"ynn den vater stand,"* commentary on the Fourth Commandment, "Honour thy father and thy mother," qtd. in Nitschke, *Der öffentliche Vater*, 103. On the German tradition of addressing sovereigns as "fathers," see Paul Münch, "Der Landesvater. Historische Anmerkungen zu einem Topos der deutschen politischen Kultur," *Journal Geschichte* 5 (1986), 37–43, and "Die 'Obrigkeit im Vaterstand.' Zu Definition und Kritik des 'Landesvaters' während der frühen Neuzeit," *Daphnis: Zeitschrift für mittlere deutsche Literatur* 11 (1982), 15–40.

61. References in this paragraph are to texts collected in Deutsches Textarchiv (DTA) by the Berlin-Brandenburgische Akademie der Wissenschaften, http://www.deutschestextarchiv.de, retrieved May 31, 2016.

62. Bryan, *Washington in American Literature*, 87n2.

63. Schiller, *William Tell*, trans. William Peter (2nd edn. Luzern, Switzerland: Printed for A. Gebhardt, 1857), Act 4, Scene 2, 127. The German original reads as follows: *"Des Landes Vätern zähl' ich mich jetzt bei, / Und meine erste Pflicht ist, euch zu schützen."* *Wilhelm Tell*, with Explanatory Notes by J. C. Oehlschläger (Philadelphia: John Weik, 1851), 129.

64. Butter, *Der "Washington-Code,"* 36. On "political fathers" in Schiller, see Nitschke, *Der öffentliche Vater*, 112–17 and, specifically on *Wilhelm Tell*, 185–89.

65. On Schiller's defense of republican virtues, see Nitschke, *Der öffentliche Vater*, 150. For a more recent reimportation of republicanism, see Frey, "Washington in American Fiction," 25. On *Wilhelm Tell's* popularity in the American South, see Jennifer Ratner-Rosenhagen, *The Ideas That Made America A Brief History* (New York: Oxford UP, 2019), 53.

66. John Adams, qtd. in Fliegelman, *Prodigals and Pilgrims*, 223.

67. As Marcus Cunliffe demonstrated in "The Two Georges," the difference was played out not only in America, but also in Britain. Lord Byron for instance contemptuously dismissed George III's burial service as merely representing "the rottenness of eighty years in gold" (57).

68. *Ibid.*, 58.

69. "The Trenton Ladies' Sonata," in Kaminski and McCaughan, eds., *A Great and Good Man*, 117–18.

70. Irving was not the only one for whom the name of Washington was adopted. One of Walt Whitman's brothers was called *George Washington* Whitman; and for the former slave Booker Taliaferro to adopt *Washington* as his last name was a symbolic way of taking on American citizenship. Cunliffe, *George Washington*, 23. Henry Lee, qtd. in Bryan, *Washington in American Literature* 64. Lee's speech was delivered in Philadelphia and was printed several times in 1800.

71. Washington, "Rules of Civility," *WWR* 3–10. For "underlying hunger for posthumous glory," see Chernow, *Washington*, 471. On the significance of the *Rules of Civility*, see Brookhiser, *Founding Father*, 127–29; on Washington's "self-education," see Adrienne M. Harrison, *A Powerful Mind: The Self-Education of George Washington* (Lincoln: U of Nebraska Press / Potomac Books, 2015).

Chapter 4

1. George Washington to Robert Cary & Company, July 18, 1771, *Founders Online*, National Archives,

http://founders.archives.gov/documents/Washington/02-08-02-0339-0002, retrieved January 8, 2019. For a photograph of the seal, see *Colonial Williamsburg Journal*, Winter 2013, 13.

2. For Washington, only virtuous and reasonable citizens who would accept and fulfill their responsibilities to their nation and to others, who understood that the interests of their fellow citizens were inseparable from their own, and who, working together, were able to balance their own interests with the common good, could be sure of a reward—happiness. As he said in his first inaugural address, there was "an indissoluble union between virtue and happiness, between duty and advantage, between the genuine maxims of an honest and magnanimous policy, and the solid rewards of public prosperity and felicity [and of] happiness." *WWR*, 733–34. For Washington's "burning ambition," see John E. Ferling, *The Ascent of George Washington: The Hidden Political Genius of an American Icon* (London-New York: Bloomsbury P, 2009), 9.

3. Washington to the Marquis de Lafayette, May 28, 1788, *WWR*, 680, 681.

4. Washington to the Marquis de Lafayette, May 28, 1788, *WWR*, 680. Washington also was among the subscribers (together with Lafayette, Franklin, Paine, and the French king Louis XVI, who ordered 25 copies) to Barlow's epic. Silverman, *Cultural History of the American Revolution*, 489, 519, and 603. For Barlow's Independence Day oration, see Bryan, *Washington in American Literature*, 53; for his *Vision of Columbus*, see *ibid.*, 138–39.

5. Wick, *American Icon*, 125–27. The music for "Hail Columbia" was composed by Philip Phile and was first played ceremonially in April 1789 in Trenton, New Jersey, to honor president-elect George Washington. Hopkinson's words were added nine years later, and the song was then published as "The Favorite New Federal Song Adapted to the Presidents March." The first issue of the song bore the image of President John Adams; when in July 1798 Washington was appointed Commander in Chief of the American forces in anticipation of war with France, his portrait was substituted for Adams's. Washington's letter to Hopkinson is dated May 27, 1798. *Founders Online*, National Archives, last modified April 12, 2018, https://founders.archives.gov/documents/Washington/06-02-02-0227.

6. Chernow, *Washington*, 472.

7. Washington to Chastellux, April 25–May 1, 1788, *Founders Online*, National Archives, http://founders.archives.gov/documents/Washington/04-06-02-0202, retrieved February 20, 2017.

8. Humphreys' "Life" has been edited by Rosemarie Zagarri.

9. Washington to John Augustine Washington, May 31, 1754, *WWR*, 48. For "revealing," see Brumwell, *Gentleman Warrior*, 430.

10. Washington, "I am a warrior," in "Address to the Delaware Nation," May 12, 1779, *Founders Online*, National Archives, http://founders.archives.gov/documents/Washington/03-20-02-0388, retrieved November 26, 2017.

11. *Ibid.*

12. Tobias Lear, December 4, 1799, *Founders Online*, National Archives, August 15, 2017, http://founders.archives.gov/documents/Washington/06-04-02-0406-0002, retrieved November 21, 2017.

13. George III, qtd. in Brookhiser, *Founding Father*, 103; John Adams, qtd. in Brumwell, *Gentleman Warrior*, 192.

14. The officer's remark was published in London's *Gentleman's Magazine* of August 1778, here qtd. in Brumwell, *Gentleman Warrior*, 4.

15. Qtd. *ibid.*, 5, emphasis added.

16. Chernow, *Washington*, 206, 211, 224, 256, 264, and passim; for "much broken and dispirited" and "war of posts," see Brumwell, *Gentleman Warrior*, 263, 243. Writing to John Hancock on September 8, 1776, Washington gave a classic statement of what would come to be characterized as his "Fabian" strategy: "that we should on all occasions avoid a general action or put anything to the risk unless compelled by a necessity into which we ought never to be drawn." *WWR*, 241.

17. Brumwell, *Gentleman Warrior*, 238–42, and Chernow, *Washington*, 303–307.

18. Higginbotham, "Afterword," *Washington Reconsidered*, 313.

19. Washington, letters respectively to James Madison (November 5, 1786), Benjamin Lincoln (November 7, 1786), and David Humphreys (December 26, 1786), all in *Founders Online*, National Archives, https://founders.archives.gov, retrieved February 18, 2017.

20. Washington thus confided to John Jay on August 15, 1786, that the nation could survive only when there was a power that would pervade the entire union in an "energetic manner." *WWR*, 605. Washington struck the theme again in his "Farewell Address," saying that, ideally, the country would be run by "a Government of as much vigour as is consistent with perfect security of Liberty." *WWR*, 969. For "braced and held with a steady hand" see Washington's letter to Henry Lee, October 31, 1786, *Founders Online*, National Archives, https://founders.archives.gov, retrieved February 18, 2018. On Washington's "conservative republicanism," see Glenn A. Phelps, "The Republican General," *George Washington Reconsidered*, ed. Don Higginbotham (Charlottesville: UP of Virginia, 2001), 165–97, here 168–69, and Richard Norton Smith, *Patriarch*, 279, 281. For further discussion of Washington's political philosophy, see Jeffry H. Morrison's eponymous book.

21. Good credit for instance allowed Albert Gallatin, Jefferson's Treasury Secretary, to borrow money in Europe to finance the Louisiana Purchase in 1803. For an exhaustive analysis of how Washington established the national economy on a solid footing, see Lengel, *First Entrepreneur*, esp. chapters 7 and 8.

22. Qtd. in Thomas P. Slaughter, *The Whiskey Rebellion: Frontier Epilogue to the American Revolution* (New York: Oxford UP, 1986), 187. On the unrest in western Pennsylvania, see William Hogeland, *The Whiskey Rebellion: George Washington, Alexander*

Hamilton, and the Frontier Rebels Who Challenged America's Newfound Sovereignty (New York: Scribner's, 2006).

23. On Washington's misgivings about slavery, see Richard Norton Smith, *Patriarch*, 346, and, for further discussion and analysis, Dorothy Twohig, "'That Species of Property': Washington's Role in the Controversy over Slavery," *George Washington Reconsidered*, ed. Don Higginbotham (Charlottesville: UP of Virginia, 2001), 115–32.

24. For "Town Destroyer," see Ferguson, *The American Enlightenment*, 165; for the "Address to the Cherokee Nation," see *WWR*, 956–60; for Washington's Indian policy, see Burns and Dunn, *George Washington*, 98–101.

25. John Adams, qtd. in Ferguson, *The American Enlightenment*, 152; for "black swans," see *ibid.*, 182. For a discussion of politicized motherhood and marginalized fatherhood, see Linda K. Kerber, "The Republican Mother: Women and the Enlightenment—An American Perspective," *American Quarterly* 28 (1976), 187–202, and her *Women of the Republic: Intellect and Ideology in Revolutionary America* (Chapel Hill: U of North Carolina P, 1980), as well as Kann, *The Gendering of American Politics*, and Norton, *Liberty's Daughters*. On women's role in the wake of Washington's death, see Kahler, *The Long Farewell*, 17–18 and Chap. 4, 73–85.

26. Much of what the Founders did not do is told in Gary B. Nash, *The Unknown American Revolution: The Unruly Birth of Democracy and the Struggle to Create America* (New York: Viking, 2005). On what George Washington did do during his presidency, see Richard Norton Smith, *Patriarch*. Even more radical is Jill Lepore, who in her recent book *These Truths: A History of the United States* (New York: Norton, 2018) advances the view that George Washington was involved in two revolutions, not just one: the familiar successful rebellion against British monarchical rule and a less remembered one to abolish slavery that would not succeed until 1865.

27. Ron Chernow, *Alexander Hamilton* (New York: Penguin, 2004), 435–42, quotation ("cause of Anglomany") 436. On America's neutrality politics, see Mlada Bukovansky, "American Identity and Neutral Rights from Independence to the War of 1812," *International Organization* 51:2 (Spring 1997), 209–43.

28. Washington to Thomas Jefferson, August 23, 1792, Founders Online, National Archives, http://founders.archives.gov/documents/Washington/05-11-02-0009, retrieved January 28, 2018.

29. On the political intrigues of Washington's cabinet, see Richard Norton Smith, *Patriarch*, especially 44–60. On Washington's ordeals, see a. Brookhiser, *Founding Father*, 75–104. For a close study of party organization during Washington's presidency, see Noble E. Cunningham, Jr., *The Jeffersonian Republicans: The Formation of Party Organization, 1789–1801* (Chapel Hill: U of North Carolina P, 1957).

30. Thomas Jefferson to George Washington, May 23, 1792, Founders Online, National Archives, http://founders.archives.gov/documents/Washington/05-10-02-0267, retrieved January 26, 2018.

31. Qtd. in Bryan, *Washington in American Literature*, 152.

32. Freneau, "monarchical farce," qtd. in Chernow, *Washington*, 687. For poems written on the occasion of Washington's birthday in 1790, see Kaminski and McCaughan, eds., *A Great and Good Man*, 41–44.

33. The French writer Chateaubriand, for instance, was quite startled by the absence of pretension in the "small house, just like the adjacent houses," that served as "the palace of the President of the United States" in Philadelphia, then the nation's capital. Qtd. in Chernow, *Washington*, 645–55.

34. For the full story, see Lengel, *Inventing George Washington*, 1–7 and Bryan, *Washington in American Literature*, 12n12.

35. Qtd. in Cunliffe, *George Washington*, 147. For "chameleon-colored thing," see Cunliffe, "Two Georges," 63; for "Royal Brute," see Paine, *Common Sense*, 99.

36. Qtd. in Chernow, *Washington*, 765.

37. Richard Hofstadter, *The Paranoid Style in American Politics* (New York: Knopf, 1965), 3–40.

38. Washington's overall score is 80 points out of a maximum 100. Faber and Faber, *American Presidents Ranked by Performance*, 32–33. Ron Chernow, in contrast, no doubt would have placed Washington at the top, for in his estimate Washington's accomplishments as president were "no less groundbreaking than his deeds in the Continental Army." *Washington*, 602 and, for a summary, 602–607. On Washington's "failings," see Albanese, *Sons of the Fathers*, 147–48, 148–53, 160–65, and Gordon S. Wood's preface to the catalog published for the Huntington Library Washington exhibition on the occasion of the bicentennial of Washington's death. John Rhodehamel, *The Great Experiment: George Washington and the American Republic* (New Haven: Yale UP, 1998), viii.

39. Wecter, "President Washington and Parson Weems," the same, *The Hero in America: A Chronicle of Hero-Worship* (New York: Charles Scribner's Sons, 1941), 99–147.

40. On the "halo effect," see Phil Rosenzweig's book of that title.

41. Dexter, *Reminiscences*, 95. The Senate address is qtd. in David Ramsay, *Life of Gerorge Washington Commander in Chief of the United States of America … and First President of the United States* (New York: Hopkins & Seymour, 1807), 322.

42. Kahler, *The Long Farewell*, 134. Kahler's partial listing of funeral rites runs to approximately 400 for the period December 18, 1799 through March 9, 1800. *Ibid.*, 10–13, 137–49. For an overview of the many forms of observances commemorating Washington's death see a. Meredith Eliassen, "George Washington, Death, and Mourning," *A Companion to George Washington*, ed. Edward G. Lengel (Malden, MA: Wiley-Blackwell, 2012), 576–91.

43. Of this plethora of verse and oratory, a few survive in manuscript, some in the collected works of recognized poets, such as Susanna Rowson, in volumes of Washingtonia and, last but not least, in the University of Freiburg's database "Poems on American Presidents, 1789–1865," https://presidents.ub.uni-freiburg.de/index.php, last accessed July 14,

2017. For "Lady Washington's Lamentation," which is in the possession of the Peabody Essex Museum, Salem, Massachusetts, see Cavitch, "Remembering George Washington," 263. For a discussion of the 346 funeral orations known to have been printed, see Bryan, *Washington in American Literature*, 55–64; for poetic eulogies, see *ibid.*, 154–56; for *Washingtons Ankunft in Elisium*, ibid., 180 and, for the text of the sketch, Evans, *Early American Imprints, Series I*, no. 39020.

44. Cavitch cites a poem in which a Pennsylvanian woman, lamenting the king's death, "joins a Nation's sigh." Her "Nation," in 1760, of course was England. "Remembering George Washington," 272n18.

45. *Pennsylvania Gazette*, January 8, 1800, qtd. in Schwartz, *American Symbol*, 81.

46. Timothy Dwight, "A Discourse, Delivered at New Haven, Feb. 22, 1800; On the Character of George Washington, Esq.," qtd. in Kahler, *The Long Farewell*, 121.

47. Kahler, *The Long Farewell*, Chap. 3, 55–72.

48. "Mount Vernon Hymn" qtd. in Eliassen, "Death, and Mourning," 585.

49. Kahler, *The Long Farewell*, 19; "mortal part of … the Father of His Country" qtd. *ibid.*, 1.

50. Representative Clairborne, in *Annals of Congress*, 1799–1801, 858–59, qtd. in Miller and Schwartz, "The Icon of the American Republic," 529. The statue was to have been an equestrian one; Congress gave the prestigious commission to artist Joseph Wright, who constructed a preparatory bust, then did a portrait, but did not live to complete the statue. Chernow, *Washington*, 508–509.

51. Washington to Colonel Lewis Nicola, May 22, 1782, *WWR*, 468–69.

52. See, for instance, his letter to John Jay, August 15, 1786, *WWR*, 606: "What astonishing changes a few years are capable of producing! I am told that even respectable characters speak of a monarchical form of government without horror. From thinking proceeds speaking, thence to acting is often but a single step. But how irrevocable & tremendous! What a triumph for the advocates of despotism to find that we are incapable of governing ourselves, and that systems founded on the basis of equal liberty are merely ideal & falacious! Would to God that wise measures may be taken in time to avert the consequences we have but too much reason to apprehend." In a letter to James Madison of March 31, 1787, Washington expressed similar sentiments, writing that "those who lean to a Monarchical government have either not consulted the public mind, or live in a region where the levelling principles in which they were bred [had been] irradicated…" *Founders Online*, National Archives, last modified June 13, 2018, http://founders.archives.gov/documents/Washington/04-05-02-0111, retrieved July 7, 2018.

53. Ray Raphael, *Mr. President: How and Why the Founders Created a Chief Executive* (New York: Knopf Doubleday, 2012). For Eric Nelson, writing a powerful chief executive into the Constitution was a victory of the "Royalist Revolution," "royalist" because enthusiasm for executive power among revolutionaries like James Wilson, John Adams, or Alexander Hamilton owed much to seventeenth-century arguments in favor of Stuart royal powers and prerogatives. Nelson, *The Royalist Revolution: Monarchy and the American Founding* (Cambridge: Harvard UP, 2014).

54. Lowering the "p" in "President" to "president" of the United States has become a quasi-universal standard only in the post-Watergate period, Richard J. Hardy and David J. Webber have argued. See "Is It 'President' or 'president' of the United States?" *Presidential Studies Quarterly* 38:1 (March 2008), 159–82.

55. In William Liddle's view, "a republicanized version of Bolingbroke's patriot king" is the "very heart" of the Constitution of 1787. "A Patriot King, or None,'" 969.

56. Washington to David Stuart, July 26, 1789, *Founders Online*, National Archives, http://founders.archives.gov/documents/Washington/05-03-02-0180, retrieved August 15, 2017.

57. Sidney Milkis and Michael Nelson, *The American Presidency: Origins and Development, 1776–2011*, 6th edn. (Washington, DC: CQ P, 2011), 74, and, for further description and discussion, Kathleen Bartoloni-Tuazon, *For Fear of an Elective King: George Washington and the Presidential Title Controversy of 1789* (Ithaca: Cornell UP, 2014); Gordon S. Wood, *Empire of Liberty: A History of the Early Republic* (Oxford–New York: Oxford UP, 2009), chap. 2 ("A Monarchical Republic").

58. Letter to George Washington, March 29, 1789, *Founders Online*, National Archives, last modified June 13, 2018, http://founders.archives.gov/documents/Washington/05-01-02-0357. For contemporary records of Washington's triumphal journey to New York City, see Kaminski and McCaughan, eds., *A Great and Good Man*, 114–28; for "long live George Washington," see *ibid.*, 105. For illustrations of triumphal arches, published in *The Columbian Magazine* and, later, by Nathaniel Currier, see Cuningham, *Popular Images of the Presidency*, 205–209.

59. All qtd. in Chernow, *Washington*, 568.

60. Washington, "First Inaugural Address (30 April 1789)," *WWR*, 733.

61. The coat George Washington wore on the occasion also was a political statement. Its color, brown, was a clear marker of independent republicanism. Moreover, the cloth was home-made, coming from the Hartford Woolen Manufactory, which had been founded by Jeremiah Wadsworth, a former supplier to the Continental Army. Washington was pleased. As he wrote to Henry Knox on April 10, 1789, a mere two weeks before the inauguration, "The cloth & Buttons … really do credit to the Manufactures of this Country." *Founders Online*, National Archives, http://founders.archives.gov/documents/Washington/05-02-02-0045, retrieved November 27, 2017. Edward Lengel disputes this account, adding that when Washington visited the manufactory in the fall of 1789, he found that its products were "not of the first quality" (*First Entrepreneur*, 181).

62. Neil MacNeil, *The President's Medal, 1789–1977* (New York: Clarkson N. Potter in association

Chapter 5

1. William Barton to the Continental Congress, qtd. in Aron, *Why the Turkey Didn't Fly*, 16. When Barton wrote this, in 1782, there was no president; the government of the United States was that of the Articles of Confederation, and the Continental Congress was both the executive and legislative branch. Barton introduced the eagle, but the ultimate source for the national bird, Cornelius Vermeule found, was the Flavian relief set over the door of the Church of the Twelve Apostles (Santi Apostoli) in Rome. The Flavians were emperors of the first century AD. As the followers of Nero, they first engaged in rebuilding the imperial city—hence rebirth seems a legitimate meaning also for the American eagle. Vermeule, *Numismatic Art in America*, 45.

2. On the "cult of antiquity" in the early republic, Meyer Reinhold, *Classica Americana: The Greek and Roman Heritage of the United States* (Detroit: Wayne State UP, 1984).

3. See Aron, *Why the Turkey Didn't Fly*, 40–41. The standard reference to the *Magna Carta Libertatum* is by the Cambridge medievalist James C. Holt: *Magna Carta*, 1992; rev. edn. (Cambridge: Cambridge UP, 2015). Also useful is David Carpenter's commentary to the 2015 Penguin Classics edition of the Magna Carta. As Carpenter writes, while Langton's input into the Magna Carta was mostly indirect, "it was Langton who crafted and inserted what now became the first clause," which was "of overwhelming importance for the Charter's future." *Magna Carta*, trans. with a new commentary by David Carpenter (London: Penguin, 2015), 349.

4. See T. H. Breen, *The Character of the Good Ruler: A Study of Puritan Political Ideas in New England, 1630–1730* (New Haven: Yale UP, 1970), and Edmund S. Morgan, "The Puritan Ethic and the American Revolution," *William and Mary Quarterly*, 3rd Ser. 24 (1967), 3–43.

5. "[W]hich sets us free from so many inborn Tyrannys," Anthony Ashley Cooper, Third Earl of Shaftesbury, *Characteristicks of Men, Manners, Opinions, Times*, 2nd edn. 1714, 3 vols. (repr. Farnborough, UK: Gregg International Publishers, 1968), 2:252; "Tyranny," *ibid.*, 1:107; on Shaftesbury's eulogy on England, see 1:108, and 216–22.

6. Shaftesbury, *Characteristicks*, 3:143n., and *ibid.*, 143: "A People, as enjoying the Happiness of a real Constitution and Polity, by which they are Free and Independent."

7. Washington to George Mason, April 5, 1769, *Founders Online*, National Archives, http://founders.archives.gov/documents/Washington/02-08-02-0132, retrieved April 20, 2017. See a. Brookhiser, *Founding Father*, 141–43. Jeffry Morrison, too, argues that Washington's political philosophy was shaped both by the classical republican tradition and by English liberal thought. *The Political Philosophy of George Washington*, 3, 62–106, 107–54.

8. The print is reproduced in Philip J. Deloria, *Playing Indian* (New Haven: Yale UP, 1998), 52. The original is owned by the Fenimore Art Museum, formerly the New York State Historical Association, Cooperstown.

9. Richard Doty, *Pictures from a Distant Country: Images on 19th-Century U.S. Currency* (Raleigh, NC: Boson Books, 2004), 146–45.

10. George Bennet to his mother, April 15, 1783, *The Writings of George Washington*, ed. Fitzpatrick, 26:321n.

11. James Madison to Thomas Jefferson, qtd. in James Thomas Flexner, *The Indispensable Man* (Boston: Little, Brown, 1974), 203.

12. There is a caveat, though, formulated by Ron Chernow, in that the unremitting emphasis on *Cato* as being Washington's favorite play has obscured his love of many other plays, most notably ribald comedies such as Sheridan's *School for Scandal*. See *Washington*, 126. Ironically, *Cato* seems to have been the favorite play also of George III. Cunliffe, "The Two Georges," 59. On *Seneca's Morals* as a source of inspiration for Washington, see Brookhiser, *Founding Father*, 122–23.

13. Leverenz, *Manhood and the American Renaissance*, 215–16.

14. *Cato*, 1.1. On the impact of Addison's play on eighteenth-century America, see Frederic M. Litto, "Addison's *Cato* in the Colonies," *William and Mary Quarterly*, 3rd Ser. 23 (July 1966), 431–49. On the significance of *Cato* for George Washington, see Henry C. Montgomery, "Addison's Cato and George Washington," *Classical Journal* 55:5 (1960), 210–12; on Washington's power politics, see Wills, *Cincinnatus*, 17–25 und 162–71.

15. Marshall, *The Life of George Washington*, 5:773 and, for "real republican," 577.

16. *Ibid.*, 773.

17. Wills, *Cincinnatus*, 116, with ill.

18. Clark, "An Icon Preserved," 42.

19. On Glass's *Georgii Washingtonii*, see Jeff Smith, *The Presidents We Imagine*, 36–38.

20. Architect of the Capitol, "General George Washington Resigning His Commission," April 29, 2016, https://www.aoc.gov/art/historic-rotunda-paintings/general-george-washington-resigning-his-commission, August 3, 2017. For an account of the actual event at the Statehouse, see Schwartz, *American Symbol*, 139–43.

21. Schwartz, *American Symbol*, 138–39 and Fig. 28. Engravings of Barralet's painting, executed by Alexander Lawson, are both in the National Portrait Gallery and the Metropolitan Museum of Art.

22. Wills, *Cincinnatus*, 217–41, quotation 225.

23. "When I painted him," Stuart recalled, "he had just had a set of false teeth inserted, which accounts for the constrained expression so noticeable about the mouth and lower part of the face." Barratt and Miles, *Gilbert Stuart*, 139. To connoisseurs, Stuart's result has been known as "the postage slot mouth." Richard Norton Smith, *Patriarch*, 264.

24. Schwartz, *American Symbol*, 160.
25. *Ibid.*, and Figs. 30–32.
26. Clark, "An Icon Preserved," 42, 44. For Asher Durand, visit the 2007 New York Public Library exhibition, *From Revolution to Repblic*, http://web-static.nypl.org/exhibitions/revolution/captions/mcalpin16.html, last accessed September 19, 2017. For the 1876 "after Houdon" bust, see George W. Nordham, *George Washington: Vignettes and Memorabilia* (Philadelphia and Ardmore, PA: Dorrance, 1977), 59.
27. Clark, "An Icon Preserved," 39, and *ibid.* for the Smithsonian's Inventory of American Sculpture.
28. "[A] servile adherence to the garb of antiquity might not be altogether so expedient, as some little deviation in favor of modern custom." Letter to Thomas Jefferson, August 1, 1786, *WWR*, 601. On Houdon in America, see Howard, *The Painter's Chair*, 90–103, on his work on the statue *ibid.*, 103–106.
29. Wright's portrait was in preparation for an equestrian statue commissioned of him by Congress in 1783. While the statue was never completed, the finished portrait shows Washington in uniform. Chernow, *Washington*, 508–509.
30. For an image of the statue, go to State Artwork Collection, Library of Virginia, http://www.virginiamemory.com/online_classroom/shaping_the_constitution/doc/washington, last accessed September 4, 2014.
31. On identifying Washington with the Roman gentleman, as well as on the commonly held idea that the nation's pillar—republican virtue—emerged from working the land, see Wills, *Cincinnatus*, 225–30 and 248–49, and Bruce S. Thornton and Victor David Hanson, "'The Western Cincinnatus': Washington as Farmer and Soldier," *Patriot Sage: George Washington and the American Political Tradition*, ed. Gary L. Gregg II und Mathew Spalding (Wilmington, DE: ISI Books, 1999), 39–60.
32. Thomas Jefferson to Governor Patrick Henry of Virginia, qtd. in Cunliffe, "The Two Georges," 73n24. On the controversy over the Society of the Cincinnati see Kahler, *The Long Farewell*, 106–107.
33. On Houdon's master piece, see John S. Hallam, "Houdon's Richmond Statue of Washington," *American Art Journal* 10 (November 1978), 73–80.
34. Schwartz, *American Symbol*, 122.
35. Washington, June 26, 1775, *WWR*, 174.
36. On the lost portraits by Trumbull and the elder Peale, see Wills, *Cincinnatus*, 13. Wills (*ibid.*, 70) also lists a statue executed by Antonio Canova between 1815 and 1821; Canova's Washington, commissioned by the Congress of the State of North Carolina, looks rather like Caesar, the quill pen and the writing tablet notwithstanding.
37. Chernow, *Washington*, 453–54.
38. Qtd. *ibid.*, 249, with further examples. Freneau, "Verses Occasioned by General Washington's Arrival in Philadelphia, on His Way to His Seat in Virginia," in Kaminski and McCaughan, eds., *A Great and Good Man*, 32. For the *Virginia Gazette*, see Bryan, *Washington in American Literature*, 148.
39. Humphreys, "A Poem on the Happiness of America," qtd. in Bryan, *Washington in American Literature*, 129. Quite similarly, a poem titled "A Rare Phaenomenon" ends by calling Washington, "A private citizen, who might be king." Kaminski and McCaughan, eds., *A Great and Good Man*, 39.
40. Weems, *Life of Washington*, 217, 219. Samuel Low, "Ode on the Death of General Washington," qtd. in Bryan, *Washington in American Literature*, 156. For later renderings of Washington as Cincinnatus, see Thistlethwaite, *The Image of George Washington*, 121–27.
41. Gay, *The Enlightenment*, 32, 40–41.
42. Cunliffe, *George Washington*, 165.
43. Byron, "Ode to Napoléon," qtd. in Bryan, *Washington in American Literature*, 167–68.

Part III

1. Charles Francis Adams, "The State of the Currency II," *Hunt's Merchants' Magazine* (December 1839), 505–17, here 515.
2. Edgar Allan Poe, *Poetry and Tales*, ed. Patrick Quinn (New York: Library of America, 1984), 380.
3. Poe, "Diddling Considered as One of the Exact Sciences," *Ibid.*, 607–17, quotations 607, 608.
4. Philip B. and Peter W. Kunhardt, *P. T. Barnum: America's Greatest Showman* (New York: Knopf, 19095), vi, and Claude Richard, "Poe and the Yankee Hero," *Mississippi Quarterly* 21 (Spring 1968), 93–109.
5. Benjamin Reiss, *The Showman and the Slave: Race, Death, and Memory in Barnum's America* (Cambridge: Harvard UP, 2001), 135–67.
6. Walt Whitman in an editorial published in 1858, in *I Sit and Look Out: Editorials from the Brooklyn Daily* Times, edd. Emor Holloway and Vernolian Schwarz (New York: Columbia UP, 1932), 59.
7. New England Historical Society, "Ethan Allen and the Tale from the Outhouse," updated in 2018, http://www.newenglandhistoricalsociety.com/ethan-allen-tale-outhouse/, accessed August 3, 2018. The anecdote as told by Lincoln is qtd. in David Herbert Donald, *Lincoln* (New York: Simon & Schuster, 1995), 196. There's also a wonderful rendition of the story in Spielberg's biopic on Lincoln. My thanks to "Steve" Rabitsch for drawing my attention to the Ethan Allan story.
8. Hawthorne, *The English Notebooks*, qtd. in Bryan, *Washington in American Literature*, 235. On Jefferson's pantheon of Washingtons see Wills, *Cincinnatus*, 110–17; Emerson ("I cannot keep my eyes off it") qtd. in Miller und Schwartz, "The Icon of the American Republic," 539n12. For more details on the antebellum deification of Washington, see Frank Craven, *The Legend of the Founding Fathers* (New York: New York UP, 1956).

Chapter 6

1. Bryan, *Washington in American Literature*, 83–84; Willard, *History of the United States*, 300.
2. Baker, *Bibliotheca Washingtoniana* (Philadel-

phia: Robert M. Lindsay, 1889), and Bryan, *Washington in American Literature*, 96–120; for "no Boswell," see *ibid.*, 86.

3. Bryan, *Washington in American Literature*, 92–96. These are Washington's "Great Virtues" according to Weems: "1 His Veneration for the Diety [*sic*], or Religious Principles. 2 His Patriotism. 3^d His Magninmity [*sic*]. 4 his Industry. 5 his Temperance and Sobriety. 6 his Justice, etc., etc." Letter to Matthew Carey, Weems's Philadelphia publisher, January 12 or 13, 1800, qtd. *ibid.*, 93.

4. John Adams, Letter to Thomas Jefferson, July 1813, qtd. in Bryan, *Washington in American Literature*, 14; for further discussion of Marshall's *Life*, see *ibid.*, 89–91, and Mitnick, "Parallel Visions," 60–61.

5. Bryan, *Washington in American Literature*, 98–100. Sparks had done even worse damage working towards his twelve-volume edition of *The Writings of George Washington*, completed in 1837. Lengel, *Inventing George Washington*, 16–18. For a general discussion of Washington biographies through Irving, see Jeff Smith, *The Presidents We Imagine*, 28–31.

6. Irving, *Life of Washington*, 5:320.

7. *Ibid.*, 4:517. Cotemporaneous with Irving's rendering of Washington as Cincinnatus is an engraving by James Smillie, after Alonzo Chappel, which appeared on the title page of volume 2 of John Frederick Schroeder's *Life and Times of Washington*. See Thistlethwaite, *The Image of George Washington*, 125 and 275 (fig.105).

8. Irving, *Life of Washington*, chap. XXVI, 1:309–24, quotation 311.

9. Donald A. Ringe, "New York and New England: Irving's Criticism of American Society," *American Literature* 38 (1967), 455–67, quot.'s. 463, 467. For "outposts of the English aristocracy," see Irving, *Life of Washington*, 1:321.

10. Irving, *Life of Washington*, 1:310, 4:215. Longfellow, "In the Churchyard at Tarrytown [1876]," *A Century of Commentary on the Works of Washington Irving*, ed. Andrew B. Myers (Tarrytown, NY: Sleepy Hollow Restorations, 1976), 38–39, here 39.

11. Mary Weatherspoon Bowden, *Washington Irving* (Boston: Twayne, 1981), 179. For "knew no divided fidelity…," see Irving, *Life of Washington*, 5:319; for "paternal appeal" and "watchword of our Union" see *ibid.*, 5:320, emphases added.

12. Andrew B. Myers, "The New York Years in Irving's *Life of George Washington*," *Early American Literature* 11 (1976), 68–83, here 81–82n3. The outside wrapper for part 12 of the "Illustrated Edition" (1857) showed a reproduction of a medal featuring a Roman-looking portrait of George Washington. *Ibid.*, 122.

13. See Bryan, *Washington in American Literature*, 103–105 and Stanley Thomas Williams, *The Life of Washington Irving*, 2 vols. (New York: Oxford UP, 1935), 1:10 and 2:227–31.

14. Bryan, *Washington in American Literature*, 100–101.

15. James K. Paulding, *A Life of Washington*, 2 vols. (New York: Harper & Brothers, 1835), 2:231.

16. Bryan, *Washington in American Literature*, 106–107; Lengel, *Inventing George Washington*, 61–63.

17. Bryan's selected bibliography lists over three hundred titles for the period 1775 to 1865 alone. *Washington in American Literature*, 247–65. John R. Frey's "George Washington in American Fiction," *Virginia Magazine of History and Biography* 55:4 (October 1947), 342–49, provides an overview, from Cooper's *The Spy* (1821) through Howard Fast's *The Unvanquished* (1942), of the numerous narratives portraying George Washington, either as the actual hero or as a secondary character. Max Cavitch's "Remembering George Washington" is mainly about texts from the Revolutionary and Early National eras, though he does address some more recent novels, including Thomas Pynchon's *Mason & Dixon* of 1973.

18. Bryan, *Washington in American Literature*, 121.

19. Sewall, "War and Washington," *Poems on American Presidents, 1789–1865*," Universität Freiburg, n.d., https://presidents.ub.uni-freiburg.de/index.php, July 14, 2016. See a. Bryan, *Washington in American Literature*, 130–36 and, for "effusions," *ibid.*, 132.

20. Bryan, *Washington in American Literature*, 179. For "Darby's Return," see Bryan, *Washington in American Literature*, 178; for *The Fall of British Tyranny, ibid.*, 173, emphasis added.

21. *Ibid.*, 188; for *America: a Dramatic Poem*, see 187–88. Later plays dealing with the Father of His Country are treated in Samual Shirk's *The Characterization of George Washington in American Plays Since 1875*. Shirk's estimation is similar. Although he finds "moments of dramatic intensity" in some of the plays, overall there is a "dearth of worthwhile Washington drama" (*ibid.*, 116).

22. James Fenimore Cooper, *The Spy: A Tale of the Neutral Ground* (New York: Wiley and Halstead, 1821); repr. with an Introduction by Tremaine McDowell (New York: Charles Scribner's, 1931), 8. The novel was dramatized in 1822 and made into a movie in 1914. Bolam and Bolam, *The Presidents on Film*, 14; Bryan, *Washington in American Literature*, 180. A lonely exception to portrayals of Washington as a military man is Hugh Henry Brackenridge's *Modern Chivalry* of 1799, which portrays Washington as president. Bryan, *Washington in American Literature*, 193–94.

23. Cooper, *The Spy*, 449–50.

24. Bryan, *Washington in American Literature*, 203 and, for further discussion of this and similar works, 206–25, and Frey, "George Washington in American Fiction."

25. Paulding, *The Old Continental; or, The Price of Liberty*, 2 vols. (New York: Paine and Burgess, 1846), 1:190.

26. Thackeray, qtd. in Bryan, *Washington in American Literature*, 16.

27. Bryan, *Washington in American Literature*, 230; for the *Southern Literary Messenger*, see 229. For a discussion of *The Virginian*, see *ibid.*, 225–30.

28. John R. Thompson, *Southern Literary Messenger*, qtd. *ibid.*, 233.

29. Nathaniel Hawthorne, *Notes of Travel*, 1871, 4 vols. (Boston-New York: Houghton Mifflin, 1900), 4:43; on the magazine piece, see Bryan, *Washington in American Literature* 84n94.

30. Cavitch, "Remembering George Washington," 248.

31. Shirk, *Washington in American Plays*, 116–21 and, for fiction and literature in general, Bryan, *Washington in American Literature*, 86, 121.

32. Susan Warner (Elizabeth Wetherell). *The Wide, Wide World* (New York: Putnam, 1852), 270. For Washington as "good for feeling," see Albanese, *Sons of the Fathers*, 144.

33. Frederick Douglass, *The Heroic Slave*, qtd. in Casper, "The Washington Image in American Culture," 599–600. John C. Calhoun, "one of us—a slaveholder and a planter," qtd. in Bryan, *Washington in American Literature*, 75.

34. Harriet Beecher Stowe, *Uncle Tom's Cabin*, ed. Elizabeth Ammons, 2nd edn. (New York: Norton, 2010), 25.

35. *American Magazine* and Dickens, *American Notes*, qtd. in Ayres, "At Home with George," 100.

36. Stowe, *Uncle Tom's Cabin*, 25; and see Mitnick, "Parallel Visions," 63. For "Washington-centric," see Howard, *The Painter's Chair*, viii.

37. Krimmel's watercolor, which also goes by the title *Dance in a Country Tavern*, was published as a lithograph by Childs and Lehman in the 1830s. Thistlethwaite, *The Image of George Washington*, 216, fig. 4. Already Krimmel's *The Quilting Frolic* from 1813 had shown a roomful of people frolicking under a framed print of Washington in the place of honor above the mantel. For an illustration of the painting, from the Winterthur Museum, see *ibid.*, 214, fig. 2.

38. Schwartz, *American Symbol*, 36–37 and Figs. 9–11 and 36. Today the painting is in the possession of the Brooklyn Museum in New York.

39. For Ira D. Gruber, the biographer of the British commanders General William Howe and Vice Admiral Richard Howe, the Princeton campaign was *the* turning point in the war. Not only had Washington's victory guaranteed the revolution's survival, but, after Princeton, "the British government had very little chance of winning the war and retaining tis colonies." *The Howe Brothers and the American Revolution*, 154, 157, qtd. in Brumwell, *Gentleman Warrior*, 296.

40. Chernow, *Washington*, 65. It has been estimated that Washington administered an average of six hundred lashes in each flogging, and at one point he even had gallows erected to instill terror in anybody contemplating desertion. *Ibid.*, 73. For "the Life and Soul of an army," see "General Orders, Cambridge, January 1, 1776, *WWR*, 196. For more examples of "cruel and usual punishment," see Logan Beirne, *Blood of Tyrants: George Washington and the Forging of the Presidency* (New York: Encounter Books, 2013), especially 49–98.

41. Brumwell, *Gentleman Warrior*, 93, 198, 218, 252; and see Trevor Nevitt Dupuy, *The Military Life of George Washington, American Soldier* (New York: Franklin Watts, 1969); and Higginbotham, "Washington and the Colonial Military Tradition," in *George Washington Reconsidered*, ed. the same (Charlottesville: UP of Virginia, 2001), 38–66.

42. Chernow, *Washington*, 287.

43. Washington to Virginia Governor Robert Dinwiddie, September 23, 1756, *Writings*, ed. Firtzpatrick, 1:466. On drinking habits during Washington's times, see Sreven Grasse, *Colonial Spirits: A Toast to Our Drunken History* (New York: Harry N. Abrams, 2016).

44. Luke Spencer, "Exploring America's Largest Collection of Early Tavern Signs," *Atlas Obscura*, April 22, 2015, http://www.atlasobscura.com/articles/exploring-america-s-largest-collection-of-early-tavern-signs?utm_source=facebook.com&utm_medium=atlas-page, retrieved May 14, 2017.

45. Benjamin Rush, qtd. in Brumwell, *Gentleman Warrior*, 311.

46. From George Washington to Anthony Wayne, June 9, 1781, *Founders Online*, National Archives, last modified June 13, 2018, http://founders.archives.gov/documents/Washington/99-01-02-06020. For Washington's determination that the "dangerous spirit" running through the ranks must be "suppressed by force," see Brumwell, *Gentleman Warrior*, 373–74.

47. Letter to Rochambeau, October 10, 1780, *Founders Online*, National Archives, last modified June 13, 2018, http://founders.archives.gov/documents/Washington/99-01-02-03532. For "a deadly wound, if not a fatal stab," see Washington's "General Orders" for September 26, 1780, *Writings*, ed. Fitzpatrick, 20:95. On the Arnold-André affair, see Chernow, *Washington*, 378–87.

48. Stephen Brumwell has written eloquently—and passionately—about Peale's "limitations." *Gentleman Warrior*, 5–7.

49. The Nassau Hall copy had been commissioned by the trustees as a substitute for "the picture of the late king [George III] of Great Britain, which was torn away by a ball from the American artillery in the battle of Princeton." Qtd. in Cunliffe, *George Washington*, 21.

50. A special exhibition produced by the National Portrait Gallery in the late 1990s bears this out. See Ellis G. Miles's exhibition catalog, *George and Martha Washington: Portraits from the Presidential Years*, with a Preface by Edmund S. Morgan (Charlottesville: UP of Virginia / Washington, DC: National Portrait Gallery, Smithsonian Institution, 1999).

51. Diary entries qtd. in Kinnaird, *George Washington*, 134. The story of the 1772 portrait is vividly retold in Howard, *The Painter's Chair*, 37–46. For illustrations of Peale's miniatures see Chernow, *Washington*, between 394 and 395.

52. Higginbotham, "The Colonial Military Tradition," 39.

53. Peale's painting of "Virginia's most distinguished soldier," as Washington's biographer Douglas Southall Freeman called him, now is in the Lee Chapel Museum of Washington and Lee University in Lexington, Virginia. For "Virginia's most distinguished soldier," see Brumwell, *Gentleman Warrior*, 155. For the "Goldsborough" portrait, see Mitnick, ed., *American Symbol*, 11, plate 3.

54. George Washington, letter to Joseph Reed, January 31, 1776, *Founders Online*, National Archives, http://founders.archives.gov/documents/Washington/03-03-02-0163, retrieved January 30, 2018. Illustrations of the prints "after Campbell" in Wick, *American Icon*, 18–22. For Peale's mezzotints, see *ibid.*, 2, 14–16, and 85.

55. George Washington, qtd. in Meschutt, "Life Portraits," in Mitnick, ed., *George Washington: American Symbol*, 25. Washington was enthusiastic about Pine's work—which included a risqué print Pine had done in England during the Revolutionary War, which showed Washington as the country's heroic liberator—and readily sat for the artist. Tuckerman, *Character and Portraits*, 39–40; Chernow, *Washington*, 508. For an illustration of Pine's 1785 portrait of Washington, see Meschutt, "Life Portraits," 29, Fig. 2.

56. Qtd. in Kinnaird, *George Washington*, 142.

57. Meschutt, "Life Portraits," 27, Fig. 1. For engraved prints of Wright's Washington, see Wick, *American Icon*, 36–39, 101–102.

58. Thomas Jefferson to Isaac Barre, June 3, 1785, *Thomas Jefferson Papers*, qtd. in John L. Cotter et al., *The Buried Past: An Archaeological History of Philadelphia* (Philadelphia: U of Pennsylvania P, 1992), 192.

59. Bushrod Washington, qtd. in Tuckerman, *Character and Portraits*, 41.

60. Letter to Solms, January 3, 1784, *Founders Online*, National Archives, http://founders.archives.gov/documents/Washington/04-01-02-0005, retrieved January 6, 2015.

61. For an illustration of Wright's design for the quarter dollar, see Richard Doty, *America's Money—America's Story*, Second Edition (Atlanta, GA: Whitman, 2008), 65.

62. Washington to Henry Lee, July 3, 1792, *Founders Online*, National Archives, http://founders.archives.gov/documents/Washington/05-10-02-0348, retrieved November 30, 2017.

Chapter 7

1. Wendy Bellion, "Heads of State: Profiles and Politics in Jeffersonian America," *New Media*, ed. Lisa Gitelman and Geoffrey B. Pingree (Cambridge: MIT P, 2003), 31–59, quot. 45. The term "presentation of self" belongs to Erving Goffman and is qtd. in Peter Burke, *Eyewitnessing: The Uses of Images as Historical Evidence* (Ithaca: Cornell UP, 2001), 26.

2. As Washington remarked to Henry Lee, he had grown "so heartily tired of the attendance which from one cause or the other has been given <to> these kind of people that it is now more than two years since I have resolved to sit no more for any of them and have adhered to it, except in instances where it has been requested by public bodies, or for a particular purpose (not of the Painters) and could, not without offense be refused." July 3, 1792, *Founders Online*, National Archives.

3. Chernow, *Washington*, 613–14.

4. Kinnaird, *George Washington*, 141; quotations respectively from Stuart and Washington *ibid.*, 144. Two later artworks depict the situation, Carl H. Schmolze's *Washington Sitting for His Portrait to Gilbert Stuart* (1858), which shows the President within an almost aristocratic setting, and Jean Leon Gerome Ferris's *The Painter and the President* (ca. 1930), which idealizes the situation for an audience entranced by the romance of colonial America. Marling, *Washington Slept Here*, 10, Fig. 1.12; Mitnick, ed., *American Symbol*, 20, plate 22.

5. For "strongest and most ungovernable passions," see Aron, *Why the Turkey Didn't Fly*, 15; for "amplitude and grandeur," see John Neal, *Randolph: A Novel* (Philadelphia: Charles I. Jack, 1823), 1: 63; for "compression of the mouth and indentation of the brow," see Brookhiser, *Founding Father*, 116; for Lavater's analysis, see Catherine E. Kelly, "Face Value: George Washington and Portrait Prints," *Common-place* 7:3 (April 2007), http://www.common-place-archives.org/vol-07/no-03/kelly/, retrieved March 21, 2017, and Howard, *The Painter's Chair*, 187; for "general effect of the countenance," see Bellion, "Heads of State," 48. Ron Chernow, too, focuses on Washington's inner tensions. His "unerring judgment, sterling character, rectitude, steadfast patriotism, unflagging sense of duty, and civic-mindedness—these exemplary virtues were achieved only by his ability to subdue the underlying volatility of his nature and direct his entire psychological makeup to the single-minded achievement of a noble cause." *Washington*, xx. For a discussion of the genius of Gilbert Stuart, see Dorinda Evans's eponymous book (Princeton: Princeton UP, 1999).

6. Unsurprisingly, it was copied numerous times, most notably by Valentine Green in 1781, whose print served not only as purveyor of Washington's likeness to the European public but also provided visual evidence of the decline of British rule in the North American colonies. Today Trumbull's original is owned by the Metropolitan Museum of Art in New York. William Alfred Bryan briefly comments on "The Genius of America" in *Washington in American Literature*, 142–43.

7. Trumbull always emphasized that all the details are as he had seen them: "Every part of the detail of the dress, horse, furniture, etc., as well as the scenery, from the real objects." John Trumbull, qtd. in Kinnaird, *George Washington*, 144–46, and, for an illustration, 145.

8. George Washington, letter to Lafayette, November 21, 1791, *Founders Online*, National Archives, http://founders.archives.gov/documents/Washington/05-09-02-0123, retrieved January 30, 2018.

9. Qtd. in Brumwell, *Gentleman Warrior*, 4.

10. Qtd. *ibid.*, 381–82.

11. Major James Wilkinson, qtd. in Brumwell, *Gentleman Warrior*, 293. Trumbull's words are from *Catalogue of Paintings, by Colonel Trumbull … in the Gallery of Yale College* (New-Haven: J. Peck, 1835), 21. For a discussion of these two paintings, see Fischer, *Washington's Crossing*, 429–31.

12. Brumwell, *Gentleman Warrior*, 11.

13. Other examples are Junius Brutus Stearns's

Washington as Soldier (c. 1851), which shows the hero as a young Colonel in the French and Indian War, and Emanuel Gottlieb Leutze's *Washington Rallying the Troops at Monmouth* (1854), which depicts the general assuming sudden responsibility, and his later *Washington at the Battle of the Monongahela* (1858). For a discussion of these and related artworks, see Thistlethwaite, *The Image of George Washington*, 71–115, 247 (figs.57 and 58), and 255 (fig.71).

14. Brumwell, *Gentleman Warrior*, 3; for Brumwell's reasons, see *ibid.*, 5–7.

15. Kelly, "Face Value," web document.

16. Schwartz, *American Symbol*, 163–65, quotation 163. For the military flavor of the funeral processions, see Kahler, *The Long Farewell*, Chap. 2, 38–54.

17. For an illustration of *Washington at Dorchester Heights*, see Schwartz, *American Symbol*, Fig. 34. Today, the painting is on exhibit in the Museum of Fine Arts, Boston.

18. Clark, "An Icon Preserved," 44–47.

19. Bolam and Bolam, *The Presidents on Film*, 12, 13, and 37, and John D. Thomas, "George Washington," 198–203.

20. Shirk, *Washington in American Plays*, 100–101. The play is completely devoid of dramatic force, though it shows Washington as commander-in-chief-to-be, after the battle of Bunker Hill, and at Valley Forge.

21. Wick, *American Icon*, 4 and 82 (ill.6). In 1779, John Norman advertised in the *Pennsylvania Evening Post* "a Primer adorned with a beautiful head of general Washington." No copy of the primer has been found, though a small engraving of Washington (again after Peale) has been identified as Norman's frontispiece. *Ibid.*, 10.

22. *Ibid.*, x and 12. The standard verse for "W" read, "Whales in the sea God's voice obey."

23. Clark, "An Icon Preserved," 44–47.

24. Klaus Lubbers, "The Construction of Collective Identity in Early Republican Folk Art," *The Construction and Contestation of American Cultures and Identities in the Early National Period*, ed. Udo J. Hebel (Heidelberg: Winter, 1999), 273–301, here 287.

25. *Ibid.*, 277–78.

26. *Ibid.*, 285–86 and 281, Fig.6, and the same, "*The Virgin's Seed*: A Note on Intercultural Perspectives in American Art," *Intercultural America*, ed. Alfred Hornung (Heidelberg: Winter, 2007), 257–83, here 266–67.

27. On folk art, see also Holger Cahill, *American Folk Art: The Art of the Common Man in America 1750–1900* (New York: Museum of Modern Art, 1932).

28. Kinnaird, *George Washington*, 148–53; University Archives, http://www.universityarchives.com/Find-an-Item/Results-List/Item-Detail.aspx?ItemID=54810, last accessed October 17, 2014.

29. *Philadelphia Aurora* and *The Federal Gazette*, January 4, 1800, qtd. in Wick, *American Icon*, 144; for an illustration of a mourning ring, see *ibid.*, 67.

30. Kelly, "Face Value," web document. Baker classified the prints first according to the painter responsible for the original portrait and then according to the engraver. In 2007, the New York Public Library's C. W. McAlpin Collection put on display a collection of "Fictitious Portraits of Washington." To view the collection, visit Section IV, http://web-static.nypl.org/exhibitions/revolution/selection4.html, last accessed August 3, 2017.

31. Kelly, "Face Value," web document. For "Textbook for the Washington collector" and "the nobility of his character…," see William S. Baker, *The Engraved Portraits of Washington* (Philadelphia: Lindsay & Baker, 1880), Preface, v.

32. Thistlethwaite, "The Face of the Nation," 41, Fig. 18. The print is on view in Independence National Historical Park in Philadelphia.

33. Marcus Tullius Cicero, *On the Republic. On the Laws*, trans. Clinton W. Keyes (Cambridge: Harvard UP, 1928), Loeb Classical Librrary 2018, https://www.loebclassics.com/view/LCL213/1928/volume.xml, retrieved June 5, 2018. On the genealogy and usages of *patriae pater*, see Andreas Alföldi, *Der Vater des Vaterlandes im römischen Denken* (Darmstadt, Germany: Wissenschaftliche Buchgesellschaft, 1971), especially 3 80–101.

34. William Ellery Channing, *Remarks on the Character of Napoleon Bonaparte* (Boston: Bowles and Dearborn, 1827), 48. John Marshall, qtd. in Morrison, *The Political Philosophy of George Washington*, 62, 81–84. On Byron's "Ode to Napoléon," which likewise juxtaposes the two men (Washington wins), see above, Chap.5. Also of interest are "Lines on the Statue of Washington in the Capitol" (1836), in which the anonymous writer pronounced the Father of His Country "A perfect hero, free from all excess, / Above Napoleon, though he dazzled less." Qtd. in Bryan, *Washington in American Literature*, 160. On the identification, in the 1820s and 1830s, of Napoleon with Andrew Jackson, see below, Chap.9.

35. Rembrandt Peale, "Washington and His Portraits," qtd. in Gustavus A. Eisen, *Portraits of Washington*, 3 vols. (New York: Robert Hamilton, 1932), 1: 312.

36. Charles Wilson Peale, qtd. in Kelly, "Face Value," web document.

37. Lillian B. Miller and Carol Eaton Hevner, *In Pursuit of Fame: Rembrandt Peale, 1778–1860* (Washington, DC: National Portrait Gallery, Smithsonian Institution in association with the U of Washington P, 1992), 144. For Peale's sessions with George Washington in 1795, see Chernow, *Washington*, 745–46. For an illustration of Peale's 1795 portrait, see Meschutt, "Life Portraits," 34, Fig. 7.

38. Charles Wilson Peale, qtd. in Chernow, *Washington*, 225.

39. Rembrandt Peale, letter to William Dunlap, December 27, 1834, reprinted in *Magazine of American History* 5 (1880), 129–32. For the comments in the 1824 pamphlet, see Peale, *Portrait of Washington*, 9–18, for his disparaging remarks about Stuart's "Athenaeum," see *ibid.*, 7.

40. Egon Verheyen, "'The most exact representation of the Original': Remarks on Portraits of George Washington by Gilbert Stuart and Rembrandt Peale," *Retaining the Original: Multiple Originals, Copies,*

and Reproduction, ed. Kathleen Preciado (Washington, DC: National Gallery of Art / Hanover, NH: UP of New England, 1989), 127–39, here 127–28. After its purchase, *Patriae Pater* was hung at the gallery level in the Senate Chamber, where it remained until 1859. It was returned to the Old Senate Chamber in 1976, following its restoration as a museum room. The Vanderlyn Washington of 1834, which closely resembles Stuart's "Lansdowne," still is in the House Chamber.

41. Rembrandt Peale, qtd. in *United States Senate Catalogue of Fine Arts*, ed. Jane R. McGoldrick (Washington, DC: U.S. Government Printing Office, 2002), 395. The oil replicas of the original porthole portrait constitute "four distinct categories: those identical to the original, with the subject's face turned proper right and featuring civilian dress; those similar to the original, but with face turned to the left; those with Washington's face turned right, but featuring military dress; and those facing left, with military dress. The example at the Pennsylvania Academy is believed to be the original of the second type. The New-York Historical Society owns a late 1853 version in which Washington wears a military uniform." (*Ibid.*)

42. Peale, *Portrait of Washington*, 7–8.

43. Edward Everett, "The Youth of Washington," *Orations and Speeches on Various Occasions*, Vol. 1 (Boston: Little, Brown, and Co., 1865), 564–98, here 575.

44. Tuckerman, *Character and Portraits*, 88–89.

45. *Ibid.*, 91–93.

46. Peale, *Portrait of Washington*, 3.

47. Charles Wilson Peale, qtd. in Kelly, "Face Value," web document.

48. Durkheim, *The Elementary Forms of the Religious Life*, 263.

Chapter 8

1. Karl Marx and Friedrich Engels, *The Communist Manifesto* [1848]. Authorized English trans., ed. and annotated by Friedrich Engels (New York: New York Labor News Co., 1908), 11.

2. On "fatherlessness" as the result of modernization, see, for instance, Michael S. Kimmel, *Manhood in America: A Cultural History* [1996], 3rd edn. (New York: Oxford UP, 2012), 25, and Dieter Thomä, *Väter. Eine moderne Heldengeschichte* (München: Carl Hanser, 2008), 20–45.

3. Fliegelman, *Prodigals and Pilgrims*, 210. For accounts of the social and cultural changes between the War of Independence and the mid-nineteenth century, see Douglas C. North, *The Economic Growth of the United States 1790–1860* (New York: Norton, 1966); Charles Sellers, *The Market Revolution: Jacksonian America 1815–1846* (New York: Oxford UP, 1994); and David Anthony, *Paper Money Men: Commerce, Manhood, and the Sensational Public Sphere in Antebellum America* (Columbus: Ohio State UP, 2009).

4. Gordon-Reed and Onuf, *"Most Blessed of the Patriarchs*, 80–81 and passim.

5. Among the copiers were Henry Inman and George C. Lambdin; a modified version was executed by Christian Schuessele. Thistlethwaite, *The Image of George Washington*, 131–32 and 281 (figs.115 and 116). For a more detailed discussion, see Scott E. Casper, "First First Family: Seventy Years with Edward Savage's *The Washington Family*," *Imprint* 24:2 (Autumn 1999), 2–15.

6. For a reading of the painting, see Ellen G. Miles, "Edward Savage and *The Washington Family*," in Ellen G. Miles, Patricia Burda, Cynthia J. Mills, and Leslie Kaye Reinhard, *American Paintings of the Eighteenth Century* (Princeton: Princeton UP, 1995), 145–59.

7. I have drawn for this reading of Savage's painting on Ross Barrett's NPG lecture, "Capital Likenesses: George Washington, the Federal City, and Economic Selfhood in American Portraiture," The Edgar P. Richardson Symposium: New Perspectives on Portraiture at the National Portrait Gallery, Washington, DC, Sept. 20, and Sept. 21, 2018, You Tube, November 19, 2018, https://www.youtube.com/watch?v=HvCl-PDYwH4&feature=youtu.be, retrieved November 21, 2018.

8. George Washington was not just the leader of the capital venture. As Adam Costanzo has shown, it was Washington's original vision for a grand national capital on the Potomac that found form first in L'Enfant's plan of 1790 and then in Ellicott's embellished version, depicted by Savage. Costanzo, *George Washington's Washington: Visions for the National Capital in the Early American Republic* (Athens: U of Georgia P, 2018).

9. The Washingtons never lived to see any occupants of the "President's House," as the White House was originally called. Stymied by ideological clashes, land speculation, and economic uncertainties, the nation's new capital would qualify as a "work in progress" for decades to come. Costanzo, *George Washington's Washington*, passim.

10. On Washington's involvement in the development of the nation's new capital see Lengel, *First Entrepreneur*, 192–94 and 244–46. On the close links between patriarchal authority, based on property that is held *de jure* (as opposed to mere *de facto* possession), and monetary systems, see Gunnar Heinsohn and Otto Steiger, *Ownership Economics: On the Foundations of Interest, Money, Markets, Business Cycles, and Economic Development*, trans. and ed. Frank Decker (Abingdon, UK-New York: Routledge, 2013), especially chapters 3 and 4.

11. Qtd. in Brumwell, *Gentleman Warrior*, 430; for "complete gentleman," see Congressman Thomas Cushing, June 21, 1775, qtd. *ibid.*, 430.

12. On Washington and his family, see Patricia Brady's eponymous article in Edward Lengel's *Companion to George Washington* (Malden, MA: Wiley-Blackwell, 2012), 86–103. For "peans to domestic felicity," see Chernow, *Washington*, 102. For a description of the southern variant of patriarchal fatherhood see Daniel Blake Smith, *Inside the Great House: Planter Family Life in Eighteenth-Century Chesapeake Society* (Ithaca: Cornell UP, 1980).

13. Nelly Custis, qtd. in Brookhiser, *Founding Father*, 165. Abigail Adams, qtd. in Chernow, *Washington*, 199.

14. Nelly Custis, qtd. in Chernow, *Washington*, 463; for "thankless task," see *ibid.*, 154–55.

15. E. Anthony Rotundo, "American Fatherhood: A Historical Perspective," *American Behavioral Scientist* 29:9 (September/October 1985), 9.

16. Chernow, *Washington*, 162; for duties towards his children, *ibid.*, 101.

17. Norton, *Liberty's Daughters*, 99–100.

18. Chernow, *Washington*, 615; for the adoptions, see *ibid.*, 421.

19. Massachusetts Cincinnati, qtd. in Minor Myers, *Liberty without Anarchy: A History of the Society of the Cincinnati* (Charlottesville: UP of Virginia, 1983), 137; David Ramsay, *The History of the American Revolution* [1789], 2 vols. (Indianapolis, IN: Liberty P, 1990), 2:266, http://oll.libertyfund.org/titles/1870, retrieved February 13, 2018. On the idea of the family as the state in microcosm, see Melvin Yazawa, *From Colonies to Commonwealth: Familial Ideology and the Beginnings of the American Republic* (Baltimore: Johns Hopkins UP, 1985).

20. Henry St John, 1st Viscount Bolingbroke, *The Idea of a Patriot King*, 1738, ed. Sydney Wayne Jackman (Indianapolis: Bobbs-Merrill, 1965), 46.

21. Brookhiser, *Founding Father*, 173.

22. Morrison, *The Political Philosophy of George Washington*, 74–79.

23. James I, qtd. in Edwin G. Burrows and Michael Wallace, "The American Revolution: The Ideology and Psychology of National Liberation," *Perspectives in American History* 6 (1972), 167–306, here 170.

24. Sir Robert Filmer, *Patriarcha and Other Writings*, ed. Johann P. Somerville (Cambridge: Cambridge UP, 1991), 7, 16, 11.

25. "Can it be reason to say that God, for the preservation of fatherly authority, lets several new governments with their governors start up…?" Locke, *Two Treatises of Government* [1698], with a Supplement, *Patriarcha by Robert Filmer*, ed. Thomas I. Cook (New York: Hafner Press / London: Collier Macmillan, 1947), I, §147; "[T]hat the power of a magistrate over a subject may be distinguished from that of a father over his children…" *Ibid.*, II, §2; "[No] one can be put out of his estate and subjected to the political power of another without his own consent. The only way whereby any one divests himself of his natural liberty, and puts on the bonds of civil society, is by agreeing with other men to join and unite into a community…" *Ibid.*, II, §95; "[T]he beginning of politic society depends upon the consent of the individuals to join into and make one society…" *Ibid.*, II, §10.

26. Brookhiser, *Founding Father*, 175. For Filmer's Virginia connection, see Peter Laslett, "Sir Robert Filmer, The Man and the Whig Myth," *William and Mary Quarterly* 5:4 (October 1948), 523–46.

27. "Land is the most permanent estate we can hold, and the most likely to increase in value," Washington wrote to his stepson John Parke Custis on February 1, 1778. *Writings*, ed. Fitzpatrick, 10:414. And on May 26, 1778, he wrote, again to his stepson: "Money … will melt like Snow before a hot Sun [but] Lands are permanent, rising fast in value." *Ibid.*, 10:457. The biographer James T. Flexner concluded: "In no other direction did Washington demonstrate such acquisitiveness as in his quest for the ownership of land." *George Washington*, vol.1 (Boston: Little, Brown, 1965), 289. On Washington's economic struggles in pre–Revolutionary Virginia, see Bruce A. Ragsdale, "George Washington, the British Tobacco Trade, and Economic Opportunity in Pre-Revolutionary Virginia," in *George Washington Reconsidered*, ed. Don Higginbotham (Charlottesville: UP of Virginia, 2001), 67–93. For other instances of financial difficulties, see Richard Norton Smith, *Patriarch*, 9–11, 66–67, 137–38, and 312–13.

28. As Heinsohn and Steiger argue, mortgaging or loaning, to name the premier economic activities, imply the temporary burdening (by a creditor) or hypothecating (by a debtor) of rightfully held property. This creates a temporary loss both to the creditor and to the debtor, who can no longer freely dispose of their burdened or hypothecated property during the period of such activities. See *Ownership Economics*, 55–65, 101–103.

29. The term "racial patriarchy," in the sense of a hierarchy based on differences in race, culture, class, and gender, belongs to Pauline E. Schloesser, *The Fair Sex: White Women and Racial Patriarchy in the Early American Republic* (New York: New York UP, 2002), 12–13.

30. Fritz Hirschfeld, *George Washington and Slavery: A Documentary Portrayal* (Columbia and London: U of Missouri P, 1997), 226. On Washington, race, and the patriarchal family, see a. Russ Castronovo, *Fathering the Nation: American Genealogies of Slavery and Freedom* (Berkeley and Los Angeles: U of California P, 1995).

31. "Interesting Specimen of African Eloquence," *New Bedford Columbian Courier*, January 17, 1800, 4, qtd. in Cavitch, "Remembering George Washington," 271n15.

32. Edmund Burke, "Speech on Conciliation with America," March 22, 1775, *The Works of the Right Honourable Edmund Burke*, 2 vols. (Boston: John West & O. C. Greenleaf, 1807), 1:17–82, quot. 36.

33. *Ibid.*

34. Washington to Bryan Fairfax, July 20, 1774, *Writings*, ed. Fitzpatrick, 3:234.

35. Gordon-Reed and Onuf, *"Most Blessed of the Patriarchs,"* esp. 19–21, 263–64, 289–96, and passim; the phrase "most blessed of the patriarchs" is from Jefferson's letter to Angelica Church, November 27, 1793, qtd. *ibid.*, xiii and 47–48.

36. *Ibid.*, 307 and, for "meeting of hearts and minds," 214; for "elemental building block," see 174.

37. John G. A. Pocock, "The Classical Theory of Deference," *American Historical Review* 81 (1976), 516–23, quot. 516. For the notion that George Washington not only built his own prosperity but also that of the nation, see Lengel, *First Entrepreneur*, chapters 7 and 8.

38. During the ratification of the Constitution

parades in 1788, for instance, one contingent of artisans displayed a bust of Washington (in Philadelphia), while another carried a flag with Washington's picture and the words "may he be the first President of the United States" (in New York City). Silverman, *Cultural History of the American Revolution*, 584 and 601. Both the relative absence of conflict and the construction of personal identity in terms of duties owed to the community have led E. Anthony Rotundo to conflate patricians and craftspeople under the label "communal manhood." *American Manhood: Transformations in Masculinity from the Revolution to the Modern Era* (New York: Basic Books, 1993), 2–3, 11–18.

39. Tocqueville, *Democracy in America*, 464.

40. Leverenz, *Manhood and the American Renaissance*, 74 and, on the "patrician paradigm," 35–39. Michael S. Kimmel's typology of American manhood (masculine archetypes) is similar to Leverenz's. Taking his cue from Royall Tyler's five-act comedy *The Contrast*, Kimmel distinguishes the "Genteel Patriarch," the "Heroic Artisan," and the "Self-Made Man." *Manhood in America*, 11–13.

41. Tocqueville, *Democracy in America*, 477. On the surge of the homicide rate from the late 1840s to the 1870s, which transformed the United States into the most homicidal affluent nation, see Randolph Roth, *American Homicide* (Cambridge: Harvard UP, 2009), especially chapters 6 and 7, respectively 250–96 and 297–385.

42. Rotundo, "American Fatherhood," 10–12.

43. I am indebted here to David Jaffee, "Visual Evidence in Jacksonian America," *Picturing United States History*, 2017, https://picturinghistory.gc.cuny.edu/visual-evidence-in-jacksonian-america/, retrieved February 8, 2017.

44. Anne McClintock, *Imperial Leather: Race, Gender and Sexuality in the Colonial Contest* (New York: Routledge, 1995), 357.

45. Laura Wexler, "Techniques of the Imaginary Nation: Engendering Family Photography," *Looking for America: The Visual Production of Nation and People*, ed. Ardis Cameron (Malden, MA: Blackwell, 2005), 94–117, quot. 103. For an illuminating discussion of photography as nationalist iconography, see Trachtenberg, *Reading American Photographs* (New York: Hill & Wang, 1999), esp. chap. 1.

46. Wexler, "Techniques of the Imaginary Nation," 103–104.

47. *Ibid.*, 105–108.

48. Qtd. in Samuel, *American Fatherhood*, 52.

49. Rev. John S. C. Abbott, "Paternal Neglect," *The Parents' Magazine and Young People's Friend* (March 1842), 147–48, qtd. in Blankenhorn, *Fatherless America*, 14. I have also drawn in this paragraph on John Putnam Demos, "The Changing Faces of American Fatherhood," *Father and Child: Developmental and Clinical Perspectives*, ed. Stanley H. Cath et al. (Boston: Little, Brown, 1982), 425–45, here 442–43, and Leverenz, *Manhood and the American Renaissance*, 4, 73.

50. See Armengol-Carrera, "Where are Fathers in American Literature?" *Journal of Men's Studies* 16:2 (2008), 211–26.

51. Poe, letter to Beverly Tucker, *Letters*, 1:116. "I have no father—nor mother," qtd. in Ian Walker, ed., *Edgar Allan Poe: The Critical Heritage* (1986. London-New York: Routledge, 1997), 68.

52. Horatio Hastings Weld, qtd. in Bryan, *Washington in American Literature*, 101; for Poe's praise of Paulding, see *ibid.*, 100–101. On images of orphanhood in antebellum literature, see Diana Loercher Pazicky, *Cultural Orphans in America* (Jackson: UP of Mississippi, 1998), 149–77.

53. Reference to "father of the fatherless" is to Psalms 68:5: "A father of the fatherless [...] is God in his holy habitation."

54. Qtd. in Cunliffe, *George Washington*, 24; for "a napkin lying in his lap," see Miller et al., *American Encounters*, 144. Greenough's statue was on display in the Capitol Rotunda from 1841 to 1843, when it was relocated to the east lawn. In 1908 Congress transferred the statue to the Smithsonian Institution, where it was exhibited in the Smithsonian Castle until its relocation to the new National Museum of American History in 1964. It has resided on the second floor of the Museum ever since. When the Museum reopened November 21, 2008, the Washington statue became the signature artifact for a section in the west wing of the museum focused on American lives. National Museum of American History, "Landmark Object: George Washington Statue, 1841," n.d., http://americanhistory.si.edu/press/fact-sheets/landmark-object-george-washington-statue-1841, retrieved February 27, 2017.

55. Qtd. in Cunliffe, *George Washington*, 13.

56. Bryan, *Washington in American Literature*, 67 and, for a versifier's regret of the nation's failure to provide an appropriate monument for the first President, 159: "Thy country, spirit of the mighty dead, / To thee a lasting monument imparts; / She rears, great Washington, above thy head, / A monument of most ungrateful hearts."

57. *Ibid.*, 19. For the congressional action of 1832, see *ibid.*, 69.

58. Bryan, *Washington in American Literature*, 73–74; and Boime, *The Unveiling of the National Icons*, 317–24. The history of the Washington Monument and the National Monument Society is treated more fully in Frederick L. Harvey's eponymous book (Washington, DC: Government Printing Office, 1903).

59. Henry Wadsworth Longfellow, "To a Child," *The Belfry and Other Poems* (1845), *The Complete Works* (London: Delphi Classics, 2012), n.p., lines 67–69.

60. Thomas Carlyle, *On Heroes, Hero-Worship and the Heroic in History* (New York: Frederick A. Stokes, 1893), 253.

61. See, on Frost's book as well as on Edmond's *The Image Peddler*, Thistlewthaite, *The Image of George Washington*, 26–27 and 189.

62. Stephen M. Frank, "'Their Own Proper Task': The Construction of Meanings for Fatherhood in Nineteenth-Century America," conference paper, 1992, qtd. in Blankenhorn, *Fatherless America*, 104.

63. *Ibid.*

64. Lippard, *Paul Ardenheim*, 158–65, in Lengel, *Inventing George Washington*, 36–43, quotation 41.
65. Thistlethwaite, *The Image of George Washington*, 116–22 and 270 (fig.95). The painting is now in the Virginia Museum of Fine Arts, Richmond.
66. Ibid., 129 and 280 (fig.113). Currier's lithograph is now owned by the Historical Society of Pennsylvania, Philadelphia.
67. Fitzhugh, *Cannibals All! Or Slaves without Masters*, qtd. *ibid.*, 131.
68. All in Mitnick, "Parallel Visions," 63. An illustration of Stearns's *Marriage* is in Mitnick, ed. *American Symbol*, 14, plate 9; see a. Thistlethwaite, *The Image of George Washington*, 31 and 40–47, and, for Lambert Sachs, 99–101, and 263–64 (figs. 85 and 86).

Part IV

1. Ciunningham, *Popular Images of the Presidency*, 275, 280.
2. William Alfred Bryan, "George Washington: Symbolic Guardian of the Republic, 1850–1861," *William and Mary Quarterly*, 3rd ser. 7 (January 1950), 53–63, quot. 63.
3. Clay and Calhoun, qtd. in Bryan, *Washington in American Literature*, 75.
4. Lengel, *Inventing George Washington*, 93–100, quotations 94, 96, 97.
5. Ibid., 97–99. The 1880 version, published in the December edition of the *National Tribune*, became the most popular one. It was reprinted in 1931 and 1950. It was made into an anti–Communist pamphlet in the 1950s, distributed by a Christian organization for almost two decades, retold in Susy Smith's book *Prominent American Ghosts* (1967), bowdlerized for the science fiction television series *One Step Beyond* (1961), and reinterpreted to suit the so-called War on Terror in Janice Connell's best-selling book *Faith of Our Founding Father* (2004, new edition 2007). *Ibid.*, 99–100.

Chapter 9

1. Holmes, "Ode for Washington's Birthday," *The Poetical Works of Oliver Wendell Holmes*, rev. and with a new introd. by Eleanor M. Tilton (Boston: Houghton Mifflin, 1975), 98.
2. Tuckerman, qtd. in Kammen, *Mystic Chords of Memory*, 71.
3. Daniel Webster, "The Character of Washington (February 22, 1832), *The Works of Daniel Webster*, 6 vols. (Boston: Little and Brown, 1851) 1:217–33, quot. 1:221.
4. For the reading out of the Farewell Address, which soon became a tradition that was done annually until the 1970s, see National Archives, "George Washington's Birthday," August 24, 2016, https://www.archives.gov/legislative/features/washington, retrieved June 9, 2017. For the Union as "the great object" of Washington's thoughts, see Webster, "The Character of Washington," *Works*, 1:229. For "no such thing as a peaceable secession," see *Key Concepts in American Cultural History: From the Colonial Period to the End of the 19th Century*, 2nd edn., ed. Bernd Engler and Oliver Scheiding (Trier, Germany: Wissenschaftlicher Verlag Trier, 2007), 623.
5. Rufus Wilmore Griswold, *The Republican Court; or, American Society in the Days of Washington* (New York: D. Appleton, 1855), 67, emphasis added.
6. For a discussion of Stearns's painting, see Thistlethwaite, *The Image of George Washington*, 152–59.
7. Ibid., 199 and 317 (fig.169).
8. Ibid., 200 and 317 (fig.170).
9. Mitnick, "Parallel Visions," 63–64.
10. Peale, "Washington and His Portraits," qtd. in Gustavus A. Eisen, *Portraits of Washington*, 3 vols. (New York: Robert Hamilton, 1932), 1:299.
11. Edward Everett, "The Character of Washington," *Orations and Speeches on Various Occasions*, vol. 4 (Boston: Little, Brown, and Co., 1868), 3–51, quot. 50. Other references to the lecture in this paragraph are, respectively, to 52, 28, 34–35, 36, and 49.
12. Richter, *The Quaker Soldier*, and "Rebels," qtd. in Bryan, *Washington in American Literature*, 165. For a fuller treatment of the role of Washington in prewar controversy, see Bryan, "George Washington: Symbolic Guardian of the Republic."
13. Henry Adams, *Democracy. An American Novel* [1880], Foreword by Henry D. Aiken (New York: New American Library / Signet Classics, 1961), 70–82. Cunningham, qtd. in Marling, *Washington Slept Here*, 83; for the early years of Mount Vernon, see *ibid.*, 77–84. On the importance of the place for the Father of His Country, see Robert F. Dalzells, Jr., and Lee Baldwin Dalzell, *George Washington's Mount Vernon: At Home in Revolutionary America* (New York: Oxford UP, 1999).
14. Cunningham, qtd. in Marling, *Washington Slept Here*, 84. For current activities of the association, see the Mount Vernon Ladies' Association of the Union's *Annual Reports*, available from www.mountvernon.org. For *lieu de memoire*, see Nora, "Between Memory and History: Les lieux de mémoire [1984]," *Representations* 26 (Spring 1989), 7–25, and, for the larger picture, *Realms of Memory: Rethinking the French Past*, 3 vols., ed. Lawrence D. Kritzman, trans. Arthur Goldhammer (New York: Columbia UP, 1996–1998). For pictorial renderings of Mount Vernon as well as of scenes of family life there, see Thistlethwaite, *The Image of George Washington*, 132–44.
15. Yancey, qtd. in Bryan, *Washington in American Literature*, 80–81.
16. Matthew Karp, *This Vast Southern Empire: Slaveholders at the Helm of American Foreign Policy* (Cambridge: Harvard UP, 2016), 78–80, 229–48. Quotation from the *New York Herald* in David S. Reynold, "The Slave Owners' Foreign Policy," *The New York Review of Books* 64:11 (June 22, 2017), http://www.nybooks.com/issues/2017/06/22/, retrieved July 6, 2017. On the North's amnesia, see Wolfgang Schivelbusch, *Die Kultur der Niederlage. Der amerikanische Süden 1865, Frankreich 1871, Deutschland 1918* (Darmstadt: Wissenschaftliche Buchgesellschaft, 2001), 59.

17. Abraham Lincoln, letter to George Robertson, August 15, 1855, *The Collected Works of Abraham Linccoln*, ed. Roy P. Basler, 9 vols. (New Brunswick: Rutgers UP, 1953–1955), 2:318.

18. James M. McPherson, *Battle Cry of Freedom: The Civil War Era* (New York: Ballantine, 1988), 318.

19. Mitchell, *The Coloniad, a Narrative in Verse on Washington's War*, qtd. in Bryan, *Washington in American Literature*, 142.

20. John R. Thompson, "Inauguration of the Equestrian Statue of Washington ... Opening Ode," qtd. *ibid.*, 164.

21. John Wise, qtd. *ibid.*, 79–80. The Richmond statue monument was commissioned by the state of Virginia in 1849; its unveiling took place two years after Henry Kirke Brown's bronze equestrian statue had been installed in New York's Union Square Park. On the Great Seal of the Confederacy, see Morrison, *The Political Philosophy of George Washington*, 120–21.

22. Morrison Heady, *The Farmer Boy, and How He Became Commander-In-Chief, by Uncle Juvinell*, ed. William M. Thayer (Boston: Walker Wise, 1864), 4–5; other references to the book are to 28–31.

23. "Ode on the Death of President Lincoln" (1865), qtd. in Butter, *Der "Washington-Code,"* 96.

24. Qtd. in Schwartz, *American Symbol*, 197.

25. Hobsbawm, "Introduction" to *The Invention of Tradition*, 13, 9.

26. On Brumidi's *Apotheosis* as well as on other artistic and sculptural decoration of the U.S. Capitol, see Donald R. Kennon and Thomas P. Somma, *American Pantheon: Sculptural and Artistic Decoration of the United States Capitol* (Athens, OH: U.S. Capitol Historical Society—Ohio UP, 2004), passim.

27. Adapted from "The Image Recapitulated," http://xroads.virginia.edu/~cap/gw/gwrecap.html, retrieved March 2, 2017.

28. Cunningham, *Popular Images of the Presidency*, 128.

29. Stoddard, "Abraham Lincoln, a Horatian Ode," qtd. in Bryan, *Washington in American Literature*, 166.

30. Butter, *Der "Washington-Code,"* quotations 40 (Adams and Jefferson), 68 and 70–71 (Jackson). Jackson, John William Ward has shown, was also frequently portrayed as Napoleon. *Andrew Jackson: Symbol for an Age* (New York: Oxford UP, 1955), 8.

31. Butter, *Der "Washington-Code,"* quotations 78 (Harrison), and 88 (Taylor).

32. Cunningham, *Popular Images of the Presidency*, 35–82, passim. Portraits of Washington as well as of his successors also served as decorative elements in ornate prints of the Declaration of Independence. *Ibid.*, 91–108. For pictures associated with "Union," see *ibid.*, 119–29 and 216–18, plates 15–17.

33. Lincoln, qtd. in Bryan, *Washington in American Literature*, 82.

34. Hillard, *The Last Men of the Revolution*, 13, qtd. in Marling, *Washington Slept Here*, 9.

35. "Ode on the Death of President Lincoln" (1865), qtd. in Butter, *Der "Washington-Code,"* 96; for "principles of Washington," see Schwartz, *American Symbol*, 197.

36. Schwartz, *American Symbol*, Fig. 40.

37. Rutherford Hayes, qtd. in Casper, "The Washington Image," 600.

Chapter 10

1. Louis J. Kern, "'A New Gospel to This Continent…,'" paper given to "American Foundational Myths" conference, Swiss Association for American Studies (SANAS) / Austrian Association for American Studies Joint Conference (University of Zurich, November 19–21, 2000). The painting is on view at the Michele & Donald D'Amour Museum of Fine Arts, Springfield, Massachusetts.

2. Eric Hobsbawm, "Mass-Producing Traditions: Europe, 1870–1914," *The Invention of Tradition*, ed. the same and Terence Ranger (Cambridge: Cambridge UP, 1983), 263–307, quot.'s 280, 279.

3. See Matthew Dennis, *Red, White, and Blue Letter Days: An American Calendar* (Ithaca: Cornell UP, 2002).

4. William McKinley, "Inaugural Address," March 4, 1897, online by Gerhard Peters and John T. Woolley, *The American Presidency Project*, http://www.presidency.ucsb.edu/ws/?pid=25827.

5. New York high school principal, qtd. in Higham, *Strangers in the Land*, 235. On the educational activities by the D.A.R. and other societies, see *ibid.*, 236–37.

6. Treasury Secretary Salmon P. Chase, "national in their character"; John Sherman, "a sentiment of nationality," both qtd. in Tschachler, *The Greenback*, 110, 112.

7. Spencer M. Clark, qtd. in Q. David Bowers, *Obsolete Paper Money Issued by Banks in the United States, 1782–1866* (Atlanta, GA: Whitman Publishing, 2006), 406.

8. American history books of the nineteenth century commonly represented Burgoyne as the one British general from the War of Independence who was the most responsible for plundering and looting, massacres, unspeakable cruelties, and destruction—and for stirring up the native tribes against the Americans. Eugen Kotte, "USA. Konsens und Mission [Consensus and Mission]," *Mythen der Nationen. Ein europäisches Panorama*, ed. Monika Flacke (Berlin: Deutsches Historisches Museum, 1988), 557–75, here 564–65.

9. National Monetary Commission, qtd. in Andrew McFarland Davis, *The Origin of the National Banking System* (Washington, DC: Government Printing Office, 1910), 106. On the power of currency imagery for constructing a collective national identity, see Eric Helleiner, "National Currencies and National Identities," *American Behavioral Scientist* 41:10 (October 1998), 1409–36, here 1412–1414.

10. See, on the artworks, Ann Uhry Abrams, "National Paintings and American Character: Historical Murals in the Capitol Rotunda," in *Picturing History: American Painting 1770–1930*, ed. William Ayres (New York: Rizzoli International, 1993), 65–80. For the currency notes, see Tschachler, *The Greenback*, 112–14.

11. Bellion, "Politics in American Art," Chicago Humanities Festival, November 1, 2015, *YouTube*, https://www.youtube.com/watch?v=zKyvCaKpWc0&feature=youtu.be, accessed December 11, 2015; for further discussion, see Simon P. Newman, *Parades and the Politics of the Street: Festive Culture in the Early American Republic* (Philadelphia: U of Pennsylvania P, 1997).

12. Qtd. in Philip Davidson, *Propaganda and the American Revolution, 1763–1783* (Chapel Hill: U of North Carolina P, 1941), 373. I have also drawn in this and the preceding paragraph on Bellion, "Politics in American Art," web document; and Schwartz, *American Symbol*, 53 (for an illustration of the wooden replica of Washington, see Fig. 13).

13. One picture, from the holdings of the New York Historical Society, is reprinted in Herbert J. Bass et al., *America and Americans*, vol. 1 (Morristown, NJ: Silver Burdett P, 1983), 106.

14. Bellion, "Politics in American Art"; to view the event in Baghdad, go to https://www.theguardian.com/world/video/2013/mar/09/saddam-hussein-statue-toppled-bagdhad-april-2003-video, last accessed September 26, 2017.

15. George Washington, "General Orders," July 10, 1776, *Founders Online*, National Archives, http://founders.archives.gov/documents/Washington/03-05-02-0185, retrieved September 26, 2017.

16. George Washington to Henry Knox, March 8, 1787, *WWR*, 642.

17. George Washington, November 5, 1786, *Founders Online*, National Archives, http://founders.archives.gov/documents/Washington/04-04-02-0299, retrieved September 26, 2017.

18. Benson J. Lossing, *A Primary History of the United States: For Schools and Families* (1858; New York: Sheldon & Co., 1870), 94.

19. Salma Hale, *History of the United States* (New York: Charles Wiley, 1825), 155.

20. Jesse Olney, *A History of the United States States, on a new plan; adapted to the capacity of youth* (1836; New-Haven, CT: Durrie & Peck 1839), 144.

21. On the critical reception of Leutze's epic painting and its performative function as "visual ideology" see Mark E. Thistlethwaite, "*Washington Crossing the Delaware*: Navigating the Image(s) of the Hero," in *George Washington in and as Culture*, ed. Kevin L. Cope et al. (New York: AMS P, 2001) 39–63. I have also drawn here on Louis Kern's conference paper, "'A New Gospel to This Continent….'"

22. Kern, "'A New Gospel to This Continent….'" Ferdinand Freiligrath not only marched with Leutze in the Festival of German Unity on August 6, 1848; he also wrote a poem, "Vor der Fahrt," in which "Revolution" is the name of a ship on its way to America in search of freedom. There is a direct reference in the poem to Washington as the ship's captain or helmsman: "Ha, wie Washington es / geleitet!" ("Ha, how Washington did lead.") The poem is collected in Freiligrath's *Ça Ira! Sechs Gedichte*, qtd. and trans. in Barbara S. Groseclose, *Emanuel Leutze, 1816–1868: Freedom Is the Only King* (Washington, DC: Smithsonian Institution P, 1975), 36, 65n32. The newspaper is quoted in Natalie Spassky, *American Paintings in the Metropolitan Museum of Art* (New York: Metropolitan Museum of Art, 1985), 2:18.

23. Fischer, *Washington's Crossing*, 1.

24. Karsten Fitz, *The American Revolution Remembered, 1830s to 1850s* (Heidelberg: Winter, 2010), 265–97.

25. Bingham's *Washington Crossing the Delaware* is currently located at the Chrysler Museum of Art, Norfolk, Virginia.

26. The film, which was directed by Robert Harmon, stars Jeff Daniels as George Washington. See William McDonald, "The General, The River, The Famous Boat Ride," *The New York Times*, January 10, 2000, http://www.nytimes.com/2000/01/10/arts/television-review-the-general-the-river-the-famous-boat-ride.html, accessed March 2, 2017. For *The Miller of New Jersey*, see Bryan, *Washington in American Literature*, 183.

27. Marling, *Washington Slept Here*, 136; other references in this paragraph are to *ibid.*, 383, 378, 160, and 336.

28. Cunningham, qtd. in Casper, "The Washington Image," 601–602.

29. Marling, *Washington Slept Here*, 87.

30. See *ibid.*, 38–51; Thistlethwaite, *The Image of George Washington*, 167, 173, and 300 (fig.146). For Welles's 400-page tome, see Kat Eschner, "This Nineteenth-Century Genealogist Argued Norse God Odin Was George Washington's Great-Great-Great … Father," *Smithsonian Magazine*, September 8, 2017, http://www.smithsonianmag.com/smart-news/nineteenth-century-genealogist-argued-norse-god-odin-was-george-washingtons-great-great-great-grandfather-180964742/?utm_source=facebook.com&utm_medium=socialmedia, retrieved September 11, 2017.

31. Lowell, "Under the Old Elm," qtd. in Bryan, *Washington in American Literature*, 169.

32. *Ibid.*, 168.

33. Marling, *Washington Slept Here*, 25–37; for an illustration of a "Century Vase," see Miller et al., *American Encounters*, 293.

34. Marling, *Washington Slept Here*, 51.

35. W. Herbert Burk, *Washington's Prayers* (Norristown, PA: Published for the Benefit of the Washington Memorial Chapel, 1907), respectively 13 and 15, qtd. in Lengel, *Inventing George Washington*, 73 and 75.

36. *Ibid.*, 13, emphases added.

37. *Ibid.*, 76. For Manship's "Prayer Warrior," go to http://prayerwarriorwashington.blogspot.co.at, last accessed August 11, 2017.

38. Schwartz, *American Symbol*, 197.

39. Marling, *Washington Slept Here*, 143.

40. Ford, *The True Washington*, 5, qtd. in Casper, "The Washington Image," 603.

41. *Ibid.*, 603–604.

42. Martha Washington's portrait was designed by Thomas F. Morris after a painting by Charles François Jalabert and engraved by Charles Burt. George Washington's portrait was engraved by Alfred Sealey after Gilbert Stuart. Burt's head of Martha Washington

also appeared as the central feature on the $1 Silver Certificates, Series 1886 and, slightly redesigned, Series 1891, making Martha Washington the first and only woman to grace the primary portrait of the currency. Q. David Bowers, *Whitman Encyclopedia of U.S. Paper Money* (Atlanta, GA: Whitman publishing, 2009), 124–26. For the celebration of the Washingtons' wedding anniversary, see Schwartz, "A New Man for a New Century," 125–26. A photograph in Mary Northend's book *Colonial Homes and Their Furnishings* of 1912 shows an inviting dining room doorway with George and Martha portraits on separate sides. Marling, *Washington Slept Here*, 167, Fig. 6.11.

43. *Indiana Democrat*, qtd. in "Martha on $1," *George Washington's Mount Vernon*, n.d., http://www.mountvernon.org/george-washington/martha-washington/martha-on-1/, retrieved September 20, 2017.

44. Vermeule, *Numismatic Art in America*, 167. On the Philadelphia monument, see Schwartz, "A New Man for a New Century," 128–29, and Association for Public Art, "Washington Monument," 2017, http://www.associationforpublicart.org/artwork/washington-monument/, March 2, 2017.

45. Higham, *Strangers in the Land*, 45–52, 87–96. For the "miracle of America" pageant, see Marling, *Washington Slept Here*, 121–38, quotation 130. For the imitation Inaugural Ball, held in 1887, see *ibid.*, 114–20. (At the Ball, one woman, said to be George Washington's great-grandniece, wore a buckle containing a lock of her great-grand uncle's hair.)

46. Adams, *Democracy*, 82. For a discussion of Haberle's *Changes of Time*, on display at the Manoogian Collection, New York, see Miller et al., *American Encounters*, 363–64.

47. *Chicago Daily Tribune* and Lorado Taft qtd. in Schwartz, "A New Man for a New Century," 130, 131. For the two plays, see Shirk, *Washington in American Plays*, respectively 131 and 130, with *King Washington* listed as a "lost" play.

48. Casper, "The Washington Image," 602–603. For "Washington on a Lark," see Marling, *Washington Slept Here*, 50.

49. *Samantha at the Centennial* (1879), qtd. in Marling, *Washington Slept Here*, 30.

50. Ambrose Bierce, "George the Made-Over" (1899), in *Tangential Views. The Collected Works of Ambrose Bierce*. Vol. IX. New York-Washington: Neale Publishing, 1911. 48–52, quotations 48 and 49.

51. *Ibid.*, 50.

52. Marling, *Washington Slept Here*, 42.

53. Hughes, qtd. in Cunliffe, *George Washington*, 158.

54. Ferguson, *The American Enlightenment*, 180; Marina Warner, *Monuments and Maidens: The Allegory of the Female Form* (New York: Atheneum, 1985), xx, 277. For "fair daughters of Columbia," see Kahler, *The Long Farewell*, 82.

55. Sparks, *Life*, 99.

56. Abigail Adams, letter to Judge F. A. Vanderbilt, February 3, 1814, qtd. in Ferguson, *The American Enlightenment*, 182.

57. Paine, *An Occasional Letter on the Female Sex*, qtd. *ibid.*, 179.

58. Blackstone, *Commentaries on the Laws of England* (1765–69), qtd. *ibid.*, 160. The French expression *"femme couverte"* means that women, upon entering marriage, received a "cover," to the effect that they were at the same time "protected" and "hidden." The same notion is preserved in the German phrase *"unter die Haube kommen."*

59. Mary Poovey, *Uneven Developments: The Ideological Work of Gender in Mid-Victorian England* (Chicago: U of Chicago P, 1998), 80.

60. Eva Boesenberg, "Self-made Women, Spent Men? Money and Gender in U.S. American Novels since the 1980s," in *Almighty Dollar: Papers and Lectures from the Velden Conference*, ed. Heinz Tschachler, Eugen Banauch, and Simone Puff (Wien-Münster: LIT Verlag, 2010), 159–80, here 160–61; reference to "étalonnage" is to Luce Irigaray, "Noli Me Tangere" (1976).

61. See Marc Leepson, *Flag: An American Biography* (New York: St. Martin's P, 2005), 43 and, for a reevaluation of Betsy Ross, Marla L. Miller, *Betsy Ross and the Making of America* (New York: Henry Holt, 2010). For "comfortably domestic story," see Aron, *Why the Turkey Didn't Fly*, 61.

Chapter 11

1. Virginia H. Hewitt, "Soft Images, Hard Currency: The Portrayal of Women on Paper Money," *The Banker's Art: Studies in Paper Money*, ed. the same (London: British Museum P, 1995), 156–65, quot. 156 and, for further discussion and analysis within the American context, Tschachler, *The Greenback*, 77–81.

2. The figures are impressive: Between 1861 and 1900 more than 160 different types, classes, and varieties of bank notes were put in circulation. By 1929, the number was cut in half; as of 1930, only 15 were left. For an overview of the development of America's paper money since the Civil War, see Josh Lauer, "Money as Mass Communication: U.S. Paper Currency and the Iconography of Nationalism," *The Communication Review* 11 (2008), 109–32, here 121–24.

3. United States Bureau of Engraving and Printing (USBEP), "FAQs," n.d., https://www.moneyfactory.gov/resources/faqs.html, January 16, 2018. The word "presidents" is, strictly speaking, a misnomer. The committee's decision was somewhat altered by the Secretary of the Treasury, the USBEP explains, to include Hamilton (on the new $10 bill), the fledgling nation's first Secretary of the Treasury; Salmon P. Chase (on the new $10,000 bill), Secretary of Treasury under Lincoln and credited with promoting the National Banking System; Benjamin Franklin (on the new $100 notes, the "Benjamins"), one of the signers of the Declaration of Independence and, together with John Adams and John Jay, of the Paris Peace Treaty of 1783. "All three of these statesmen," the USBEP concludes, "were well known to the American public."

4. Coolidge, "Great Virginians," *The Price of*

Freedom: Speeches and Addresses (1924; Amsterdam: Fredonia Books, 2001), 173.

5. Coolidge, "Address to a Joint Session of Congress in Anticipation of Celebration of the Two Hundredth Anniversary, in 1932, of the Birth of George Washington," February 22, 1927, online by Gerhard Peters and John T. Woolley, *The American Presidency Project*, http://www.presidency.ucsb.edu/ws/?pid=418, June 5, 2018.

6. Recreation of Wakefield was counted among the most worthwhile actions the Bicentennial Commission could undertake. It soon became an item of the highest national priority and was completed as a National Memorial in 1931. Marling, *Washington Slept Here*, 264–65.

7. Alfred Kazin, qtd. *ibid.*, 365.

8. Michael Schudson, "the past is constantly being retold," qtd. in Schwartz, "A New Man for a New Century," 137.

9. Kreitner, "Shifting the Grounds of Monetary Politics," in *Culture and Money in the Nineteenth Century*, ed. Daniel Bivona and Marlene Tromp (Athens: Ohio UP, 2016), 66–97, quotation 66.

10. Ralph LaRossa, *The Modernization of Fatherhood: A Social and Political History* (Chicago: U of Chicago P, 1997), 17.

11. Woodrow Wilson, qtd. in Schwartz, "A New Man for a New Century," 124.

12. Marling, *Washington Slept Here*, 257.

13. Calvin Coolidge, "Address to the American Society of Newspaper Editors, Washington, D.C.," January 17, 1925, online by Gerhard Peters and John T. Woolley, *The American Presidency Project*, http://www.presidency.ucsb.edu/ws/?pid=24180, June 6, 2018.

14. Casper, "The Washington Image," 604. For the Claude Gernade Bowers quote, see Marling, *Washington Slept Here*, 253.

15. In 1939, a pro–Hitler rally packed Madison Square Garden, where the leader of the German-American Bund spoke in front of a thirty-foot image of General Washington surrounded by swastikas hanging from the wall. Sarah Kate Kramer, "When Nazis Took Manhattan," NPR, February 20, 2019, https://www.npr.org/sections/codeswitch/2019/02/20/695941323/when-nazis-took-manhattan, February 21, 2019.

16. Hiram Evans, qtd. in Perlstein, "I Thought I Understood the American Right," *The New York Times Magazine*, April 11, 2017, https://www.nytimes.com/2017/04/11/magazine/i-thought-i-understood-the-american-right-trump-proved-me-wrong.html?_r=0, retrieved April 17, 2017.

17. Higham, "The Tribal Twenties," *Strangers in the Land*, 264–99; on the rise of anti–Semitism, see *ibid.*, 277–86.

18. On the resurgence of the Klan, see Linda Gordon, *The Second Coming of the KKK: The Ku Klux Klan of the 1920s and the American Political Tradition* (New York: W. W. Norton, 2017), and Higham, *Strangers in the Land*, 286–99 and, on the riot in West Frankfort, 323–24.

19. The most thorough account of the Fred Trump story is Mike Pearl's "All the Evidence We Could Find About Fred Trump's Alleged Involvement with the KKK," *Vice*, March 10, 2016, https://www.vice.com/en_us/article/mvke38/all-the-evidence-we-could-find-about-fred-trumps-alleged-involvement-with-the-kkk, January 7, 2018..

20. For *The Birth of a Nation* catalysing the eruption of the second Klan, see Gordon, *The Second Coming of the KKK*, 11–12.

21. *Ibid.*, 205. For the warning in the *New York Times* ("The Uprising of the Women"), see Sandra Adickes, "Sisters, not Demons: The influence of British Suffragists on the American Suffrage Movement," *Women's History Review* 11:4 (2002), 675–690, quot. 681.

22. Griswold, *Fatherhood in America*, 87.

23. *Ibid.*, 115; for "masculine development," see *ibid.*, 110.

24. David Cannadine, "The Context, Performance and Meaning of Ritual: The British Monarchy and the 'Invention of Tradition,' c. 1820–1977," *The Invention of Tradition*, ed. Eric Hobsbawm and Terence Ranger (Cambridge: Cambridge UP, 1983), 101–164, quot. 141.

25. MacMonnies, qtd. in Douglas Ullman, Jr., "The Princeton Battle Monument," *Civil War Trust*, n.d., https://www.civilwar.org/learn/articles/princeton-battle-monument, March 3, 2017. Subsequent quotations are to the same source.

26. A companion project in the South—a Confederate monument that Borglum began on Stone Mountain in northern Georgia in 1923—was halted in 1928 for lack of money. It was finally completed in 1970. Vermeule, *Numismatic Art in America*, 157–59. On the sculpture in South Dakota, see Susan Grove Hall with Dennis Hall, "Mount Rushmore," *American Icons: An Encyclopedia of the People, Places, and Things that Have Shaped Our Culture*, ed. the same, vol. II (Westport, CT: Greenwood P, 2006), 493–500.

27. "Patriarchy Fixed in Stone" is the title Boime chose for the Mount Rushmore chapter in his *The Unveiling of the National Icons*.

28. *Ibid.*, 153.

29. Boime, *The Unveiling of the National Icons*, 175–79. For Borglum's November 1930 description of the monument's scale as truly "soul-stirring," see *ibid.*, 137. On Borglum's association with the Ku Klux Klan, see Jesse Larner, *Mount Rushmore: An Icon Reconsidered* (New York: Thunder's Mouth Press / Nation Books, 2002), 187–231.

30. Cass Gilbert, qtd. in Cannadine, "The Context, Performance and Meaning of Ritual," 127n.

31. Vermeule, *Numismatic Art in America*, 224–25.

32. Boime, *The Unveiling of the National Icons*, 151; for "national shrine," see *ibid.*, 136.

33. See Jeff Smith, *The Presidents We Imagine*, 115–16.

34. John Ward Dunsmore, Henry A. Ogden, Percy Morgan, and Howard Pyle are among the other prominent painter-illustrators who contributed to the series. Barbara J. Mitnick, "Paintings for the People: American Popular History Painting, 1875–1930,"

in *Picturing History: American Painting 1770–1930*, ed. William Ayres (New York: Rizzoli International, 1993), 137–76.

35. Mitnick, ed., *American Symbol* 20, color plate 22; for an illustration of Schmolze's painting, in the possession of the Pennsylvania Academy of Fine Arts, Philadelphia, see Marling, *Washington Slept Here*, 10, Fig. 1.12. For "commemorative period," see Thistlethwaite, *The Image of George Washington*, 6. For Washington's own record of the sitting, see above, Chap.7.

36. Qtd. in Schwartz, *American Symbol*, 197; for "grand dukes of debunkery," see Lengel, *Inventing George Washington*, 68. It is also a matter of record that the values ascribed to Washington after 1945 often borrowed from those typically associated with Lincoln, "compassion for wounded soldiers and hatred of racial and religious bigotry." Casper, "The Washington Image," 606.

37. Schwartz, *American Symbol*, 198.

38. Vermeule, *Numismatic Art in America*, 164.

39. For details of some of the more outrageous activities of the Bicentennial see Marling, *Washington Slept Here*, chap. 11, 325–64. For a complete record of the bicentennial activities see the five-volume history edited by the United States George Washington Bicentennial Commission.

40. *Special News Releases*, qtd. in Marling, *Washington Slept Here*, 337.

41. Marling, *Washington Slept Here*, 337–41. Houdon's bust originally stood in Washington's mansion at Mount Vernon. A copy created in 1932 is in the Indiana Statehouse in Indianapolis.

42. See Vermeule, *Numismatic Art in America*, 165–69.

43. Vermeule, *Numismatic Art in America*, 165.

44. Other stamps of the set bore renderings by Charles Wilson Peale, Saint-Memin, Trumbull, and Houdon. The 1932 red two-cent stamp was, for its date, the most widely circulated stamp ever printed. Later in the year it became a three-cent issue when postal rates rose. Skaggs, "Postage Stamps as Icons," *Icons of America*, ed. Ray B. Browne and Marshall W. Fishwick (Bowling Green, OH: Bowling Green State University Popular P, 1978), 198–208.

45. Marling, *Washington Slept Here*, 343.

Part V

1. Grant Wood, qtd. in Thistlethwaite, "Hero, Celebrity, and Cliché," 143, emphasis added. I have also drawn from Marling, *Washington Slept Here*, 335–36 and 345–46.

Chapter 12

1. View the image at *Saturday Evening Post*, "Artists Gallery," https://www.saturdayeveningpost.com/issues/1935-02-23/.

2. Weems, *Life of Washington*, 181–82.

3. Marling, *Washington Slept Here*, 1–8, which also lists other, sometimes bizarre, forms of the prayer image. For Friberg's *The Prayer at Valley Forge*, go to Friberg Fine Art at https://www.fribergfineart.com, where framed lithographs (image size 8 x 13 in.) are sold for $59.95 a piece. For the films, see Bolam and Bolam, *The Presidents on Film*, 12, 13, 15, 19. For Quinley's novel, see John R. Frey, "George Washington in American Fiction," *Virginia Magazine of History and Biography* 55:4 (October 1947), 342–49, here 343. For the Valley Forge plays, see Shirk, *George Washington in American Plays Since 1875*, 39–43, 123, 126, and 130. For *Tales of the Revolution, Washington and His Men*, and *Blanche of Brandywine*, see Bryan, *Washington in American Literature*, 209, 219, and 183–84.

4. Bolam and Bolam, *The Presidents on Film*, 25.

5. Franklin D. Roosevelt, "Inaugural Address," March 4, 1933, online by Gerhard Peters and John T. Woolley, *The American Presidency Project*, http://www.presidency.ucsb.edu/ws/?pid=14473, retrieved September 21, 2017.

6. The term "fireside chat" was first used by Robert Trout of the CBS's Washington station, who introduced Roosevelt on the occasion of his first radio address. At ten o'clock on the evening of March 12, 1933, Trout told sixty million people, seated before twenty million radios, that "the President wants to come into your home and sit at your fireside for a little fireside chat." Kenneth S. Davis, *FDR: The New Deal Years, 1933–1937* (New York: Random House, 1986), 60. To listen to the "fireside chats," go to the University of Virginia's Miller Center, https://millercenter.org/the-presidency/presidential-speeches/march-12-1933-fireside-chat-1-banking-crisis, last accessed December 16, 2018.

7. Griswold, *Fatherhood in America*, 143–44.

8. *American Home* qtd. in Samuel, *American Fatherhood*, 13.

9. Bolam and Bolam, *The Presidents on Film*, 25–26.

10. Whit Ridgway, "George Washington and the Constitution," *A Companion to George Washington*, ed. Edward G. Lengel (Malden, MA: Wiley-Blackwell, 2012), 413–29 here 413–14.

11. Griswold, *Fatherhood in America*, 161.

12. Admiral Thomas C. Hart, qtd. in Casper, "The Washington Image," 606.

13. Qtd. in Marling, *Washington Slept Here*, 376–77; for the Eisenhower quotation, see *ibid.*, 376.

14. "The Man Who Stole the Sun," *Superman*, vol.1, #48, September 1947, DC Database, http://dc.wikia.com/wiki/Superman_Vol_1_48, last accessed September 11, 2018.

15. Shirk, *Washington in American Plays Since 1875*, 77–81, quotation 80.

16. Howard Fast, *The Unvanquished* (New York: Duell, Sloan and Pearce, 1942), 313; for "…new beginnings," see *ibid.*, 312.

17. *Ibid.*, 313–14.

18. Both Dixon Wecter's *The Hero in America* and Gerald Johnson's *American Heroes and Hero-Worship* were published in 1941.

19. Durkheim, *The Elementary Forms of the Religious Life*, 420.

20. Bolam and Bolam, *The Presidents on Film*, 27–28. For the number of commemorative activities in 1932, see Bodnar, *Remaking America*, 174.

21. Jeff Smith, *The Presidents We Imagine*, 188–90.

22. Fishwick, "Did Anyone Ever See Washington Nude?" 305.

23. Jeff Smith, *The Presidents We Imagine*, 190.

24. *Boston Herald*, February 22, 1944, qtd. in Bryan, *Washington in American Literature*, 242.

25. Cunliffe, *George Washington*, 160.

26. Wood, "The Greatness of George Washington," in *George Washington Reconsidered*, ed. Don Higginbotham (Charlottesville: UP of Virginia, 2001), 309–24. 312; the essay originally appeared in the *Virginia Quarterly Review* of 1992.

27. On the transformations, in the 1960s and 1970s, of the cultural landscape on which American manhood was played out, see Michael S. Kimmel, *Manhood in America: A Cultural History* [1996], 3rd edn. (New York: Oxford UP, 2012), 263–71.

28. Casper, "The Washington Image," 608, and Dorothy Twohig, "'That Species of Property': Washington's Role in the Controversy over Slavery," *George Washington Reconsidered*, ed. Don Higginbotham (Charlottesville: UP of Virginia, 2001), 115–32.

29. See, in this connection, James W. Loewen, *Lies My Teacher Told Me: Everything Your American History Textbook Got Wrong* (1995; New York: Simon & Schuster, 2007), 288–89.

30. Washington, qtd. in Susan Dunn, "Slaves in the White House," *The New York Review of Books* LXIV, number 8 (May 11, 2017), 55–57, here 55.

31. Schwartz, *American Symbol*, 203 and Fig. 43. For the Lichtenstein painting, see Thistlethwaite, "Hero, Celebrity, and Cliché," 149–50; for Larry Rivers, see Marling, *Washington Slept Here*, 379 and, for a full-color image, Mitnick, ed., *American Symbol*, 22, color plate 28.

32. Thistlethwaite, "Hero, Celebrity, and Cliché," 147–48.

33. Trevor Noah, *The Donald J. Trump Presidential Twitter Library* (New York: Spiegel & Grau, 2018), 295. Among the people depicted are Vice President Mike Pence, Chief of Staff John Kelly, Jeff Sessions, Jared Kushner, Kellyanne Conway, and, not to forget, Trump's daughter Ivanka. I'm grateful to Stefan "Steve" Rabitsch for alerting me to the book.

34. Thistlethwaite, "Hero, Celebrity, and Cliché," 149. The sculpture is owned by the Stedelijk Museum, Amsterdam; to view an illustration, go to https://www.stedelijk.nl/en/collection/64-robert-arneson-george-and-mona-in-the-baths-of-coloma, last accessed June 7, 2018. On Peter Saul's painting, see Thistlethwaite, "Hero, Celebrity, and Cliché," 146–47. On Arneson's *Pinot noir*, see Clark, "An Icon Preserved," 51 and, for a full-color illustration, Mitnick, ed., *American Symbol*, 22, plate 27.

35. Frank Moore, *Diary of the American Revolution* (New York: Charles Scribner, 1860), 2:492, qtd. in Miller and Schwartz, "The Icon of the American Republic," 533.

36. Fishwick, "Did Anyone Ever See Washington Nude?" 306.

37. Thistlethwaite, "Hero, Celebrity, and Cliché," 148.

38. Guy Debord and Gil J. Wolman, "A User's Guide to Détournement [1956]," trans. Ken Knabb, *Bureau of Public Secrets*, 2006, http://www.bopsecrets.org/SI/detourn.htm#1, January 15, 2018, and Stefan Hartmann, "Faites vos jeux: subversive Banknoten-Fakes," *Der schöne Schein. Symbolik und Ästhetik von Banknoten*, ed. Stefan Hartmann und Christian Thiel (Regenstauf, Germany: Gietl-Verlag, 2016), 245–76.

39. Sidra Stich, *Made in U.S.A.: An Americanization in Modern Art, the 50s and 60s* (Berkeley: U of California P, 1987), 40, and Klaus Lubbers, "*The Virgin's Seed*: A Note on Intercultural Perspectives in American Art," *Intercultural America*, ed. Alfred Hornung (Heidelberg: Winter, 2007), 257–83, here 266–67, here 264.

40. Get the sticker from Santa Fe Hemp at $2.50 a piece. Santa Fe Hemp, http://www.santafehemp.com/products/i-grew-hemp-sticker. Also available are rubber stamps (priced at $6.95 a piece) that make Washington say, "I grew hemp."

41. See, for an illustration and further description, Barry Schwartz, "'Collective Memory and Abortive Commemoration: Presidents' Day and the American Holiday Calendar," *Social Research* 75.1 (2008), 75–110, here 97–98.

42. Thomas Pynchon, *Mason & Dixon* (New York: Henry Holt, 1997), 280.

43. For an illustration, see Fishwick, "Did Anyone Ever See Washington Nude?" 304.

44. A John Armstrong, who described the preparations for Washington's reception to Horatio Gates, thought the caricature demonstrates "that wit spares nothing—neither Washington nor God—and that the former like the latter will have something to suffer and much to forgive." Cunningham, *Popular Images of the Presidency*, 180.

45. Barry Schwartz, *George Washington: The Making of an American Symbol* (New York: Free P, 1987), 199.

46. Americans find humor in other cartoons, too. A preliminary search at CartoonStock.com, for instance, yielded 1,568 results; also useful is Sandra Czernek, "Political Cartoons and Comic Strips," *The American President in Popular Culture*, ed. John W. Matviko (Westport, CT—London: Greenwood P, 2005), 141–54.

47. Marling, *Washington Slept Here*, viii.

48. Thomas Lask, qtd. in Lengel, *Inventing George Washington*, 178.

49. James Thomas Flexner, *Maverick's Progress: An Autobiography* (New York: Fordham UP, 1996), 483.

50. Lengel, *Inventing George Washington*, 181.

51. Flexner, qtd. *ibid.*

52. Lengel, *Inventing George Washington*, 188 and, for the full story, 182–88.

53. Bryant, *I Cannot Tell a Lie*, xii, qtd. *ibid.*, 190.

54. "All the Presidents' Girls" refers to a series of paintings the British pop artist Annie Kevans exhibited in New York City's Volta gallery in 2009. The series included Sally Fairfax and, predictably, Venus. *Ibid.*, 192.

55. Bruce Wilson calls the Washington Prayer "a bastardized version of text excerpted from the end of Washington's Circular Letter and then substantially altered." Wilson, "How Fake American History Feeds Christian Nationalism," *Talk2action. org*, January 5, 2008, http://www.talk2action.org/story/2008/1/5/155457/0298, August 11, 2017.

56. Michele Bachmann, qd. in Chris Rodda, "Bachmann Uses Fake George Washington Prayer to Bash Obama," *Huffpost*, June 3, 2009, updated December 6, 2017, https://www.huffingtonpost.com/chris-rodda/bachmann-uses-fake-george_b_194960.html, retriecved January 16, 2018.

57. Kahler, *The Long Farewell*, Chap. 3, 55–72.

58. David Domke and Kevion Coe, *The God Strategy: How Religion Became a Political Weapon in America* (New York: Oxford UP, 2007, updated edn. 2010).

59. U.S. Treasury Bureau of Engraving and Printing (USBEP), "FAQs," n.d., https://www.moneyfactory.gov/resources/faqs.html, January 16, 2018. See a. Tschachler, *The Greenback*, 189–91 and, on the origin and history of the motto, 54–55.

60. Wilbur Brucker, qd. in Lengel, *Inventing George Washington*, 88.

61. Fishwick, "Did Anyone Ever See Washington Nude?" 307.

62. "Time Is On My Side," *Time Masters*, 1, #4 (May 1990), web document, http://dc.wikia.com/wiki/Time_Masters_Vol_1_4. Thank you, "Steve" Rabitsch, for drawing my attention to this.

63. Irving Kristol, qtd. in Marling, *Washington Slept Here*, 388. For "could not decently be ignored," see *ibid*., 385.

64. I list several of these events in this chapter, below.

65. Family Research Council, qtd. in Lengel, *Inventing George Washington*, 86. On the FRC, see a. Daniel J. B. Hofrenning, "Religious Lobbying and American Politics," *In God We Trust? Religion and American Political Life*, ed. Corwin E. Smidt (Grand Rapids, MI: Baker Acad., 2001), 118–41, quot. 125.

66. Griswold, *Fatherhood in America*, 259.

67. Richard Klein, "Why Washington is 'The Father of our Country,'" The Christian Broadcasting Network, n.d., http://www1.cbn.com/churchandministry/why-washington-is-%22the-father-of-our-country%22, March 21, 2016.

68. Go to www1.cbn.com. On Colson's career, see Lengel, *Inventing George Washington*, 86.

69. William J. Bennett, *Our Sacred Honor: Words of Advice from the Founders in Stories, Letters, Poems, and Speeches* (New York: Simon & Schuster, 1997.

70. *Deseret News*, "Firearms are Vital for Society" (April 25, 1994) and "About us" (2017), respectively http://www.deseretnews.com/article/349243/FIREARMS-ARE-VITAL-FOR-SOCIETY.html?pg=all and http://www.deseretnews.com/about-us#about, August 13, 2017. William James, *The Constitution and What It Means* (Bloomington, IN: iUniverse, 2012), 155. I have also drawn in this paragraph on Steve Randall, "George Washington on Guns … According to Sean Hannity," *FAIR*, January 9, 2013, http://fair.org/home/george-washington-on-guns-according-to-sean-hannity/, August 13, 2017.

71. Washington, "First Annual Message to Congress," January 8, 1790, *WWR*, 748–51, quotation 749.

72. Charles C. Haynes, "What part of 'secular nation' do we not understand?" *First Amendment Center*, September 16, 2007, http://www.firstamendmentcenter.org/what-part-of-'secular-nation'-do-we-not-understand/, January 16, 2018; see a. Lengel, *Inventing George Washington*, 72–105, and Bruce Wilson, "How Fake American History Feeds Christian Nationalism," web document.

73. Lengel, *Inventing George Washington*, 195–96. For Semkiw's IISIS, go to http://www.iisis.net/index.php?page=reincarnation-deepak-chopra-kevin-ryerson-walter-semkiw, last accessed August 13, 2017.

74. *Ibid*., 198–200.

75. *Ibid*., 200.

76. As the colonial historian Michael Kammen argues, American novelists, artists, poets, journalists, and politicians have consistently de-Revolutionized the Revolution Washington led. *A Season of Youth: The American Revolution and the Historical Imagination* (New York: Knopf, 1978), 214–15 and passim.

77. Vitaly Komar and Alex Melamid, "Washington Lives! 1799–1999," *ArtForum International* 33:5 (1995), 74–75, qtd. in Casper, "Washington's Image," 608–609. For an illustration of *Washington Lives II*, see Mitnick, ed., *American Symbol*, 23, plate 30.

78. See Frame, *The American President in Film and Television*, 67–68.

79. For more information, visit http://1776themusical.us.

80. Decker, "Paintings and Sculptures," 26–28.

81. ThisNation.com, "Why is George Washington considered the Father of this nation?" N.d., http://www.thisnation.com/question/017.html, retrieved March 21, 2016.

82. George Washington, letter to Henry Lee, September 22, 1788, *Founders Online*, National Archives, last modified June 13, 2018, http://founders.archives.gov/documents/Washington/04-06-02-0469, quoted in somewhat different form in ThisNation.com, "Why is George Washington considered the Father of this nation?"

83. In a book on "why aren't there any great presidents anymore?" Aaron David Miller, *The End of Greatness: Why America Can't Have (and Doesn't Want) Another Great President* (New York: Palgrave Macmillan, 2014), 25–34.

84. Perry, "The Presidency: What Makes a Great President?" C-SPAN3, Sunday, April 9, 2017, 8pm, https://www.c-span.org/video/?423970-1/makes-great-president, accessed May 15, 2017.

85. C-SPAN, "Presidential Historians Survey 2017," February 19, 2017, https://www.c-span.org/presidentsurvey2017/, retrieved February 20, 2017; and see Lamb et al., *The Presidents*.

86. Faber and Faber, *The American Presidents Ranked by Performance*, 1–3.

87. Polling Report, Inc., "Presidents and History," 2017, http://www.pollingreport.com/wh-hstry.htm,

retrieved February 26, 2017 (Lincoln was ranked first, Washington fifth). For the 1945 survey, see Faber and Faber, *The American Presidents Ranked by Performance*, 3.

88. *Ibid.*, 4 and, for the critique of presentism, Thomas A. Bailey, *Presidential Greatness: The Image and the Man from George Washington to the Present* (New York: Appleton-Century, 1966), 21. The actual popularity of the presidents is reflected in the breakdown of their appearances in film. Of the 407 films studied by the Bolams, Lincoln leads with 123, followed by Washington with 52, and Franklin Roosevelt with 35. *The Presidents on Film*, 7.

89. Polling Report, Inc., "Presidents and History," web document.

90. Faber and Faber, *The American Presidents Ranked by Performance*, 32. In the second edn. of the book, Reagan is down one place, at 35.

91. Daniel Gilbert and Timothy D. Wilson, "Miswanting: Some Problems in the Forecasting of Future Affective States," in *The Construction of Preference*, ed. Sarah Lichtenstein and Paul Slovic (Cambridge: Cambridge UP, 2006), 550–63. For "predictably irrational," see Dan Ariely's eponymous book (rev. and exp. edn. New York: Harper, 2010). On the decline in Washington's relevance to Americans, see Schwartz, *Abraham Lincoln in the Post-Heroic Era: History and Memory in Late Twentieth-Century America* (Chicago: U of Chicago P, 2008), 148, and Casper, "The Washington Image," 607. On the problematics of polls and presidential rankings, see respectively, Jon R. Bond and Richard Fleisher, "The Polls: Partisanship and Presidential Performance Evaluations," *Presidential Studies Quarterly* 31:3 (2001), 529–40, and Curt Nichols, "The Presidential Ranking Game," *Presidential Studies Quarterly* 42:2 (2012), 275–99. For a brief history of Presidential rankings, see Douglas Brinkley, in Lamb et al., *The Presidents*, 10–17.

92. Faber and Faber, *The American Presidents Ranked by Performance*, 6–7 and, in detail, 9–32; in the second edn. of 2012, "Presidential Comportment" was substituted for "Personal" Qualities (28–31). Likewise in the second edn., President Obama was tentatively (by the time book went to press, he had completed only 3 years of his first term) ranked 16th (266–75).

93. *Ibid.*, respectively 23, 26, 12, and 29.

94. James Rees, with Stephen Spignesi, *George Washington's Leadership Lessons* (Hoboken, NJ: Wiley, 2007). For the Fabers' account, see *The American Presidents Ranked by Performance*, 27–29 and 37–38.

95. Faber and Faber, *The American Presidents Ranked by Performance*, 31. Overall, George Washington received 77 points out of a maximum 100 (Lincoln received 78); in the 2nd edn., Washington's 78 points leave him two points behind Lincoln, who received 80 (*ibid.*, 33).

96. Robert G. Denton, *The Symbolic Dimensions of the American Presidency* (Prospect Heights: Waveland P, 1982), 46.

97. Faber and Faber, *The American Presidents Ranked by Performance*, 4.

98. Bailey, *Presidential Greatness*, 262, 267, emphasis added.

99. Wood, "The Inventor of the Presidency," *The New York Review of Books* LXIV (May 25, 2017), 34–37, quot. 34 and, similarly, "The Greatness of George Washington," 310: If polls of historians "are to be taken seriously, then Washington fully deserved the first place he has traditionally held."

Chapter 13

1. For an overview of scholarship see Don Higginbotham's introduction to *Washington Reconsidered*, 1–12.

2. Brookhiser, *Founding Father*, 12.

3. *Ibid.*, 13.

4. Higginbotham, Afterword to *Washington Reconsidered*, 328.

5. Higginbotham, *Washington Reconsidered*, 326–29. A roster of the several large exhibitions during the decade of the bicentennial includes *George Washington: American Symbol* (Museum of Stony Brook, Long Island; and Museum of Our National Heritage, Lexington, Massachusetts); *The Great Experiment: George Washington and the American Republic* (Huntington Library, Los Angeles; and Morgan Library, New York City); *"His True and Impressive Image": Portraits of George Washington* (Mead Art Museum, Amherst, Massachusetts); *The Power and the Glory: George Washington and the Birth of Fame in America* (New-York Historical Society, New York City); *Treasures from Mount Vernon: The Man behind the Legend* (New-York Historical Society, New York City; Huntington Library, Los Angeles; Virginia Historical Society, Richmond; Atlanta Historical Society; and Chicago Historical Society); *Washington in Glory: America in Tears* (Fraunces Tavern Museum, New York City); *George Washington: The Man Behind the Myths* (Washington and Lee University, Lexington, Virginia).

6. Raymond Williams, *Marxism and Literature* (Oxford: Oxford UP, 1977), 132; Edmund S. Morgan, "Mr. W. on Show," *The New York Review of Books* (March 4, 1999), 23–25, here 24.

7. Schwartz, *Abraham Lincoln in the Post-Heroic Era*, xi.

8. J. S. Wolfe, qtd. in Wilbur Zelinsky, *Nation into State: The Shifting Symbolic Foundations of American Nationalism* (Chapel Hill: U of North Carolina P, 1988), 79.

9. Campbell and Jamieson, *Presidents Creating the Presidency*, 12, 13.

10. Zelinsky, *Nation into State*, 79.

11. James Madison, "Inaugural Address," March 4, 1809, online by Gerhard Peters and John T. Woolley, *The American Presidency Project*, http://www.presidency.ucsb.edu/ws/?pid=25805. For context, argument, and effect, see James Martin, *Politics and Rhetoric* (London-New York: Routledge, 2014), 52–57 and 100–102.

12. Martin Van Buren, "Inaugural Address," March 4, 1837, online by Gerhard Peters and John

T. Woolley, *The American Presidency Project*, http://www.presidency.ucsb.edu/ws/?pid=25812.

13. James K. Polk, "Inaugural Address," March 4, 1845 online by Gerhard Peters and John T. Woolley, *The American Presidency Project*, http://www.presidency.ucsb.edu/ws/?pid=25814.

14. Zachary Taylor, "Inaugural Address," March 5, 1849, online by Gerhard Peters and John T. Woolley, *The American Presidency Project*, http://www.presidency.ucsb.edu/ws/?pid=25815, emphases added.

15. Taylor qtd. in Butter, *Der "Washington-Code,"* 88.

16. Franklin Pierce, "Inaugural Address," March 4, 1853, online by Gerhard Peters and John T. Woolley, *The American Presidency Project*, http://www.presidency.ucsb.edu/ws/?pid=25816.

17. James Buchanan, "Inaugural Address," March 4, 1857, online by Gerhard Peters and John T. Woolley, *The American Presidency Project*, http://www.presidency.ucsb.edu/ws/?pid=25817. In his speech, Buchanan also alluded to a pending Supreme Court case, *Dred Scott v. Sandford*, the outcome of which he already knew as he had managed to win over at least three justices. Jean H. Baker, *James Buchanan* (New York: Times Books, 2004), 80–85; for Buchanan's Fourth Annual Message to Congress, see *The American Presidency Project*, http://www.presidency.ucsb.edu/ws/?pid=29501, retrieved November 14, 2017.

18. Bryan, *Washington in American Literature*, 82.

19. Rutherford B. Hayes, "Inaugural Address," March 5, 1877, online by Gerhard Peters and John T. Woolley, *The American Presidency Project*, http://www.presidency.ucsb.edu/ws/?pid=25822.

20. James A. Garfield, "Inaugural Address," March 4, 1881, online by Gerhard Peters and John T. Woolley, *The American Presidency Project*, http://www.presidency.ucsb.edu/ws/?pid=25823.

21. Grover Cleveland, "Inaugural Address," March 4, 1885, online by Gerhard Peters and John T. Woolley, *The American Presidency Project*, http://www.presidency.ucsb.edu/ws/?pid=25824.

22. Benjamin Harrison, "Inaugural Address," March 4, 1889, online by Gerhard Peters and John T. Woolley, *The American Presidency Project*, http://www.presidency.ucsb.edu/ws/?pid=25825.

23. Grover Cleveland, "Inaugural Address," March 4, 1893, online by Gerhard Peters and John T. Woolley, *The American Presidency Project*, http://www.presidency.ucsb.edu/ws/?pid=25826.

24. William McKinley, "Inaugural Address," March 4, 1897, online by Gerhard Peters and John T. Woolley, *The American Presidency Project*, http://www.presidency.ucsb.edu/ws/?pid=25827.

25. William McKinley, "Inaugural Address," March 4, 1901, online by Gerhard Peters and John T. Woolley, *The American Presidency Project*, http://www.presidency.ucsb.edu/ws/?pid=25828.

26. Theodore Roosevelt, "Inaugural Address," March 4, 1905, online by Gerhard Peters and John T. Woolley, *The American Presidency Project*, http://www.presidency.ucsb.edu/ws/?pid=25829. The standard history of Roosevelt's domestic and foreign policy is Lewis L. Gould's *The Presidency of Theodore Roosevelt*, second edn. (Lawrence: UP of Kansas, 2011).

27. Warren G. Harding, "Inaugural Address," March 4, 1921, online by Gerhard Peters and John T. Woolley, *The American Presidency Project*, http://www.presidency.ucsb.edu/ws/?pid=25833. For the "Return to Normalcy" speech, delivered in Boston, MA, on May 14, 1920, go to *TeachingAmericanHistory.org*, n.d., http://teachingamericanhistory.org/library/document/return-to-normalcy/, November 15, 2017.

28. On Harding's dealings with the League of Nations, see Eugene P. Trani and David L. Wilson, *The Presidency of Warren G. Harding* (Lawrence: UP of Kansas, 1977), 142–47.

29. Calvin Coolidge, "Address to the American Society of Newspaper Editors, Washington, D.C.," January 17, 1925, online by Gerhard Peters and John T. Woolley, *The American Presidency Project*, http://www.presidency.ucsb.edu/ws/?pid=24180, June 6, 2018.

30. Franklin D. Roosevelt, "Inaugural Address," March 4, 1933, web document.

31. Franklin D. Roosevelt, "Second Inaugural Address," January 20, 1937, online by Gerhard Peters and John T. Woolley, *The American Presidency Project*, http://www.presidency.ucsb.edu/ws/?pid=15349.

32. Franklin D. Roosevelt, "Third Inaugural Address," January 20, 1941, online by Gerhard Peters and John T. Woolley, *The American Presidency Project*, http://www.presidency.ucsb.edu/ws/?pid=16022.

33. Jimmy Carter, "Inaugural Address," January 20, 1977, online by Gerhard Peters and John T. Woolley, *The American Presidency Project*, http://www.presidency.ucsb.edu/ws/index.php?pid=6575.

34. Dwight D. Eisenhower, "Inaugural Address," January 20, 1953, online by Gerhard Peters and John T. Woolley, *The American Presidency Project*, http://www.presidency.ucsb.edu/ws/?pid=9600.

35. On critiques of the father since the 1950s, see Blankenhorn, *Fatherless America*, 57–58, 86–88.

36. "William Faulkner—Banquet Speech," *Nobelprize.org*, 1950, http://www.nobelprize.org/nobel_prizes/literature/laureates/1949/faulkner-speech.html, August 9, 2017. For "idolized" George Washington, see Richard Norton Smith, *Life Portrait of George Washington*, https://www.c-span.org/video/?121783-1/president-life-portraits-series, last accessed February 12, 2018.

37. Dwight D. Eisenhower, "Second Inaugural Address," January 21, 1957, online by Gerhard Peters and John T. Woolley, *The American Presidency Project*, http://www.presidency.ucsb.edu/ws/?pid=10856.

38. John Thomas, "George Washington," 201.

39. John F. Kennedy, "Inaugural Address," January 20, 1961, online by Gerhard Peters and John T. Woolley, *The American Presidency Project*, http://www.presidency.ucsb.edu/ws/?pid=8032.

40. Lyndon B. Johnson, "The President's Inaugural Address," January 20, 1965, online by Gerhard Peters and John T. Woolley, *The American Presidency Project*, http://www.presidency.ucsb.edu/ws/?pid=26985.

41. Richard Nixon, "Inaugural Address," January

20, 1969, online by Gerhard Peters and John T. Woolley, *The American Presidency Project*, http://www.presidency.ucsb.edu/ws/index.php?pid=4141.

42. Richard Nixon, "Oath of Office and Second Inaugural Address," January 20, 1973, online by Gerhard Peters and John T. Woolley, *The American Presidency Project*, http://www.presidency.ucsb.edu/ws/?pid=4141.

43. Ronald Reagan, "Inaugural Address," January 20, 1981, *Ronald Reagan Presidential Library*, n.d., https://reaganlibrary.archives.gov/archives/speeches/1981/12081a.htm, January 30, 2017.

44. Ronald Reagan, "Remarks at a White House Ceremony in Observance of National Day of Prayer," May 6, 1982, *Ronald Reagan Presidential Library*, n.d., https://www.reaganlibrary.archives.gov/archives/speeches/1982/50682c.htm, August 10, 2017.

45. Ronald Reagan, "Inaugural Address," January 21, 1985, *Ronald Reagan Presidential Library*, n.d., https://www.reaganlibrary.archives.gov/archives/speeches/1985/12185a.htm, January 30, 2017. See a. Jan Hanska, *Reagan's Mythical America: Storytelling as Political Leadership* (New York: Palgrave Macmillan, 2012), esp. chap. 4.

46. George H. W. Bush, "Inaugural Address, January 20, 1989," online by Gerhard Peters and John T. Woolley, *The American Presidency Project*, http://www.presidency.ucsb.edu/ws/?pid=16610, emphasis added.

47. William J. Clinton, "Inaugural Address," January 20, 1993, online by Gerhard Peters and John T. Woolley, *The American Presidency Project*, http://www.presidency.ucsb.edu/ws/?pid=46366.

48. William J. Clinton, "Inaugural Address," January 20, 1997, online by Gerhard Peters and John T. Woolley, *The American Presidency Project*, http://www.presidency.ucsb.edu/ws/index.php?pid=54183.

49. Barack Obama, "Inaugural Address," January 20, 2009.

50. Lengel, *Inventing George Washington*, 102–105.

51. Family Research Council, "George Washington Takes the Oath: 'So Help Me God,'" April 30, 2014, http://www.frcblog.com/2014/04/george-washington-takes-oath-so-help-me-god-april-30-1789/, August 10, 2017. For U.S. Presidents from Carter through George W. Bush wearing God on their sleeves, see Jeff Walz, "Religion and the American Presidency," *In God We Trust? Religion and American Political Life*, ed. Corwin E. Smidt (Grand Rapids, MI: Baker Acad., 2001), 191–212.

52. William H. Wilbur, *The Making of George Washington* (1970; 3rd edn. Baltimore, MD: Patriotic Education, 2005), 17, 25.

53. Campbell and Jamieson, *Presidents Creating the Presidency*, 30–31. There are two additional functions to an inaugural address, to set forth the political principles that will guide the new administration, and to demonstrate that the new president appreciates the requirements and limitations of the executive functions. (*Ibid.*)

54. See Travers, "Washington, Lincoln, and Presidents' Day," *Encyclopedia of American Holidays and National Days*, vol.1 (Westport, CT: Greenwood P, 2006). Washington's birthday, Barry Schwartz found, also did not much arouse people even at the peak of Washington reverence in the 1850s. See *American Symbol*, 198.

55. Diana Pederson, "A Father's Importance," BellaOnline[SM], 2009, http://www.bellaonline.com/articles/art51420.asp, retrieved February 2, 2009.

56. See "Father's Day," *New World Encyclopedia*; January 12, 2009, http://www.newworldencyclopedia.org/entry/Father's_Day, last accessed February 8, 2009.

57. "TV Guide's '50 Greatest TV Dads of All Time,'" *TVWeek*, January 3, 2014, http://www.tvweek.com/in-depth/2014/01/tv-guides-50-greatest-tv-dads/, January 21, 2017. For Jimmy Carter's Father's Day speech, see "Carter Proclaims Father's Day," *The New York Times*, May 1, 1979, B8, qtd. in Samuel, *American Fatherhood*, 45.

58. George W. Bush, "Father's Day, 2001," *Whitehouse.gov*, n.d., http://georgewbush-whitehouse.archives.gov/news/releases/2001/06/20010615.html, June 15, 2001.

59. Philip Longman, "The Return of Patriarchy," *Foreign Policy* (October 20, 2009), 56–65, http://foreignpolicy.com/2009/10/20/the-return-of-patriarchy/#, February 7, 2018. I have also drawn in this paragraph on Griswold, *Fatherhood in America*, 249 and, on the "new father" as largely a middle-class phenomenon, *ibid.*, 252–54.

60. Leonard Benson, *Fatherhood: A Sociological Perspective* (New York: Random House, 1968), 12. Frank L. Mott, qtd. in Blankenhorn, *Fatherless America*, 71.

61. Blankenhorn, *Fatherless America*, 62 and, for further discussion and description of the "Unnecessary Father," 65–83.

62. Solnit, "From Lying to Leering," *London Review of Books* 39:2 (January 19, 2017), 3–7, http://www.lrb.co.uk/v39/n02/rebecca-solnit/from-lying-to-leering, retrieved January 29, 2017. Alan Abramowitz, too, in *The Great Alignment* argues that Trump won the 2016 election by exploiting the deep divisions in American society.

63. Robert P. Jones, "The Rage of White, Christian America," *The New York Times*, November 10, 2016, http://www.nytimes.com/2016/11/11/opinion/campaign-stops/the-rage-of-white-christian-america.html?_r=0, retrieved December 23, 2016. On the general tendency to idealize the family life of previous generations, see John R. Gillis, *A World of Their Own Making: Myth, Ritual, and the Quest for Family Values* (Cambridge: Harvard UP, 1997), 225–40.

64. Schwartz, *American Symbol*, 198.

65. Frances Davis Whittemore, *George Washington in Sculpture* (Boston: Marshall Jones, 1933).

66. See, for instance, the cover for Heinz Tschachler, *The Greenback: Paper Money and American Culture*, at https://mcfarlandbooks.com/product/the-greenback/.

67. Marling, *Washington Slept Here*, 20–24. For discussions of the commercialization of the Washington image, see a. Robinson, "The Marketing of an Icon," and Ayres, "At Home with George."

68. Brookhiser, *Founding Father*, 193.

69. Thistlethwaite, "'Where Am I?': Tracking George Washington's Dollar Bill Image," Paper given to "Rethinking National Foundations: Using/Abusing History," American Comparative Literature Association Conference, Harvard University, March 17–20, 2016. To view the dollar bill boots, go to https://www.balenciaga.com/us/ankle-boot_cod114258011n.html#/us/women/shoes, last accessed March 15, 2018.

70. See Annegret Stalder, *Max Weber—Die Veralltäglichung des Charismas* (Norderstedt, Germany: GRIN Verlag, 2007), 9–11; for "trivialization," see Don Higginbotham's Afterword to *Washington Reconsidered*, 325.

71. "The Captioned Adventures of George Washington," LadyHistory, Tumblr, http://ladyhistory.tumblr.com/tagged/the%20captioned%20adventures%20of%20george%20washington, last accessed February 13, 2018.

72. Richard Lim, "Father of His Country," *George Washington Digital Encyclopedia*, George Washington's Mount Vernon, n.d., http://www.mountvernon.org/digital-encyclopedia/article/father-of-his-country/, March 21, 2016. For the George Washington Facebook site, go to https://www.facebook.com/President-George-Washington-12117978561/, last accessed February 3, 2018.

73. "The Garden of Eden," *BioShock Infinite*, BioShock Wiki, http://bioshock.wikia.com/wiki/Garden_of_New_Eden, accessed August 6, 2018; for "Motorized Patriots," see http://bioshock.wikia.com/wiki/Motorized_Patriot and https://youtu.be/GHlNyOc5iW8?t=11s, in which some of the game designers speak to the character's visual aesthetics. For a recording of gameplay, go to https://youtu.be/JgqQ2pQ7X-k?t=9m20s. My thanks to Stefan "Steve" Rabitsch for drawing my attention to this game.

74. Nice Peter & EpicLloyd, http://genius.com/Nice-peter-and-epiclloyd-george-washington-vs-william-wallace-lyrics, retrieved March 3, 2016. "Willy" of course refers to William Wallace, the subject, *inter alia*, of the 1995 film *Braveheart*. Wallace was a Scottish knight who became one of the main leaders during the Wars of Scottish Independence. After defeating the English at Stirling Bridge in 1297, he was himself defeated at Falkirk. Captured in 1305, he was handed over to the English King Edward I, who had him hanged, drawn, and quartered for high treason.

75. Audible Originals, *Presidents are People Too!* April 3, 2017, https://itunes.apple.com/at/podcast/presidents-are-people-too/id1168237590?l=en&mt=2&i=1000383759362, January 7, 2018.

76. "Be Washington: It's Your Turn to Lead," *MountVernon.Org*, February 2018, http://www.mountvernon.org/site/bewashington/?utm_source=facebook&utm_medium=social&utm_campaign=bewashington, January 7, 2018.

77. The phrase, used by Karal Ann Marling as a book title, most likely originated from the title of a play by George Kaufman and Moss Hart, produced at New York's Lyceum Theatre on October 18, 1940. Shirk, *George Washington in American Plays*, 129.

78. Brookhiser, *Founding Father*, 166.

79. Washington to Lieutenant Colonel Tench Tilghman, April 24, 1783, *Founders Online*, National Archives, http://founders.archives.gov/documents/Washington/99-01-02-11161, retrieved December 8, 2017; Circular to State Governments, June 14, 1783, in *WWR*, 518. In 1805, the "Millions yet unborn" reappeared on a memorial medal engraved by Thomas Webb and commissioned and distributed by the British merchant Daniel Ecclestone. In 1807 Ecclestone sent one of the medals to Thomas Jefferson, along with two others that he wished forwarded to Bushrod Washington, George Washington's nephew, and John Marshall, chief justice of the Supreme Court. The legend on the medal's reverse contains the phrase "INNUMERABLE MILLIONS YET UNBORN WILL VENERATE THE MEMORY OF THE MAN WHO OBTAINED THEIR COUNTRY'S FREEDOM." Ray Williams, "'He Is in Glory.' Washington medals commended the country's first official leader," *The Numismatist* 131:2 (February 2018), 67–68, quot. 68.

80. Brookhiser, *Founding Father*, 167.

81. Lengel, *Inventing George Washington*, ix; for "adopted political heirs," see Brookhiser, *Founding Father*, 168.

82. The "America, I am your father" likeness of Washington (originally created for May Fourth or Star Wars Day in 2017) was posted on Mount Vernon's Instagram on June 15, 2018, https://www.instagram.com/p/BkDfo1Ojl6_/?hl=en&taken-by=mount_vernon. For a picture of a George Washington meatloaf, go to Instagram, https://www.instagram.com/p/BeHfZvJFXAy/. For the story about the strands of Washington's hair, see the *New York Post* of February 18, 2018, https://nypost.com/2018/02/13/strands-of-george-washingtons-hair-found-in-book/, retrieved February 15, 2018. The "hair-raising" discovery was made at Union College's library in Schenectady in upstate New York. The strands of white hair had belonged to Elizabeth Schuyler, wife of Alexander Hamilton, who gave it to their third son, James A. Hamilton. Elizabeth Schuyler was the daughter of General Philip Schuyler, who served in the Revolutionary War.

83. For reenactments of the Delaware River crossing, see Bodnar, *Remaking America*, 238–43. On the Society of the Cincinnati donation, see Kahler, *The Long Farewell*, 116.

84. "Dream Big," *The Numismatist*, July 2016, 27. For the Americana Totem Pole, see Decker, "Paintings and Sculptures," 21–22. The story of the faithful representative is retold in Schwartz, *American Symbol*, 200.

85. Brookhiser, *Founding Father*, 161 and, on the subject of internalizing one's parents, *ibid.*, 193.

Epilogue

1. William Shakespeare, *The Merchant of Venice*, III: ii, *The Yale Shakespeare*, ed. Wilbur L. Cross and Tucker Brooke (New York: Barnes & Noble, 1993), 153–183, quot. 170.

2. In the Renaissance, portrait painting became "empirical," the art historian John Wyndham Pope-Hennessey wrote in *The Portrait in the Renaissance* (New York: Pantheon Books, 1966), 3.

3. Peter Parshall, "Imago controfacto. Images and Facts in the Northern Renaissance," *Art History* 19 (1993), 554–79.

4. Michael Baxandall, *Giotto and the Orators: Humanist Observers of Painting in Italy and the Discovery of Pictorial Composition; 1350–1450* (Oxford: Clarendon P, 1971), 172–76.

5. "[T]he very innermost essence of a man." Pavel Svinin, qtd. in Miller und Schwartz, "The Icon of the American Republic," 528.

6. Lavater was a contemporary and friend of Goethe's, whom he deeply influenced. His writings on physiognomy were translated into English during the author's lifetime (Lavater died in 1801). Egon Verheyen, "'The most exact representation of the Original': Remarks on Portraits of George Washington by Gilbert Stuart and Rembrandt Peale," *Retaining the Original: Multiple Originals, Copies, and Reproduction*, ed. Kathleen Preciado (Washington, DC: National Gallery of Art / Hanover, NH: UP of New England, 1989), 127–39, here 131 and, for further discussion, *The Faces of Physiognomy: Interdisciplinary Approaches to Johann Caspar Lavater*, ed. Ellis Shookman (Columbia, SC: Camden House, 1993).

7. "But we are cursed with the common, miserable representations of our Great Hero…" William Whitley, *Gilbert Stuart*, 180, qtd. in Miller und Schwartz, "The Icon of the American Republic," 525. Martha Washington, "true resemblance," qtd. in Chernow, *Washington*, 747.

8. William J. Hubard, "A National Standard for the Likeness of Washington," *Magazine of American History* 4 (1880), 83–108, quot. 85; John Marshall, qtd. in Gustavus A. Eisen, *Portraits of Washington*, 3 vols. (New York: Robert Hamilton, 1932), 1: xvii; John Neal, *Randolph: A Novel*, 1: 63.

9. Cunliffe, *George Washington*, 15. For "matchless Washington … next unto the Trinity," see Kaminski and McCaughan, eds., *A Great and Good Man*, 143–44.

10. Gustave de Beaumont, qtd. in Seymor Martin Lipset, *The First New Nation: The United States in Historical and Comparative Perspective* (New York: Basic Books, 1963), 19, italics in original.

11. John Adams, qtd. in John A. Schutz und Douglas Adair, eds., *The Spur of Fame: Dialogues of John Adams and Benjamin Rush, 1805–1813* (San Marino, CA: Huntington Library, 1966), 229.

12. John Quincy Adams, December 11, 1831, qtd. in Kammen, *Mystic Chords of Memory*, 19.

13. Langston, *With Reverence and Contempt*, passim.

14. Ralph Waldo Emerson ("I cannot keep my eyes off it"), qtd. in Miller und Schwartz, "The Icon of the American Republic," 539n12.

15. Walt Whitman in an editorial published in 1858, in *I Sit and Look Out: Editorials from the Brooklyn Daily Times*, ed. Emor Holloway and Vernolian Schwarz (New York: Columbia UP, 1932), 59.

16. Hubard, "A National Standard for the Likeness of Washington," 85.

17. "Every American considers it his sacred duty to have a likeness of Washington in his home, just as we have images of God's saints." Pavil Svinin, *Picturesque United States of America*, qtd. in Thistlethwaite, "The Face of the Nation," 38.

18. Mitnick, ed., *American Symbol*, 23, plate 29 and, on Wesselmann's as well as other modern and postmodern appropriations of the face of the nation, Thistlethwaite, "Hero, Celebrity, and Cliché," 141–52.

19. Bolam and Bolam, *The Presidents on Film*, 271–72.

20. Wakoski, *Emerald Ice*, 44–48, quotation 46.

21. On Wakoski's "conservatism," see Gary Lenhart's review of *Emerald Ice* in *The American Book Review* 12:4 (September-October, 1990), 16–26, and, as well, Carole Ferrier, "Sexual Politics in Diane Wakoski's Poetry," *Hecate* 1:1 (July 1975), 89–94.

22. Reference to William Carlos Williams is to the central chapter in his collection of essays, *In the American Grain*, qtd. in Marling, *Washington Slept Here*, 295. On the ERA, see Sarah Slavin, *The Equal Rights Amendment: The Politics and Process of Ratification of the 27th Amendment to the Constitution* (New York: Haworth P, 1982) and, for the 1920s, Susan D. Becker, *The Origins of the Equal Rights Amendment: American Feminism between the Wars* (Westport, CT: Greenwood P, 1981).

23. For Frazer, see de Beauvoir, *The Second Sex*, trans. and ed. H. M. Parshley (London: New English Library, 1960), 331; for "magic male essence," "heavenly father," and "against all denial," see *ibid.*, 332. For Washington as "good for feeling," see Albanese, *Sons of the Fathers*, 144.

24. Gerbner, "Society's Storyteller: How TV Creates the Myths by Which We Live," *Media & Values* 40–41 (Los Angeles: Center for Media and Values, Summer/Fall 1987), 8–9, quot. 9.

25. Blankenhorn, *Fatherless America*, 1. On war-related father absences, see *ibid.*, 60, 253n51. Reference to Allen Ginsberg is to his poem "American Change," *Reality Sandwiches: 1953–1960* (1963; San Francisco: City Lights Books, 1976), 67–69.

26. Marche, "Manifesto of the New Fatherhood," *Esquire* (June 13, 2014), http://www.esquire.com/lifestyle/news/a28987/manifesto-of-the-new-fatherhood-0614/, retrieved November 28, 2017.

27. Blankenhorn, *Fatherless America*, 94.

28. Jack Schaefer, *Shane and Other Stories* (Harmondsworth: Penguin, 1980), 98.

29. *Ibid.*, 109.

30. Wini Breines, *Young, White, and Miserable: Growing Up Female in the Fifties* (1992; Chicago: U of Chicago P, 2001), 40.

31. Bernard Montgomery, *The Memoirs of Field-Marshal the Viscount Montgomery of Alamein* (London: Collins, 1958), 484.

32. "[A]ll the eggheads are for Stevenson, but how many eggheads are there?" John Alsop, qtd. in Martin Halliwell, *American Culture in the 1950s* (Edinburgh: Edinburgh UP, 2007), 21. On the election of

1952, see John Robert Greene, *I Like Ike* (Lawrence: UP of Kansas, 2017).

33. Daisy Bates, *The Long Shadow of Little Rock: A Memoir* (New York: David McKay, 1962).

34. The phrase "financial atheism" belongs to Jean-Joseph Goux, whose summary is pertinent: "As if an explicit affirmation of faith in God could somehow magically reverse the loss of convertibility to the unique presence of gold, the State uses this solemn motto to restore faith in the currency." *The Coiners of Language*, trans. Jennifer Curtiss Gage (Norman: U of Oklahoma P, 1994), 134.

35. The phrase "esoteric political theology" ("*esoterische Polittheologie*") is from Jochen Hörisch, *Kopf oder Zahl. Die Poesie des Geldes* (Frankfurt am Main: Suhrkamp, 1996), 76. For a discussion and analysis of interest in the dollar bill's "esoteric political theology," see Tschachler, *The Greenback*, 153–56.

36. Jeff Smith, *The Presidents We Imagine*, 217. John Huston made *Independence Day* specifically to celebrate the Bicentennial at Independence Hall, Philadelphia.

37. *Ibid.*, 219. A new brand of action heroes emerged in the aftermath of 9/11, including firefighters, police, and other rescue workers, and with them, came a rehabilitation of heroic manhood in the culture at large. Kimmel, *Manhood in America*, 249, and Ahu Tanrisever, *Fathers, Warriors, and Vigilantes: Post-Heroism and the U.S. Cultural Imaginary in the Twenty-First Century* (Heidelberg: Universitätsverlag Winter, 2016), 1–6.

38. Smith, *The Presidents We Imagine*, 219 and, for a discussion of similar films, 219–23.

39. John D. Thomas, "George Washington," 202. To watch the George Washington segment, which first went on air on Monday, March 15, 1999 and has since become the most popular in the series, go to https://www.c-span.org/video/?121783-1/president-life-portraits-series, last accessed February 12, 2018. C-SPAN at the time of the broadcast also invited people to become participants in their "Classroom" section on its website, which offered teachers' guides, classroom, and other materials.

40. Marling, *Washington Slept Here*, 23. "Whatsoproudlywehail.org" is a Washington, DC, based forum described as a "one-stop source for free, literary-based curricula to aid in the classroom instruction of American history, civics, social studies, and language arts." See https://www.whatsoproudlywehail.org; for Holmes's "Ode for Washington's Birthday," see *The Poetical Works of Oliver Wendell Holmes*, rev. and with a new introd. by Eleanor M. Tilton (Boston: Houghton Mifflin, 1975), 98, and https://www.whatsoproudlywehail.org/curriculum/the-american-calendar/ode-for-washingtons-birthday, retrieved January 30, 2018. On the power of symbolic acts to suspend the—increasingly common—"24/7" business week, see Amitai Etzioni, "Holidays and Rituals," *We Are What We Celebrate: Understanding Holidays and Rituals*, ed. the same and Jared Bloom (New York: New York UP, 2004), 3–40, here 3–15.

41. President Roosevelt used the phrase "unity of purpose" in his Annual Message to Congress (State of the Union Address) on January 6, 1941. Franklin D. Roosevelt Presidential Liberary and Museum, File No. 1353-A, "Message to Congress," January 6, 1941, http://www.fdrlibrary.marist.edu/_resources/images/msf/msf01407, retrieved January 6, 2019.

42. George Washington to John Adams, May 10, 1789, *WWR*, 738.

43. Wilentz, "They Were Bad. He May be Worse," *The New York Times Sunday Review*, January 20, 2018, https://www.nytimes.com/2018/01/20/opinion/sunday/trump-bad-presidents-history.html, January 23, 2018.

44. Schlesinger, qtd. in Burns and Dunn, *George Washington*, xvi.

45. Hillary Clinton, *What Happened*, 224–25.

46. Uri Friedman, "Why It's So Hard for a Woman to Become President of the United States," *The Atlantic*, November 12, 2016, https://www.theatlantic.com/international/archive/2016/11/clinton-woman-leader-world/506945/, March 11, 2018. Sexism and stereotypes are, of course, only one obstacle to be overcome. Another, related one, is that women have always found it extremely difficult to raise funds sizeable enough for a prolonged and successful campaign. On this issue see Ellen Fitzpatrick, *The Highest Glass Ceiling: Women's Quest for the American Presidency* (Cambridge: Harvard UP, 2016), 276–77 and, on the wide literature addressing women and the American presidency, 295n2.

47. Annette Gordon-Reed, "Female Trouble," *The New York Review of Books* LXV:2 (February 8, 2018), 12–14, quot. 13.

48. Hillary Clinton, *What Happened*, 223.

49. Homer, *The Odyssee with an English Translation* by A.T. Murray, Book 1, lines 356–59, http://data.perseus.org/texts/urn:cts:greekLit:tlg0012.tlg002.perseus-eng1, March 11, 2018, emphasis added. Mary Beard quotes from a different source, as see *Women & Power* (London: Profile Books, 2017), 3–4.

50. Thomas Jefferson to Albert Gallatin, January 13, 1807, *Founders Online*, National Archives, http://founders.archives.gov/documents/Jefferson/99-01-02-4862, retrieved March 12, 2018.

51. Reid Mitchell, *The Vacant Chair: The Northern Soldier Leaves Home* (New York: Oxford UP, 1993), 116.

52. Robin Lakoff, qtd. in Maureen Dowd, "The 1992 Campaign," *The New York Times* (October 10, 1992), http://www.nytimes.com/1992/10/10/us/1992-campaign-political-memo-knights-presidents-race-mythic-proportions.html?pagewanted=all&pagewanted=print, retrieved February 9, 2018.

53. Friedman, "Why It's So Hard for a Woman to Become President of the United States," web document.

Bibliography

Abramowitz, Alan I. *The Great Alignment: Race, Party Transformation, and the Rise of Donald Trump.* New Haven: Yale University Press, 2018.

Albanese, Catherine L. *Sons of the Fathers: The Civil Religion of the American Revolution.* Philadelphia: Temple University Press, 1976.

Anderson, Benedict. *Imagined Communities: Reflections on the Origin and Spread of Nationalism.* London: Verso Press, 2006.

Aron, Paul. *Why the Turkey Didn't Fly: The Surprising Stories Behind the Eagle, the Flag, Uncle Sam, and Other Images of America.* Lebanon, NH: University Press of New England, 2013.

Ayres, William. "At Home with George: Commercialization of the Washington Image." *George Washington: American Symbol.* Ed. Barbara L. Mitnick. New York: Hudson Hills Press, 1999. 91–107.

Bailyn, Bernard, ed. *The Debate on the Constitution: Federalist and Antifederalist Speeches, Articles, and Letters During the Struggle Over Ratification.* 2 vols. New York: Library of America, 1982.

Barratt, Carrie Rebora, and Ellen G. Miles. *Gilbert Stuart.* New York: Metropolitan Museum of Art / New Haven: Yale University Press, 2004.

Blankenhorn, David. *Fatherless America: Confronting Our Most Urgent Social Problem.* New York: Basic Books, 1995.

Bodnar, John E. *Remaking America: Public Memory, Commemoration, and Patriotism in the Twentieth Century.* Princeton: Princeton University Press, 1992.

Boime, Albert. *The Unveiling of the National Icons: A Plea for Patriotic Iconoclasm in a Nationalist Era.* Cambridge: Cambridge University Press, 1998.

Bolam, Sarah Miles, and Thomas J. Bolam. *The Presidents on Film: A Comprehensive Filmography of Portrayals from George Washington to George W. Bush.* Jefferson, NC: McFarland, 2007.

Breen, T.H. *George Washington's Journey: The President Forges a New Nation.* New York: Simon & Schuster, 2016.

Brookhiser, Richard. *Founding Father: Rediscovering George Washington.* New York: Free Press, 1996.

Brumwell, Stephen. *George Washington: Gentleman Warrior.* New York–London: Quercus, 2012.

Bryan, William Alfred. *George Washington in American Literature 1775–1865.* New York: Columbia University Press, 1952; repr. Westport, CT: Greenwood Press, 1970.

Burke, Edmund. *Reflections on the Revolution in France.* New York: Holt, Rinehart and Winston, 1959.

Burns, James MacGregor, and Susan Dunn. *George Washington.* American Presidents Series. New York: Henry Holt / Times Books, 2004.

Butter, Michael. *Der "Washington-Code": Zur Heroisierung amerikanischer Präsidenten, 1775–1865.* Göttingen, Germany: Wallstein Verlag, 2016.

Campbell, Karlyn Kohrs, and Kathleen Hall Jamieson. *Presidents Creating the Presidency: Deeds Done in Words.* Chicago: University of Chicago Press, 2008.

Casper, Scott E. "The Washington Image in American Culture." *A Companion to George Washington.* Ed. Edward G. Lengel. Malden, MA: Wiley-Blackwell, 2012. 592–611.

Cavitch, Max. "The Man That Was Used Up: Poetry, Particularity, and the Politics of Remembering George Washington." *American Literature* 75:2 (June 2003): 247–74.

Chernow, Ron. *Washington: A Life.* New York: Penguin, 2010.

Clark, H. Nichols B. "An Icon Preserved: Continuity in the Sculptural Images of Washington." *George Washington: American Symbol.* Ed. Barbara L. Mitnick. New York: Hudson Hills Press, 1999. 39–53.

Clinton, Hillary Rodham. *What Happened.* New York: Simon & Schuster, 2017.

A Companion to George Washington. Ed. Edward G. Lengel. Malden, MA: Wiley-Blackwell, 2012.

Cunliffe, Marcus. *George Washington: Man and Monument.* New York: New American Library, 1958.

_____. "The Two Georges: The President and the King." *American Studies International* 24:2 (October 1986): 53–73.

Cunningham, Noble E., Jr. *Popular Images of the Presidency: From Washington to Lincoln.* Columbia: University of Missouri Press, 1991.

Decker, Juilee. "Paintings and Sculptures." *The American President in Popular Culture.* Ed. John W. Matviko. Westport, CT–London: Greenwood Press, 2005. 15–32.

Durkheim, Émile. *The Elementary Forms of the Religious Life.* New York: Free Press, 1965.

Faber, Charles F., and Richard B. Faber. *The American Presidents Ranked by Performance.* Jefferson, NC: McFarland, 2006; 2nd edn. 2012.

Ferguson, Robert A. *The American Enlightenment, 1750–1820.* Cambridge: Harvard University Press, 1997.

Fischer, David Hackett. *Washington's Crossing.* New York: Oxford University Press, 2004.

Fishwick, Marshall W. "Did Anyone Ever See Washington Nude?" *The Hero in Transition.* Ed. Ray B. Browne and Marshall W. Fishwick. Bowling Green, OH: Bowling Green University Popular Press, 1983. 297–307.

Fliegelman, Jay. *Prodigals and Pilgrims: The American Revolution Against Patriarchal Authority, 1750–1800.* Cambridge: Cambridge University Press, 1982.

Frame, Gregory. *The American President in Film and Television: Myth, Politics, and Representation.* Oxford et al.: Peter Lang, 2014.

Freeman, Douglas S. *George Washington: A Biography.* 7 vols. New York: Scribner's, 1948–1957.

Gordon-Reed, Annette, and Peter S. Onuf. *"Most Blessed of the Patriarchs": Thomas Jefferson and the Empire of the Imagination.* New York–London: Liveright, 2016.

Griswold, Robert L. *Fatherhood in America: A History.* New York: Basic Books, 1993.

Higginbotham, Don, ed. *George Washington Reconsidered.* Charlottesville: University Press of Virginia, 2001.

Higham, James. *Strangers in the Land: Patterns of American Nativism, 1860–1925.* New Brunswick: Rutgers University Press, 1955; repr. New York: Atheneum, 1981.

History of the George Washington Bicentennial Celebration. 5 vols. Washington, D.C.: United States George Washington Bicentennial Commission, 1932.

Hobsbawm, Eric. "Introduction: Inventing Traditions." *The Invention of Tradition.* Ed. the same and Terence Ranger. Cambridge: Cambridge University Press, 1983. 1–14.

Howard, Hugh. *The Painter's Chair: George Washington and the Making of American Art.* New York: Bloomsbury Press, 2009.

Hyneman, Charles S., and Donald S. Lutz. *American Political Writing During the Founding Era, 1760–1805.* 2 Vols. Indianapolis, IN: Liberty Fund, 1983. Online Library of Liberty. Web. February 13, 2018 http://oll.libertyfund.org/titles/hyneman-american-political-writing-during-the-founding-era-1760-1805-2-vols.

Irving, Washington. *Life of George Washington.* 5 vols. New York: Putnam, 1856–1859.

Kahler, Gerald E. *The Long Farewell: Americans Mourn the Death of George Washington.* Charlottesville: University of Virginia Press, 2008.

Kaminski, John P., and Jill Adair McCaughan, eds. *A Great and Good Man: George Washington in the Eyes of His Contemporaries.* Madison, WI: Madison House Publishers, 1989.

Kammen, Michael G. *Mystic Chords of Memory: The Transformation of Tradition in American Culture.* New York: Knopf, 1991.

Kann, Mark E. *The Gendering of American Politics: Founding Mothers, Founding Fathers, and Political Patriarchy.* Westport, CT–London: Praeger, 1999.

_____. "Manhood, Immortality, and Politics During the American Founding." *Journal of Men's Studies* 5:2 (November 1996): 79–103.

Ketcham, Ralph. *Presidents Above Party: The First American Presidency, 1789–1829.* 1984; Chapel Hill: University of North Carolina Press, 1987.

Kinnaird, Clark. *George Washington: The Pictorial Biography.* New York: Bonanza Books, 1967.

Lakoff, George. *Moral Politics: How Liberals and Conservatives Think.* 2nd ed. Chicago: University of Chicago Press, 2002.

Lamb, Brian, Susan Swain, and C-SPAN. *The Presidents: Noted Historians Rank America's Best—and Worst—Chief Executives.* New York: Public Affairs, 2019.

Langston, Thomas S. *With Reverence and Contempt: How Americans Think About Their President.* Baltimore: Johns Hopkins University Press, 1995.

Larson, Edward. *The Return of George Washington: 1783–1789.* New York: William Morrow, 2014.

Lengel, Edward G. *First Entrepreneur: How George Washington Built His—and the Nation's—Prosperity.* New York: Da Capo Press, 2016.

_____. *Inventing George Washington: America's Founder, in Myth and Memory.* New York: HarperCollins, 2011.

Leverenz, David. *Manhood and the American Renaissance.* Ithaca: Cornell University Press, 1989.

Liddle, William D. "'A Patriot King, or None': Lord Bolingbroke and the American Renunciation of George III." *Journal of American History* 65:4 (March 1979): 951–70.

Longmore, Paul K. *The Invention of George Washington.* Berkeley: University of California Press, 1988.

Luther, Martin. *Der Große Katechismus*. Gütersloh, Germany: Gütersloher Verlagshaus, 1998. Text im Projekt Gutenberg-DE. N.d. Web. February 17, 2018. http://gutenberg.spiegel.de/buch/-266/4.

Marche, Stephen. "Manifesto of the New Fatherhood: Why fathers matter now more than ever before. A charge." *Esquire*. June 13, 2014. Web. November 28, 2017. http://www.esquire.com/lifestyle/news/a28987/manifesto-of-the-new-fatherhood-0614/.

Marling, Karal Ann. *George Washington Slept Here: Colonial Revivals and American Culture, 1876–1986*. Cambridge: Harvard University Press, 1988.

Marshall, John. *The Life of George Washington*. Philadelphia: C. P. Wayne, 1804–1807.

Marx, Karl. *The Eighteenth Brumaire of Louis Bonaparte*. Trans. Daniel De Leon. 1897; Chicago: Charles H. Kerr, 1913.

McCullough, David. *1776*. New York: Simon & Schuster, 2005.

Meschutt, David. "Life Portraits of George Washington." *George Washington: American Symbol*. Ed. Barbara L. Mitnick. New York: Hudson Hills Press, 1999. 25–37.

Miller, Angela L., Janet C. Berlo, Bryan Wolf, and Jennifer L. Roberts. *American Encounters: Art, History, and Cultural Identity*. Upper Saddle River, NJ: Pearson, Prentice Hall, 2008.

Miller, Eugene F., and Barry Schwartz. "The Icon of the American Republic: A Study in Political Symbolism." *The Review of Politics* 47:4 (October 1985): 516–43.

Mitnick, Barbara J, ed. *George Washington: American Symbol*. New York: Hudson Hills Press, 1999.

_____. "Parallel Visions: The Literary and Visual Image of George Washington." *George Washington: American Symbol*. Ed. Barbara J. Mitnick. New York: Hudson Hills Press, 1999. 55–69.

Morgan, Edmund S. *Inventing the People: The Rise of Popular Sovereignty in England and America*. New York: W. W. Norton, 1988.

Morrison, Jeffry H. *The Political Philosophy of George Washington*. Baltimore: Johns Hopkins University Press, 2009.

Nitschke, Claudia. *Der öffentliche Vater. Konzeptionen paternaler Souveränität in der deutschen Literatur*. Berlin-Boston: de Gruyter, 2012.

Norton, Mary Beth. *Liberty's Daughters: The Revolutionary Experience of American Women, 1750–1800*. 1980; Ithaca: Cornell University Press, 1996.

Obama, Barack. *The Audacity of Hope: Thoughts on Reclaiming the American Dream*. New York: Vintage, 2008.

_____. *Dreams from My Father: A Story of Race and Inheritance*. 1995; New York: Crown Publishers, 2004.

Paine, Thomas. *Common Sense on the Origin and Design of Government in General ... Together with the American Crisis*. New York: G. P. Putnam's Sons, 1912.

Rakoff, Jed S. "The Magna Carta Betrayed?" *The New York Review of Books* LXIII, Number 2 (February 11, 2016): 18–19.

Rasmussen, William M. S., and Robert S. Tilton. *George Washington: The Man Behind the Myths*. Charlottesville: University Press of Virginia, 1999.

Robinson, Raymond H. "The Marketing of an Icon." *George Washington: American Symbol*. Ed. Barbara L. Mitnick. New York: Hudson Hills Press, 1999. 109–21.

Samuel, Lawrence R. *American Fatherhood: A Cultural History*. Lanham, MD et al.: Rowman & Littlefield, 2016.

Sandoz, Ellis. *Political Sermons of the Founding Era, 1730–1805*. 2 Vols. Foreword by Ellis Sandoz. 1991. Second edn. Indianapolis, IN: Liberty Fund, 1998. Online Library of Liberty. Web. February 12, 2018. http://oll.libertyfund.org/titles/816.

Schwartz, Barry. "George Washington: A New Man for a New Century." *George Washington: American Symbol*. Ed. Barbara L. Mitnick. New York: Hudson Hills Press, 1999. 123–39.

Shirk, Samuel Blaine. *The Characterization of George Washington in American Plays Since 1875*. Doctoral thesis. Philadelphia: University of Pennsylvania, 1949.

Silverman, Kenneth. *A Cultural History of the American Revolution: Painting, Music, Literature, and the Theatre in the Colonies and the United States from the Treaty of Paris to the Inauguration of George Washington, 1763–1789*. New York: Thomas Y. Crowell, 1976.

Smith, Jeff. *The Presidents We Imagine: Two Centuries of White House Fictions on the Page, on the Stage, Onscreen, and Online*. Madison: University of Wisconsin Press, 2009.

Smith, Richard Norton. *Patriarch: George Washington and the New American Nation*. Boston–New York: Houghton Mifflin, 1993.

Sons of the Father: George Washington and His Protégés. Ed. Robert M. S. McDonald. Charlottesville: University of Virginia Press, 2013.

Thistlethwaite, Mark E. "The Face of the Nation: George Washington's Image and American Identity." *Visual Cultures—Transatlantic Perspectives*. Ed. Volker Depkat and Meike Zwingenberger. Publications of the Bavarian American Academy, 14. Heidelberg: Universitätsverlag Winter, 2012. 35–52.

_____. "Hero, Celebrity, and Cliché: The Modern and Postmodern Image of George Washington."

George Washington: American Symbol. Ed. Barbara J. Mitnick. New York: Hudson Hills Press, 1999. 141–52.

_____. *The Image of George Washington: Studies in Mid-Nineteenth-Century American History Painting.* New York: Garland, 1979.

Thomas, John D. "George Washington." *The Columbia Companion to American History on Film: How the Movies Have Portrayed the American Past.* Ed. Peter C. Rollins (New York: Columbia University Press, 2004), 198–203.

Tocqueville, Alexis de. *Democracy in America.* The Henry Reeve Text. Abr. with an Introduction by Thomas Bender. New York: Random House / Modern Library, 1980.

Tschachler, Heinz. "George Washington: Gallant Revolutionary." *The Numismatist.* Colorado Springs, CO, 131:2 (February 2018): 39–44.

_____. *The Greenback: Paper Money and American Culture.* Jefferson, NC: McFarland, 2010.

_____. *The Monetary Imagination of Edgar Allan Poe: Banking, Currency and Politics in the Writings.* Jefferson, NC: McFarland, 2013.

Tuckerman, Henry T. *The Character and Portraits of Washington.* New York: Putnam, 1859; facs. edn. New York: Adamant Media Corp., 2006.

United States George Washington Bicentennial Commission. *History of the George Washington Bicentennial Celebration.* 5 vols. Washington, D.C.: Bicentennial Commission, 1932.

United States Senate. "Art and History. George Washington (Patriae Pater)." N.d. Web. March 17, 2014. http://www.senate.gov/artandhistory/art/artifact/Painting_31_00001.htm.

Vermeule, Cornelius C. *Numismatic Art in America: Aesthetics of the United States Coinage.* 2nd edn. Atlanta, GA: Whitman, 2007.

Wakoski, Diane. *Emerald Ice: Selected Poems 1962–1987.* Santa Rosa, CA: Black Sparrow Press, 1988.

Washington, George. *The Papers of George Washington.* Digital edition. *Founders Online,* National Archives. Ed. Theodore J. Crackel et al. Charlottesville: University of Virginia Press, Rotunda, 2007. https://founders.archives.gov/content/volumes#Washington. (Original source: *The Papers of George Washington.* Ed. W. W. Abbot et al.).

_____. *The Papers of George Washington.* Ed. W. W. Abbot et al. 5 ser., 70 vols. to date. Charlottesville: University of Virginia Press, 1987. www.gwpapers.virginia.edu.

_____. *The Writings of George Washington from the Original Manuscript Sources, 1745–1799.* Ed. John C. Fitzpatrick. 37 vols. Washington, D.C.: United States Government Printing Office, 1931–1944.

_____. *Writings.* Ed. John Rhodehamel. New York: Library of America, 2011; abbr. as *WWR.*

Weems, Mason Locke. *The Life of Washington.* Ed. Marcus Cunliffe. Cambridge: Belknap Press of Harvard University Press, 1962.

Wick, Wendy C. *George Washington, an American Icon: The Eighteenth-Century Graphic Portraits.* Charlottesville: University of Virginia Press for the Smithsonian Institution Traveling Exhibition and the National Portrait Gallery, 1982.

Willard, Emma. *History of the United States.* New York: White, Gallaher & White, 1829.

Wills, Garry. *Cincinnatus: George Washington and the Enlightenment.* Garden City, NY: Doubleday, 1984.

Woodward, William E. *George Washington: The Image and the Man.* New York: Boni & Liveright, 1926.

Zagarri, Rosemarie, ed. *David Humphreys' "Life of General Washington" with George Washington's "Remarks."* Athens, GA: University of Georgia Press, 1991.

Index

Numbers in ***bold italics*** indicate pages with illustrations

Adams, Abigail 65, 226n13, 231n56; on George Washington 108
Adams, Henry: *Democracy* 126, 144
Adams, John 7, 10, 37, 54, 59, 63, 65, 67, 81, 83, 89, 91, 131, 137, 172, 173, 195, 210n43, 212n76, 215n53, 216n5, 216n13, 217n25, 218n53, 221n4, 231n3, 240n11, 241n42
Adams, John Quincy 10, 81, 195, 240n12
Addison, Joseph: *Cato* (1712) 55, 74, 86, 203n18, 214n45, 219n14
African Americans 9, 87, 111, 165, 168; and the Constitution 64; *see also* slavery
allegories, depictions of 30, 38, 71, 72, 102, 129, 133, 143, 150; *see also* Eagle, American; Liberty
Allen, Ethan 32, 82–83
Allen, Levi 32, 203n15
America Inimica Tyrannis 71; *see also* mottoes
American Indians *see* Native Americans
American Revolution 2, 3, 5, 7, 12, 23, 30, 34, 47, 50–53, 57–58, 64, 66, 71, 78, 85–89, 95, 117, 124, 126, 132, 134–38, 150, 159, 160, 167–68, 183, 184, 205n21, 213n4, 222n39, 235n76; *see also* War of Independence
"Americans for George" 2, 203n5; *see also* one-dollar bill
Anderson, Alexander 7, 99, 135–37
annuit coeptis motto 41, 211n68; *see also* mottoes
apotheosis 38, 129, 138, 139, 192; *see also* Barralat, John James; Brumidi, Constantino
Arthur, Chester A. 185
Articles of Confederation 33, 47, 54, 63, 219n1
"Athenaeum" portrait *see* Stuart, Gilbert
An Autobiography of George Washington 169

Baker, William S. 101, 128, 209n20, 224n30

Barlow, Joel 61, 213n12
Barralet, John James 38, 75, 219n21; *Apotheosis of Washington* 38
Belcher, Jonathan (governor of Massachusetts) 17, 205n14
Bennett, William J. 171
Bible 4, 37, 58, 74, 87, 110, 182–84, 192, 215n58
Bierce, Ambrose: "George the Made-Over" 144
Blackstone, William: *Commentaries on the Laws of England* 145
Bloom, Sol 154–55, 157
Bolingbroke, Viscount Henry St. John 55–57, 109–10, 218n55
Bonaparte, Napoleon 79, 102, 224n34, 229n30
Borglum, Gutzon *see* Mount Rushmore
Bowling Green (New York City) 7, 36, 136–37; *see also* Celebration of Independence
Brackenridge, Hugh Henry 221n22
Bradshaw, Wesley: "Washington's Vision" 121–22
Britain, Great Britain *see* George III; War of Independence
Brumidi, Constantino: *The Apotheosis of George Washington* 129, 210n49, 229n26
Buchanan, James 121, 180, 237n17
Bunker Hill, Battle of 138, 224n20
Burgoyne, General John 135, 229n8
Burke, Edmund 111
Bush, George H.W. 4, 10, 24, 175, 182, 184
Bush, George W. 14, 22, 28, 163, 172, 184, 185, 186–87, 238n51
Butter, Michael *see* "Washington-Code"
Byron, Lord (George Gordon) 79, 215n67

cabinet: Washington's 54, 65, 163
Caesar, Julius 57, 74, 75, 102, 209n10, 214n42, 220n36
Calhoun, John C. 7, 87, 121, 126, 131

Campbell, Alexander 92, 223n54
capitalism 106–7, 127, 189
caricatures 167–68, 234n44; *see also* Washington, George: caricatures and cartoons of
Carter, Jimmy 13, 182, 186
Carver, George Washington 140, 166
Cato: A Tragedy see Addison, Joseph; Washington, George: and Cato
Celebration of Independence 7, 135–36; *see also* Anderson, Alexander
Ceracchi, Giuseppe 36, 75, 78
Chase, Salmon P. 134, 231n3
Cherry Tree legend 35, 83, 159, 199
Christian Broadcasting Network 9, 171
Christy, Howard Chandler: *Scene at the Signing of the Constitution* 161
Cicero, Marcus Tullius 55, 102, 214n42; as Roman *Pater Patriae* 55, 102, 224n33
Cincinnatus, Lucius Quinctus 5, 32–33, 77–79; *see also* Washington, George: as C.
Circular to State Governments 52–53, 169, 190; *see also* Washington, George: Circular to State Governments
Civil War, American 6, 7, 12, 85, 86, 98, 126, 127–31, 169; *see also* Confederacy; Davis, Jefferson; Lincoln, Abraham; North and South
Claremont Institute 25; *see also* Trump, Donald J.
Clark, Spencer M. 134–35
Clay, Henry 121
Cleveland, Grover 180–81
Clinton, Hillary Rodham 200–201
Clinton, William Jefferson 4, 10, 13, 24, 26, 28, 175, 184, 185
colonial era 17, 30, 35, 48, 49, 56–57, 92, 97, 107–11, 138, 140; *see also* War of Independence
"colonial revival" 8, 9, 141, 144–45, 152–53, 180, 231n42

247

"Columbia's Noblest Sons," lithograph 7
Columbus, Christopher 67, 115, 214*n*40
Common Sense see Paine, Thomas
Confederacy 127, 149, 172; Southern nationalism 126–27, 132; *see also* Civil War
Congress *see* United States Congress
Constitution, federal 31, 40, 43, 53–57, 63, 64–65, 133, 171–72, 179–80, 182, 200, 218*n*53; Washington on 74, 233*n*10
Constitutional Convention 5, 33, 47, 53–54, 63–64, 68, 74, 123, 161, 174, 182, 213*n*32
Continental Army 35, 36, 41, 61, 74–75, 78, 88, 97, 98, 117, 132, 137, 141, 150, 190
Continental Congress, first 29, 40, 135, 173
Continental Congress, second 31, 32, 62, 219*n*1
Coolidge, Calvin 147–48, 151, 154, 175, 181–82
Cooper, James F.: *The Spy* (1821) 86, 2221*n*22
Copley, John Singleton 88
Country Party *see* Bolingbroke, Henry St. John
Crawford, Thomas: equestrian statue of Washington 76, 98, 127–28
Crossing of the Delaware 8, 9, 11, 51–52, 135, 138–40, 159, 160, 163, 166, 168, 172, 189, 190–91, 230*n*21; *see also* Hicks, Edward; Leutze, Emanuel; Rivers, Larry; Saul, Peter; Sorel, Edward; Sully, Thomas
Cunliffe, Marcus 3, 4, 79, 164–65, 178, 203*n*11
Cunningham, Ann Pamela *see* Mount Vernon Ladies' Association of the Union
currency and coins, Washington depicted on 6, 10–12, 36, 37, 62, 83, 88, 99, 127, 142–43, 155, 188
currency, and national identity 11, 88, 127–28, 134–35, 147, 169, 191, 198, 231*n*2
Currier, Nathaniel 87, 129–30; *General George Washington* 51; *Washington at Mount Vernon* 118; *Washington's Reception by the Ladies* **69**
Custis, Daniel Parke 56
Custis, Eleanor Parke ("Nelly") 100, 108–9
Custis, George Washington Parke ("Washy") 109
Custis, John Parke ("Jacky") 108
Custis, Martha Parke ("Patsy") 108

Daughters of the American Revolution 134, 139, 159

Davies, Samuel, Reverend 17, 29, 55
Davis, Jefferson 122; portraits of, on currency 127; *see also* Civil War; Confederacy
"dead presidents" *see* "portraits of presidents"
debunkers, debunking 141, 145, 153, 163, 166, 168; *see also* Hughes, Rupert; Woodward, William E.
Declaration of Independence 29, 40, 52, 62, 94, 132, 136, 180, 229*n*32; *see also* War of Independence
The Declaration of Independence see Trumbull, John
Democratic Republicans 66, 67; *see also* Federalism; Jefferson, Thomas
Depression, Great 8, 149, 152, 159, 160, 161, 174; *see also* New Deal; Roosevelt, Franklin Delano
"*des Landes Vater*" *see* Washington, George as; *see also* Luther, Martin; Schiller, Friedrich von
de Tocqueville, Alexis 6, 35, 112, 195
Dexter, Samuel 67
Dickinson, John: *Letters from a Farmer in Pennsylvania* 30, 57, 214*n*52
dollar: as national currency 26, 133, 143, 165, 166, 188–89, 191, 193, 198, 231*n*60, 241*n*35
Doolittle, Amos 40; *Display of the United States* 102
Dunsmore, John Ward 8, 142, 153
Durand, Asher 73, 76, 220*n*26

E pluribus Unum (motto) 31, 40–41, 211*n*68; *see also* mottoes
Eagle, American 70, 71, 73, 75, 124, 129–30, 141, 144, 173, 191, 219*n*1; *see also* allegorical depictions
Educational Series 133; *see also* Silver Certificates
Eisen, Gustavus 101–2
Eisenhower, Dwight 9, 162, 174, 182–83, 198; *see also* "In God We Trust"
Emerson, Ralph Waldo 41, 82
Engels, Friedrich 106; *see also* Marx, Karl
"esoteric political theology" ("*esoterische Polittheologie*," Jochen Hörisch) 198, 241*n*35
ethnicity *see* immigrants and immigration
Everett, Edward 104, 122, 124–26
exhibitions 7, 43, 133, 138, 141, 143, 144, 170, 178–79, 205*n*16, 217*n*38, 222*n*50, 236*n*5

Fairfax, Bryan 111
Fairman, Gideon: "Phillips" portrait of Washington 167
fame 32, 37; *see also* allegories, depictions of

Family Research Council 9, 171, 185
"Farewell Address" 20, 24–25, 37, 43, 121, 123, 124–25, 128, 132, 180, 188, 191, 216*n*20, 228*n*4; *see also* Washington, George
Fast, Howard 87, 139, 163
Father Knows Best (radio and TV series) 27, 195
Father of His Country: Roman origin 3, 55, 102, 192, 214*n*42, 224*n*33; Washington as *see* Washington, George: as Father of His Country
fatherhood: political fatherhood 3–5, 17, 24, 28, 47, 56, 201; roles of 13–16, 19, 26, 35, 106, 109, 112–14, 117, 148, 161–62, 187–88, 191, 197–98, 208*n*75
fatherlessness 2–3, 10, 14, 17, 26–27, 106, 115, 117, 191, 197, 225*n*2
fathers: biblical 15–16; biological and metaphorical 3, 16, 36, 192, 201; and public rhetoric 12, 48, 56, 201; "strict" father and "nurturant parent" 3, 18–20, 24, 25, 27, 112, 137, 181, 192, 198–99; *see also* Lakoff, George
Father's Day 186, 238*n*57
Faulkner, William 182, 237*n*36
Federal City (Washington, D.C.) 107
federal government *see* Constitutional Convention
The Federalist Papers 25, 43, 206*n*39, 215*n*57
Federalist Party 66–67, 121; *see also* Democratic Republicans; Hamilton, Alexander
feminism 196, 240*n*22; *see also* woman suffrage
Ferris, Jean Leon Gerome. 8, 142, 152, **153**, 223*n*4
Field, Erastus Salisbury: *Historical Monuments of the American Republic* 133; *Joseph Moore and His Family* 112, **113**
Filmer, Sir Robert: *Patriarcha* 110
Fitzpatrick, John C.: *The Writings of George Washington* 155, 178
Flanagan, John 155
Flexner, James Thomas: *George Washington* 9, 42, 168–69, 178, 226*n*27
folk art 32, 52, 88, 99, 100, 133, 190, 224*n*27
Ford, Paul Leicester 139, 142
Ford, Worthington Chauncey 142
Fourth of July celebrations 6, 41, 65, 83, 116, 134, 173, 196
Franklin, Benjamin 57, 67, 77, 91, 93, 161, 189, 216*n*4; political thought of 68, 215*n*54
Fraser, Laura Gardin 155
Fraunces Tavern (New York City): Washington bidding farewell to his officers 52, 78, 213*n*19

Index

Freeman, Douglas Southall: *George Washington* 84, 178, 222*n*53
Freneau, Philip 50, 65, 78
Fugitive Slave Act 64

Gallatin, Albert 201
Garfield, James 180
gender 4, 12, 64, 72, 107, 145, 147, 165, 178, 187, 188, 200, 201
General Washington 99; *see also* Anderson, Alexander
George II: as "father of his country" 17, 29, 55
George III: as "father of his country" 4, 17, 29, 32, 47, 56, 106, 192; as "tyrant" 3, 29–30, 57, 71, 209*n*14
George Washington Bicentennial Commission 154–55, 233*n*39
"Georges" *see* one-dollar bill
"*Geschichtsbruch*" *see* rupture, historic
the Gilded Age 7, 134, 140, 143–44
Glass, Francis: *Georgii Washingtonii ... Vita* 75
Goethe, Johann Wolfgang von 59, 240*n*6
Gore, Al 26
Grant, Ulysses S. 180
Great Britain *see* Britain
Greene, General Nathanael 53
Greenough, Horatio: marble statue of Washington 6, 75, 87, **115**, 116, 173, 227*n*54
Griffith, D.W.: *America* 8, 148, 160; *The Birth of a Nation* 149
Griswold, Rufus 123, 140, 185; *see also* "Republican Court"
"Gunpowder notes" 31; *see also* Maryland

Hamilton, Alexander 5, 49, 54, 65, 137, 161, 163, 218*n*53, 231*n*3, 239*n*82; economic policy of 63; influence on Washington 190; *see also* federalism; Jefferson, Thomas
Hancock, John 7, 88, 135, 216*n*16
Hardie, James 34, 55
Harding, Warren G. 148, 150, 181
Harrison, Benjamin 140, 143, 180
Harrison, Gabriel 113, 117
Harrison, William Henry 131
Hart, Charles Henry 95, 99, 101
Hawthorne, Nathaniel 83, 86, 87
Hayes, Rutherford B. 132, 180
Hefferton, Phillip: *Sweet Funk* 165, 167
hegemony, political 39–40, 197
hemp, George Washington and 9, 167, 199
Henry, Patrick 213*n*8, 220*n*32
Hicks, Edward: *Washington at the Delaware* 52, 213*n*15
Hillard, Elias Brewster: *The Last Men of the Revolution* 132
Hobbes, Thomas 16

Holmes, Oliver Wendell 7, 123, 199
Hoover, Herbert 24, 154, 175, 182
Hörisch, Jochen 241*n*35; *see also* "esoteric political theology" ("*esoterische Polittheologie*")
Houdon, Jean-Antoine 5, 8, 36, 76–78, 86, 97, 103, 113, 116, 143, 151, **154**, 155, 173, 190, 233*n*41
Hughes, Rupert 8, 145; *see also* debunkers and debunking
Humphreys, David 5, 50, 63, 75, 79, 167, 213*n*12; as Washington's authorized biographer 62, 216*n*8
Hütter, Christian Jacob: *Washingtons Ankunft in Elisium* 67

icon: definition 2–3, 41; Washington as national icon 2, 6, 9, 10, 11, 36, 45, 76, 78, 88, 98, 100, 103, 113, 117, 124, 128, 144, 166, 168, 188–90, 192, 194, 203*n*7
iconography 31, 64, 71; political 5, 134, 173, 190, 227*n*45, 233*n*44
image 3, 6, 15, 16, 24, 33, 34, 38–43, 50, 60, 74, 82, 88, 99, 101, 105, 117, 121, 123, 128, 131, 137, 143, 147, 155, 163, 167, 168, 171–73, 176, 185, 188, 189, 191, 194, 195, 212*n*77; *see also* picture
"imagined community" (Benedict Anderson) 27, 39–40
immigrants and immigration 7–8, 12, 19, 114, 133–34, 143, 148, 150, 181; *see also* Ku Klux Klan
"In God We Trust" 198, 241*n*34; *see also* mottoes
Inaugural Centennial celebration (1889) 7, 140, 142, 143, 144
"Inscribed to the Father of His Country" 33, 34, 85, 209*n*27
"invented" tradition (Eric Hobsbawm) 7, 129, 204*n*28
Irving, Washington 59, 99–100, 136, 185, 215*n*70; *Life of Washington* 6, 50–52, 83–85

Jackson, Andrew 7, 9, 121, 131, 175, 177, 207*n*49; as guiding influence for Donald J. Trump 22–24; *see also* populism
Jay, John 94, 216*n*20, 218*n*52; Jay Treaty 42, 66, 231*n*3
Jefferson, Thomas 7, 9, 12, 54, 65, 75, 77, 78, 82, 93, 111, 131, 135, 151, 160, 175–77, 179, 186, 189, 190, 202; as classical republican 31, 206*n*39; and farming 106–7; as patriarch 111, 226*n*35; *Summary View of the Rights of British America* 29–30, 214*n*49; on Washington 49, 50, 54, 212*n*1; *see also* Declaration of Independence; War of Independence
Johnson, Andrew 180
Johnson, Lyndon B. 183

Kennedy, John F. 22, 28, 175, 177–78, 183, 185, 198

Kennedy, John Pendleton 86
Kingsley, Sidney: *The Patriots* 163
Kirkland, Caroline Matilda: *Memoirs of Washington* 85
KKK *see* Ku Klux Klan
Knox, Henry 32, 33, 52, 54, 55, 64, 137, 213*n*32, 218*n*61
Komar, Vitaly: *Washington Lives II* 173; *see also* Melamid, Alex
Krimmel, John Lewis: *Barroom Dancing* 88, **89**, 222*n*37
Ku Klux Klan 148–50, 232*n*18

Lafayette, Gilbert du Motier, Marquis de: and Washington 5, 49, 61, 212–13*n*4
Lakoff, George 19, 198, 203*n*9; *see also* fathers
Lange, Dorothea 161, **162**
Lavater, Johann Kaspar 95, 194, 240*n*6
Lear, Tobias 62, 63
Lee, Henry (Light Horse Harry) 59, 62, 68, 73
Lee, Robert 132, 149
Le Mire, Noël: *Le Général Washington* 45–46
Leonardo da Vinci 102
Leutze, Emanuel Gottlieb: *Washington Crossing the Delaware* 11, 138–40, 159, 166, 189, 230*n*21
Leyendecker, J. C.: Washington at Prayer, cover of *Saturday Evening Post*, February 23, 1935 160
Liberty 30, 36, 71–73, 129, 136, 145, 170, 171–72, 173, 191; *see also* allegorical depictions
liberty cap 30, 31, 38
Lincoln, Abraham 7, 9, 22, 23, 53, 127, 133, 143, 174–77, 186; and George Washington 7, 50, 66, 82, 124, 128–29, **130**, 131, 142, 153–54, 160, 164, 180, 200, 236*n*95; on George Washington 131–32; Lincoln Memorial 8, 150, 151; *see also* Civil War
Locke, John 16, 94, 110, 226*n*25
Longfellow, Henry Wadsworth 84, 117
Lowell, James Russell 141
Loyalists, loyalism 12, 94; *see also* colonial era; Patriots
Luther, Martin: "*des Landes Vater*" 58, 192, 215*nn*58–60

Madison, James 40, 65, 68, 116, 137, 161, 179, 206*n*39; as advisor to Washington 54, 163, 190
Magna Carta, *Magna Carta Libertatum* 5, 71, 72, 219*n*3
Marshall, John 102, 116, 123, 127, 194; *Life of Washington* 6, 74, 83–84
Marx, Karl 24, 207*n*64; "The Communist Manifesto" 106; *see also* Engels, Friedrich

Maryland: revolutionary paper issue of 1775 **30**, 30–31, 71
Mason, George 72, 209*n*10
McKinley, William 134, 181
medals *see* Washington, George
Melamid, Alex: *Washington Lives II* 173; *see also* Komar, Vitaly
middle classes: rise of 112, 194
Monmouth, Battle of 41, 128, 224*n*13
Monroe, James 212*n*76
Morris, Gouverneur 33, 37, 68
Morris, Robert 152
mothers, republican 35, 72, 217*n*25
mottoes 30, 31, 41, 71, 169, 170, 198; *see also* specific mottoes ("In God We Trust")
Mount Rushmore 8, 150–51
Mount Vernon 6, 107, 111, 116, 123, 125, 128, 132, 153, 167, 189; importance in Washington's life 54, 74, 79; preservation of 7, 126, 170; visitors to 83, 178, 190; *see also* Washington, George
Mount Vernon Ladies' Association of the Union 2, 118, 124, 126, 140, 228*n*14

"nation-as-family" metaphor 19, 203*n*9; *see also* Lakoff, George
Native Americans 39, 143, 229*n*8; and the Constitution 5, 64
Neal, John 194
New Deal 182; *see also* Roosevelt, Franklin Delano
New York (city) 33, 36, 52, 59, 63, 69, 70, 78, 95, 98, 107, 123, 124, 136, 138, 140, 167
Newburgh conspiracy 49, 190
Niles, Nathaniel 17, 29
Nixon, Richard M. 25, 140, 166, 183, 186, 207*n*61
Norman, John 224*n*21; *The True Portraiture of His Excellency* 46, 73, 93
North *see* Civil War

Obama, Barack: as "Father of the Year 2009" 1, 204*n*1; on fatherhood 14, 20, *21*, 184; inaugural addresses 4, 10, 13, 26
Ogden, Henry A. 8, 142, 153
one-dollar bill 2, 28, 165, 167, 182, 193
opinion polls *see* rankings, presidential

pageants 137, 143, 152, 153, 154
Paine, Thomas: *American Crisis* 41; *Common Sense* 29, 30; and George Washington 66; on women 145; *see also* War of Independence
paper money 2, 29, 81, 135; portraits on 102, 231*n*1; *see also* "portraits of presidents"
parades 8, 54, 136, 140, 143, 149, 188, 226–27*n*38, 230*n*11

Paris Peace Treaty (1783) 53, 231*n*3
participation mystique 3, 191; *see also* Washington, George, as "Father of His Country"
pater patriae, Roman honorary title 3, 35, 55, 102, 214*n*42, 224*n*33
Patriae Pater, portrait *see* Peale, Rembrandt
patriarchism, patriarchy 6, 11, 16, 17, 18, 47, 48, 65, 72, 114, 145, 151, 161, 187, 201, 212*n*2
Patriot king *see* Bolingbroke, Henry St. John
Patriots 31, 32, 39, 41, 50, 54, 57, 61, 71, 73, 109, 124, 128, 163, 203*n*13, 209*n*14; *see also* Loyalists; War of Independence
Paulding, James Kirke: *Life of Washington* 85, 86; *see also* slavery
Peale, Charles Wilson 32, 42, 61, 78, 88, 91–93, 98, 99, 173; *George Washington at Princeton* 11, 34, 36, *90*
Peale, Rembrandt 102–5, 124, 151, 224*n*37; *George Washington, Patriae Pater* 6, 11, 23, **103**
photographs 28, 104, 113, 117, 132, 155, 161, 227*n*45; *see also* Harrison, Gabriel
Phrygean cap *see* liberty cap
physiognomy *see* Lavater, Johann Kaspar
physiognotrace (drawing machine) 88
picture 2, 11, 22, 37, 38, 42, 67, 83, 92, 99, 102, 128, 135, 137, 147, 153, 170, 184, 189, 210; *see also* image
Pierce, Franklin 179–80
pileus see liberty cap
Pine, Robert Edge 92, 223*n*55
planter aristocracy 124; *see also* Virginia aristocracy
Plutarch 75, 178, 209*n*10
Poe, Edgar Allan 81–82; absence of father 115
political fatherhood *see* fatherhood
political iconography *see* iconography, political
Polk, James 116, 177, 179
populism, populist 22, 24; *see also* Jackson, Andrew; Trump, Donald J.
portraits 2–3, 6, 7, 10, 11, 22–24, 28, 32, 36, 42–46, 61–62, 76–78, 82–83, 88, 91–93, 94, 95, 97, 100, 101, 114, 124, 127, 131, 142, 187; debates over 87, 103–5, 155, 193–94; *see also* "portraits of presidents"
"portraits of presidents" 147; *see also* paper money
postage stamps 11, 36, 37, 151, 154, 155, 160, 188, 233*n*44
prayer in the snow legend 160, 170, 171; *see also* Valley Forge, legend of

"Prayer Journal," Washington's putative 141, 171, 235*n*55
presidency 4, 17, 21, 24, 47, 57, 62–63, 71, 74, 127, 164, 176, 177, 185, 192, 200, 203*n*6, 204*n*2, 218*n*57, 241*n*46
Presidents' Day 185–86
Princeton Battle Monument 150
Princeton, Battle of 88, 95, 97, 128, 138, 150, 174
providence 36–37; Washington's acknowledgment of 41
Pyle, Howard 8, 142, 153
Pynchon, Thomas 87, 167
pyramid and all-seeing eye 41; *see also* seal, Great Seal of the United States

quarter dollar: Washington quarter 155, 189, 191
Quiroz, Alfred J.: *George Washington Inspects the Hemp Crop* 167

race *see* African Americans; slavery
Ramsay, Allan: *King George III* 45
Randolph, Edmund 54
rankings, presidential 28, 66, 174–77
Reagan, Ronald 4, 9, 10, 13, 24, 162, 169, 170, 174, 175, 183, 184, 192, 196; inauguration of 1985 170
Reed, Joseph 5, 49
reincarnation of Washington 172, 184
relics of Washington 7, 141, 143, 178; *see also* Washington, George: Washingtoniana
republic, Roman, symbolic tradition 5, 6, 31, 45, 55, 68, 72–79, 97, 214*n*45, 219*n*2, 220*n*31
"Republican Court" 7, 140–41, 180; *see also* Griswold, Rufus
republicanism 5, 25, 50, 59, 71, 74, 128, 214*n*45
Revere, Paul 71, 99
Revolutionary War *see* War of Independence
Rittenhouse, David 34, 209*n*20
Rivers, Larry: *Washington Crossing the Delaware* 9, 139, 166; *see also* Leutze, Emanuel Gottlieb
Rockwell, Norman: *The Guiding Influence* 8, 155, **156**, 157, 159
Rogers, Will 24
romance, historical 8, 86, 126, 152, 160, 199, 223
Rome *see* republic, Roman, symbolic tradition
Roosevelt, Franklin Delano 9, 148, 160–61, 174–75, 182, 196, 199, 207; *see also* New Deal
Roosevelt, Theodore 9, 151, 160, 175, 181; *see also* Mount Rushmore
Ross, Betsy 146, 152, **153**, 155, 231*n*61
Rousseau, Jean-Jacques 35, 54, 210*n*36

rupture, historic ("*Geschichtsbruch*"): Independence and early republic as 39, 211*n*58
Rush, Dr. Benjamin 32, 91
Rushmore, Mount *see* Mount Rushmore

Saint-Gaudens, Augustus 143, 150
Saint-Mémin, Charles de 100–1
"Samantha at the Centennial" 207
Saul, Peter 140, 166
Savage, Edward: *The Washington Family* 6, 36, 76, 100, 107, **108**, 112, 124, 189
"Save the Greenback" 2; *see also* "Americans for George"
Schaefer, Jack: *Shane* 197
Schiller, Friedrich von: *Wilhelm Tell* 58, 215*n*63; *see also* "*des Landes Vater*"
Schlesinger, Arthur M. 175, 176
Schlesinger, Arthur M., Jr. 175, 200
Schmolze, Carl H. 152, 223*n*4
seal, Great Seal of the United States 41, 61, 102
Sealey, Alfred 230*n*42
Shaftesbury, Anthony Ashley Cooper, Earl of 5, 17, 72
Shakespeare, William: *The Merchant of Venice* 193–94
Shays' Rebellion 54, 63
Sherman, John 134
"*Sic Semper Tyrannis*" 31, 109*n*10; *see also* mottoes
Silver Certificates 7, 133, 134, *142*, 143; *see also* Educational Series
Slavery Sanctioned by the Bible (John Richter Jones) 126
slavery, slaves 9, 64, 87, 111, 121, 124, 126–27, 131, 165, 168, 179, 180; Washington on 165, 217*n*23; *see also* African Americans
Smillie, James 221*n*7
Smith, Adam: *Wealth of Nations* 127
Society of the Cincinnati 77–78, 94, 109, 140, 190
Sorel, Edward 140
South *see* Civil War; Confederacy
Sparks, Jared: *Life of Washington* 6, 83, 145
Stamp Act 71, 136
Stearns, Junius Brutus 118, 121, 123, 152, 223–24*n*13
Stowe, Harriet Beecher: *Uncle Tom's Cabin* (1852) 87–88
Stuart, Gilbert 2, 6, 75, 83, 87, 94, 97, 100, 103, 131, 152, 166, 173, 187, 194, 195; "Athenaeum" portrait 2, 11, 28, 45, 76, **77**, 87, 88, 95, 98, 103, 151, 152, 155, 166, 185, **187**, 188, 193, 199; "Lansdowne" portrait 10, 11, 42, 43, **44**, 62, 98, 118, 173, 190, 212*n*78
Sully, Thomas 6
Super Bowl XIX 9, 170
symbols 2, 7, 10, 12, 24, 32, 40–42, 45, 58, 59, 66, 71, 73, 75, 77–78,
87–88, 101–3, 105, 106, 123, 124, 128, 136, 145, 153, 165, 173, 179, 191, 195, 196, 199

Taylor, Zachary 7, 10, 131, 179
Thackeray, William Makepeace 86, 87
Tiebout, Cornelius: *Sacred to Patriotism* 36, 137
Townshend Acts (1767) 57, 136
Truman, Harry 177, 182, 198
Trumbull, John: *The Death of General Mercer at the Battle of Princeton* 50, 97, 174; *General Washington at Trenton* 50, 97, 135; *Jefferson Presenting the Declaration of Independence* 7, 135; *Washington at Verplanck's Point* 50, **96**
Trump, Donald J. 4, 10, 17, 20, 166, 185, 187, 200; and Andrew Jackson 22–23, **23**; inaugural address 19; as "strict father" 24–26, 28
Trump, Fred 149, 185, 232*n*19
Tuckerman, Henry 36, 104, 123

union: Washington as symbol of 4, 6, 7, 23, 39, 41, 55, 65, 85, 94, 121–23, **125**, 128, 131, 177, 228*n*4
United States Bicentennial 160, 165, 166, 183
United States Bureau of Engraving and Printing (USBEP) 2, 134; *see also* Chase, Salmon P.; "portraits of presidents"
United States Congress 53–54, 64, 71, 75, 93, 121, 123, 133, 135, 138, 148, 149, 164, 169, 170, 171, 179, 181, 196
United States Constitution 31, 40, 64–65, 133, 149, 171, 172, 180, 182, 185, 191, 200, 233*n*10; constitutional debates 47, 53–54, 57, 63
United States George Washington Bicentennial Commission 155, 232*n*6, 233*n*39

Valley Forge, legend of 8, 35, 74, 117, 118, 135, 148, 160, 170, 184; *see also* prayer in the snow legend
Van Buren, Martin 66, 131, 176, 179
Vanderlyn, John 43, 104
Virginia aristocracy 84, 124
Virginia Regiment 88, 92, 209*n*21
virtue, republican 5, 24, 25, 33, 43, 50, 57, 61, 62, 64, 76, 79, 98, 102, 104, 112, 128, 140, 145, 215*n*65, 220*n*31

Wakefield, Virginia 147, 190, 232*n*6
Wakoski, Diane: "The Father of My Country" 10, 196, 240*n*21
War of 1812 131, 140
War of Independence 36, 38, 62, 94, 152, 163; Washington's role during 21, 33, 52, 62; *see also* Declaration of Independence; George III; Jefferson, Thomas; Paine, Thomas; Washington, George
Warner, Susan: *The Wide, Wide World* 87
Washington, Augustine (father of George Washington) 185
Washington, George: as anachronism 165; appearance of 48, 62, 86, 87, 50–51; assessment of 15, 42, 50, 66, 89, 97–98, 144, 153, 163, 165, 174, 177, 178, 188, 190, 191, 203*n*11, 217*n*38; "Athenaeum" portrait of 2, 11, 28, 45, 76, **77**, 87, 88, 95, 98, 103, 151, 152, 155, 166, 185, **187**, 188, 193, 199; Battle of Monmouth 41, 128, 224*n*13; bicentennial celebration 4, 101, 140, 141, 152–57; biographies of 4, 6, 9, 34, 35, 52, 66, 74, 79, 83, 84–87, 118, 142, 145, 148, 168, 174, 189, 210*n*30; birthday as holiday 37, 62, 123, 185–86, 188, 238*n*54; birthday celebrations 6, 10, 59, 83, 104, 117, 123, 127, 132, 144, 154, 170, 171, 199, 217*n*32; caricatures and cartoons of 9, 11, 29, 166, 167, 168, 188, 234*n*46; catalogs of paintings and prints 99, 101, 102, 141, 222*n*50; and Cato 55, 74, 86, 203*n*18, 214*n*45, 219*n*14; centennial of birth 83, 104, 115–16, 123, 155; centennial of inauguration 7, 140, 142, 143, 144; as Cincinnatus 5, 32–33, 77–79; "Circular to State Governments" 52–53, 169, 190; and civic virtue 32–34, 47, 57–59, 98, 104, 110, 112, 129, 140; and civil-military relations 50, 52, 75, 78, 97; on coins, medals, and currency 6, 10–12, 36, 37, 41, 62, 70, 83, 88, 99, 127, 142–43, 155, 188, 195, 218–19*n*62, 221*n*12; as commander in chief of the Continental Army 32, 49, 50, 52, 61, 62, 68, 75, 92, 108, 128, 174, 190, 217*n*41; confronts Newburgh Conspiracy 49, 190; at Constitutional Convention 5, 33, 47, 53–54, 63–64, 68, 74, 123, 161, 174, 182, 213*n*32; death and mourning of 37–38, 65, 67–68, 98, 100, 118, 210*n*48, 217*n*42; as disciplinarian 109; in drama 85–87, 99, 160, 163, 222*n*31; as entrepreneur and investor 107–8, 145, 148, 173; and executive power 63, 68, 174, 215*n*57, 218*n*53; exhibitions 7, 43, 133, 138, 141, 143, 144, 170, 178–79, 205*n*16, 217*n*38, 222*n*50, 236*n*5; as "Fabius" 63, 216*n*16; as "face of the nation" 2, 37, 38, 76, 100, 185; "Farewell Address" 20, 24–25, 37, 43, 121, 123, 124–25, 128, 132, 180, 188, 191, 216*n*20, 228*n*4; as Father of His Country

2, 3, 5, 7, 9, 10, 11, 12, 17, 31, 33–35, 37–42, 47–50, *51*, 52–53, 55, 57, 61–62, 65, 67–68, 74–76, 82–89, 95, 98, 102–5, 106, 113, 115–18, 121–22, 125–26, 128, **130**, 132, 142–43, 144–45, 152, 154–55, 163–76, 178–86, 188–91, 192–93, 196, 200–1, 239n72; in fiction 85–87, 139, 160, 163, 167, 194, 215n65, 235n76; in film 8, 98–99, 139, 148, 160, 161, 163, 164, 173, 183, 195, 207n54; as "gallant revolutionary" 6, 50; idolization of 36, 182, 195; inauguration of 1789 59, **69**, 70, 98, 152, 167, 169; journey through the states 5, 54–55, 62, 176; as "*des Landes Vater*" 4, 32, 57, 58, 192, 214n39, 215nn58–60, 215n63; library of 56, 137, 141; and military discipline 89–91; and "monarchical" practices 65, 66, 212n80, 218n52; as Moses 40, 211n62; and Mount Vernon 54, 74, 79; and national capital 6, 107; as nonpartisan 11, 34, 54, 56, 65, 66, 214n48; in oratory 33, 34, 83, 121, 124, 126, 217n43; as patriarch 6, 118, 199; poems about 33, 42, 50, 61, 67, 78, 79, 83, 85, 171, 196, 209n27; political philosophy of 24, 25, 53–54, 216n20; portraits of *see* "Athenaeum" portrait of, individual artists, and Stuart, Gilbert, "Lansdowne" portrait; "Prayer Journal" 141, 171, 235n55; as President 34, 37, 40, **44**, 54, 57, 63–67, 70; in presidential rankings 9, 28, 66, 174–77; reincarnation of 172, 184; resignation as commander in chief 34, 38, 63, 74, 75, 219n20; retirement 54, 59, 66, 101; sculptures of 36, 66, 75, 76, 98, **115**, 116, 129, 150, 155, 166, 229n26, 228n65; Shays' Rebellion, handling of 54, 63; as slaveowner 111, 145, 165, 167, 169, 199; and slavery 64, 131, 165, 217n23; and spiritualism 169, 172–73; as symbol of national unity 4, 6, 7, 23, 39, 41, 55, 65, 85, 94, 121–23, **125**, 128, 131, 177, 228n4; urges resistance against Britain 111; and Valley Forge legend 8, 35, 74, 117, 118, 135, 148, 160, 170, 184; veneration of 5, 29, 34, 38, 65, 68, 71, 168, 195; and Virginia Regiment 88, 92, 209n21; as Virginian 84, 124; visual representations of *see* portraits in War of Independence 21, 33, 52, 62; Washington cult 38, 65, 153; Washington memorials 38, 68, 116, 147, 153; Washington Monument 7, 8, 75, 116–17, 124, 133, 148, 151, 168, 190; Washingtoniana 6, 83, 121, 128, 141, 143, 220n2; Whiskey rebellion, handling of 64, 176, 190, 216n22; *see also* Anderson, Alexander; Arneson, Robert; Christy, Howard Chandler; Dunsmore, John Ward; Fairman, Gideon; Ferris, Jean Leon Gerome; Hefferton, Philip; Hicks, Edward; Le Mire, Noël; Leutze, Emanuel Gottlieb; Norman, John; Ogden, Henry A.; Peale, Charles Wilson; Peale, Rembrandt; Pyle, Howard; Quiroz, Alfred J.; Rockwell, Norman; Saint-Gaudens, Augustus; Saint-Mémin, Charles de; Saul, Peter; Savage, Edward; Schmolze, Carl H.; Sorel, Edward; Stuart, Gilbert; Sully, Thomas; Trumbull, John; Vanderlyn, John
Washington, John Augustine (brother of George Washington) 41
Washington, Martha Custis (wife of George Washington) 56, 83, 91–95, 100, 107–9, 118, 140, 141, 143, 145, 152, 189, 194; Martha Washington tea 159; portrait on paper money 7, 133, **142**
Washington Bank: dollar bill of 1800, with Washington portrait 102, 210n32
"Washington-Code" (Michael Butter) 131

Washington Crossing the Delaware see Leutze, Emanuel Gottlieb; Rivers, Larry; Sorel, Edward
Washington Monument (Washington, DC) 7, 8, 75, 116–17, 124, 133, 148, 151, 168, 190
Wayne, "Mad" Anthony 91
Weber, Max 19, 189
Webster, Daniel: on Washington 123
Webster, Noah: *American Spelling Book* 99
Weems, "Parson" Mason L.: *The Life of Washington* 4, 6, 8, 34–37, 79, 85–87, 111, 121, 144, 148, 159, 160, 170, 184, 217n39
The West Wing (TV series) 28, 173
Wheatley, Phillis 85
Whig Party 57, 121, 131
Whiskey Rebellion 64, 176, 190, 216n22; *see also* Washington, George: Whiskey rebellion, handling of
Whitman, Walt 1, 82, 195
Willard, Emma 6, 42, 83
Williamsburg, Virginia 33, 172, 183
Wilson, Woodrow 142, 148, 149, 161, 181
Wise, John (Virginia Governor) 128; *see also* Civil War; North and South
woman suffrage 64, 146, 149, 165; *see also* feminism
women: and the Constitution 5, 64–65; *see also* mothers, republican
Wood, Grant: *Parson Weems' Fable* 8, 139, 159–60
Woodward, William E. 8, 145; *see also* debunking
Wright, Joseph 36, 73, 77, 92–93, 102, 218n50

Yancey, William Lowndes 126, 131; *see also* Civil War; North and South
Yorktown, Virginia 41, 133, 180

www.ingramcontent.com/pod-product-compliance
Lightning Source LLC
Chambersburg PA
CBHW080802300426
44114CB00020B/2802